Alexander the Great: A Battle for Truth and Fiction

Alexander the Great: A Battle for Truth and Fiction

The Ancient Sources and Why They Can't Be Trusted

David Grant

PEN & SWORD
HISTORY
AN IMPRINT OF PEN & SWORD BOOKS LTD.
YORKSHIRE - PHILADELPHIA

First published in Great Britain in 2022 by
Pen & Sword History
An imprint of
Pen & Sword Books Ltd
Yorkshire – Philadelphia

ISBN 978 1 39909 471 9

Printed and bound in the UK by CPI Group (UK) Ltd, Croydon, CR0 4YY.

Pen & Sword Books Limited incorporates the imprints of Atlas, Archaeology,
Aviation, Discovery, Family History, Fiction, History, Maritime, Military, Military
Classics, Politics, Select, Transport, True Crime, Air World, Frontline Publishing,
Leo Cooper, Remember When, Seaforth Publishing, The Praetorian Press,
Wharncliffe Local History, Wharncliffe Transport, Wharncliffe True Crime and
White Owl.

For a complete list of Pen & Sword titles please contact

PEN & SWORD BOOKS LIMITED
47 Church Street, Barnsley, South Yorkshire, S70 2AS, England
E-mail: enquiries@pen-and-sword.co.uk
Website: www.pen-and-sword.co.uk

Or
PEN AND SWORD BOOKS
1950 Lawrence Rd, Havertown, PA 19083, USA
E-mail: Uspen-and-sword@casematepublishers.com
Website: www.penandswordbooks.com

Contents

Author's Foreword

Two decades ago, as part of a Master's degree, I commenced a three-year study of the 'sources and methodologies' that shaped the history of Alexander the Great. The research was enlightening, but deeply frustrating, as my preconceptions and assumptions fell apart one by one.

A decade later, I found the time to pull my thoughts together; it was a process that felt like unravelling an intricately knotted ball of historical string, with illusive threads exposed everywhere but without a clear beginning or end. Somewhere in the middle, I was sure, lay an ossuary of hidden secrets.

Finally, in 2017, I self-published a highly controversial book titled *In Search of the Lost Testament of Alexander the Great* which challenged the 'standard model' of Alexander (as I termed it), and in particular the accounts of his death. At 917 pages with over 4,000 footnotes, it was never destined for commercial bookshelves, and its online presence remained obscure, except for a brief notoriety from the *Daily Mail Online* which found my argument intriguing.

The book was, however, read by academics in Greece, who invited me to meet and discuss a possible new research project with many parallels. From mid-2017, I spent considerable time with them, in person or corresponding, and that collaboration resulted in my 2019 title, *Unearthing the Family of Alexander the Great, the Remarkable Discovery of the Royal Tombs of Macedon* (Pen & Sword History imprint). What I learned from both investigations is that *nothing* related to the royal line of ancient Macedon is straightforward or what it seems. The deaths of Alexander's family were just as inexplicable and suspiciously documented as Alexander's own.

The following year, and with the encouragement of my current publisher, I abridged my first book to enable a wider audience to delve into the mysterious and conflicting accounts of Alexander's death. Here I explained the covert forces which kept this cataclysmic episode in history such a well-guarded secret. *The Last Will and Testament of Alexander the Great: an Empire Left to the Strongest* (Pen & Sword History imprint) went to print in summer 2021. It embodied my original contention: Alexander's death in Babylon, recorded by the mainstream histories as his wholesale failure to nominate a successor, remains as misunderstand as any episode from the ancient world and is nothing short of the greatest succession cover-up of all time.

This latest book once again encompasses many of my conclusions from the past decade of research. As the title suggests, it serves as a guide and a warning against anyone trusting the ancient texts on Alexander too far.

Publisher's Note

A useful companion to this title is David Grant's in-depth investigation into Alexander's death. As a prime example of further conflict and manipulation within the ancient sources, the reporting of Alexander's final days in Babylon is frequently cited within this new book, and readers may wish to know more.

It is titled *The Last Will and Testament of Alexander the Great, an Empire Left to the Strongest* (Pen & Sword History imprint) and is listed in the sources references as 'Grant, *Last Will and Testament* (2021)'.

Chapter 1

Introduction: 'Study the Historian before you Study the History'

It is a naive belief that the distant past can be recovered from
written texts, but even the written evidence for
Alexander is scarce and often peculiar.

Robin Lane Fox, *Alexander the Great*[1]

Over the centuries, historians have expressed, in one way or another, the uncomfortable relationship between what they deem likely to have happened and what is claimed to have come to pass. In the modern age, this conundrum has sparked a whole industry analyzing our library of written historical sources.

In ancient Greece, however, from the dawn of the oral tradition which gave us the names of gods and heroes, down to the legendary deeds of mortals which gradually emerged from the rubble of Dark Age Greece along with a new alphabet, the convention of campfire listeners entranced by a travelling bard was to swallow this 'mythistory' whole, or risk committing impiety. In the case of the royal clan of ancient Macedon – the Temenids or Argeads, as they are alternatively known (depending upon which founding myth they are linked to) – there lies an additional challenge: the nation's warlord kings willingly fused this paradox together. And there was no greater alchemist of history than Alexander the Great.

Alexander's lineage was the perfect storm for not just sweeping aside the status quo (his father had already seen to that), but for bridging the growing divide between an ever-more rationalized present (largely thanks to his tutor, Aristotle) and the mythopoeic past (thanks to the epics of Homer). Alexander made sure that his story would forever be more enduring than a mortal lifespan, and less challengeable than fact, and his brilliantly talented entourage had everything to gain from this new apotheosis.

Today, historians are faced with the unique task of unravelling the many faces of the campaigning king: the sensitive adolescent, the ruthless warlord, the classically educated monarch and the oriental Great King-cum-Pharaoh whose legend metamorphosed into romance in the chaos of the Hellenistic world he fathered. Consequently, the age-old question remains: how do we divide

Alexander's biographical pie into the correctly characterized proportions? The answer lies in the ancient sources: that knotted and frayed ball of historically intertwined string.

Interest in the emotional language and source fidelity of the life and times of Alexander was rekindled in the Renaissance when already-ancient manuscripts, discovered lying in damp scriptoriums where they had been forgotten for centuries or ferried West in haste away from the Ottoman threat, were mined for wisdoms of old. But this process of enlightenment, unfortunately, saw a proliferation of new deceits (see chapter 9). Since then, and sped along by new forensic techniques in historiography developed over the last two centuries, classical scholars – and philologists in particular – have dedicated themselves to separating the 'historical' out of the total written evidence contained in classical literature. The quest has solicited contemplations from some of the greatest minds of the ages: the philosophers, priests, politicians, antiquarians and polymaths attempting to unlock the gates of the past. Many concluded that duplicity of one kind or another, subtle or overt, is endemic to the narrating of 'history', so that falsifications and the forensic method to unravel them competed on every page. A most fertile weapons testing ground remains the life of Alexander.

No modern scholar could complain that we had not been provided with fair warning. Two thousand years ago, the Roman geographer Strabo (*ca.* 64 BC–AD 24) voiced his concern by writing that 'all who wrote about Alexander preferred the marvellous to the true'. Even the Stoic soldier-historian Arrian (*ca.* AD 86–160), a great Alexander admirer who used 'court sources' to obtain 'reliable' detail, could not help but voice his frustration: 'no one else has been the subject of so many writers with such discrepancy between them.' He therefore attempted to set the record straight, as he saw it anyway, or wished it to be seen.

The eloquent observer of human character Plutarch (*ca.* AD 46–120), a voracious collector of detail who named twenty-four sources when profiling Alexander, provided a more general, sobering warning on earlier source material:

> So very difficult a matter is it to trace and find out the truth of anything by history, when, on the one hand, those who afterwards write it find long periods of time intercepting their view, and, on the other hand, the contemporary records of any actions and lives, partly through envy and ill-will, partly through favour and flattery, pervert and distort truth.[2]

Their frustrations could be directed to the wider history of Alexander's family line, because fundamental to any understanding of his reign is the twenty-three-year rule of his extraordinary father, Philip II, and the first twenty-three years of warfare between his equally remarkable successors who fought for a chunk of the vast Macedonian-governed empire in the post-Alexander years.[3] And yet in few such momentous periods of history has so much had to be extracted from so few scattered and time-ravaged dots: the eyewitness sources for the reigns of both Philip and Alexander have all been lost, save lonely snippets, and the regal and bloody rivalries of the Hellenistic era (popularly defined as the years from Alexander's death in 323 BC to the Battle of Actium in 31 BC) was brutal for manuscripts documenting the period immediately after.

In the case of Alexander's reign, we are reliant on five mainstream gap-ridden biographies whose authors represent an eclectic mix of social and ethnic backgrounds: an aristocratic Greek (Plutarch), a Romanized Gaul (Pompeius Trogus, late first century BC; his account survives in an epitome by Justin, likely from the third century AD), an obscure Greek-Sicilian (Diodorus, published between 60 and 30 BC), a Romanized Bithynian commander (Arrian) and a politically connected Roman (Curtius, publication date unknown but likely mid-first century AD). Each wrote under the scrutiny of a Rome which was rapidly swallowing the Macedonian-ruled territories. I refer to these as the 'mainstream' accounts to separate them from the sources we attach to 'romance'.

Written from the distance of some 300–450 years after the events they narrated, these texts were compiled from a *corpus* of earlier sources, some eyewitness and others penned a generation later, including the influential account of the Alexandrian-based Cleitarchus, who seems to have spawned the genre we refer to as 'Vulgate' due to its popularity in Rome (embodied in the accounts of Diodorus, Trogus via Justin and Curtius). Apart from surviving fragments, all of this earlier material has been lost. Indeed, without the infrequent references to these archetypal sources which are strewn sparingly across the classical library, the parental Alexander historians would otherwise be unknown, and many must still lie buried in unmarked graves.

Scholars can additionally call on an infamous collection of fragments (few of which provide useful campaign or biographical detail) from an assemblage of ancient writers who framed Alexander in the prevailing philosophical doctrine and state propaganda of their day, heavily garnished with rhetoric; these politicians, antiquarians and orators were above all promoting their own literary careers by using Alexander as a platform for their art.

Thanks to the ground-breaking forensic work undertaken through the 1800s and 1900s, today's scholars can identify almost 400 fragments directly relating to Alexander from some thirty 'lost' writers, whose works ranged from serious biography to propaganda pamphlets, by the 'good, sound and important' and 'the world's greatest liars'; paradoxically, those traits often combine in the same source.[4] But naming the narrator behind them is often problematic; after historians had sifted through the entries to divide the truly original reporting from regurgitated testimonia, many were deemed paraphrases while others have been labelled 'spuriously assigned'.

It might seem logical to expect a linear deterioration in the accuracy and detail of this material through time, and it would be reasonable to suppose that the most lamentable losses will always be those compiled by Alexander's senior staff. These eyewitnesses – including Ptolemy, Aristobulus, Nearchus, Onesicritus, Callisthenes, Eumenes and Chares – we define as the 'primary' or 'court' sources, who, as the title suggests, frequented the king's palace or campaign headquarters, and even the king's secretariat where the Royal Diaries were compiled. Yet to assume that a corruption of the truth was magnified by time would be a mistake, because evidence suggests that the magnet of political ambition and the realities of survival in a world torn apart by rivalries – along with the powerful hand of sponsorship that any publication would have required – perniciously drew fabrication, omission, exaggeration and agenda into the first-generation texts. Alexander's successors were, after all, at war. Not too far behind them chronologically, there emerged the *Greek Alexander Romance*, one of the world's most-widely read books of fables, which was inspired by and fed off the most embellished campaign accounts.

Today, we employ advanced historiographical methodologies to help us frisk the sources for weapons of deceit. Studies have become multi-disciplined processes in which papyrology, palaeography, linguistic palaeontology, osteoarchaeology, codicology, iconography, numismatics, epigraphy and even space-archaeology are being brought to bear on the evidence. Papyri and parchment palimpsests (reused scrolls or book pages) are undergoing multi-spectral imaging, and ancient bones and tomb materials are subject to DNA, stable isotope and radiocarbon dating tests. The surviving (or 'extant') written histories have always been just one part of a wider story, and their interpretation, unfortunately, has been open to modern bias – history is, after all, interpretation, not fact. Just as we need to tread carefully when listening to the ancient sources, care is also needed with the contemporary ear: 'cherish those who seek the truth, but beware of those who find it'.[5]

This investigation into the sources who gave us Alexander follows my own journey into an ocean of anecdotes, testimony and propaganda in which the tides of scholarly opinion ebb and flow. Anyone delving into these murky waters soon realizes just how frail are the facts behind the life of the man dubbed 'the Great' sometime in the late Hellenistic era.[6] Moreover, when sources are analyzed impartially, there appears evidence that those who did know him – the eyewitness historians who campaigned beside him – had much invested in keeping it that way.

The history of Alexander is a vexatious interweaving of history, personal politics, reinvention and fable, swinging like ship-wreckers' lanterns beckoning historians to perilous harbours of deduction. Many a modern reader has been lost on the rocks this way.

'History is a bag of tricks we play upon the dead,'

remarked the cynical Voltaire.

To which I propose:

'On the contrary, history is a bag of tricks

the dead have played upon historians.'

The author

Chapter 2

Primary Sources: Eyewitnesses at War

So, we see that even the most trustworthy writers, men who were
actually with Alexander at the time have given conflicting accounts of
notorious events with which they must have been perfectly familiar.[1]

Arrian, *The Campaigns of Alexander*

To understand how it all began, we need to start at the beginning, with the
eyewitnesses who accompanied Alexander on campaign across the Persian
Empire from 334–323 BC and subsequently published their accounts.

These men were a select and privileged few, most of whom were not, in fact,
trained historians or writers. There was also a band of fawning poets and courtiers
who followed their king to lands few Europeans had ever seen, where they witnessed
or partook in warfare on a scale history has rarely imagined. After that life-changing
decade on the march, they were inspired to record what they saw and eventually
fought among themselves, figuratively or literally. It is no surprise that their output
acknowledged few literary restraints or rules of reputational engagement, and that
they showed little hesitation in criticizing their literary counterparts for the sake
of self-promotion or to hamstring a rival. Yet their recollections became the stock
for every biographical stew served up in the 500 years that followed, when Rome
co-opted Alexander's story into its own imperial growing pains.

We start with an eyewitness whose deserving credentials put him at the head
of the epitaphic list: he was both the first to write and the first to die as a result of
what he saw.

Callisthenes of Olynthus

Callisthenes, the son of Demotimus of Olynthus, was the first to put pen to ink in
Alexander's name. He was appointed by Alexander as what amounted to 'official'
campaign historian, most likely through the influence of his relative, Aristotle,
who reputedly warned his protégé on his indiscreet tongue. There was reportedly
a further motive for Callisthenes joining the Macedonian adventure: to convince
Alexander to resettle his native city, Olynthus, destroyed by Philip II in 348 BC
for its part in sheltering his half-brothers, who would have challenged him for the

throne.[2] Callisthenes was actually following Aristotle's lead with this request, for he had likewise petitioned Philip to restore *his* birthplace, Stagira, destroyed in the same year when Macedonian forces annexed the Chalcidian Peninsula.[3]

Before the army set off, Callisthenes, along with another campaign philosopher Anaxarchus (*ca*. 380–320 BC), annotated Aristotle's copy of Homer's *Iliad* (known as the 'Recension of the Casket'), an editing possibly spurred by Aristotle's (now-lost) *Homeric Problems* which had highlighted Homer's inconsistences. Alexander is said to have kept these amended scrolls close, and Callisthenes' collaboration must have gained the historian bonus points.[4]

Callisthenes was now mandated to toe the royal Argead corporate line; his new role was more akin to front-line reporting by a journalist employed by a state newspaper: a Macedonian *Pravda*. Although his account was to be a political manifesto, it became something of a biographic encomium of the king which attempted to embody ideals that would appeal to Greek consumption, annexed as Greece was by Macedonian garrisons.[5] Callisthenes had already proven himself an able historian before joining Alexander, having completed a *Hellenica* (a history of Greece from *ca*. 387–357 BC), a *Periplous* (circumnavigation) of the Black Sea and *On the Sacred War* (in which Philip played a manipulative role in the internal politics in Greece), amongst other works. He, like other writers of the fourth century BC (such as Theopompus of Chios, Anaximenes of Miletus and Ephorus of Cyme, all of whose works are now lost), attempted more than one literary genre.[6]

We can assume that aside from the sycophantic and flattering content displayed in surviving fragments, his *Deeds of Alexander*, if indeed this was his title, was on the whole coherent and valuably replete with dates, names and numbers, even if a work of lower quality than his previous publications, as he himself admitted. When questioned on why his earlier *Hellenica* was superior to the campaign account, Callisthenes allegedly replied: 'Because I wrote it when I was hungry, and the other work when I was well fed.' That is until he was arrested and reportedly kept in a cage after losing favour with Alexander.[7]

Callisthenes was employed at a turning point in history. Philip II had defeated the Greek alliance at the Battle of Chaeronea in 338 BC (two years before he was assassinated and four years before Alexander's invasion of Persia). After coming to the throne in 336 BC, Alexander levelled the Greek city of Thebes, after which he enforced his father's edicts; the Boeotian League (headed by Thebes) was abolished and the Greek city-states had already been reorganized into an uneasy alliance in the form of the Hellenic League, more commonly referred to as the League of Corinth, with the imposition of a Common Peace.

The notion of 'freedom', previously underpinned by calls from the aged Athenian statesman Isocrates for Greek unity in an environment where perennial city-state war was crippling the land, was now revived in a war of revenge on the new Persian Great King, Darius III. Here, Callisthenes performed his part in modelling his reporting to both thrill and placate a resentful Greek audience. His description of the Battle of Gaugamela (331 BC), which ended Achaemenid rule, has been termed 'nothing short of a Pan-Hellenic set piece'. It was the last major campaign battle the historian would ever witness.[8]

Callisthenes reportedly proposed, in the style of the revered Thucydides (*ca.* 460–395 BC), who narrated the Peloponnesian War through his own creative mouthpiece: 'In attempting to write anything one must not prove false to the character, but make the speeches fit both the speaker and the situation.'[9] It was a self-issued permit for artistic license. Through his merging of moralizing discursions into a history steeped in antiquarian scholarship, Callisthenes was writing in 'an almost rhetorical' manner; the Greek historian Polybius (*ca.* 200–118 BC) thought Callisthenes' statements were simply 'absurd', while the Roman statesman Cicero (106–43 BC) later termed him a 'hackneyed piece of goods'.[10]

Extant fragments of Callisthenes' campaign account reveal a systematic denigration of the influential general Parmenio, a veteran of Philip's day and Macedon's most talented military strategist; he was executed on Alexander's orders in the Persian royal city of Ecbatana in Media in late 330 BC.[11] Knowing when Parmenio died, and supposing when Callisthenes was himself sent by Alexander down to Hades (conflicting reports make exact dating impossible, but no later than 327 BC), we have our termini within which the last part of his account must have been released.

Campaign-related detail is limited, and not all testimonia we have is necessarily first-hand. Fragments contain geographical digressions on Asia Minor linking sites to Homeric legend, and they do not suggest a coherent or progressive campaign log. These snippets may, in fact, be taken from Callisthenes' earlier works.

Despite his rhetorical flourishes and insertion of the fabulous designed to portray Alexander's deeds as beyond those of a mere mortal, Callisthenes' account was official, vetted and, we assume, sanctioned by Alexander before publication, and thus not easily contradicted by his contemporaries. Moreover, written in 'real time', it was a veritable campaign atomic clock when personal memories faded, as well as an invaluable historical spinal column for new anecdotal flesh to be grafted onto later.

Modern historians remain vexed by the paucity of references to Callisthenes in the extant sources. Why do the surviving accounts, which are based on the books by Alexander's contemporaries like Ptolemy and Aristobulus, stay silent on his contribution? In the case of Ptolemy's testimony, the answer is easily deduced: citing Callisthenes as the source would have undermined his own eyewitness position. Furthermore, the tactless sophist had been controversially executed in Ptolemy's presence, and possibly with his encouragement.[12]

Hemmed in on one side by his philosophical precepts, and with an ever more censorious king on the other (Alexander allegedly censored army correspondence home in bleaker campaign periods), Callisthenes should have trodden carefully when sermonizing on campaign, as Aristotle warned.[13] Yet it appears he did not, because according to Arrian he tactlessly claimed that Alexander and his exploits (along with a share of divinity) would be forgotten without him and his pen.[14] His aphorism has undertones of the more cynical quip: 'Any fool can make history, but it takes a genius to write it.'[15] Callisthenes had 'kept his superfluous wit but had thrown away his common sense', and that may have spelled the end.[16] But Callisthenes' reminder on the ink behind the making of history proved prophetic, and with him went valuable detail no one has since recovered.

As a result, it appears that only a few key episodes from Callisthenes' campaign account survived for the Roman-era historians to consult. Moreover, Arrian's references to him come with second-hand wrappings such as 'it is said that Callisthenes the Olynthan' and 'the following remark of his, if indeed it has been correctly recorded'. Plutarch only twice cited Callisthenes as a source, and he too, like Arrian, could have extracted through an intermediary.[17] He is not named as a source at all in the popular Vulgate genre accounts.

If we require further proof that Callisthenes' history disappeared early on, we simply need to recall that the famous book of fables, the *Greek Alexander Romance* – still popularly referred to as a 'Pseudo-Callisthenes' production – was at some point (in its earlier less fabulous form) credited to him; this was a misattribution only possible in the absence of the original. But this equally suggests that Callisthenes' reputation as a marvel-maker, propagated by those few encomiastic episodes, was established early on.[18]

Callisthenes was finally arrested for his reputed part in a plot involving the king's royal pages (some of whom were Callisthenes' students) to assassinate Alexander.[19] It was a huge eyewitness conundrum and one that demanded some form of public relations initiative, executed as the historian was with little evidence of guilt.[20] The episode and its outcome, and the speeches couched within, neatly set the tone for the criticism of the conqueror that were soon to emanate from Greece: Alexander, the once model student, had lost his way in the East and had now become a tyrant.[21]

Arrian noted the disunity in the reports of Callisthenes' demise, and as one scholar points out, he ultimately experienced 'five different deaths' on Alexander's orders.[22] Callisthenes' incomplete book also had an uncertain end, for it disappeared from the corpus of history too gracefully for comfort, with his only epitaph appearing in the *On Grief* by Theophrastus (a former student of Aristotle and his successors at the Lyceum), which observed that Alexander misused the good fortune sent his way.[23]

Callisthenes' position was surely compromised from the start. His disapproval of Alexander's adoption of Persian court pomp and ceremony, his lack of tact and alleged morose silences (we assume biting his tongue when witnessing indigestible episodes) led Alexander himself to brand the sophist 'a sage who is blind to his own interests', or so Plutarch claimed.[24]

Although Callisthenes was executed on Alexander's orders a few years before Alexander himself died, his campaign participation is worth remembering because his reporting DNA entered the surviving accounts. His eulogistic treatment of his king before his tragic demise most likely shaped the template of what came after, and it potentially influenced his newly hired successor, Onesicritus.

Onesicritus of Astypalea

Onesicritus, from the Greek island of Astypalea, in many ways appears to have been Callisthenes' successor, and he might have been summoned to replace him at the mobile campaign court.[25] This remains a surprisingly undeveloped theory when considering that the first references to Onesicritus appear soon after Callisthenes' death. It has been suggested that Alexander didn't require a 'political historian' after the Persian Great King, Darius III, had been overthrown, for the initial propaganda mission had by then been fully accomplished. But it is doubtful that the Macedonian king, set to campaign to the world's end, was prepared to let his future deeds go entirely unrecorded.

Onesicritus was a student of Diogenes the Cynic whom Alexander reportedly admired, and this might have propelled his credentials to the top of the application pile.[26] He and Callisthenes had benefited from dialectic training (reasoned truth through discourse) and philosophical teaching, so perhaps we should refer to them as 'philosophers with a mandate for history' rather than the reverse. The amalgam was never likely to have produced a straight-talking narrative, though Onesicritus was certainly the more tactful of the two men; his survival speaks for his political dexterity because the Cynics, and possibly the Peripatetics (followers of Aristotle's school of philosophy taught at the Lyceum), were a significant part of a decidedly hostile picture of Alexander that emerged after his death.[27]

In a 1953 translation of the surviving fragments of the campaign histories, it was noted that there are chapters in which the sources appeared 'thin' on campaign detail. More recently, a scholar probed into the existence of a gap of nearly six months in the chronicle of a total 'missing year' broadly coinciding with this changeover period.[28] Even formative episodes involving Alexander's meeting with his first wife, Rhoxane, and her father, Oxyartes, suffered from these conflicts, and if we can trust the anonymous late-Roman period manuscript known as the *Metz Epitome*, the birth and loss of a first child by Rhoxane fell into the reporting gap too.[29]

Callisthenes was executed at some indeterminate point after the Battle of Gaugamela in September 331 BC, possibly in Bactria and as late as 328/327 BC, though he had already been under arrest for some time before his death.[30] The clear lack of synchronicity between the court-sourced account of Arrian (who principally drew from Ptolemy and Aristobulus, the 'court sources') and the Cleitarchus-derived reports of the eastern campaign (which are cited by the Roman-period Vulgate-genre authors, so Diodorus, Justin and Curtius), broadly relating to the period between the winters spanning 329/328 and 328/327 BC, does suggest an absence of front-line reporting.[31] If Onesicritus was called out to replace Callisthenes (before or after his eventual execution), and factoring in the distance a 'recruitment message' and its response had to travel – from the eastern Persian satrapies to Greece and back again – Onesicritus may not have arrived until Alexander was already in the upper satrapies (covering today's northern Afghanistan, Pakistan, Tajikistan and Uzbekistan), to which some fragments linked to him refer, or perhaps even preparing to enter India through the Khyber Pass.[32] The blurring of detail suggests that the official campaign Royal Diaries, under the auspices of Alexander's Greek secretary, Eumenes of Cardia, must themselves have been far from perfectly preserved.

Onesicritus was keen to preserve the wonders of the East, and some twenty-one of the surviving thirty-eight fragments do refer to India, the 'third part of the world' as it was commonly referred to. He was, for example, the very first Greek to detail a sighting of cotton plants.[33] But his credibility is diminished by reports of 500-year-old elephants, humans 130 years old, 8ft-tall men and serpents over 200ft long, plus rather shaky reference to anthropology and geography.[34]

It was here in India, on the very edges of the Persian Empire and the known world, that Onesicritus was keen to see Alexander accepted as the 'first armed philosopher' by the gymnosophists (from the Greek, literally meaning 'naked sophists'), the Brahmin sages they encountered, though this approach was not original and is steeped in Platonist doctrine. Perhaps it captured something of an idealistic self-reflection as well as an attempt to align the Indian dogma with that of the Cynic school.[35] Strabo's branding of Onesicritus as the 'chief pilot of fantasy' was no doubt a play upon his attested role as helmsman of the royal barge on the Hydaspes-Indus river flotilla, or as pilot (under the naval captain Nearchus) of the fleet dispatched by Alexander to explore the sea route from the Indus delta to the Persian Gulf.[36]

These were the colourful roles that earned Onesicritus an immortal place in the fabled-filled *Greek Alexander Romance*. His involvement with the Brahmins hints that he was something of a spokesperson for the king's propaganda machine on ascetic matters. If new tribes and nations were to be encountered as the Macedonian-led army made its way south towards the sea, a court philosopher and counsellor on the metaphysical might win them over more effectively than a soldier and a spear, for the Indian campaign was already mired in blood. This status may also explain Onesicritus' presence with Nearchus on the naval expedition of supply and discovery through the Persian Gulf. Onesicritus' own account of that voyage did not survive, though extracts appeared in the *Natural History* of Pliny.[37]

Onesicritus' book of wonders and eastern exotica seems to have dovetailed neatly with Callisthenes' earlier colour, but we have no idea how one account met and greeted the other. If its title, *On the Education of Alexander*, is accurate it was a latter-day *On the Education of Cyrus* (*Cyropaedia*), emulating the eulogy of Cyrus the Great written by the Athenian soldier of fortune Xenophon (*ca*. 431–354 BC), who also campaigned in the Persian Empire for Cyrus the Younger, the pretender to the throne. Xenophon's works would have certainly been read by Alexander before crossing to Asia. This conclusion is not promising, for Xenophon's encomium idealized the lives of both Persian royals the same. Xenophon had also warned his readers: 'I shall pass over those actions that are not worth mentioning, dealing only with what deserves to be remembered.' And that is tragic, because what remains of Xenophon's writing represents Greek historical literature for the entire fourth century BC.[38] Yet Xenophon's statement on 'deserved' history was reused by a much-admiring Arrian, and it inevitably leads to questions on what Onesicritus may have selectively bypassed too.[39]

Although we remain uncertain of when Onesicritus' account commenced, elements of his work appear to have survived intact for Roman-period autopsy. The Greek-educated Roman antiquarian Aulus Gellius (*ca*. AD 125–post 180) claimed Onesicritus' manuscripts were available when he arrived at Brindisi in Italy and made his way to Rome, and he linked Onesicritus' texts to the many 'books of wonders' cheaply on sale in the streets.[40] Once again, his account – or what survived of it – appears to have been select titbits rather than a cogent and chronologically organized campaign history.

Like Callisthenes, Arrian's references to Onesicritus verge on the dismissive, and they additionally fail to confirm whether he actually read his original campaign account;[41] Arrian's rejection of Onesicritus' claims to naval authority, for example, looks to be sourced from Nearchus.[42] Even Plutarch's references to the Cynic-trained historian leave us unsure whether he had a copy of his *On the Education of Alexander*. Certainly, a cynical retort from Lysimachus, Alexander's prominent Bodyguard who became king of Thrace and the bordering lands, which questioned the historian's credibility over a dubious 'Amazon affair', did not come from Onesicritus' own manuscript, for that would have been wholly self-incriminating.[43]

Gellius' statement on the plentiful 'Onesicritus' material for sale may once again refer to something other than the biography of Alexander, and his campaign account may have followed Callisthenes' into oblivion rather earlier than we assume. The meagre length of the doxography (an essay capturing the doctrines of the ancient philosophers) by the Roman, Diogenes Laertius, certainly indicates he found little biographic detail worth extracting from Onesicritus, though his opinion of his work, in comparison to that of Xenophon, probably explains why 'Onesicritus, as is to be expected of an imitator, falls short of his model'.[44]

There is one further report which suggests Onesicritus remained in the thick of affairs in the post-Alexander world; or rather, it suggests someone wished him to be by implication in the dangerous politicking surrounding Alexander's death: Onesicritus is said to have refused to name those present at the last banquet hosted by Medius of Larissa and his co-conspirators accused of poisoning Alexander (see Grant, *Last Will and Testament*, 2021), being fearful of reprisals by those present. While this may be linked to a political pamphlet in circulation, his eyewitness status and intimacy with his king were never going to provide Onesicritus with immunity in the Successor Wars.[45]

Callisthenes and then Onesicritus were the official 'spin-doctors' on campaign, and it appears that, once again, partiality was never a compromising factor.

Nearchus the Cretan

Nearchus, a Cretan by birth but a citizen of the newly Macedonian city of Amphipolis (thanks to Philip's annexation of the Chalcidian Peninsula and lands to its east), was raised at the Macedonian court and was one of the coeval friends of the young Alexander. The king's other inner circle intimates were principally Macedones of noble birth and veteran officers from Philip's military ventures, though highborn Asiatics controversially entered the ranks later in Alexander's Persian campaign.

Nearchus had reputedly once been exiled from the political capital at Pella along with Ptolemy (as well as several other of Alexander's close friends) for his part in what is known as the 'Pixodarus affair' (see chapter 8), most likely in 337 or early 336 BC, in the final years of Philip's reign.[46] If true, the exile suggests Nearchus was amongst the few who were truly trusted by the then-teenage Alexander who had alienated himself from his father by interfering in court politics.

By 334/333 BC, with Philip II dead and Alexander's own invasion force in control of much of Asia Minor, Nearchus was appointed as governor of Lycia and Pamphylia, and thus he became a prominent general or pan-regional military governor (a *strategos*). The role most likely required his naval experience to deny any Persian flotilla access to the numerous harbours on that rugged coastline, and potentially (with another naval admiral, Amphoterus) to deal with pirates, the scourge of the Eastern Mediterranean since Homeric times, when the Cilician coast, Skyros and the Thracian Chersonese (peninsula) were notorious outposts of the plunderers.[47]

The Persian fleet had commenced naval attacks against Greek interests in the Aegean in 333 BC, so Athens needed well over 100 warships to protect the grain shipments arriving from Egypt. Nearchus' post, crucial to watching Alexander's back as he headed further inland, lasted some six years until 328 BC, when he was called to the East with new recruits once the naval threat had subsided with the end of Achaemenid rule with the death of Darius III (330 BC) and the subsequent capture of Bessus, the new self-proclaimed but short-lived Great King who named himself Artaxerxes V (329 BC).[48]

Nearchus became an accomplished commander of light infantry as well as a trireme (a 'trierarch' captaining and funding a Greek ship with banks of three oars) of the Indus-Hydaspes flotilla, an esteemed role that would have seen him relieved of significant wealth by Alexander to equip the troopship or barge.[49] He finally became admiral of the sea fleet and recorded the unique two-and-a-half-months, 1,700-mile coastal voyage across the Erythrean Sea (alternatively named the Red Sea by some sources, broadly spanning the Persian Gulf and Gulf of Oman) from the Indus delta to the mouth of the Euphrates, a route that allegedly (and mistakenly) provided him with calculations that 'proved' he crossed what we now call the Tropic of Cancer and the Equator.[50] His account of the voyage, the *Indica* (broadly 'about India'), took a swipe at his co-pilot, Onesicritus, along the way, for they clashed on claims of nautical authority and who bore the title chief helmsman and admiral, and thus who was subordinate to the other.[51]

Nearchus' lost work, though substantially preserved by Arrian's précis of the same name (*Indica*), was most likely written in old Ionic dialect in the style of the century-old *Histories* of Herodotus, which also wove its path through the colour of the Persian Empire. Nearchus' geographical digressions on rivers, monsoons and floods were rooted in Herodotean tradition, as well as his own understanding of the voyage of Scylax of Caryander (like Herodotus, a Greek born in a coastal city of Anatolia) through similar lands almost two centuries before.[52]

Nearchus appears to have sensibly bypassed the land campaign in his memoirs in favour of Indian geography, customs and military organizations; he may have concluded his book at a point before Alexander's death in Babylon, as Arrian deferred to the eyewitness reporting of Aristobulus for detail on the fleet preparations being carried out there at the time. But Nearchus was certainly present, as Plutarch and Diodorus claimed Nearchus warned Alexander against entering the city due to adverse portents that the self-serving Chaldean priests had observed.[53]

As one modern historian observed, the service of Nearchus, who uniquely had a major achievement of his own amongst the officers of Alexander, 'shines like a good deed in the admittedly naughty world of Alexander historians'.[54] An earlier summation considered the conclusion to his sea voyage (as it was portrayed by Arrian) unsurpassed 'in loyalty and depth of penetration into human personality'.[55]

Yet much of it appears 'epic adornment' which was inspired by Homer's *Odyssey*, while the extensive list of thirty-three trierarchs he provided for the flotilla again reads like the Catalogue of Ships from the *Iliad*.[56] Strabo grouped Nearchus, alongside Onesicritus and others who later wrote on India, as someone who could not avoid the obligatory fabulous elements on his reporting.[57] Ultimately, Nearchus' account ended up as another 'philosophical geography'.[58]

Rewarded with a golden crown at Susa for his loyal service (as was Onesicritus and other high-ranking officers), Nearchus played a prominent part in the Successor Wars following Alexander's death, in which his legacy was significant.[59] He was usefully employed by the larger-than-life veteran, Antigonus the One-Eyed, at least until the Battle of Gaza in 313/312 BC, where he was cited as one of the advisers to Antigonus' son, Demetrius the Besieger. Nearchus was in his mid-40s by then (assuming he was broadly coeval with Alexander) and was never mentioned thereafter. If he perished in the disastrous outcome when 'most of Demetrius' friends fell … the majority of which were cavalry or men of distinction', then he must have published his book in the unattested years before this renewed military activity (first attested *ca.* 318 BC) and possibly as early as 320 BC. This conclusion is supported by the fact that he may have been referred to by the loose-tongued historian Theopompus of Chios (he cited 'authors of *Indica*'), who had earlier frequented Philip's court.[60]

Nearchus was an eyewitness of events at Babylon, where he allegedly spoke up for the succession right of Alexander's older son, Heracles, by his mistress Barsine, to whom he had become related by virtue of the mass weddings at Susa, where Alexander paired his senior command to women of the Persian nobility (see chapter 8). Nearchus was additionally named as one of the attendees of Alexander's final banquet, where the king was allegedly poisoned, though he was named as one of six 'innocents' in a later politically inspired pamphlet which identified the assassins present.[61]

Today, historians and archaeologists ponder whether he and other prominent campaign figures were amongst the skeletons recently exhumed from the once-magnificent Casta Hill tomb at Amphipolis in northern Greece after its entrance and burial chambers were discovered in 2014.[62]

Ptolemy son of Lagus

Arrian's principal court source, Ptolemy I Soter (the 'Saviour'), the putative son of Lagus of the canton of Eordaea (western Macedon), has much to answer for in Alexander's story, and in particular accounts of his death (see Grant, *Last Will and Testament*, 2021). Ptolemy's mother, Arsinoe, was a former concubine of Philip II and possibly from a lesser branch of the Argead royal house. This fostered the rumour that Ptolemy was Alexander's half-brother, a loud whisper Ptolemy may have propagated himself.[63] It might explain why Ptolemy had the controversial historian Theopompus of Chios executed when he inherited governance of Egypt, for the Chian chronicler had conspicuously damned Alexander's father and the sexual exploits of what he painted as a thoroughly debauched court.[64]

In 330 BC, Ptolemy became one of Alexander's seven personal Bodyguards (in Greek, *Somatophylakes*, and distinct from other more generalized 'bodyguard' corps), after which his prominence continued to grow, at least in his own account of the campaign.[65] A statement from Curtius – that 'he was certainly no detractor of his own fame' – suggests Ptolemy's self-promotion had not gone unnoticed (though such wording was not unique and similar statements appeared in the Roman narratives of Livy and Tacitus).[66] A close friend of Alexander at the Pellan court, Ptolemy had always been one of those destined to exert influence over men if he showed loyalty, military acumen and political agility. Certainly, the latter two were on display until he died at the age of 84.

A leading Alexander scholar of the 'who's who' of the era neatly summed up the problem we face when interpreting the texts featuring Ptolemy's campaign contribution: what we read about him ultimately originated with Ptolemy himself, with all the bias and self-promotion that entailed, yet we have just thirty-five fragments of his writing.[67] A parallel autopsy of Xenophon's earlier works articulates the challenge of dealing with a self-documenting source: it 'thus requires delicate handling by the historian. What it says, and the way it says it, is always to be weighed against what it does not say, and the reason why it does not.' For example, Ptolemy appears to have avoided commenting on Alexander's darker episodes, for they in turn blackened him by close association.[68]

By the time Ptolemy published his campaign account, his unchallengeable position as king and pharaoh of Egypt provided him with the power to manipulate character portrayals; those who opposed him in the Successor Wars no doubt suffered a retrospective damnation as a consequence. Others were simply not spoken of. It was a far more enduring victory than any under arms, but for all that, Ptolemy's campaign history appears to have been a dry and pedestrian military-focused affair that failed to ignite the Roman imagination, and it was less widely read than, for example, Cleitarchus' later and more colourful Vulgate-genre account.[69]

Modern studies have conceded that Ptolemy was unreliable: he got what he wanted from 'a lie, a fraud, and an intentional omission', from a clinical suppression of details and insertion of falsehoods.[70] Another well-known Alexander historian simply branded Ptolemy 'a conniving pragmatic old shit'.[71]

Like Onesicritus and Nearchus, Ptolemy was said to be present at Babylon when Alexander doubled-up in pain at the banquet hosted by Medius of Larissa, the event which led to the spread of rumours of a conspiracy to poison the king. And like Nearchus, Ptolemy was named as an innocent bystander, but he too made sure his voice was heard at the assembly gathering of the army immediately after Alexander died, when the transfer of power was being discussed. It appears he rejected Nearchus' call for Alexander's older son to be recognized (both sons, in fact, as they were 'half-barbarian'; see Grant, *Last Will and Testament*, 2021, chapter 3), and soon he and Nearchus were at war.

Aristobulus of Cassandrea

The second of Arrian's 'court' sources – those he said he favoured drawing from when writing his campaign account – was Aristobulus, who lived to old age, beyond 90 we are told, supposedly commencing his writing when he was a tender 84. We have no title for Aristobulus' book, and the sixty-two genuine-looking fragments provide no chapter numbers, so we cannot gauge its length.[72]

Aristoboulus' interest in river systems and flood plains and his accurate descriptions of monuments (some he was tasked to repair), as well as the highly mechanized siege of Tyre, reveal a technical eye with a geographical slant and have led scholars to believe he was employed as a technician or engineer on campaign.[73] Like Nearchus and Onesicritus, he was eager to recount the colour of India, though apparently without the blatant exaggerations and overt 'wonderment'. But the gods still had their place in Aristobulus' reckoning and their divine intervention always fell on the side of his king; that is until Alexander's ill-omened return to Babylon in 323 BC.[74]

Like Ptolemy, Aristobulus appears to have avoided the negative campaign episodes, and he airbrushed those he could not completely erase; if not a full-fledged 'flatterer' of Alexander, then he might be termed an 'apologist'. The episode of the Gordian Knot, 'Fate's silent riddle' that vexed all-comers in Phrygia, may be instructive here. A famed waggon stood on the acropolis of the palace of Gordius and Midas, and had been dedicated to Sabazios, a god the Greeks associated with Zeus. Midas tied it to a post with an impossibly intricate knot, and oracular prediction held that whoever unravelled it would become the king of Asia.[75] Eyewitnesses variously reported that Alexander, driven by his 'yearning' (*pothos*), either impetuously sliced through the ancient rope in frustration or, as Aristobulus claimed, cunningly unyoked the pin of the cart to which it was bound. This appears to be face-saving propaganda to hide an embarrassing performance – what Justin described as 'a false interpretation of the oracle' – even though thunder is said to have followed, signifying the approval of the gods.[76]

So, 'how is it to be decided whether the more dramatic or the more prosaic version of a story is the original one? The question of historical probability may be irrelevant: no one can really hope to know what actually happened at Gordium any more than one can say what song the Sirens sang, comments one scholar.'[77] But Alexander's brutal cutting of the knot ultimately 'ended an ancient dispensation by placing the power of the sword above that of religious mystery'.[78]

Similarly, we have the claim by the satirist Lucian (*ca*. AD 125–180) that a newly penned chapter Aristobulus was reading aloud was tossed overboard by Alexander in an apparent rejection of its portrayal of him slaying elephants with a single javelin throw.[79] But this sounds contrived (if not exaggerated), for Onesicritus was afforded a similar retrospective in the pages of Lucian's satirical *How to Write History*.[80] Yet to become truly Homeric, a king had to be seen fighting in single combat, like the heroes of the *Iliad*. The episode does, nevertheless, confirm that Aristobulus enjoyed a well-known intimacy with Alexander, as well as a tradition that he was an unreliable historian. But as has been noted, Aristobulus' literary approach falls into no easy category.[81]

Aristobulus' post-campaign activity remains unattested, and this is unsurprising because he did not hold a military command; few engineers, architects or city planners were ever referred to in ancient scrolls, except perhaps in siege situations or concerning noteworthy funerary constructions.[82] Aristobulus' birthplace is uncertain, though Plutarch, Lucian and the rhetorician Athenaeus (late second to early third century AD) linked him to the city of Cassandrea, which led to the theory that he was a supporter of Cassander (the son of Alexander's former regent, Antipater), who had taken control of Macedon and built the eponymous city founded in 316 BC on the Chalcidian Peninsula.[83]

Cassander was responsible for the murder of both of Alexander's sons and their mothers. It was the most direct means of propelling himself to almost twenty years of power and establishing a dynasty that would last until 294 BC through two of his three ill-fated sons, who in turn were murdered by Alexander's competing successors (known as the 'Diadochi', after the Greek) and their heirs. In the process, and probably when he was fighting Alexander's mother, Olympias, and her allies – including the former royal secretary, Eumenes of Cardia – a politically charged pamphlet emerged accusing Cassander and his brother, Iollas, of Alexander's assassination in Babylon; it led to revenge killings across Macedon when Olympias targeted his family (see Grant, *Last Will and Testament*, 2021, chapter 8).

But there is no further evidence of Aristobulus' return to Europe after Alexander's death. He could equally have worked for Ptolemy through the Successor Wars; Alexandria, Ptolemy's new capital of Egypt, would have been *the* place to be for an already-established engineer, for the new city was one of the largest civic construction projects ever undertaken, though Cassandrea was a significant other.[84] The ever-advancing Alexandrian building site was (later) described by the poet Theocritus as having 'everywhere army-boots and men in military cloaks'.[85]

Although Aristobulus was not an uncommon name, the one possible link to his post-campaign service is the Aristobulus cited as Ptolemy's high-ranking diplomat operating in Asia Minor to negotiate the so-called 'Peace of the Dynasts' in 311 BC in the heat of the Successor Wars. The connection is offered in name alone, but we would expect Aristobulus to have been offered some prominent service – and especially in a role that involved dealing with former campaign comrades (as this envoy would have) – if he truly did not commence his writing until an octogenarian.[86]

The proposals are not conflicting. A career with Ptolemy, whose interests were aligned with Cassander much of the time (he had sons from his marriage to Cassander's sister and was allied with him against the threat from Antigonus), followed by retirement to Cassandrea, is supportable for Aristobulus. Moreover, Diodorus suggested that much of the city populace who survived Philip's earlier city destructions, of Olynthus for example, were absorbed by Cassandrea, as were other smaller towns, so the metropolis' footprint and notoriety would have grown fast.[87] For a brief period, from 281–279 BC, Cassandrea even became a 'Ptolemaic' city in the Macedonian kingship of Ptolemy the Thunderbolt, the passed-over son of Ptolemy I Soter.

A change of employer, as well as city, was not unique in this period. If finally publishing from Cassandrea as a noteworthy resident, Aristobulus' similarly extensive service would have also been associated with Cassandrea in retrospective literary citations; the city officials would certainly have appreciated the public relations opportunity. Although the identification of Aristobulus' employer and location is not essential, the influences exerted upon him by Cassander, who controlled Macedon and who lay at the nefarious heart of the rumours of Alexander's poisoning – alongside the influence of an already-published book by Ptolemy, who enjoyed absolute rule of Egypt as well as influence in the islands, and who made very specific claims about Alexander's death (a version which effectively exonerated Cassander; see Grant, *Last Will and Testament*, 2021, chapter 1) – cannot be underestimated. Aristobulus was straightjacketed in what he could write by at least one powerful dynast.

Evidence of that influence may still be traceable, for Arrian concluded his campaign account with a phrase suggesting that Aristobulus had no more to offer on Alexander's death than that claimed by the Eumenes-compiled Royal Diaries, and moreover, that detail corroborated with Ptolemy's account.[88] If Ptolemy (as I have argued)[89] was the originator of this supposed Royal Diaries extract, which denied any evidence of regicide and omitted any detail of Alexander nominating a legitimate successor at Babylon, then Aristobulus could not easily have provided Alexander with anything more than that: a silent, intestate and conspiracy-free death, despite what he might have witnessed there or heard after the event (see Grant, *Last Will and Testament*, 2021, chapter 6).

Furthermore, as a writer living in the political and military sphere of influence of either of these dynasts, Aristobulus would have been extremely sensitive when making references to Rhoxane and her son, Alexander IV, or to Alexander's older son, Heracles, each of whom had been executed on Cassander's direct orders or through his political reach. As has been pointed out, Aristobulus certainly 'was not encumbered by the truth' when dealing with Alexander's campaign entourage, and the reason (or one of them) is not difficult to trace.[90]

Eumenes of Cardia

Historians rarely cite Eumenes as a 'source', but in every respect he should be. His CV makes him an eyewitness to the most formative of events and a noteworthy author of the genuine Royal Diaries, fabricated oaths and royally sealed forgeries.

Philip saw Eumenes' potential early and employed him from the age of 20 (*ca.* 342 BC) at court in Pella as his personal secretary, when Alexander was in his mid-teens. There, Eumenes needed to negotiate growing tensions, firstly between Philip and Alexander's estranged mother, Olympias, with whom Eumenes would remain a lifelong ally, and then between Alexander and his father when the prince went into exile (see chapter 6). It seems that after Philip's death, Eumenes was able to continue in his post in the court archives, where the Royal Diaries were kept, and of course the secretariat that handled the growing written communications of the ever-expanding empire. Eumenes also remained a correspondent in Asia with the royal family back in Epirus and Macedon. There are references to these court archives scattered through the histories of the Macedonian kings, and on campaign as the empire expanded with each victory, the royal secretariat also grew.[91]

As the invasion ventured East, it seems that Alexander's reliance on Eumenes grew along with his influence, to the point where the confidence the king placed in him irked Alexander's second-on-command, Hephaestion. An indicator is Plutarch's statement that the tent (by now we may imagine an expansive pavilion) of Eumenes caught fire in India, or rather was set on fire by Alexander as a prank. In his regret, Alexander made every effort to assist Eumenes, who held the role expressed as the diary-keeping secretary (*hypomnematographos*), in retrieving correspondence from the generals and regional governors; much was obviously lost and its recovery was essential to the administration of the newly acquired empire. Eumenes had managed to accumulate wealth along the way, and this landed him a trierarch role in the Indus–Hydaspes river flotilla.[92]

Eumenes was granted a golden crown by Alexander for his services and paired with a wife linked to Persian nobility at the mass weddings at Susa, along with prominent courtiers who were being groomed to oversee the empire. At some point, alongside his secretarial duties, Eumenes also gained his own cavalry command and access to the highest echelon of power by the time the army finally returned to Babylon in early 323 BC; he *may* have been promoted to the king's personal Bodyguard status (see Grant, *Last Will and Testament*, 2021, chapter 7).[93]

At Alexander's deathbed in Babylon, Eumenes may have even penned the king's dictated will (despite reports of an intestate death and infamous last words leaving his kingdom 'to the strongest'), and he was certainly associated (genuinely or by mendacious design) with the final Royal Diaries entry recording Alexander's death. The Roman antiquarian Aelian (*ca.* AD 175–235) had a dubious opinion of what he read about Alexander's alleged behaviour: 'or the authors of these stories are telling lies: from them one can infer that such writers, who include Eumenes of Cardia, tell similar tales on other occasions'. He may have been referring to the forged letters from the kings and the regent in Pella that are clearly referred to, or an allegedly doctored oath which won him freedom from a later siege. But duplicities were rife in the Successor Wars (see Grant, *Last Will and Testament*, 2021, chapter 7).

In those turbulent days immediately following Alexander's death, Eumenes became a valuable, trusted mediator for the unpopular 'royalist' Perdiccas, Alexander's former second-in-command, to broker a truce between the infantry and cavalry at Babylon, each supporting different factions in their power struggle to fill the vacant throne, helping to avert an instant 'civil war'. Eumenes himself was given vast provinces to govern, and over the next eight years he remained at the centre of the Successor Wars, much of the time as an outlaw after his proscription in 320 BC following his defeat of the popular veteran Craterus, who died in Eumenes' arms. As a renegade, the Macedonian generals railed against him, and despite his brilliance on the battlefield against Antigonus the One-Eyed – along with his subterfuges off it – his own Macedonian infantrymen, including the best veteran corps of fighters in the empire, turned him in for execution at the end of 316 BC (see Grant, *Last Will and Testament*, 2021, chapter 7).

Eumenes' role in the Successor Wars influenced the history of Hieronymus of Cardia, most likely his nephew, who documented the first fifty post-Alexander years, again as an eyewitness at the centre of unravelling events. As *the* formative history of the period, Eumenes features prominently in the compression of Hieronymus' detail preserved in the Roman-period books of Diodorus detailing the same period. His bitter-sweet career uniquely earned him biographies by Plutarch and Roman writer Cornelius Nepos (*ca.* 110–25 BC). But as an eyewitness 'historian' to the reign of Alexander, Eumenes' most important contribution was as keeper of the Royal Diaries; it appears he waged not just cavalry war, but a battle of words on the nature of Alexander's death and his succession instructions, in league with Olympias, who was executed in the same year.

As a suitable, though ill-willed, epitaph, we have the taunt of the Macedonian commander Neoptolemus, who jibed that 'he had followed the king with shield and spear, but Eumenes with pen and paper'. Eumenes killed Neoptolemus in single combat on the battlefield three years later.[94] What happened to the Royal Diaries is unknown, though Ptolemy claimed to have the final entry dealing with the days leading up to Alexander's death. However, this entry looks contrived and we may logically argue that if a folio of coherent campaign records *had* survived, there would be few, if any, contradictions in the sources. And that is demonstrably not the case.

Other Court Sources and Eyewitnesses to Events

Chares of Mytilene on Lesbos has to be considered a primary or 'court' source, penning a *History of Alexander* in ten or more books. As the royal usher or chamberlain to the king, he could not resist capturing court gossip he was uniquely well placed to hear. Some nineteen fragments remain, principally in Athenaeus' *Dinner Sophists* and Plutarch's biography, ranging from lucid eyewitness memoirs of court ceremony to what are clearly tinsel-covered anecdotes.[95] The vivid descriptions of regal excesses suggest he published under a later patronage that must have been tolerant of its negative content; a location on Lesbos under Antigonus' sphere of influence might support that supposition.[96] There is no guarantee, however, that the fragments are fully representative of Chares' work as a whole, and unlike the unrestrained accusations of alcoholism credited to others, he was careful not to directly slander Alexander or his Companions.[97]

Marsyas of Pella, half-brother to Antigonus the One-Eyed and his naval captain at the Battle of Salamis off Cyprus in 307/306 BC, authored another now-lost *On the Education of Alexander* as well as a *History of Macedon* in ten books that captured detail of the early campaign. His was, almost uniquely, a Macedonian history written by a Macedonian, whereas the thirteen other authors we know of who chronicled the rise of the nation were conspicuously not.[98] One prominent modern scholar of the period concluded that, 'like the Carthaginians and the Spartans, the Macedones are among the silent people of the ancient Mediterranean basin', referring to the lack of literary output from these once-dominant powers. This might be a little over-generalized, for we know that either Alexander's regent, Antipater, or perhaps an Antipater of Magnesia, wrote a historical work titled *On the Deeds of King Perdiccas in Illyria* (a former Macedonian king), and that there once existed a *History of Alexander* by a Philip of Pella. We also have fifteen fragments from a Macedonian history by the native Theagenes.[99]

Medius of Larissa, the alleged host of the fatal party at which Alexander was poisoned, features prominently and was possibly a member of the Thessalian Aleuadae royal house. Following Alexander's death, he first served Perdiccas and then, like Nearchus, switched his allegiance to Antigonus the One-Eyed against Ptolemy. The philosopher Anaximenes of Lampsacus, a city near the Hellespont notable for its philosophers and historians, resided within Alexander's inner circle; both dipped their reeds into self-serving ink along with other less-easily identified writers.[100] References to Idomeneus, also of Lampsacus and a friend of the philosopher Epicurus, suggest an anecdotal work in the style of Duris (whom he likely knew) had once existed, and the anonymous Byzantine encyclopaedia known as the *Suda* suggested that another contemporary, Menaechmus of Sicyon, wrote a history of the campaign. Strabo captured an additional snippet of the sea voyage back from India by Androsthenes of Thasos, who was a prominent crewmember under Nearchus' command.[101]

A few of the titles attached to these lost works are tantalizing: a treatise by Ephippus, *On the Death (or Funeral) of Alexander and Hephaestion*, and Strattis of Olynthus' *Five Books on the Royal Diaries* are mouth-watering names for historians but remain no more than that.[102]

These, along with other contemporary writers associated with the campaign (such as Polycleitus of Larissa, mentioned repeatedly by Roman-era authors), no doubt constituted a corpus of authors who were later referenced by Arrian, Diodorus and Curtius under the frustrating collectives of 'some historians', 'other writers' or even 'so they say'. These indeterminate in-betweens still elude identification and dating.

We should not forget the verbal material that birthed the rumour, hearsay and anecdote that crept into Alexander's tale along with genuine eyewitness reminiscences which never made it to papyrus. One formative scholar identified what he termed a 'mercenary source' within the texts, suggesting this incendiary bundle included the reminiscences of a soldier who fought *for* the Persian king, as tens of thousands of Greek mercenaries had, against Alexander. However, we could credibly postulate that this was not an individual, but a recycling factory of information from soldiers of fortune and campaigners settling in the provinces during the Successor War years, some seeking sanctuary and others seeking silver.[103]

Both locations were magnets for campaign veterans on either side of the Persian–Macedonian divide; they had stories to tell and grudges to settle in the choppy wake of Macedon's continued domination of Greece. No doubt campfire commentary on Alexander was a favourite flytrap for soldiers' tales as the wine flowed.

We should not forget the epigraphic evidence (inscribed texts) carved into rock and stone. We have the *Parian Chronicle* (otherwise known as the Parian Marble) compiled *ca.* 264/263 BC, which covers events from 336–302/301 BC, as well as the Babylonian *Chronicle of the Successors*, a fragmentary cuneiform tablet that now resides in the British Museum. A further inscription found at Scepsis, recording the contents of a letter from Alexander's one-eyed general Antigonus to the Greek cities of Asia Minor, is an enlightening insight into the state of affairs and a fragile peace of 311 BC that did not last. Carved slabs (stelae) like these are primary witnesses too if they were inscribed by contemporaries; moreover, they had little room for the rhetoric that we find interwoven into manuscripts.

As one eminent historian put it in 1894: 'It is indeed true that the archaeologist has succeeded in exacting from dumb, cold marble or crustated metal, the interesting story of contemporaneous achievements ... while their very nature possessed well-nigh all the elements of absolute authenticity, this is far from being the case with written records. For in their transmission from century to century they are all but certain to become distorted or adulterated.'[104] His eloquent contention would hold true were it not for the Egyptian *Satrap Stele* (erected in 311 BC), which essentially reads as Ptolemaic propaganda in stone.[105]

Of course there once existed written accounts by those subjugated by Alexander and Macedonian rule, and they would have put up a challenge. We have no idea what may have been written about the Macedonian invaders by Berossus, the Babylonian Chaldean priest of Bel–Marduk who wrote just a generation later; the twenty-two quotations or paraphrases of his work and the eleven statements about him in classical sources suggest he was prolific in astronomical and philosophical references to Chaldeans, though to what extent this represented a history of events remains unknown.[106] What did the *Egyptica* (*ca.* 285 BC) of Manetho, a subjugated priest of Ra based at Heliopolis, make of Ptolemaic rule?[107] Manetho's criticism of Herodotus gives us a hint of his views on Greeks coveting the oriental past for themselves. Yet the 'standard authorities' remain the Macedonian, Greek and Roman perspectives on the conquest of the Persian Empire, like Herodotus' *Histories* which had documented the earlier rise and expansion of Persia.

Yet these 'barbarian' voices were just as entitled to a hearing; after all, the greater part of Alexander's adult life had been spent east of the Hellespont. Chaldeans from Babylonia, Indian gymnosophists, Phoenician shipwrights and traders, and embalmers from Egypt complemented the Macedonian entourage.[108] The inner circle at the court banquets included Thessalians, Cretans, Cypriots and royal Asiatics. His first wife, Rhoxane, was Bactrian, or perhaps Sogdian, and he had attachments to Carian and Persian 'mothers', adopted by one and adopting the other.[109] Alexander was not a man longing to return to the provincial pastures of Pella, and neither were his senior commanders, who had their eyes on a chunk of the Asian empire.

The Extended Family at War

These remarkable successors, the Diadochi, who became the first Hellenistic kings, had inherited more than a knowledge of sarissa drills and flying wedges from their king: they had learned Macedonian statecraft. Had Alexander's own ambition never ventured beyond the expanded borders established by his father, these Pellan court aristocrats may have contented themselves with governing one of the ancient feudal cantons of Upper or Lower Macedon they heralded from.[110] The more ambitious of them might have become *condottieri* working for a tyrant or satrap in Asia Minor. But Alexander had set the bar high, and in the process infused his court Companions (referred to as *hetairoi*) with a vision far grander than domestic state affairs or seasonal campaigning to pocket gold Darics. By now they had come to harbour a self-belief that emanated from their part in his great journey; they coveted kingdoms, not the ephemeral wealth of serving the remaining Argead line. It was an ambition that, according to Justin, left Fortune imbuing them 'with mutual emulation for their mutual destruction'.[111]

Labelling Alexander's inner sanctum of power eyewitnesses 'at war' is legitimate. For those who participated in Alexander's eleven-year campaign in Asia, it was almost impossible to avoid being drawn into what we could term 'civil war', or even 'Graeco-Persian world war', in the aftermath of his death, in which the entire Graeco–Persian world was embroiled, from the borders of the Adriatic in the West to India in the East, and the Caspian Sea in the North to Ethiopia in the South. If they were military men, they now had to fight for survival as well as territory, and if they were interested onlookers – like the campaign historians and philosophers who became attached to courts – they had to shield themselves behind a militarized tyrant or king.

This universal conflict commenced immediately, from the moment the regional provinces of the empire (referred to as 'satrapies') were contentiously divided amongst Alexander's senior command in the days after his death. Whatever his last words on the matter or his hidden succession instructions, no one was content with the outcome and the lack of central authority imploded into self-serving factions of power.

Alexander had nominated seven (as was tradition) of his most trusted men to his personal Bodyguard corps; these court aristocrats were high-ranking military officers with command over significant sections of the infantry and cavalry, and by now they had accrued significant personal wealth to boot. The most notable 'inheritors and inheritances' mentioned by the sources (although their mandates may have been over even greater regions, including bordering lands)[112] include: Ptolemy, who inherited Egypt; Lysimachus, who was given authority over Thrace; Leonnatus, the Hellespont-bordering region of Phrygia; Antigonus the One-Eyed, with the greater part of Anatolia; Peithon, who gained Media; Peucestas, who controlled the Persian heartlands; Seleucus, who gained the governorship of Babylonia (either immediately or several years later);[113] and Alexander's former second-in-command ('chiliarch'), Perdiccas, who oversaw the empire and was *de facto* regent for the co-kings (Alexander's son by Rhoxane and his halfwit half-brother, who was elevated by the army at Babylon). Eumenes was given the lands of Cappadocia and Paphlagonia, which had not yet been subdued. It is likely that other named Bodyguards such as Aristonus, as well as the prominent court notables with military experience like Nearchus and Medius, would also have been given regional governorships as part of the twenty-or-more regional divisions, but the lists are corrupt and smack of manipulation and suppression; they were, after all, drafted by historians in the fight (see Grant, *Last Will and Testament*, 2021, chapter 8).[114]

To cover the events of the next twenty to thirty years in any detail requires a book of encyclopaedic proportions (as Hieronymus' scrolls were, most readily read today in highly fragmented and compressed form in the Roman-era texts of Curtius' chapter 10, Diodorus' books 18–21, Arrian's fragmentary *Times After Alexander*, Plutarch's *Lives* of Eumenes, Pyrrhus and Demetrius, as well as Justin's epitomised books 13–17), and we cannot do justice to the political, matrimonial and military intrigues here, but some key dates and conflicts can be outlined in an appreciation of why the historians were truly 'at war'.

Within days of pronouncing Alexander dead, the infantry mutinied at the prospect of Alexander's aristocratic senior command carving out power among themselves. In the convening of the army to decide on such matters – the traditional 'Common Assembly of Macedones', as it was known – both of Alexander's Asiatic sons were rejected (Rhoxane's potential son – she was pregnant – as well as Alexander's absent older child, Heracles, promoted by Nearchus). Civil war almost erupted as the infantry and cavalry faced off and skirmishing took place.

Eventually, with the dissenters trampled to death outside the city walls by the corps of Indian war elephants, Perdiccas was forced into a dangerous compromise: he elected to support Alexander's son (if a son) by the seven-month-pregnant Rhoxane (who subsequently gave birth to 'King Alexander IV'). This move propped-up his own power, and yet he had to simultaneously agree to a co-king in the form of Alexander's halfwit half-brother, Arrhidaeus, who was crowned 'Philip III'. Worse was to come, as Perdiccas was forced to allow a pugnacious granddaughter of Philip II to marry Arrhidaeus (her uncle) in a union that would provide potential legitimate, but hostile, offspring that could in future challenge for the throne. The various dissatisfied successors departed Babylon to take up their governorships, while the royal army was herded around Cappadocia and southern Anatolia (Pisidia and Lycaonia) under an unpopular chiliarch (Perdiccas) in response to local revolts.

Two years after Alexander's death, in 321 BC, Ptolemy stole (or rescued, depending upon the interpretation from divided sources) Alexander's funeral bier in Syria and Perdiccas declared war; he had himself been intriguing with the hand of the daughter of the regent, Antipater, as well as with Alexander's sister, Cleopatra, in his bid for primacy in both Macedon and Asia. Eumenes was complicit in Cleopatra's courting through corresponding with her in Pella and then Sardis, as well as with Alexander's mother, Olympias, in Epirus, in a bid to bolster the Perdiccan cause. Antipater, Craterus and Antigonus, after defeating the Greek uprising in the Lamian War in Thessaly, crossed back to Asia to face this 'royalist' threat. Cleopatra soon followed them independently, hoping to broker power more locally from Sardis in Lydia.

Perdiccas was murdered by his own officers on the banks of the Nile after failing to penetrate Ptolemy's defences (and probably with Ptolemy's coercion and complicity), but in an unexpected twist of fate, Eumenes defeated the venerated general Craterus in battle close to Cappadocia; the popular veteran died in Eumenes' arms. Some fifty of the 'Perdiccans' (Eumenes included) were thereafter proscribed as outlaws under sentence of death when Antipater, Antigonus and their allies met for a council of war in 320 BC at Triparadeisus in northern Syria, where the empire was redistributed to account for the newly deceased and the now-damned.

Triparadeisus was formative in the episode where two generations of 'successors' were given regional authority and guardianships of the kings.

Antipater escorted the 'kings' back to Macedon and left Antigonus in charge to mop in the rebels, and there then commenced five years of spectacular warfare against Eumenes, while back in Macedon the dead regent's son, Cassander, came to power after defeating the coalition Olympias had put together. She and Eumenes were executed in the same year (316 BC). By now, through marriages to the various daughters of former regent Antipater, the powerful dynasts-in-waiting – Ptolemy, Lysimachus and Antigonus (through his son, Demetrius the Besieger) – were related, and there could have commenced a period of stability if it was not for Antigonus' ambition to control the whole of the Asian empire. He soon executed Peithon, and Seleucus, seeing the way the wind was blowing, fled to Ptolemaic Egypt.

Despite brief accords and short-lived peace treaties between the warring successors (most notably after Eumenes' death in 315 BC and then in 311 BC – the so-called 'Peace of the Dynasts', the precursor to Cassander murdering both of Alexander's sons) – an alliance of Ptolemy, Lysimachus, Seleucus and Cassander coalesced in response to the continued Antigonid threat, as borders waxed and waned and battles were fought across the empire. Both Nearchus and Medius joined Antigonus' collation.

In the years that followed, now that the legitimate royal line of Macedon had been extinguished by Cassander (who would nevertheless have sons with royal blood by Alexander's captured half-sister, Thessalonice), and with the assistance of Antigonus, who had Cleopatra killed when she was fleeing to Ptolemy for marriage, the Diadochi were to proclaim themselves kings in their own right. But rather than being quelled by the new titles, the ambitions of the successors saw them intriguing once more either to protect their own borders or as a precursor to a challenge for the throne of Macedon itself. Finally, they met for a deciding clash at Ipsus in 301 BC, when Antigonus, now in his mid-80s and with a great Asian army but devoid of significant other allies, faced the combined forces of Lysimachus, Seleucus and Cassander, with Ptolemy providing absent moral support (an alleged ruse by Antigonus had seen him withdraw his army). Some 150,000 men, 120 scythed chariots and 475 war elephants are said to have arrayed for battle on the Phrygian plain, where Antigonus was surrounded and shot through with javelins; his son, Demetrius, fled and the Asian empire was carved up once more among the victors.

In the view of many historians, the Battle of Ipsus represented the true beginning of the Hellenistic era, when the landscape of the empire was for the very first time reshaped by 'agreement' rather than by brute force.[115] In the following decades, superpowers emerged, around which the Eastern Mediterranean and former Persian Empire gravitated for generations to come. The kingdoms of Seleucus,

Ptolemy and Lysimachus (and Antigonus before them) riveted Asia, Egypt and Macedon together as never before, propagating Greek culture and language eastward, perhaps in a way Alexander had originally conceived that the final pages of his own epitaph would have done.

With the epic battle in Phrygia at Ipsus in 301 BC, the Antigonid storm passed, and if the squalls from his equally charismatic son, Demetrius the Besieger, had not quite settled, the horizon in Asia was extended, providing Ptolemy at least some security and an environment in which his historical account might finally be penned. Before then, powerful and well-informed enemies resided close by (Coele-Syria, meaning 'Hollow Syria' and referring to what is today Israel and/or Lebanon's fertile Beqaa Valley, and Phoenicia changed hands repeatedly) and an invasion of Egypt was only ever a Nile Delta crossing away. Ptolemy's grip on power was still tenuous, and those were not the years in which to publish a web of deceit, for dangerous repercussions were likely. If Ptolemy had read his Euripides, he would have known of a pertinent wisdom: 'Silence in season, speech where speech is safe.'[116]

Although it appears that in the longer term Ipsus 'created more tensions than it resolved',[117] the trio of Alexander's former Bodyguards – Ptolemy, Seleucus and Lysimachus – avoided self-destruction for the best part of the next twenty years, each living into their 80s.[118] That is not to say they didn't intrigue, use their intermarriages nefariously or sponsor some of the most famous generals in history to undermine their opponents. Responding to Seleucus' occupation of Coele-Syria in the wake of Ipsus, when governance of the empire was again reviewed, Ptolemy allegedly commented on the quiet revenge he may one day extract: 'For friendship's sake he would not for the present interfere but he would consider later how best to deal with friends who chose to encroach.'[119] And that might just have been carried out through the medium of his book.

The decades after Ipsus were not kind to the home nation of Macedon. The kingdom became divided as Pyrrhus of Epirus (another dynastic relative), Demetrius the Besieger, Cassander's sons and Lysimachus each attempted (or briefly succeeded) to take the throne. Demetrius was ousted after a failed reinvasion of Asia and was reduced to drinking himself to death in captivity. Seleucus, now in his early 80s, defeated Lysimachus at the Battle of Cyropedium (the 'Plain of Cyrus') in 281 BC and thought he had finally unified the empire, only to be killed by one of Ptolemy's equally ambitious sons, Ptolemy the Thunderbolt. The complex web of intermarriages filtered down the generations as sons married dynastic daughters, and even brothers married sisters, and the whole Graeco–Persian world of the Hellenistic period remained one 'family at war'.

In this age of widespread turbulence, it is difficult to imagine how *any* written accounts could have been published, for the generational wars continued until Rome finally occupied the former Macedon-ruled Eastern Mediterranean, Ptolemaic

Egypt and the former Achaemenid Empire, during a period that saw the wholesale loss of much Hellenistic literature.

The very first bloody years between Alexander's end in 323 BC and 320 BC had already witnessed the deaths of the vocal anti-Macedonian Athenian orators Demosthenes and Hyperides, the great polymath Aristotle, Diogenes the Cynic – who once met Alexander in Corinth – and the court philosopher Anaxarchus. The historian of Philip's court, Theopompus of Chios, had been executed by Ptolemy soon after he took control of Egypt. Perdiccas, Craterus and the Bodyguard Leonnatus all died at war, while Nearchus may well have perished at the Battle of Gaza in 313/312 BC. The necrology includes many other prominent names associated with Alexander and his family line, including Eumenes, his ally Olympias and Alexander's own wives, sons, sister and half-sister (and her offspring).

Perhaps we should finish by asking why the long-lived Seleucus and Lysimachus declined to publish campaign accounts and stake their own claims to heroics and a share in Alexander's success, for they became kings with great tales to tell and no doubt with their own hatchets to bury deep. Possibly it was because Ptolemy ended his account at Alexander's death, and until then, his pages had treated them fairly enough, if perhaps not 'frequently' enough for their liking, for Ptolemy's reluctance to attribute credit to Alexander's other nobles has long been recognized.[120] But for all we know, Seleucus and Lysimachus were felled halfway through writing their memoirs in old age, with primed court historians ready to dictate to. But manuscripts, diaries, journals, libraries and official correspondence disappeared without a trace in the face of defeat in battle, giving the impression that a literary desert had existed at their court. Along with treasuries, their wives, generals and their men, chattels, ships and cities, literary ordnance was also seized, so the history of the vanquished slipped into the folio of the victor.

After occupying Antigonus' former 'empire', which spanned Asia Minor, Lysimachus did set about repairing the crumbling walls of what he believed was Troy (the mound at Hissarlik), suggesting he harboured something of a 'caretaker' role for the Homeric past, no doubt for propaganda purposes. According to a fragment from the history of Memnon which has been preserved in a ninth-century epitome,[121] Lysimachus exiled a certain Nymphis from Thrace; he appears to have written a work titled *Concerning Alexander, the Diadochi and the Epigoni*, and this may suggest Lysimachus was sensitive to the subject as a whole, marrying as he once did into the Antipatrid house, whose figurehead, Cassander, had murdered Alexander's mother and sons.[122] Or perhaps after thirty years of bloody campaigning, these giants of the age were simply content to rule in their own name, with their dynasties unfolding before them, though they were themselves to witness – and even orchestrated – the death of a number of their own children.

A scholar who profiled these 'lost historians' concluded that the eyewitness contemporaries wrote for their own 'literary' purposes rather than for any higher 'historical' ideals.[123] But they may have had little choice, for the unceasing war had clearly forced them to 'weaponize' their accounts. It appears their retrospective words in ink, sharper-tongued than a Greek logographer, slashing reputations like scythed chariots and removing textual entrails like the blade of a deft diviner, were capable of elevating some to great deeds while character-assassinating others, leaving us a prime example of what might be termed 'history eavesdropping on legend'.[124]

Chapter 3

The Funeral Games Historian

The account given by Hieronymus is different ... for a man who
associates with royalty cannot help being a partial historian.[1]

Pausanias, *Guide to Ancient Greece*

No profiling of the formative histories of the age would be complete without
Hieronymus of Cardia. It was he who gave us a first-hand account of the
first fifty, bloody, post–Alexander years, the wars the dying king allegedly
referred to as his posthumous 'funeral games'.[2]

Hieronymus entered the frame sometime soon after Alexander's death, when he
is found in the service of his likely uncle, Eumenes of Cardia, the royal secretary.
Inevitably, in the opening to his book, Hieronymus recounted the troubled transfer
of power that took place at Babylon, and possibly recorded some of the most notable
events that led up to it along with a geographical breakdown of the empire to provide
readers with some perspective, as was the vogue.

There is good reason to believe that the extremely detailed, but rhetoric-free,
descriptions of the gargantuan funeral pyre raised for Hephaestion (who died in
Ecbatana in 324 BC) and the priceless funeral bier constructed for Alexander over
two years (323–321 BC), as well as the archetypal list of satrapies which represents
the first partition of the empire, each originated with Hieronymus. Alexander's
grandiose pending projects, his so-called 'last plans' which were supposedly
'discovered' in the king's memoranda at Babylon, may also derive from Hieronymus,
along with a summary of what was contentiously presented, proposed and rejected
at the Common Assembly of Macedones in June 323 BC, where all the fighting
commenced (see Grant, *Last Will and Testament*, 2021, chapter 9).[3]

But Hieronymus was wise enough not to attempt a retrospective Alexander
biography, even though he had access to the most intimate of eyewitnesses: Eumenes
and the veterans he recruited. After all, the events that were soon unfolding before
Hieronymus' own eyes were as momentous in scale, ambition and immediate peril
as Alexander's campaign to overthrow Persia.

In Alexander 'historiography' (the study of the sources and methodology
behind the written accounts), the Successor Wars have always played second fiddle
to Alexander's lifetime campaigns. The Macedonian conquest of the East is better
remembered than the extraordinary period that followed because it was the more

easily understood, like the stark-chiselled emotions and clean-sculpted motives that underpinned war in the *Iliad*, the edited book Alexander is said to have kept under his pillow.[4] Alexander's conquest had shape, direction and cause, operating under the banner of 'revenge' for the earlier Persian invasions of Hellas and the 'profanation of Greek temples'.[5] To this grievance Alexander added the accusation that Persian gold was behind his father's assassination.

The Successor Wars lacked these public-relations-friendly soundbites, and yet they were perpetuated by the same group of mighty personas who had helped make Alexander 'great'. In a sense, the first generation of successors – the Diadochi – were the true offspring of Alexander, or as Justin termed them, 'the many Alexanders of Macedon' and a uniquely privileged generation of 'prefects who became princes'.[6] They had learned their trade alongside their king, some as coeval youths at the Pellan court, and as a cohesive unit they proved unstoppable in the decade that saw the Macedonian military machine advance as far as India. Its leadership became a true meritocracy: the unfortunate had fallen in battle, with the non-performers side-lined, while the indiscreet and loose-tongued were executed and those with frailer constitutions died on the march. Those who survived both the campaign and Alexander were tough, brutal, ambitious, and now in the Successor Wars, they proved to be cunning politicians – and historians.

On few occasions could a circle of men so influential to the fate of an empire have congregated in a single assembly hall or king's campaign pavilion. Perhaps only the Roman Senate centuries later could compare, when attended at once by Julius Caesar, Mark Antony, Cicero, Crassus, Clodius, Pompey the Great, Lucullus and Cato the Younger. Like them, the Diadochi were friends and allies at times, drinking at the Macedonian-styled banquets known as 'symposia', and then the bitterest of enemies who fought to the last man. Hieronymus had to negotiate with them all in his account, either in person, by association or in war.

Hieronymus first operated under Eumenes and then served three successive generations of the Antigonid dynasty, commencing with Antigonus the One-Eyed, his son, Demetrius the Besieger, and finally Antigonus II 'Gonatas' (the meaning of his epithet is uncertain),[7] who by then faced a radically changed Graeco–Persian world and a very different national threat. Hieronymus' lengthy career saw him operating in Asia Minor, Syria, the central-eastern provinces of the former Persian Empire, Greece and finally in Macedon, and alliances were fluid within those years. We do not know the title of his work with any certainty, though the Romanized Jewish historian Josephus (*ca*. AD 37–100) and Dionysius of Halicarnassus (published from 7 BC onwards), who described it as 'long winded and boring', suggested it was called *A History of the Successors* (*Diadochi*) or *Offspring* (*Epigoni*).[8]

Hieronymus' account of the post-Argead-dynasty world, which neatly sequelled the monographs on Alexander's life, was a distinctive work that unified Greek, Macedonian and Asian contemporary history through his unique testimony as a participant. Yet like all histories of the time, it was an 'elitist' affair which focused on the deeds of kings, generals and their statesmen alone, with little space on the pages for the plight of the common man; this was an 'aristocratic bias' in historical writing that went back to Homer's *Iliad* and *Odyssey*.[9]

Like the other lost eyewitness accounts (with very few exceptions), 'strictly speaking, we do not possess a word' of Hieronymus' original material.[10] The eighteen or nineteen fragments we have (one is dubious), less than five pages of text in all, make any evaluation of Hieronymus' work rather speculative, unless we are prepared to accept that his account is preserved reasonably intact in the more expansive sections of books 18–22 of Diodorus' *Library of History* which deal with the same years in précised form.[11]

Although it was criticised by Dionysius, Hieronymus' work was a unique and invaluable account of the decades that may otherwise have been less thoroughly chronicled because of the instability which suppressed any flowering of the art of literature, at least initially. A number of Hellenistic and Roman-era historians (Plutarch, for example) used Hieronymus for detail in their biographies of his contemporary generals and statesmen, and Hieronymus' books were précised to various degrees in 'universal' histories of the period (Diodorus and Trogus, for example), but their severe compressions (especially Justin's epitome of Trogus) render any direct comparison with his original impossible.[12]

Hieronymus himself is said to have criticized the writing of his contemporary, Duris of Samos for its hostility towards Macedonian affairs, which in turn appears to betray Hieronymus' own political partiality to his Macedonian patrons.[13] It has even been suggested that Hieronymus published in response to Duris' critical books, though Hieronymus must have diarized events as they occurred and sketched out a broad narrative years before, when in the thick of things.[14]

However, the Cardian historian faced unique challenges, and the narrating of the years in which Eumenes battled with Antigonus constituted a particular dilemma. Serving both of the protagonists, Hieronymus literally co-joined their stories in person and in ink; as a result, his history of the Successor Wars was always destined to be a compromised narrative. Neither yet a published historian and never a military general, Hieronymus' exact role under Eumenes remains unclear, though on later occasions his title (*epimeletes*) suggested a guardian of affairs. He was clearly one of Eumenes' trusted inner circle of confidants and a messenger of the most sensitive information when Eumenes was under siege in 319 BC.

For reasons we can only speculate, Hieronymus was spared execution when captured with Eumenes after Battle of Gabiene in late 316 BC, and yet the wounds he sustained suggest he saw action in the ranks. He was summarily employed by the victor and served Antigonus the One-Eyed until his death, during which Hieronymus came to play something of a 'Polybian role', when the captive came to admire his captor as an influential client–court historian.[15]

The moment Eumenes was executed on the order of Antigonus was, as one scholar put it, the event that emancipated Hieronymus as a historian, for thereafter he joined the hunter rather than the hunted, with no more offers to defect or desperate siege mediations tugging at his loyalties. But when faced with the task of later biographizing these two opponents, Hieronymus attempted to preserve the warrior virtue of each, while permitting the deceptions that hallmarked a great general: the hero Odysseus, for example, like the Sparta-encouraged cunning that Xenophon had once espoused and Polybius seems to have later admired.[16] Hieronymus' early pages had additionally needed to salvage Eumenes from the early Perdiccan wreckage and then carefully preserve the honour of those he subsequently served while maintaining a sense of balance in their competing skills.[17]

If Hieronymus' pages were necessarily slanted towards his patrons, they were not 'encomiums' (accounts of high praise), and his admiration was anything but monotone. As one scholar points out, the Hieronymus-derived accounts of Diodorus and Plutarch include some twenty-one passages illustrating Antigonus' excessive ambition, if this profile was not the notoriously negative view of Duris once again. We can, in fact, see a subtle dimming in the image of the father (Antigonus) to the brightening of that of his son (Demetrius), in which condemnation of Antigonus' lust for power was merely an abrasion that polished the story of Demetrius' extraordinary bid for survival after battle at Ipsus in 301 BC; it was a battle which changed Hieronymus' world once more.[18] Pausanias concluded that Hieronymus was ultimately hostile to all kings except Antigonus II Gonatas. Modern studies go further still and even propose that an anti-Macedonian element underpinned Hieronymus' elitist narrative.[19]

Unsurprisingly, the enemy dynasts – Seleucus, Peucestas and Lysimachus – fared badly in Hieronymus' pages, as did Pyrrhus in the historian's desire to please his last patron king, Antigonus II Gonatas, whom Pyrrhus once defeated. However, the former state regent Polyperchon, who had supported Eumenes and Olympias, was afforded more mercurial treatment.[20] Hieronymus' agenda was clear: his portrait reflected Polyperchon's alignment with, or opposition to, his own patrons, firstly his support for Olympias and (it is claimed) Eumenes, then Antigonus from 315 BC, and finally his alliance with Cassander, who arranged the termination of Alexander's line. The historian's tone towards the turncoat, Polyperchon, changes at, or soon after, Eumenes' final capture in late 316 BC, when the previously loyal (if not dominant) regent was painted as ever more ineffectual. The final character assassination came when Alexander's son, Heracles, was murdered. The last episode may have genuinely disgusted the historian, for Polyperchon's execution of the teenage Heracles in 309/308 BC on the orders of Cassander, in return for 100 talents and a minor share of power, ended a scheme to enthrone the prince which may well have been crafted with Antigonus' support.[21]

Hieronymus' narrative, ending sometime after the death of Pyrrhus of Epirus in 272 BC, captured at least fifty-two years of war reporting through one of history's most dramatic and metamorphic eras of the Graeco–Persian world.[22] It outspanned the chronological breadth of Thucydides' *Peloponnesian War*, Xenophon's account of the ill-fated 'ten thousand' under Cyrus the Younger and Alexander's reign combined. We cannot underestimate the complexity of the task facing the Cardian historian when he finally laid out his scrolls. His career had witnessed the execution of Perdiccas, Eumenes and his backer Olympias, as well as Alexander's sons and wives, the defeat and capture of Demetrius at Gaza in 313/312 BC (with Nearchus as advisor), the early death of Antigonus' younger son, Philip, in 306 BC, then Antigonus' disastrous invasion of Ptolemaic Egypt in the same year, when 80,000 infantry, 8,000 cavalry and eighty-three elephants – supported by a fleet of 150 warships and 100 transports – fared no better than Perdiccas' attempt seventeen years before.[23] Ptolemy, who might himself have had no more than a core of 5,000 Macedones in an army of some 30,000 men, used similar tactics again; he offered rich sums of money for enemy troop defection, so Antigonus had to post slingers to deter the deserters from leaving his ranks.[24]

Hieronymus would have additionally heard reports arriving from his native city, Cardia, as it was ruined by Lysimachus in 309 BC, after which his own eponymous city, Lysimachea, emerged in its place. This might have inspired Hieronymus to claim that it was Lysimachus who desecrated the royal graves at Aegae (the old capital and site of the royal necropolis) when warring against Pyrrhus, who had briefly ruled in the western part of Macedon (rather than being destroyed by Pyrrhus' Celtic Gauls, as claimed by other sources).[25]

After the failed year-long siege of Rhodes by Demetrius in 305 BC – the campaign which earned him the epithet 'the Besieger' – came the collapse of Antigonus' Asian empire at Ipsus in 301 BC, when Hieronymus would have seen his by-now corpulent patron lying dead on the Phrygian plain.[26] He would have watched on as the once-charismatic Demetrius was reduced to drinking himself to death by 283 BC, and would have recalled that Demetrius' wife, the thrice-widowed Phila, who was the daughter of Antipater, had committed suicide by drinking poison five years earlier when Demetrius lost control of Macedon (288 BC).[27] In 281 BC, reports arrived of the death of Lysimachus at Seleucus' hand at Cyropedium, followed by the intrigues of Pyrrhus of Epirus and Ptolemy's sons for the Macedonian throne when the state was divided.

Antigonus II Gonatas finally defeated the Gallic Celts near Lysimachea in 277 BC, but suffered a defeat by Pyrrhus three years later and was forced to regroup. Under this fourth and final patron, Antigonus II Gonatas – the 'enlightened despot' who surrounded himself with philosophers, poets and writers (though undertaking the occasional execution of hostile historians) – Hieronymus was provided with a modicum of peace in which he afforded his one-eyed grandfather, Antigonus, some biographical payback for the years he campaigned for the Pellan royals.[28] After the early turbulent years of Gonatas' reign, this may have also been the environment in which Marsyas of Pella (half-brother to Antigonus) was able to publish his account. The Antigonids appear to have been tolerant of writers and historians at their courts, and more so if they towed the family propaganda line.

But when Antigonus II Gonatas finally attained the throne, a threadbare Macedon was now a shadow of its former self, reflecting upon which he became 'the first Stoic king'.[29] Hieronymus lived through the death of one of Gonatas' sons, Alcyoneus, whose passing was stoically accepted by his father, and he witnessed the self-destruction of the once-brilliant Pyrrhus (whose memoirs he used), who died at Argos in 272 BC. Ultimately, he bore witness to the last of the sons and daughters of Alexander's successors relentlessly tearing each other's kingdoms apart. The earlier 'heroic' start to the Hellenistic period had drawn to a close, and so it comes as no surprise that 'a dark thread' ran through the whole of Hieronymus' history.[30]

But there remain loose threads, missing strands and twisted fibres too in the accounts of those who extracted their detail from Hieronymus, suggesting that the Cardian historian bypassed events he did not personally witness, or omitted campaigns whose outcomes were embarrassing for his patrons. Inevitably, there must have also been occasions when Hieronymus was not able to reconcile the deeds of his masters to the realities of war and the more nefarious tactics of battle.[31]

When he finally settled down to put memories on scrolls, Hieronymus would have been looking out on a Seleucid Empire that encompassed almost all of the Asian satrapies his royal employers had fought to acquire, a bitter reflection perhaps assuaged by the knowledge that Seleucus' son, Antiochus I, was besotted with Antigonus II Gonatas' sister, Stratonice, who thus became queen of the eastern Seleucid realm.

Although Hieronymus' history appears free from much of the didactic (moralizing) digression that infected later Hellenistic-era reporting, he did see the literary value of 'fortune' (attributable to either the so-named goddess or to the less-easily definable 'fate') as well as Eumenes' use of dream visions of Alexander and the resulting cults as military ruses in what was otherwise a secular history (see Grant, *Last Will and Testament*, 2021, chapter 7). For Hieronymus, the real gods were the generals he served, and in the absence of a wider debate on the more complex causes of the conflicts and their outcome, his occasional deference to fate and omens was perhaps simply a neat means of cutting short the debate.

Professedly living to the remarkable age of 104, with his faculties about him to the end, Hieronymus was essentially a captive of his times, swept along on a Macedonian storm he could neither shelter from nor outrun.[32] His history was demonstrably and yet understandably partisan. An omitted campaign here, a swerved satrapy there, a character painted as capricious in-between were all grist to the mill for a 'court' historian with the power of judicious selection, omission and their strategic arrangement.

In negotiating the political tides washing over him, Hieronymus knew exactly which subterfuges would stick; he was, after all, the only (attested) person still alive in the 270s BC who had enjoyed such an influential eyewitness position in the Diadochi intrigues. Of the hostile dynasties, only the Ptolemies and Seleucids remained powerful enough to dispute any content that unduly promoted the claims of his patrons. But by now these warring offspring were intermarried and unlikely to have cared less how the original satrapies were portioned out at Babylon or won by the spear by their ancestors a half century before. That world was now unrecognizable.

The greatest beneficiary of Hieronymus' pen remains Eumenes, and were it not for his fellow literary Cardian, the former royal secretary might have been portrayed as an undeserving Greek pawn hounded around a hostile Macedonian chessboard. On the contrary, Hieronymus made sure he was remembered as a master strategist, consummate general, friend of the queen mother and, for a time, the most 'legitimately' backed successor east of Macedon. This was something of a 'cleaning symbiosis' between the historian and his patron for mutual historical gain.[33] 'It is not the strongest that survive, nor the most intelligent, but those most responsive to change'; this sums up the careers of both the famous Cardians who made their indelible mark with the pen rather than the sword.[34]

Pausanias, the Greek travelographer-cum-antiquarian of the second century AD, was a realist who understood Hieronymus' compromised perspective: 'For a man who associates with royalty cannot help being a partial historian.'[35] If Eumenes, Hieronymus and the family of Antigonus dominated the shaping and recording of history in the decades after Alexander's death, there was another emerging triumvirate of equally influential writers who were opposed to them in every sense: Ptolemy, Aristobulus and Cleitarchus of Alexandria. For it was their published accounts that had a monopoly on Alexander's life (and especially his death) and their words which most impressed the Roman historians.[36]

Chapter 4

The Alexandrian Monopoly

Much of what we know about his [Ptolemy's] career in Alexander's lifetime derives from Arrian and, ultimately, from Ptolemy himself.[1]

Waldemar Heckel, *The Marshals of Alexander's Empire*

He [Aristobulus] was noted for his flattering style and was not encumbered by the truth but was a blatant apologist for the King.[2]

Waldemar Heckel, *Who's Who in the Age of Alexander the Great*

Cleitarchus entertained with 'pretty fictions' and was a 'better orator than historian'; he was brilliantly ingenious but notoriously untrustworthy.[3]

Cicero, *Brutus*, and Quintilian, *Institutes of Oratory*

'Publishing' in the ancient world came with demanding and exclusive caveats: this was micro-production on papyrus scrolls or more durable 'Pergamum' parchment by an educated, literate few who could afford the time and materials. Moreover, they needed some form of notoriety to provide them a following, or a ready-made reader base that made the work worthwhile. Further, they needed the assurance that the finished transcribed scrolls would be distributed effectively to those of influence and housed for posterity in a recognized library of some kind. The lucky few had independent means and an established reputation for speech-writing or orating, as well as access to rare and carefully guarded research materials. More often than not, they were sponsored by a king, tyrant or statesman in a symbiotic interdependency that saw words strategically fashioned and prudently slanted by politics and military objectives.

Contrast this to the many who witnessed the more-toxic fallout of warfare from this period: the orphaned, crippled, raped, betrayed, bankrupted and tortured on campaign, along with the wounded and the veterans no longer fit for service who had been abandoned in distant garrison towns and had no historical voices at all. The first-hand accounts of the gnarled veterans, dispossessed townsfolk and mercenaries forced to resettle in Alexander's new mudbrick 'Alexandrias' at the ends of the empire, and the half-caste children conceived when the Macedones swept through, had no forum nor papyrus for expression either. In Alexander's day, and through the Hellenistic era, kings did, and those sponsored by kings did, and ultimately it is their voices we hear.

The digression on publication has particular relevance to our Alexander sources. With the loss of what may once have been a vast corpus of eyewitness information – whether royal diaries, personal journals or the scrolls of less well-connected writers – everything we read today comes from the Roman period, and it was pulled together almost entirely from privileged 'court-influenced' sources. If we put aside for a moment the recounting of the Successor Wars, there appears evidence of a monopoly on the story of Alexander. But the evidence comes down to just when these eyewitnesses released their claims into the Hellenistic world, and at the centre of that debate lies the elusive Cleitarchus, whose colourful account became the most popular in Rome.

Cleitarchus of Alexandria

> No one can glance through the thirty-six fragments of Cleitarchus without being struck by one thing, how little we really know about the writer who in modern times has been magnified into such an influential and far-reaching source in the Alexander story, and has attracted to himself most of the flotsam brought down by that somewhat muddy stream or streams, the so-called Vulgate.[4]

This commentary from a formative study of Cleitarchus captures an unfortunate dilemma: though his influence on the Vulgate tradition has now been established, the extent of that sway and the original shape of Cleitarchus' book remain nothing short of a mystery. Based in Alexandria in the final years of older campaign veterans, or in the early years of their offspring, Cleitarchus composed the first syncretic biography (a blended account of various assimilation sources) of Alexander by fusing primary material in circulation with the gossip, rhetoric and those negative philosophical tones emanating from Greece.[5] The fermentation vat of Alexandria did the rest in that tumultuous, creative and yet dangerous period for historians and dynasts alike.

Many veterans found their way to new employment in Egypt, for the Ptolemies knew, as did all the new generals-cum-dynasts, that you needed a hard core of Macedonian soldiers to face Macedone-led satrapal armies, and no Asiatic soldiers of the time had been able to withstand an assault by its unique phalanx. So the land-grant 'cleruch' system of incentive and remuneration became all-important in attracting new settlers who formed a 'state within a state' in Egypt, Greek mercenaries and former Macedonian campaigners alike. Under this arrangement, land was allotted on condition of continued military call-up and no doubt the enrolment of their sons into the state army.[6] This may explain why Cleitarchus was able to garner more eyewitness detail than Arrian could later obtain from his revered but long-dead and sanitizing court sources of Ptolemy and Aristobulus.[7]

The result was the most influential Greek biography of Alexander that would circulate in the Roman Republic some two centuries on. Cleitarchus became the template, if not the whole pattern, for the Latin Vulgate, even if he was at times, as Cicero thought, entertaining with 'pretty fictions' and a 'better orator than historian'. Although the Roman rhetorician Quintilian (*ca.* AD 35–post-96) considered him 'brilliantly ingenious but notoriously untrustworthy',[8] Cleitarchus nonetheless appears to have been a talent that eclipsed the eyewitness histories written without his flair, for neither Ptolemy and Aristobulus nor Nearchus and Onesicritus had any formal literary training or journalistic experience we know of.

Cleitarchus' father, Deinon, came from Colophon in Lydia, one of the cities claiming to be the birthplace of Homer and another city destroyed by Alexander's former Bodyguard Lysimachus. Deinon was a colourful historian who had based himself in Egypt and produced a non-extant history of Persia (a *Persica*) that was later praised in Rome by Cornelius Nepos (*ca.* 110–24 BC) and much referenced in Athenaeus' *Dinner Philosophers* as well as in Plutarch's biography of Artaxerxes II.[9] The *Persica*, however, frequently contradicted the Greek physician–historian Ctesias, who had been an actual resident at the Persian court from *ca.* 405–398 BC, though according to Plutarch he too 'put into his work a perfect farrago of extravagant and incredible tales … often his story turns aside from the truth into fable and romance'.[10] Deinon's son, it seems, was born in the same mould, setting out to 'improve on the facts'.[11] Alexandria was to become *the* centre of creative reporting, and elements of Deinon's work might well have found their way into his son's book, especially detail concerning Babylon and Persian lands that Cleitarchus may never have visited himself.

The acquaintance of Ptolemy I with the philosopher Stilpo of Megara, whom he (unsuccessfully) invited to Egypt around 307 BC, suggests Cleitarchus, who is attested to have studied under Stilpo, would himself have been personally acquainted with Ptolemy or his son, Ptolemy II Philadelphus, in the years that followed.[12] Ptolemaic authority, while progressive in terms of architecture, the arts and trade, was also ruthless, and the new Macedonian dynasts proved to be manipulative politicians.[13] So it would have been impossible for Cleitarchus to publish a work under Alexander's former Bodyguard or his son unless it was politically benign and did not undermine Ptolemy's claims on the nature of Alexander's life and death or Ptolemy's own campaign contribution.

If the Ptolemaic regime could not control or regulate the inbound flow of information available to Cleitarchus in Alexandria from veterans, the repeated flattering of Ptolemy we see in the Vulgate texts (especially the closing chapters) indicates Cleitarchus was prudently sensitive with the outbound production and its references to the dynast.[14] The burgeoning city would have been full of scurrilous propaganda and allegations emanating from a patchwork of personal campaign memories, and if this material could not be rebroadcast in the original form, it could be cloned, cropped and grafted by Cleitarchus onto a suitable new and colourful root.

Yet a more malevolent profiling of Alexander did, nevertheless, appear; Cleitarchus may have been influenced by Theopompus' earlier harsh moralizing on the Macedonian court, as well as the earlier negative Peripatetic-school noises that had been aired from Athens under the protection of Cassander's control of the city.[15] For through the period from 317–307 BC, Cassander installed as his administrator (later termed a 'tyrant') Demetrius of Phalerum, a student of Theophrastus, in a role that was 'in theory an oligarchy, but in practice a monarchy'. We should note, however, that Stilpo, Cleitarchus' philosophy teacher, had himself been influenced by Diogenes the Cynic, whose movement had little good to say about the Macedonian king.[16] It is not impossible that tragic elements of Duris' *Samian Chronicle*, if not his later Macedon-centred history, also infiltrated Cleitarchus' account, if it was published sufficiently late.[17]

Besides these influences in circulation, disgruntled veterans and their offspring reared on stories of the campaign sagas may well have recalled the gradual deterioration in Alexander's behaviour when the troubled campaign was quagmired in the East. Like many who had taken part in the decade-long invasion of the Persian Empire, veterans surely faced the dilemma of wanting to be associated with, and yet disassociated from, select episodes of the story. As time passed, the second-generation Ptolemies had nothing to lose from seeing a more tarnished image of Alexander manifest itself, as this in turn highlighted their own 'benign' rule, and 'not every monarch has an interest in preserving the immaculate purity of their predecessor's reputation'.[18] Thus the compromised, politicized and carefully re-characterized template of what we term the 'Vulgate' genre of Alexander was born.

The Proximity Infatuation

The stature of Cleitarchus' biography of Alexander – as a conduit between the earlier eyewitness histories and the later Roman-era derivative accounts – helps us address an inconvenient reality: the dividing line between primary sources (eyewitnesses) and the secondary historians who drew from their testimony is often indistinct. If Ptolemy and Aristobulus were influential on campaign, they were nevertheless writing some decades after the events they were putting on papyrus, and though the 'real organ of history is memory', these aged court sources must have leaned on either personal memoirs or on other already published eyewitness accounts to complete their own books. We thus have detailed descriptions (if often contradictory) of the rank-by-rank battle orders, troop numbers, section commanders and the intricate manoeuvres in the rivers, valleys and plains at the Granicus, Issus, Gaugamela and the Hydaspes River, as well as the numerous skirmishes and sieges in mountain passes and 'unassailable' rocks of the upper satrapies of the Persian Empire.[19]

Significantly more military actions had taken place in the Successor Wars, probably before Ptolemy and Aristobulus published, some eclipsing even the campaign battles fought by Alexander in complexity and others in strategic importance to the survival of the emerging dynasts. While the Roman-period satirist Lucian did refer to a collection of letters to and from Ptolemy – suggestive that he maintained communication with Seleucus at least – these veteran luminaries would have wished to consult any surviving logs from the campaign Royal Diaries, alongside any extracts they still had of Callisthenes' history, as far as it went before he was executed.[20] And it didn't go far: the contradictions between Ptolemy and Aristobulus that Arrian cites are frequent; some are minor and some relate to the most fundamental of detail.[21]

The earlier published accounts of Onesicritus, Chares and Nearchus were already in circulation, so Ptolemy and Aristobulus would have been able to extract from them, but the result, like Cleitarchus' book, would have effectively been another syncretism. Moreover, there is the observation Polybius later made when he was attempting to probe earlier sources to unravel the past:

> For since many events occur at the same time in different places, and one man cannot be in several places at one time, nor is it possible for a single man to have seen with his very own eyes every place in the world and all the peculiar features of different places.[22]

A modern scholar who profiled these lost historians sarcastically added: 'Indeed, it is hard to imagine how history could have been written at all in ancient times, except by men with great powers of memory.'[23] He also doubted, for example, that Nearchus could have kept a useful log on his almost-fatal sea voyage, though this seems a little unfair; the Indus-Hydaspes fleet had a secretary, Evagoras, and surely the sea fleet did too.[24] But the relative value of a 'primary' source to a 'secondary' offspring is not always as clear as the label suggests, rendering the definition of 'tertiary sources' (those even further removed from events) even more opaque.

The consequences of this are not always disastrous, for we are also faced with the myopic symptoms of long-sighted historical perspective, an apparent contradiction in terms explained by one historian's comment: 'Proximity as well as distance, can distort the vision.'[25] Historians in the thick of things might be compromised by their direct involvement. In contrast, later historians, and even coetaneous writers compiling from the 'privileged' position of 'reflective' distance and even exile, often provided a more holistic and balanced narrative, if not entirely free from bias; these definitions could include Xenophon, Thucydides and Hieronymus, as well as the Greek Sicilian historian Timaeus and Polybius who followed them, all of whom commenced or completed their historical writing in forced absences from their city-state.[26] Capture and exile, by definition, obliged the authors to live in the sphere of an opposite, or at least neutral, regime.

Should we therefore value refugee reportage over that of the statesman-historian who dispossessed him of his home? And do we credit the account of the embattled general with more authenticity than the narrative of the civilian onlooker? Which primary is 'prime' material and which is 'primed' by the threat of war? The answer to the last question if of course both, and these questions bring us back to Alexandria in the vibrant and dangerous years that saw the insoluble and permanent dyes of Alexander's first blueprints stain papyrus.

Logic and the Illogical Behind the Earliest Publishing Dates

The conflicts that frequently appear in the extant accounts, many of them relating to names, numbers and relative chronology, suggest that neither Callisthenes' official account nor the Royal Diaries survived to the Roman period, except in fragments and through second- or third-hand testimonia. If they had survived, no contradictory reporting should ever have appeared, for together they would have provided a near-perfect campaign log, while any archetypal inaccuracies would have been uniformly carried forward into later narratives.[27]

One modern study of this recurring source problem points out that agreement on campaign detail ends with the arrest of Callisthenes (thus that reporting gap until Onesicritus arrived), so it is evident that historians had these early campaign facts from Callisthenes and not directly from the Royal Diaries. And regarding the troubled reporting post-327 BC when Alexander was in the Upper Satrapies and then India, the study went on to reason that the Royal Diaries were probably lost before *any* account (except Callisthenes') was written.[28]

The conclusion to be drawn here is that the books of the Alexandrian and possibly Cassandrean-influenced historians – Ptolemy, Aristobulus and Cleitarchus – dominated the Roman-era perceptions of Alexander, and in turn the Roman-era derivatives are the basis of the interpretations we make today.

If Ptolemy and Aristobulus were at the foundation of Arrian's court-sourced biography (as Arrian himself stated on his opening page), and if Cleitarchus' book substantially templated the Vulgate-genre accounts, our suggestion of an 'Alexandrian' monopoly seems to hold. The combined tradition carried forward by these three historians became a robust pesticide on the tenuous roots of any other version of events, for example claims relating to a Last Will and Testament or succession attempt by Alexander from his deathbed at Babylon; it was a Hellenistic literary inheritance tax the conqueror had to pay (see Grant, *Last Will and Testament*, 2021).[29] This is the suggested publication order for these three influential books: Ptolemy first, then Aristobulus and lastly Cleitarchus; it is a discussion not without contention and discord.

We do not have space here to cite the full extent of previous arguments, and they are in any case inconclusive, but a few serve to illustrate the disparity of opinion.[30] The prevailing scholarly opinion from the 1800s to early 1900s suggested Cleitarchus' book was in circulation before those of Ptolemy and Aristobulus.[31] Since then, many scholars have concurred, believing Cleitarchus published within twenty years of Alexander's death.[32]

In contrast, another important study (published in 1948) saw the order as Aristobulus and then Ptolemy, with Cleitarchus writing last, after Ptolemy's death and possibly as late as 260 BC. The author further believed Cleitarchus had little later impact on the Roman Vulgate genre and on Curtius in particular, whose principal source therefore remained obscure.[33] Other historians similarly argued that Cleitarchus published late and used Aristobulus as a source, while proposals that these writers published gradually in instalments straddle the dating divide. For example, it has been argued that Ptolemy circulated his account between 320 and 295 BC, with 'chapter-packets' being issued at intervals (as Livy did three centuries later), though the earlier end of this dating conflicts with Arrian's claim that Ptolemy was a 'king' when he published, as no dynast proclaimed himself a king until 307 BC or later.[34]

Scholars underpin their publishing-date arguments with geographic evidence (prevailing knowledge, or ignorance, on the relative sizes of the Caspian and Black Seas, for example), sketchy statements of acquaintance (so, Ptolemy with Stilpo) and these self-appointed throning dates (when each dynast assumed the title 'king' after Alexander's sons were executed). But above all, their arguments on the publishing dates are determined by author declarations of 'conflict', in other words, when one ancient source refuted the testimony of another, for that seems to point to a clear 'who wrote erroneously before the other corrected them'.[35]

Unfortunately it doesn't, and there are several examples of how these arguments can be turned on their head to support the 'Alexandrian monopoly'.

Alexander's Near-Death Episode in India

Although the geographical arguments, titular dissections and acquaintance evidences that underpin the chronology debate each fall short of 'proof', the mantra for those concluding that Cleitarchus published first is his report of the alleged heroics of Ptolemy in a gruesome battle against a city of the Mallians in India in 326 BC, when Alexander was stranded alone inside the city walls.[36] The episode was treated rather vocally by both Arrian and Curtius, who both went to the trouble of uncharacteristically describing Cleitarchus (and also Timagenes, who wrote later in Alexandria – he was captured by Romans *ca*. 55 BC) as 'careless' and 'gullible', when on the whole Arrian forgave source discrepancies, and more so if they were inclined to flatter Alexander.[37]

The interpretation to be made, stemming from the critique by Curtius and Arrian, is that when Ptolemy stated in his own book that he was not present at the battle (as he apparently did), he was making a deliberate, and thus later, correction to Cleitarchus, whose account placed Ptolemy in the thick of the fighting and saving Alexander's life; this was supposedly just one version of how Ptolemy gained the title 'Saviour' (Soter). But if this correction of events – or the full wording of the polemic against Cleitarchus – did originate with Ptolemy, we would have expected Arrian and Curtius to be more specific on its origin (something like, 'as Ptolemy himself pointed out'), or their own mirror critique would have appeared a rather obvious and unimaginative plagiarism of their source. Moreover, as has been pointed out: 'Ptolemy never contradicted anybody; things he believed to be wrong he usually omitted altogether.'[38]

A reverse interpretation seems more valid. Curtius and Arrian knew all about conflicting accounts; Arrian recounted numerous other discrepancies in a matter-of-fact way.[39] Here, however, their parallel chastisement of Cleitarchus indicates Ptolemy had published his version of events first, in which he claimed to have been absent from the battle. That would have been, as they voiced, a careless and egregious contradiction for Cleitarchus to have made. It also suggests that there existed in the Roman era an unambiguous certainty on the publication order, which argues for a gap of some years between Cleitarchus' and Ptolemy's publication dates. It further confirms Cleitarchus' desire to eulogize the memory of Ptolemy, in whose city, Alexandria, he was based.

In this interpretation, it follows that in Rome, Curtius must have read Ptolemy's book to have criticized Cleitarchus in this way (which argues for Cleitarchus' influence or even archetyping of the Vulgate Roman genre epitomized by Curtius' style). It is also highly suggestive that Arrian read Curtius (who had likely published a century before him) and he thought the value of Curtius' criticism too good to pass up, for their wording is unique and strikingly similar.[40]

The campaigns in India and the voyage down the Hydaspes-Indus were nothing short of wholesale slaughter, and so not easily reported by Nearchus, Onesicritus, Ptolemy and Aristobulus – who were either the court sources at the heart of Alexander's policy decisions or complicit in some way in their implementation. As Curtius' account and Arrian's narrative remain in close agreement on major place names at this point, it does suggest their parallel (self-admitted) use of Cleitarchus at this point, for he had garnered testimony that originated outside court sources – the campaign veterans in Alexandria, for example – with which he filled their reporting gaps.[41]

A final, though rather cynical possibility does need voicing: Ptolemy *was* present at the battle, but he felt the whole Mallian affair (like the earlier reported massacre of the Branchidae in Sogdia) was too gruesome to be a part of, when, as even Arrian reported, many unarmed men were slaughtered and 'neither women, nor children were spared'. So, in his own book, Ptolemy spirited himself away on an expedition elsewhere.[42] That would have additionally exonerated him from failing to protect Alexander from being isolated and wounded, for other accounts had claimed it was the future Bodyguard, Peucestas (or Leonnatus in other versions), in his role as one of the royal shield bearers, who reportedly held a shield above his fallen king.[43] Somewhat suspiciously, Ptolemy did provide a most detailed description of Alexander's wound, which issued 'both blood and breath', but perhaps he garnered the detail from the attending physician who patched up his king. Ptolemy's description points to a lung piercing, which is at odds with other reports claiming the nearly fatal projectile lodged in Alexander's breastbone.[44]

One unnamed writer used by Arrian claimed that Perdiccas, already prominent among the king's Bodyguards, cut out the arrow blade. The source is unlikely to have been Cleitarchus, for reading between the lines of Curtius' closing narrative of events at Babylon, it appears Cleitarchus was rather hostile to Perdiccas, in contrast to his laudatory treatment of Ptolemy (see Grant, *Last Will and Testament*, 2021, chapter 3).

The Burning of Persepolis

A further formative event in the chronology debate provides a parallel autopsy. It concerns Thais, the Athenian courtesan who became Ptolemy's mistress, the mother of three of his children and, according to Athenaeus, eventually his wife.[45] Vulgate texts credited Thais with instigating the fire that burned the palace of Persepolis to the ground in a bacchanal that took place in May 330 BC. The royal complex completed *ca*. 518 BC by Darius the Great was no more, and the firing was supposedly the conclusion to a drunken celebration, though it came some months after the Macedones had arrived in the city (in December 331/January 330 BC). In contrast, once more, Arrian claimed the burning was a political decision and no accident at all. So, again it is argued that Ptolemy, who was Arrian's principal source, had corrected Cleitarchus on the matter.[46]

But surely Ptolemy had little choice when adopting the reporting line he did, for he could hardly have implicated his mistress (or wife) in a regrettable incident in which 'the enormous palaces, famed throughout the whole civilised world, fell victim to insult and utter destruction'.[47] Arrian's sanitized version stems from here, in which the 'political decision' appears a scapegoat for an act that might have been arrived at under the influence of alcohol. Cleitarchus' narrative, captured most vividly by Diodorus and Curtius, does paint Thais as a somewhat heroic and patriotic figure who urged Alexander to avenge Xerxes' burning of the Temple of Athena in her own native city, Athens. So the two accounts are not as irreconcilable as they first appear.[48]

Thais' Dionysian revelry was possibly setting out to emulate Herostratus, the Greek arsonist whose blaze at the Temple of Artemis at Ephesus was supposed to bring him immortal fame; this was an infamous inferno portentously linked to Alexander's birth.[49] If Cleitarchus published his book 'late' (in the late 270s or 260s BC), so in the reign of Ptolemy II Philadelphus, Thais' heroic imagery would have suited a dynasty that had propelled her children into prominent positions in the Successor Wars.[50]

Onesicritus at the Court of Lysimachus

A further pointer to a late Cleitarchean publication date is Onesicritus' alleged reading of his own account aloud to the Thracian dynast Lysimachus 'when he was king':

> And the story is told that many years afterwards Onesicritus was reading aloud to Lysimachus, who was now king, the fourth book of his history, in which was the tale of the Amazon, at which Lysimachus smiled gently and said: 'And where was I at the time?'[51]

One scholar argues this suggests that 'Onesicritus stood on the same footing with Lysimachus as Cleitarchus did with Ptolemy'.[52] Others conclude this does indeed capture a key date marker: the publishing of Onesicritus' book once the Diadochi had crowned themselves 'kings'.

The earliest date Lysimachus could have been referred to as 'king' was 305 BC, by which time Onesicritus might have been in his 70s. But he had no obvious reason to publish so late as he took no active part that we are aware of in the Successor Wars.[53] As it has been firmly established that Cleitarchus took detail from Nearchus' book,[54] which itself appears to have been published after Onesicritus' work (judging by his criticism of Onesicritus' claims on naval command), and if the Lysimachus episode did portray the reading of a *freshly completed* chapter by Onesicritus (the fourth book in this case, probably of eight),[55] it is likely Cleitarchus published a good number of years after 305 BC for Onesicritus to have completed his subsequent chapters, and for Nearchus to have published between them.[56]

And yet this all hangs on the reference to 'kingship', which could have just as credibly meant 'when Lysimachus had established himself over Thrace' (which had been no easy task), and there is no further evidence the reading came from Onesicritus' newly inked scrolls. Furthermore, as it becomes clear, the Diadochi *acted* as kings soon after leaving Babylon in 323 BC.

Fearful Historians, Conspiracy and Fearful Portents at Babylon

The claim that Onesicritus was 'fearful' of naming the supposedly guilty guests at Medius' banquet, where Alexander was allegedly poisoned, comes from an anonymous manuscript from the fourth or fifth century AD known as the *Metz Epitome*, which recorded campaign events broadly from 330–325 BC. More specifically, it is mentioned at the end in what is commonly referred to as the 'Book of Death and Alexander's Last Will and Testament', which was pinned to the end of the manuscript as a fitting conclusion to what is otherwise a Vulgate-styled text. Like the final chapter of the *Greek Alexander Romance*, this section details the plot to poison Alexander, along with the guilty and the innocent. It was Cleitarchus who imported this detail into his own final pages, providing the wrap-up to the Vulgate biographies of Alexander. But the original detail of the conspiracy appears to have come from a stand-alone political pamphlet which was released during the Successor Wars, probably in the first ten years after Alexander's death, to damn those accused of regicide when alliances were fickle.[57] But once the detail found a home in Cleitarchus' account, it proliferated in the Roman-era books of the historians who used him as their source (see Grant, *Last Will and Testament*, 2021).

This brings our attention to the corroborating comments from Diodorus and Curtius on other 'fearful historians' who avoided commenting on Cassander's reported part in the poisoning of Alexander at Babylon.[58] Cassander and his younger brother, Iollas, who was the king's cupbearer, were at the centre of the conspiracy; both were sons of the regent Antipater who governed Macedon in Alexander's absence, after which Cassander ruled Macedon from 316 BC until his death in 297 BC. His murder of Alexander's sons exhibits his ruthless path to power. If, as scholars have logically concluded, this 'fear of reprisals' can only refer to writers publishing *before* Cassander's death, then Cleitarchus, who *did* detail the plot and name Cassander in the alleged central role, must have published later, assuming he was the common source behind these Vulgate allegations.

More convincing still is a first publication after Cassander's sons had been killed (by 294 BC), and his nephews too (by 279 BC, with the death of Ptolemy the Thunderbolt), as well as Cassander's former brothers-in-law who had sons by his sisters: this category included Ptolemy I Soter himself, who died in 283 BC, and Lysimachus, who died in 281 BC, the year in which the still-dangerous Seleucus, *possibly* named as a banquet plotter, was also killed.[59] Thereafter, those who might have defended the reputation of Cassander and his extended family, and theirs by association, were gone. It is in this environment, logically focusing on the period after 280 BC, that the rebroadcasting without repercussions of these allegations of poison and regicide would have first been possible by a historian seeking fame without the fear of execution. Consequently, Cleitarchus published 'late', but there is yet another clue.

Aristobulus' penchant for the portentous was hardly unique in the Alexander story, but we have a specific example which pushes back Cleitarchus' publication date. Aristobulus reported the presence of a mysterious Syrian prophetess when the royal pages made an attempt on Alexander's life (327 BC, the episode that Callisthenes was implicated in and which led to his eventual execution), and Aristobulus was additionally the source for the supernatural episodes and divinations heralding Alexander's death, the detail interwoven, along with other corroborating augural detail, into the Vulgate-styled accounts.[60] As we have no indication that the Roman-period Vulgate historians used Aristobulus directly, we assume their source was once again Cleitarchus, who created this genre.[61] But for Cleitarchus to have read Aristobulus, who commenced his book in his 80s (or at least late in life) and who was yet sufficiently young to complete challenging assignments for Alexander on campaign, once more suggests Cleitarchus published his book later than many scholars have concluded.

The First Mention of Rome

A final dating clue to the publishing order of these early Hellenistic historians, who templated 'Alexander' for the historians of Rome, involves the emergence of the 'eternal city' itself. According to Roman naturalist Pliny the Elder (AD 23–79), Cleitarchus claimed a Roman deputation visited Alexander at (or on the way to) Babylon, presumably sent to pay homage to the Macedonian king and avert his expansionist eye.[62] Arrian named Aristus of Cyprus and Asclepiades (who is otherwise unknown) as the historians behind the detail (though he referenced 'other writers' too when discussing Italian delegations), and it was accompanied by revealing pro-Roman ambassadorial propaganda: Alexander recognized the 'proud freedom of their bearing', with 'greatness prophesised for their country'.[63]

No Roman legation was mentioned by Diodorus, whose Greek–Sicilian origins suffered in the Roman politics of his troubled day, though it has been argued that he may have omitted the detail for political expediency, writing as he was in the dangerous Roman era of the Second Triumvirate (43–33 BC), and when Antony and Cleopatra, the last ruler of the Macedonian-originating Ptolemaic dynasty in Egypt, still posed a threat. Some scholars think that the bias of Roman authors (including Trogus, as evidenced in the epitome of Justin) invented embassies from all the lands by then subject to Rome – though not to Macedon centuries before! – and listed them as paying tribute to Alexander.[64] Furthermore, modern historians still uphold the anonymity of Rome in Cleitarchus' day, but that is on the premise that he published *early*. The contention falls apart, however, if his book entered circulation in the 270s, and moreover, if we analyze Rome's ascent, its 'anonymity' is clearly unsupportable.

Polybius believed that as early as 509 BC, Rome had already signed a treaty with Carthage (modern opinion suggests 348 BC is more likely), but certainly by 338 BC – the year of Philip II's Macedonian victory over the Greek alliance at Chaeronea – Rome had reached an accord with the Italian states that had revolted in the Second Latin War; the dissolution of the Latin League was a major step towards Rome's pre-eminence in the Italian peninsula.[65] And that is unlikely to have gone unnoticed overseas, as the south of Italy and Sicily were populated by many Greek colonies which were trading with mainland Greece.

The discrediting of Cleitarchus' claim of Roman ambassadors additionally ignores the significance of the peace treaty recorded by Livy (ca. 64/59 BC–AD 17) between Alexander Molossus, the king of Epirus (who was both Alexander's uncle and brother-in-law), and Rome in 332 BC, a year or two before Molossus was killed campaigning in Italy.[66] His death, apparently fulfilling a prediction from the oracle at Dodona, was mourned in Asia by Alexander, who threw three full days of funeral games, so communications via Macedon were clearly intact.[67] Strabo additionally believed that Alexander (though which one is not clear), and later Demetrius the Besieger, petitioned Rome to take steps against the piracy of Antium (modern Anzio) in which they were apparently participating (or perhaps simply tolerating for political gain).[68]

After Alexander Molossus' misadventure in Italy almost a decade before Alexander's death in Babylon, Rome surely watched the rise of Macedonian power with interest, noting how easily the Adriatic was being crossed by its westward-looking Epirote neighbour on the pretext of protecting Tarentine interests in Italy. What is accepted is that the Italian tribes – the Lucanians and Bruttians (and Samnites) who felt the Epirote blade and successfully turned it back on the Molossian king – wisely sent a delegation to 'apologize' to Alexander, because Arrian further stated that 'other writers' claimed Italy was a future target for the Macedonian war machine.[69] So it is not impossible that the Latins harboured the same fear. Trogus' generalized list of ambassadors at Babylon (as it appears in Justin) also included 'some from Italy', and Diodorus' reference to 'those who dwell around the Adriatic' may well have been meant (guardedly) to include Rome.[70]

Although a Rhodian trade negotiation with Rome dating to 306 BC is widely regarded as the city's first known formalized contact with a Greek (rather than Epirote) state,[71] the rhetorical On the Soul by Heracleides of Pontus (died ca. 310 BC), the Greek philosopher–astronomer, had already claimed Rome was founded as a 'Greek city'. A later tradition even held that a Corinthian from Greece named Demaratus went on to sire Tarquinus Priscus, the fifth king of Rome.[72] Moreover, both Hecataeus (ca. 550–476 BC) and Hellanicus had detailed the legends of Rome's founding some two centuries (or more) before the rise of the Macedonian state.

Closer to Alexander and his entourage, the sack of Rome by the Gauls under Brennus in ca. 387/386 BC was known, it seems, in Aristotle's school.[73] His successor, Theophrastus, the Greek historian Callias of Syracuse (third century BC), as well as Timaeus (*ca*. 345–250 BC) and the poet Lycophron in his *Alexandra* (likely written pre-264 BC at the court of Ptolemy II Philadelphus), also touched on the rising presence of Rome; the city was certainly not the 'unknown' that its absence from early Hellenistic history suggests.[74] And just forty-three years after Alexander's death, the dispatches of Pyrrhus of Epirus were broadcasting Rome's presence to the Hellenistic world in no small way; Hieronymus most likely had a hand in that when using Pyrrhus' memoirs.[75]

So the whole chronological debate is rather questionable. Whether Pliny's claim that Cleitarchus mentioned a Roman delegation is based on truth or a fiction, if Cleitarchus was publishing as late as the 270s BC, the name of Rome, which invaded Sicily in 264 BC, would have been ringing in the ears of the second-generation Diadochi, and the idea of the city's submission or allegiance to the Macedonian king may have been useful propaganda for the Ptolemies.

In conclusion: the evidence suggests Cleitarchus published after both Ptolemy and Aristobulus, perhaps by several decades. If Aristobulus, as is claimed, commenced writing his memoirs at age 84, possibly from Cassandrea – the new city of Cassander who ruled Macedon – Ptolemy likely published first by some measure of years, in the relative peace of years after the Battle of Ipsus (301 BC), if not before. As a powerful dynast related to Cassander by marriage and in a military alliance with him for much of the period, Ptolemy's account of Alexander was the 'Cranmer's Bible' of the day, and Aristobulus would have been unlikely to underline the 'Alexandrian archetype'. Cleitarchus, who was based in Alexandria, had a more obvious censorship and appears to have prudently upheld or even exaggerated Ptolemy's campaign contribution.

With the Royal Diaries destroyed or kept safely out of circulation under lock and key by Ptolemy, and Callisthenes' account only running to 327 BC at the latest; with Onesicritus tight-lipped on what he deemed unsafe and Nearchus restricting his writing to his naval voyage from India; with half of the Bodyguards dead and Alexander's sons and wives executed, and when royal secretary Eumenes was cremated back in early 315 BC, the first wave of historians – so the Alexandrian–Cassandrean-linked trio of Ptolemy, Aristobulus and Cleitarchus – were overwhelmingly influential in fixing the chemical formula of Alexander's compound.

Although we may be accusing them of gross historical manipulation, they themselves would have thought quite differently on the matter, for the known world was itself in flux: geography, astronomy, the calendars, philosophy, scientific classification and even currencies were all being replaced, reorganized and recalibrated.[76] The present was finally obscuring the earlier preoccupation with the Homeric past, for Heraclean tasks were being presented to the new generation of kings who were determined to be the last man standing.

So it is doubtful that Cleitarchus lay awake over passages that captured Alexander's darker hues, or that Aristobulus felt pangs of guilt for surgically removing unsavoury campaign episodes, and surely Ptolemy wasted no sleepless nights over his manipulative self-serving methodology when broadcasting his significance to the warring world of Macedonian dynasts. Aristotle reasoned that men are by nature political animals; historians the more so, it seems.[77] Here at the dawn of the Hellenistic Age, the result from Alexandria was literary alchemy and what the Romans excavated from the sources was fool's gold.

Chapter 5

Secondary Sources: the Roman Alexander

It is hardly surprising if this material [the polished arrangement of
words] has not yet been illustrated on this language, for not one of our
people dedicated himself to eloquence, unless he could shine in court
cases and in the forum. The most eloquent of the Greeks, however,
removed from judicial cases, applied themselves first to other matters
and then especially to writing history.[1]

Marcus Antonius in Cicero, *On the Orator*

Eusebius, like any other educated man, knew what proper history was.
He knew that it was a rhetorical work with a maximum of invented
speeches and a minimum of authentic documents.[2]

Arnaldo Momigliano, *Essays in Ancient and Modern Historiography*

The early eyewitness accounts of Alexander's contemporaries and those
sponsored by their courts had to straddle the chaos of a Hellenistic world
that saw the kingdoms of the Diadochi and their offspring rise and fall,
eventually being absorbed by the expanding Roman super-state. The bloody
process swallowed much of the literary output of the age, so that the century before
Polybius remains something of a barren reporting landscape as far as the history
of Macedon is concerned. For almost seventy years after the Battle of Ipsus in 301
BC, there is no surviving continuous coherent account, Justin's severe epitome
aside.

Polybius stoically reflected in the opening of his book that the 'writings of the ...
"numerous historians" ... whom the kings had engaged to recount their exploits
have fallen into oblivion'.[3] He also doubted that what had been written captured
absolute truths, 'because there are so many various conditions and circumstances,
yielding to which men are prevented from uttering or writing their real opinions'.[4]

Diodorus, whose *Library of History* survives only in tattered fragments for
the post-Ipsus period and without the useful chapter synopses we see in his other
volumes, also mourned the poorly documented years:

And of those who have undertaken this account of all peoples, not one has continued his history beyond the Macedonian period. For while some have closed their accounts with the deeds of Philip, others with those of Alexander, and some with the Diadochi or the Epigoni, yet, despite the number and importance of the events subsequent to these and extending even to our own lifetime which have been left neglected, no historian has essayed to treat of them within the compass of a single narrative, because of the magnitude of the undertaking.[5]

The literary wasteland gives the superficial impression there was lack of interest in recording history through this era, which, as one scholar reminds us, was neither 'proper Greek history, which lost its appeal after Alexander [and his immediate successors], nor yet the vital part of proper Roman history'.[6] But Rome had been establishing itself over the twelve-city confederation of the intensely pious Etruscans and other neighbouring tribes, which was clearly the early priority, and the war against Carthage occupied its attention for the latter part of the period. Any trade delegations, government embassies, treaties and skirmishes that did take place between Rome and the Macedonian-dynasty-dominated Hellenic East in the post-Ipsus years were simply lost with intervening literature.

The narratives that did once knit the two worlds together were contained in the now-lost works of Phylarchus (*ca.* 280–215 BC), Aratus (*ca.* 271–213 BC), Philochorus (*ca.* 340–261 BC), Diyllus (*ca.* 340–280 BC) and Demochares the nephew of Demosthenes (*ca.* 355–275 BC), among a clutch of other names that have come to us through fragments. The loss includes Hieronymus' voluminous account which ended sometime soon after 272 BC, and the non-extant history of Timaeus written in fifty years of exile in Athens (care of Agathocles the Sicilian tyrant) which closed at 264 BC, the year Rome invaded his homeland of Sicily (he was from Tauromenium, modern Taormina). Diodorus' fragmentary *Library of History* had hardly made any mention of Rome until this point, which, significantly, marked the beginning of its control of his place of birth in Sicily too.

But it was Polybius, whose own account commenced in 264 BC with the First Punic War between Rome and Carthage, who saw first-hand the final fall of the former Macedonian-governed empire to the Roman legions at the Battle of Pydna in 168 BC. However, he failed (at least in what text survives) to acknowledge Hieronymus as a source of the post-Alexander years, which, as one scholar notes, is remarkable given their parallel themes: the rapid expansion of superpowers that had risen from obscurity, and with the one subsuming the other.[7]

Escorted back to Rome after the victory at Pydna by the Roman general Aemilius Paullus were a chained King Perseus, captured after fleeing, 250 waggons of booty and 1,000 notable Greeks as good-behaviour hostages, including Polybius himself, the politically connected cavalry commander from Megalopolis in Arcadia, who, as a member of the Achaean League (in fact, second-in-command), was technically in league with the Italians but on the wrong side of domestic politics which had advocated neutrality, not direct support for Rome.[8]

Now in his early 30s, Polybius would also educate Paullus' sons, and he soon perfected for the Roman legions a telegraphic aid that sent messages by torches and which came to be known as the 'Polybius Square'. During the next seventeen eventful years as a hostage in Rome (despite at least five pleas by the Achaean League for his return to Greece), or on the march with Roman generals which included a stint in Africa, he rubbed shoulders with senators and influential families and completed his military *Tactics*; it prompted Scipio to petition the city praetor that he be allowed to remain there for good. In return, Polybius' diplomacy is said to have 'stayed the wrath' of the Romans against a now toothless Greece.[9]

Recalling the clash at Pydna when he later penned his *Histories*, and summing up a fate that saw King Perseus die in prison in Rome, Polybius claimed the last ever dynastic Macedonian king recalled a prophecy that the goddess Fortuna favoured the Macedones only until she favoured others:

> So then often and bitterly did [King] Perseus call to mind the words of Demetrius of Phalerum [Cassander's tyrant in Athens]. For he, in his treatise *On Fortune*, wishing to give men a striking instance of her mutability asks them to remember the times when Alexander overthrew the Persian Empire, and speaks as follows: 'For if you consider not countless years or many generations, but merely these last fifty years, you will read in them the cruelty of Fortune. I ask you, do you think that fifty years ago either the Persians and the Persian king or the Macedones and the king of Macedon, if some god had foretold the future to them, would ever have believed that at the time when we live, the very name of the Persians would have perished utterly – the Persians who were masters of almost the whole world – and that the Macedones, whose name was formerly almost unknown, would now be the lords of it all? But nevertheless this Fortune, who never compacts with life, who always defeats our reckoning by some novel stroke; she who ever demonstrates her power by foiling our expectations, now also, as it seems to me, makes it clear to all men, by endowing the Macedones with the whole wealth of Persia, that she has but lent them these blessings until she decides to deal differently with them.' And this now happened in the time of Perseus. Surely Demetrius, as if by the mouth of some god, uttered these prophetic words.[10]

The words of Demetrius of Phalerum, Cassander's 'tyrant' in Athens who later took refuge with Ptolemy, were repeated almost word for word by Diodorus and also précised by Livy (*ca.* 64 BC–AD 17), so that no one in Rome could fail to acknowledge Alexander's part in Rome's own conquest of the East.[11] But Polybius was always looking at the wider picture (except when promoting himself). Possibly influenced by his 'tour of duty' with Scipio, Polybius – who defined his work as 'pragmatic history' – believed the recording of history meant subordinating 'the topics of genealogies and myths ... the planting of colonies, foundations of cities and their ties of kinship' to the greater significance of the 'nations, cities and rulers'.[12]

Clearly familiar with (and influenced by) Herodotus, Thucydides and Xenophon, and highly opinionated on what 'history' should be, Polybius contended that 'monographs' (like the dedicated biographies of Alexander) were inferior to his 'universal' approach. This was supposed to highlight that the earlier Greek accounts, especially those of the fourth century BC, leaned to 'the great leader theory of history', focusing on single individuals and revealing just 'dissected parts', whereas the 'whole body' needed a post-mortem.[13] The Greek historians had placed war, with its victors, the vanquished and the proponents of war, centre-stage in their perception of epochal change. His criticism of Theopompus' *Philippica* brought the point home: 'It would have been much more dignified and more just to include Philip's achievements in the history of Greece, than to include the history of Greece in that of Philip.'[14]

Polybius began his main 'holistic' narrative of affairs in the Mediterranean Basin, in which he recorded Rome's contact with the Successor Kingdoms to the East, in the 140th Olympiad, so 221/220 BC,[15] the year Philip V (a descendant of the line of Antigonus and father of King Perseus) ascended the throne of Macedon and Hannibal Barca was appointed commander of Carthaginian forces in Spain. Polybius never actually named the Alexander-era historians at all, save Callisthenes and in a somewhat disparaging manner;[16] his fourteen digressions on Alexander's behaviour (besides five passing references), which offered little unique material, provided him with little more than a somewhat stoical mixed review, though he did finally concede Alexander's soul had, 'as all admit, something of the superhuman in it'.[17]

Nevertheless, the Alexander monographs he openly despised provided Polybius with the anonymous essences he slotted into the 'entire network' of his universal body of history.[18] True to his polemical literary ancestral roots, Polybius didn't shy away from attacking 'competing' historians (near-contemporaries like Phylarchus, Philinus and Fabius Pictor, for example, who covered the wars with Carthage),[19] and he was also highly critical of his forerunner, the long-lived Timaeus, whose Olympiad reckoning system Polybius nevertheless adopted to calibrate his own chapters, which commenced at the point at which Timaeus had closed his (the 129th Olympiad).[20] His loud invective against Timaeus (who may have been born in the same year as Alexander, 356 BC) ironically preserved much of the detail he had set out to destroy, and yet Polybius' lack of charity seems hypocritical because he also proposed: 'We should not find fault with writers for their omissions and mistakes, and should praise and admire them, considering the times they lived in, for having ascertained something on the subject and advanced our knowledge.'[21]

Timaeus' account, rich in detail of colonies, city foundations and genealogies (and highlighted coincidences – all the detail Polybius absorbed but 'subordinated'), was probably worthy of a place on the shelves,[22] but the exiled Sicilian had himself famously criticized everyone and gained the title 'slanderer' along the way. Timaeus must have invited additional criticism when he spuriously dated Rome's founding to 814/813 BC (the thirty-eighth year before the first Olympiad) to synchronize it to Carthage's beginnings in order to imply the cities enjoyed twinned fates.[23] Possibly despising Timaeus for his self-declared lack of military experience, Polybius' summing up, nevertheless, elucidated the principal problem of the day: Timaeus 'was like a man in a school of rhetoric, attempting to speak on a given subject, and show off his rhetorical power, but gives no report of what was actually spoken'.[24]

But Polybius didn't remain faithful to his own critiques; he is branded a prejudiced eyewitness to the calamitous events of his day, and the frequent reconstituted speeches we read in his account were the product of his 'subjective operations'. His directionless last ten books read like personal memoirs 'focused on himself' in order to 'write himself into Roman history'.[25] In the opinion of one modern Greek scholar, Polybius could be 'as unreliable as the worst sensationalist scandalmonger historians of antiquity, provided that he is out of sympathy with his subject matter'.[26]

As part of his perception of change on what has come to be known as 'anacyclosis' (the theory and even the prediction of the evolution of governance through time and how empires will rise and fall as a result),[27] Polybius expressed an appreciation of what we might term 'globalism':

> Now in earlier times the world's history had consisted so to speak of a series of unrelated episodes, the origins and results of which being as widely separated as their localities, but from this point onwards history becomes an organic whole: the affairs of Italy and Africa are connected with those of Asia and of Greece, and all events bear a relationship and contribute to a single end.[28]

While Polybius credited Alexander's Asian empire with opening up the East, to him this 'organic whole' now meant 'Rome' in its stellar fifty-three-year rise to rule the then-known world; 'Fortune's showpiece', as he described it.[29] Whether he was truly in awe of Rome and its conquests, or simply disdainful of its sway over Greece, we may never know, but (indirect) vexatious references we see in his books suggest the Romans were considered among the barbarian tribes.[30]

It would be convenient if Polybius was the bridge between the fall of the dynasties formed by Alexander's generals and the interest in the follow-on period exhibited by written accounts in Rome. Unfortunately, the pre-Polybius 'barren reporting zone' had its sequel when 'an even more vexatious twilight descends' on Hellenistic history after Polybius passed away.[31] Although homebred Roman historians were spurred into action after the Second Punic War (or 'Hannibalic War', 218–201 BC), they focused on the progress of the mother city in the form of Rome's record of published events, the *Annales Maximi*, and not on gathering in the detail of the broader Hellenistic story.[32] But Rome's early history commenced on shaky ground. The invasion by Gauls in 390 BC and the fire that followed it left much of the city and its records in ruins. The vacuum let in falsehoods which made their way sometimes innocently, sometimes deliberately, into its founding story. Good examples of the latter are the formative speeches in Livy's volumes commonly titled the *Early History of Rome*.[33]

This has been termed 'reflective history', where Livy 'puts into the mouths of the old Roman kings, consuls and generals, such orations as would be delivered by an accomplished advocate of the Livian era, and which strikingly contrast with the genuine traditions of Roman antiquity'.[34] In an attempt to justify his dialogue with the past and even a republic he did not know, Livy, who 'praised and plundered' Polybius' books along the way, explained that: 'By intermingling human actions with divine they may confer a more august dignity on the origins of states.'[35] The challenge he articulated sounds familiar and was a fate that applied to much of the Hellenistic Eastern Mediterranean as well:

> The subject matter is enveloped in obscurity; partly from its great antiquity, like remote objects which are hardly discernible through the vastness of the distance; partly owing to the fact that written records, which form the only trustworthy memorials of events, were in those times few and scanty, and even what did exist in the pontifical commentaries and public and private archives nearly all perished in the conflagration of the city.[36]

So the chronicles to which Livy, amongst others, had access, including the dubious Linen Rolls, were filled with 'battles that were never fought, and Consuls that were never inaugurated … such, or nearly such, appears to have been the process by which the lost ballad-poetry of Rome was transformed into history.[37] There was an earlier Latin literature, a literature truly Latin, which has wholly perished, which had indeed almost wholly perished long before those whom we are in the habit of regarding as the greatest Latin writers were born.'[38]

The early historians of Rome had more often than not appeared on the *fasti*, the list of city magistrates. These were the wealthy elite, and once again like the court histories of Greece and Macedon, we have to deal with the reality that 'the histories of mankind that we possess are – in general – histories only of the higher classes', though the unfortunate woes of those below are inevitably exposed in passing.[39] There appeared the expression '*Classicus scriptor, non proletarius*' ('a distinguished, not a commonplace writer' – social standing was being linked to the quality of writing in this phrase), which came to represent the works of a distinguished group of authors (writing in Greek or Latin) who were considered meritorious in Rome, and it was those that were destined to be copied, distributed and preserved; or, in the case of the Alexander biographies, given a Roman overhaul.[40]

By the time the private Roman collectors who *were* interested in Greek and Macedonian affairs got their hands on the papyri containing the earlier accounts, much had already decrepitated. These antique seeds, rotting on a classical literary compost heap, did however fertilize new Roman rootstock, and in that grafted form the genes of some of them survived. Although Rome did become the most enduring beneficiary of Alexander's sweat and blood, his reception in the city was something of a mixed one; while Rome displayed respect for the scale of the Macedonian conquests – they had after all paved the way for its own Eastern Empire – that appreciation was tainted by a condescending superiority educated Romans showed towards Greece's humiliating decline. For Greece and Macedon were now garrisoned and administered as almost one subject nation.

This detour into the early history of Rome has a bearing on what we now read about Alexander, and the bar was set low. The surviving biographies of the great Macedone and his successors are the output of Roman-era historians and were no more forensic than their Greek counterparts when reporting on campaign episodes. These are 'secondary' or even 'tertiary' sources whose testimony may have come to us through intermediary historians, some of them still anonymous. They were products of a no-less challenging environment than their Greek and Macedonian predecessors, as Rome's republic was transformed into an empire and free speech all but disappeared. Vulnerable to the censorship of warring dictators or a lengthening imperial shadow, these writers overlaid their own contemplations, biases and ideologies – and inevitably those of the state – on Alexander's story.

Beware Greeks Bearing Gifts

A damaging process had already been at work on the legacy of Alexander before Roman-era authors added their contemplations to the pages. Modern scholars bemoan, as did Polybius, that since the fourth century BC, history had become the servant of rhetoric, the 'science of speaking well', according to Quintilian. The power of artful speech had been appreciated as a political tool as far back as Hesiod's *Theogony* (late eighth century BC), when a king's persuasiveness was portrayed as a gift of the Muses: 'Upon his tongue they shed sweet dew, and honeyed words flow from his mouth.'[41] These were the same Muses who explained to him: 'We know how to tell many falsehoods which are like truths, but we know also how to utter the truth when we wish.'[42]

The pejoratives associated with this type of 'artful speech' of poets and orators, as the Muses hinted, remind us that it involved a less than clinical approach to capturing the facts. The writers of the period had a utilitarian view of history itself, considering their overriding responsibility to be the edification of the reader, or to 'eristic' argument (one that sets out to successfully dispute another's view, rather than searching for the truth). 'As for history', said Cicero, perhaps with a hint of irony, 'with what voice other than the orator's can it be entrusted to immortality?'[43] Strabo added that 'persuasion through words is not a characteristic of kings but of orators'. Both knew where true influence resided.[44]

As witnessed by the above extract from *On the Orator*, Cicero *did* contend that orators alone should be entrusted with the past, and he outlined a series of noble tenets on how it should be recorded: 'The first is not daring to say anything false, and the second is not refraining from saying anything that is true. There should be no suggestion of suspicion of prejudice for, or bias against, when you write.'[45] Cicero was a trained rhetorician who assumed imperial posts, and he knew his noble tenet was asking too much of the day. But, as had already been pointed out to Cicero, 'it is the privilege of rhetoricians to exceed the truth of history'.[46]

Elsewhere, Cicero praised plain speaking and likened the rhetorical overlay to 'curling irons' on a narrative, further remarking that 'All the great fourth century orators had attended Isocrates' school, the villain who ruined fourth century historiography.'[47] It was Isocrates who urged Philip II to take on the role of uniting the Greeks in an overdue conquest of Persia, and Isocrates who starved himself to death after Philip had crushed the Greeks at the Battle of Chaeronea.[48] Alexander was the century's greatest son, and his story was bound to come under the influence of the rhetorical 'whetstone', as Isocrates described himself.[49] As a result, there emerged 'a sort of tragic history' that merged together rhetorical narrative and tragic poetry, a result that describes reasonably well the Roman Vulgate genre on Alexander.[50]

We can only touch lightly on a historiographical theme that runs deep and was even back then a subject without conclusion, for neither Cicero nor Marcus Antonius (died 87 BC, grandfather of the Triumvir better known today as Mark Antony) finished their treatises on an art that encompassed what Ennius termed 'the marrow of persuasion'. Rhetoric is embedded in the nature of a man and his desire to throw his persuasive cloak over another.[51] Diodorus even suggested that the Egyptians had long been fearful of the influence of such honey-coated speeches in legal proceedings, so that everything was conducted in writing in court. Later papyri fragments suggest the Ptolemies maintained a sophisticated paper trail of written testimony through court clerks and scribes as a legacy of that:

> For in that case there would be the least chance that gifted speakers would have an advantage over the slower, or the well-practised over the

inexperienced ... for they knew that the clever devices of orators, the cunning witchery of their delivery ... at any rate they were aware that men who are highly respected as judges are often carried away by the eloquence of the advocates, either because they are deceived, or because they are won over by the speaker's charm.[52]

Timaeus claimed that Syracuse in Sicily was the birthplace of rhetoric.[53] If so, then its flowering in Athens was more of an 'awakening' than a beginning, and brought with it a new appreciation of its method and potential application, for its development was firmly rooted in pre-history and Greece's Homeric past. Homer provided us with a vivid image of Odysseus' skill with words, 'snowflakes in a blizzard', while Phoenix – the tutor to Achilles – encouraged him to 'be both a speaker of words as well as a doer of deeds'. Here in the *Iliad*, the power of discourse was thought to persuade souls to take the direction of the 'truth'.[54]

The etymology of rhetoric was formed from *rhetor* – typically describing a speaker in a court or assembly – and *ike*, linking it to art or skill, and the compound of the two was possibly first seen in Plato's dialogue *Gorgias* (*ca*. 380 BC). Aristotle claimed that Empedocles (*ca*. 490–430 BC) had developed an 'art' that was already expressed as 'skills of speeches'.[55] Like Timaeus, Cicero thought the first manual of rhetoric was written by a Sicilian Greek, Corax of Syracuse, in the fifth century BC.[56] Then Gorgias of Leontini (*ca*. 485–380 BC), 'the father of sophistry' (the skilful use of false but persuasive arguments, often employed to present the merits of both sides of a case), ferried it to Athens, where Tisias and Antiphon dragged rhetoric and sophistry into the Court of Appeal or citizen council when pitting individual rights against the legal code. With them there did indeed appear 'arguments on both sides'.[57] Inevitably, this didn't help the jurors identify the verity of what was being pleaded.

The great Isocrates and Protagoras (*ca*. 490–420 BC) 'clarified' truth in the streets as well as in the courts for fees previously unheard of, for logographers (speechwriters) were extremely well paid 'to make the weaker argument stronger'.[58] Protagoras is said to have charged 10,000 drachmas per pupil for a single course in his 'double-argument' sophistry; its value was no doubt persuasively justified with the phrase 'man is the measure of all things'.[59] Ironically, at that time, *On Nature* by Anaxagoras (*ca*. 510–428 BC), a revolutionary book full of ground-breaking cosmic theories (including the impiety that the sun was, in fact, a ball of fire), could be purchased for just one drachma in the street.[60]

By Alexander's day, the Academy at Athens had been drawn in and Aristotle was not immune. Rhetoric was being vitiated by rhetoric to the detriment of literature in general, and as Aristotle argued, fine language was being disarmed by fine argument, skills that the bitterly opposed orators, Demosthenes and Aeschines, were to refine against one another. Isocrates and the so-titled 'Ten Attic Orators' had much to answer for in Athens, because the political and forensic show-speeches, along with the declamations we encounter throughout classical works, were originally crafted here. Demosthenes, Aeschines, Hyperides, Lycurgus and Deinarchus (all broadly contemporary) each had something to say about Philip and Alexander, as well as their successors, and none of it was straight talk. Whichever way it was bottled, the tumult of rhetoric was drowning out the simpler tones of truth.

The Return of the Rhetorical Son

A century-and-a-half on, when Rome was beginning to swallow the Successor Kingdoms, the newly imported seductive oratorial arts, and the attendant new philosophies, were not universally accepted, and neither was Greece itself. The sapient Cato the Elder (234–149 BC, also known as Cato the Censor), who started life as a rigid Sabine farmer, warned his son:

> I shall explain what I found out in Athens about these *Graeci* and demonstrate what advantage there may be in looking into their writings (while not taking them too seriously). They are a worthless and unruly tribe. Take this as a prophecy: when those folk give us their writings, they will corrupt everything.[61]

Cato did, nevertheless, appreciate the *practical* advantages of rhetoric.[62]

In the case of Alexander, a Macedonian 'orientalist' who fell into the barbarian trappings of the Persian Great Kings, he was not a figure to be rolled out at banquets in the presence of Cato, who had fought at Thermopylae in 191 BC thwarting the invasion of Antiochus III (a descendant of Alexander's general, Seleucus); it was a battle that ended Seleucid influence in Greece and suffocated the last gasps of Alexander's Diadochi. Cato blamed the campaign against Macedon in 168 BC, leading to battle at Pydna, for importing more Greek moral laxity into Rome.[63]

Cato's austerity continued to prevail for a while, and rhetoricians were expelled from the city in 161 BC. Some seven years earlier, the still-circulating Alexander-styled currency had also been banned.[64] But in 155 BC, Athens impressed Rome with a 'philosophical embassy' sent to argue for the repeal of a 500-talent fine. They included representatives of the 'new philosophies': the Stoic, Diogenes of Babylon (*ca.* 230–145 BC); the Peripatetic, Critolaus (*ca.* 200–118 BC); and the Sceptic, Carneades (214–129 BC).

Between them, they disarmed all opposition by the magic of their eloquence so that the youth of Rome flocked to hear them plead their cases and became immediately 'possessed'.[65] Although Cato, now almost 80, arranged their speedy departure, the door to new ideas had been irreversibly opened, and soon Rome was schooled by the Greeks. When the official philosophical schools at Athens were closed in 88 BC by edict of the Roman Senate, Greece experienced a 'brain drain' as philosophers and rhetoricians journeyed west to become 'household philosophers' in Rome.[66] With them arrived the topic of Alexander on a tide of new philosophical doctrines and their associated 'wisdoms'. Romans had finally 'submitted to the pretensions of a race they despised'.[67] So there appeared the claim from Horace: 'Captive Greece conquered its fierce conqueror and civilised the peasant Latins.' Virgil had been right to warn of Greeks bearing gifts.[68]

The Hellenistic era had witnessed the emergence of the philosophical schools of the Cynics, Stoics, Sceptics and the happier followers of Epicurus at the expense of the Academy and Lyceum of Plato and Aristotle, as thinkers tried to rationalize a radically changing world, or as Epicurus proposed, 'withdraw from it', for he suffered from perennial bad health. Inevitably, Alexander became the perfect canvas on which to project their new ideas for Roman contemplation. The life of the Macedonian king was used as an exemplum and soon became something of a whiteboard for a full-blown syllabus on rhetoric as manuals appeared on the subject. In the process, Alexander became a punch-bag for a Roman conscience being newly tested by its own aggressive expansion in the East. As one scholar put it, the Macedone was 'both a positive paradigm of military success and a negative paradigm of immoral excess – of virtue and vice in a single classroom incantation'.[69]

When searching for the remains of the original Alexander, we have to deal with the realities of historians living within the literary '*Pax Romana*', for censorship was tangible and authors were fair game.[70] Precedents had been set and the sound of Praetorian Guards marching into the atrium was never difficult to imagine, and neither was the drifting stench of the Tullianum, Rome's notorious prison.

If Livy was attached to the idea of a Republic without an emperor, he never quite told that to Augustus, who had by then suppressed publication of the official records of senatorial debates at the dawn of imperial Rome.[71] Livy had by now published much of his monumental 142-book *Early History of Rome*. He was given the young Claudius to tutor and sweetened his history lessons by suggesting the Macedones 'had degenerated into Syrians, Parthians and Egyptians' when referring to the Hellenistic kingdoms of Alexander's successors.[72]

It seems that there was still sensitivity to the lingering power of the Diadochi-founded dynasties in the wake of the self-serving propaganda of Octavian which held that 'the last of the Ptolemaic dynasty was threatening to hold sway in Rome itself'; that is, with the help of Mark Antony, who fell under the spell of Cleopatra.[73] Livy, who commenced his long work when Diodorus (broadly) ended his,[74] felt he needed to defend Rome from insinuations that it would have fallen to the Macedones:

> Anyone who considers these factors either separately or in combination will easily see that as the Roman Empire proved invincible against other kings and nations, so it would have proved invincible against Alexander ...

The aspect of Italy would have struck him as very different from the India which he traversed in drunken revelry with an intoxicated army; he would have seen in the passes of Apulia and the mountains of Lucania the traces of the recent disaster which befell his house when his uncle Alexander, King of Epirus, perished.[75]

Livy, the celebrated young poet–rhetorician Lucan (AD 39–65), Cicero and the stoical Seneca ('the Younger', 4 BC–AD 65) managed to frame Alexander as an example of moral turpitude when highlighting the depravity of absolute power, and their *Moral Letters* and rhetorical declamations (*sausoriae*) flowed. Arrogance and false pride were the two principal vices of Stoic doctrine, and the opening pages of Seneca's *On the Shortness of Life* could be an unfriendly dedication to Alexander, with its rejection of insatiable greed and political ambition, the squandering of wealth and the foolhardiness of inflicting dangers on others.

In the case of Seneca, a tutor to Nero, the Alexander–Aristotle relationship was clearly being relived. He, along with his nephew Lucan, was treading dangerous polemical ground until Nero commanded them both to commit suicide. Alexander had been termed 'the madman offspring of Philip, the famed Pellan robber', and was further described as nothing short of mankind's 'star of evil fate'. Lucan added: 'He rushed through the peoples of Asia leaving human carnage in his wake and plunged the sword into the heart of every nation.'[76] The problem was that Nero rather admired the Macedonian conqueror, the emperor forming an elite personal unit staffed exclusively by men over 6ft tall and naming it 'The Phalanx of Alexander the Great'.[77]

Seneca had also taken at face value a claim in Trogus' account (preserved by Justin) that Alexander caged his Bodyguard, Lysimachus, with a lion as punishment for his pitying Callisthenes; he had allegedly handed poison to him to end his suffering.[78] It was useful as a character defamation, and yet Curtius clearly stated the report was nothing but a scandal. Moreover, *this* Lysimachus was likely Alexander's tutor from Arcania and not the famous Bodyguard who inherited Thrace.[79] Seneca likewise accepted the ill-fated quip made by the Rhodian, Telesphorus, about Lysimachus' wife, Arsinoe (the daughter of Ptolemy by Berenice), along with his subsequent mutilation at Lysimachus' hand.[80] Athenaeus had read no evidence of mutilation and Plutarch credited the remark to Timagenes.[81] Neither episode was challenged, for each provided the perfect dish for a polemic on the corruption of kings, tyrants and ultimately Alexander.

Alexander's deeds inspired the republican iconoclasts to vilify him publicly and the city's first men to emulate him privately. In Valerius Maximus' nine books of *Memorable Deeds and Sayings* (published sometime under Tiberius), the Macedonian king appears at the centre of the frequent exempla on behaviour encompassing both virtues and vices, suggesting a transition was in progress.[82] And despite their thunderous tirades and the continuous cloud-cover of the earlier Greek invective, the rays of grudging admiration managed to shine through.

As unbridled power manifested itself ever more comfortably through dictators in Rome, and as independent power was stripped from the legal assembly of people, council, the plebeian tribune and finally from the Senate, the diluted conscience of the Roman Republic was more easily assuaged. When imperial 'divinity' was finally muttered and Eastern campaigns planned, Alexander emerged once more into the sunlight of imperial emulation when philhellenism returned to fashion, a somewhat ironic result in light of Macedon's own suppression of Greek freedom.[83] Finally, emperors embraced Alexander in earnest, portraying him as a giant who turned the course of Hellenic history, and ultimately that of Rome. They besieged his name, stormed his historical pages and inhabited his very footsteps.

In this environment, a period commonly referred to as the 'Second Sophistic' (broadly commencing with Nero's reign in AD 54 to AD 230, late in the reign of Alexander Severus, who locked up Alexander' tomb to deny anyone else a glimpse of his corpse) when there existed nostalgia for Hellenic glory, it was inevitable that a new wave of historians felt compelled to reconstruct the story of the Argead king. This period also saw the transition in literature from what is known as the Golden Age of Latin (dates debated, but broadly 80 BC–AD 14, 'the highest excellence in prose and poetry') to the Silver Age (AD 14–117, see chapter 9), which represents a general decline as freedom of speech vanished from Rome with successive emperors. The nineteenth-century scholars who defined these categorizations explained how and why:

> the continual apprehension in which men lived caused a restless versatility ... . Simple or natural composition was considered insipid; the aim of language was [now] to be brilliant ... . Hence it was dressed up with abundant tinsel of epigrams, rhetorical figures and poetical terms ... . Mannerisms supplanted style, and bombastic pathos took the place of quiet power.[84]

A contemporary linguist added:

> the foremost of these [characteristics of the Silver Age] is unreality, arising from the extinction of freedom ... . Hence arose a declamatory tone, which strove by frigid and almost hysterical exaggeration to make up for the healthy stimulus afforded by daily contact with affairs. The vein of artificial rhetoric, antithesis and epigram ... owes its origin to this forced contentment with an uncongenial sphere. With the decay of freedom, taste sank.[85]

The Silver Age witnessed the end of the true Roman Republic, and the triumvirates that preceded it were no less fatal for politically insensitive writers of the Golden Age. Through this period, Alexander was being subsumed into the essence of Rome; as one prominent commentator put it: *the* unifying leitmotiv of the Caesars is Alexander the Great.[86] As Diodorus, Trogus, Curtius, Plutarch and Arrian were publishing under successive Roman dictators and emperors, that took its toll on what could be written and how.

The Surviving Sources; 'Secondary' at Best

The Roman-era writers who 'preserved' Alexander's story inevitably bemoaned the archaic unreliability of their Greek literary ancestors, in the same way Greek historians had been critical of their own forerunners. But the biggest Roman-period disservice was not to name their sources at all. Even when considered worth preserving, these literary ancestors were, more often than not, publicly assassinated, quietly assimilated and destined to servitude as an anonymous section in a voluminous *Library of History* or a series of biographical *Lives*. Moreover, any methodology (rare) for working with sources remained a highly personalized affair.

Arrian, for example, announced a basic and instinctive form of judicious source choice: 'Wherever Ptolemy and Aristobulus in their histories of Alexander, the son of Philip, have given the same account, I have followed it on the assumption of its accuracy; where their facts differ I have chosen what I feel to be the more probable and worthy of telling.'[87] But did Arrian appreciate the responsibility that came with the statement? For the version he selected stuck, and all else has vanished for eternity. If Arrian unconsciously let the nostalgia of the Second Sophistic slant his prose, and recalling that his primary sources had been politically intriguing, then both conscious and unconscious damaging processes were at work on Alexander.

The Roman-era historians inevitably re-rendered Alexander in their own philosophies and words. Although individual ideology was not subject to state control (though clearly it was threatened by it), the wider biases of class, value and culture were as prominent then as today. It is against this backdrop that the surviving accounts of Diodorus, Justin, Curtius, Plutarch and Arrian were written under successive Roman dictators and emperors. Their information could not have been better than that which they had inherited (though perhaps they thought otherwise), and at this point Rome was not devoid of primary and intermediary sources on Alexander's campaigns (in contrast to the loss of detail on the Hellenistic period post-Ipsus), as evidenced by the many contributing historians named in Plutarch's accounts.[88]

Arrian explained his particular motivation for tackling the subject: no extant Alexander history appeared to be trustworthy, as a group they conflicted, and no single work captured the detail satisfactorily, at least not to his taste: 'There are other accounts of Alexander's life – more of them, indeed, and more mutually conflicting than of any other historical character.' He added that the 'transmission of false stories will continue ... unless I can put a stop to it in this history of mine'.[89] One modern scholar has suggested that Arrian's tirade was nothing less than a protest against the popularity of Cleitarchus' 'unsound history' which was already circulating in Rome.[90]

But the forensic eye of modern scholarship is revealing that what have been often termed 'good' sources – those behind the so-called 'court tradition' used by Arrian, for example – include what are now considered deposits of highly dubious material. On the other hand, writers who were once deemed 'dubious' provide us, on occasion, with a core of credible information from genuine lost texts. But identifying where that core separates from the mantle and the crust remains a challenge, so as far as the value of these secondary sources to Alexander's story is concerned, 'the old custom of dividing their writings into "favourable" and "unfavourable" has now been abandoned for a more sceptical, cautious and nuanced approach'. The commentator added, 'The truth of the matter is that there has never been a "good" or a "bad" source-tradition concerning Alexander, simply testimonia contaminated to a greater or lesser degree, which invariably need evaluating, wherever possible, by external criteria of probability.'[91] Taking this under consideration, let's look at what we have.

Diodorus the Sicilian

The Greek Sicilian Diodorus, the earliest of the five extant writers dealing with the exploits of Alexander, was constructing a 'universal' narrative along the lines of Polybius and, before him, the 'first universal historian' Ephorus (a pupil of Isocrates' school of rhetoric, along with Theopompus, both of whom covered the latter part of Philip's reign), with no monographic pretensions towards the Macedonian king.[92] Noting that events 'lie scattered about in numerous treatises and in divers authors', Diodorus provides us a rather Polybius-like case for his thirty years of research and compilation as part of the introduction we cited above:

> Most writers have recorded no more than isolated wars waged by a single nation or a single state, and but few have undertaken, beginning with the earliest times and coming down to their own day, to record the events connected with all peoples.[93]

With less space allocated to the extended moralizing (didactic) speeches we find in Thucydides, for example, and yet clearly influenced by what appears to be Ephorus' sentiment (derived from Isocrates) on 'moral utility', Diodorus once more focused on 'great men', and in the process he seems to have scorned democracy with its 'vast numbers that ruin the work of the government'.[94] Polybius had already commented on Athens' political system and perhaps set the tone: 'It [democracy] naturally begins to be sick of present conditions and next looks out for a master, and having found one very soon hates him again, as the change is manifestly for the worse.' This is a statement that conveniently appears to back-up his anacyclosis model (the cycle of inevitable political change). The concept of democracy (limited as it was in Ancient Greece: more of an oligarchy in Athens and unrecognizable today) was far from popular in the ancient world.[95]

In his philosophical introduction, Diodorus informed us that his *Library of History* covered 1,138 years and was arranged into three distinct sections.[96] The first was the 'mythical', in which he introduced Greek and Egyptian creation theories and narrated events through to the Trojan War. The second was a compendium of accounts ending at Alexander's death, and he originally planned the third – the last twenty-three books – to run past the first 'unofficial' Roman Triumvirate of 60/59 BC, formed between Julius Caesar, Crassus and Pompey, and through to Caesar's Gallic Wars of 46/45 BC. But he ceased at the earlier terminus, though later events were mentioned; the halt was probably prudent, considering the danger of commenting on contemporary events during the bloody Second Triumvirate.[97]

Of his original 'library', only books 1–5 and 11–20 survive anywhere near intact, though fragments from the remaining sections can be found in the 280 surviving epitomes of Photius the Patriarch of Constantinople (*ca.* AD 810–893), who collected and summarized many other now-lost works.[98] Fortunately, Philip II, Alexander and the Successor Wars years under scrutiny reside in books 16–20.

Diodorus' work has been a weapons testing ground for modern forensic disciplines deployed on written sources, and yet we know little about his life beyond what he himself told us, along with one further reference by the Illyrian historian–theologian, Eusebius Sophronius Hieronymus (*ca.* AD 347–420), otherwise known as St Jerome: 'Diodorus of Sicily, a writer of Greek history, became illustrious.'[99] Diodorus hailed from one of the oldest and formerly wealthiest, and yet by Roman times (according to Cicero) one of the most impoverished, settlements in the interior of Sicily, Agyrium, where a surviving tombstone inscription is dedicated to a similar-named 'son of Appollonius' – we assume the historian. In 36 BC, in the decade in which Diodorus was likely publishing, Octavian stripped the Sicilians of their Roman citizen rights, '*Latinitas*', previously granted to them by Sextus Pompey, which must have impacted Diodorus' 'freedom of expression'.[100]

Nevertheless, Diodorus afforded Agyrium – which may have suffered as a result of opposing Roman interests in the First Punic War – and its Heraclean cult (Heracles had supposedly visited the town) an importance out of context in the scale of his overall work (Timaeus was accused of much the same); he made 'events in Sicily finer and more illustrious than those in the rest of the world', perhaps as a deliberate rebuff to the domination of Rome.[101] Ephorus, too, had repeatedly assured his readers that the population of his home city, Cyme in north-west Asia Minor, was 'at peace', and apart from giving it attachments to Homer and Hesiod, Ephorus inferred every Spartan or Persian military action had some strategic link with Cyme. So when Diodorus digresses into a saga about Cyme we can confidently pinpoint his source (Ephorus), for Diodorus rarely named them.[102]

Evidence suggests Diodorus' information gathering took place broadly between 59 BC and the publication date somewhere between 36 and 30 BC, the decades in which Roman authority reached 'to the bounds of the inhabited world', a state of affairs that concerned him (now Sicily was occupied) despite his admiration for Rome's earlier achievements.[103] But parts of his first books appear to have circulated earlier, released as a separate chapter packet.[104] He seems to have spoken imperfect Latin (though living on Sicily gave him a 'considerable familiarity' with the language) and the jury remains out on whether he drew from Latin texts at all for detail on Roman affairs.

Like Herodotus, Diodorus claimed to have travelled widely in the continents he would have termed 'Europa' and 'Asia', but at times his geography is just as shaky as that of Herodotus, in whose *Histories* we see the first references to those continental names. It is clear from his eyewitness testimony, however, that he did spend time in Egypt (from *ca.* 60/59 BC), and he appears to have consulted the 'royal records' in Alexandria before basing himself in Rome (from *ca.* 46/45 BC) for a 'lengthy' time, though no patrons or reading circle associates were ever mentioned.[105]

Admitting he followed 'subject-system' subdivisions, Diodorus dealt with the fate of individuals sequentially, separating biographical threads rather than developing them in parallel, a method that complicates our understanding of the chronological progression. The result is at times akin to what has been described as a 'kaleidoscopic disjunctiveness'.[106] While dubbed 'universal' in its approach – and indeed at times he *was* panoramic in his scope – Diodorus all too often provided us with a monographic narrative that Polybius would have termed history 'bit by bit'. This was a definition close to that afforded to Thucydides by Dionysius of Halicarnassus, the Greek historian-cum-teacher-of-rhetoric, whose books, beside those of Polybius and Diodorus, represent the only surviving works of the Hellenistic era sufficiently intact to be of use to modern historians.[107]

Diodorus was cutting and pasting 'the numerous treatise from divers authors' and squeezing them into a highly generalized timeframe, though he was not blind to the shortcomings of his method, as he himself explained:

> it is necessary, for those who record them, to interrupt the narrative and to parcel out different times to simultaneous events contrary to nature, with the result that, although the actual experience of the events contains the truth, yet the written record, deprived of such power, while presenting copies of the events, falls far short of arranging them as they really were.[108]

Polybius had encountered a similar problem, and Ephorus had preceded Diodorus with this approach: a balancing act of grouping related events together and yet fitting the whole into a rigid annalistic (year-by-year) framework.[109]

In Diodorus' chronological progression, Alexander's achievement sat like a huge boulder – the greatest in history, he believed – in the literary road from prehistory to the increasingly turbulent present.[110] In his opinion, 'Alexander accomplished greater deeds than any, not only of kings who lived before him but also of those who were to come later down to our time.'[111] And that would have been a dangerous slap in the face to the career of Julius Caesar, had not Diodorus expediently stated that Caesar was the historical character he admired the most.[112]

The chapters focusing on Alexander in Diodorus' *Library of History* are considered to be about one-tenth as long as Cleitarchus' narrative of the same period (estimated from scant evidence), whereas Curtius' biography of Alexander roughly tracked Cleitarchus' original length; this uneven abridgement would explain many of the discrepancies within otherwise-similar Vulgate profiles.[113] And though a subject of intense debate, it remains easier (though less tantalizing) to swallow the idea that the tones and nuances attachable to other Roman-era Vulgate historians *also* came from Cleitarchus, who, publishing in the 370s or 360s BC, had absorbed earlier opinions into his more colourful, syncretic account. The alternative requires us to accept that each Vulgate historian flitted between a number of earlier sources and yet still produced a markedly homogenous result. Any remaining variation in commentary we see simply reflects the ethnic backgrounds and social climates attachable to the latter-day authors and the varying degrees to which they compressed Cleitarchus' scrolls.

For information on the first decades of the post-Alexander world, scholars have reached a 'somewhat uneasy agreement' that Diodorus shifted sources to Hieronymus of Cardia, once again with a heavy compression of his text.[114] Faced with the complete loss of Hieronymus' original account, the slant of Diodorus' useful chapter-opening prologues (which sometimes, however, conflict with his narrative) and the identification of unique diction he sometimes uses may provide a valuable path back to his original but unnamed sources.[115] As examples, *idiopragia* ('private power' rather than 'mutual gain') and the technical terms *katapeltaphetai* (literally 'catapultists') and *asthippoi* (elite cavalry units whose role is still debated), uniquely used by Diodorus to describe episodes we believe Hieronymus was eyewitness to, act as tell-tales to Hieronymus' presence as a source when we see them reused elsewhere.[116]

Inevitably, in this shifting of sources at the point of Alexander's death (made necessary because his main source, Cleitarchus, ended his main account here – he did briefly reference future events as a 'wrap-up'), Diodorus faced an overlap in information, and the resulting effort to reconcile them left us an untidy narrative which conflicted with his later chapters (see Grant, *Last Will and Testament*, 2021).[117]

In his opening preamble (known as a 'proem'), Diodorus expressed his apprehension that future compilers may copy or mutilate his work; perhaps this is suggestive of his own guilty conscience.[118] Classical writers frequently regurgitated their sources uncreatively, and Diodorus, the 'honest plodding Greek' who adopted a utilitarian and stoical approach, was no exception.[119]

Termed an uncritical compiler, Diodorus walked the path of least resistance in completing the 'immense labour' (as he himself described it) behind his interlocking volumes.[120] It has long been reasoned that Diodorus habitually followed single sources due to the practical difficulties of delving into multiple scrolls for alternative narratives, and as far back as the seventeenth century, scholars determined he had been plagiarising them to a scandalous degree, which was no better illustrated than in his digressions on Fortune.[121] It has even been suggested that Diodorus took his information through intermediaries in an already epitomized form. But there is little proof, and to what extent he did use middle sources or showed true independence of thought or opinion remains out for debate.[122]

Diodorus' own declaration of method suggests he was not entirely mechanical, and the title of his work, *Library of History*, was honest to the content, for it suggested nothing more than a collection of available texts, which, under the strict definition of more-critical scholarship, would classify him as a 'compiler' rather than a 'historian'.[123] In a sense this is fortunate and we might thank him for lacking any great gift of originality, for a more personal interpretation might have rendered his sources unrecognizable, whereas instead (we believe) we receive a fair impression of Cleitarchus' underlying account of Alexander, and of Hieronymus' narrative of the years that followed. As has been observed, some 'universal' historians were more 'universal' than others.[124]

Justin the Epitomizer

We would like to say much about Gnaeus Pompeius Trogus, a Romanized Vocontian Gaul writing 'in old fashioned elegance' in the rule of Augustus, and the least possible about Justin (Marcus Junianus Justinus), in whose epitomized books Trogus' cremated ashes are compacted.[125] The problem with epitomes, as one scholar has proposed, is that they 'reflect the interests of the authors who cite or summarise the lost works as much or more than the characteristics of the works concerned'.[126]Unfortunately, little remains of Trogus' curiously titled *Philippic History* (the full title may be translated as *Philippic History and the Origins of the world and Descriptions of the Earth*).[127] Justin did, however, provide useful prologues or summaries of the contents of each chapter in a similar manner to Trogus himself.

Trogus' family had made its mark in Rome; his grandfather and uncle served under Pompey the Great, and Trogus claimed his father was some kind of secretary–diplomat to Julius Caesar. This last detail suggests a switched allegiance, for Pompey and Caesar were opponents until the final decisive battle at Pharsalus in June 48 BC, after which Pompey fled to Egypt and assassination.[128]

Trogus' work, like Diodorus', stretched back to the dawn of time, covering the successive great kingdoms in the style of Herodotus, but now extending further forward, through the empires of Assyria, Media, Persia, Macedon and to Rome with its present Parthian challenge. Justin's précis exhibits a clear bias in content towards Spain, Gaul (which reportedly sent envoys to Alexander in Babylon), Carthage and the western provinces of the Roman Empire, which is understandable considering Trogus was born in Gallia Narbonensis, broadly modern Provence.[129]

Of Trogus' forty-four books, those numbered 7–33 focused on the rise and fall of Macedon, and six of them on the deeds of first Philip II and then Alexander. If Ptolemaic Egypt is considered the legacy of their influence, then Macedonian dynasties dominated the texts through to book 40. All in all, Philip came off badly, which was a typical rhetorical stance of the late Roman Republic: he was the terminator of Greek liberty, though both Polybius and Trogus did credit him with laying the foundation stone of Alexander's success.

Trogus' annalistic history did not pander to the audience in Rome, whose imperialism is criticized through the device of rhetorical speeches, and Parthia is positioned as the moral heart of the Persian Empire, casting doubts on Roman incursions. Here, Fortuna, the new incarnation of the Greek goddess Tyche, played her part in Alexander's quest to be named king of the world.[130] Justin's epitome suggests Trogus' original work, though eloquent (sufficiently so for Trogus to have confidently criticized both Livy and Sallust),[131] appears to have reinforced the darker themes attached to Alexander, as well as other influences already embedded in Cleitarchus.[132] Of course, the closer-to-home exhortations of Roman republican polemic had their effect as well; corruption by wealth is blamed for the downfall of the Lydians, the Greeks and ultimately Alexander himself.[133]

How much of the vocabulary in Justin's epitome was his own rather than Trogus' remains debatable, though scholars are now inclining to credit Justin with some originality and even linguistic creativity.[134] He was not naively epitomizing; in his preface, which took the form of an epistle (a letter to his audience), Justin suggested he was arranging an anthology of instructive passages, omitting 'what did not make pleasant reading or serve to provide a moral'.[135] These selections were akin to the Greek preparatory exercises, but now arranged as a history, and for all we know Justin might have simply been a student on such a syllabus. As has been recently pointed out, Romans grew up with Alexander, who 'as a schoolroom staple ... was a key figure in hortatory [those structured to encourage] texts'.[136]

The petals of what Justin termed his 'little body of flowers' have sadly fallen too far from the original roots to tell us more about Trogus' pages. Nonetheless, Justin's brief résumé of his history is, sadly, the only surviving continuous narrative of events in the Eastern Mediterranean that spans the whole of the Hellenistic Age.

Less optimistic is another modern (and somewhat Shakespearean) conclusion of Justin's efforts: 'Is there any bread at all to this intolerable deal of sack?'[137]

Curtius, the Roman Entertainer

Scholars have also forensically assaulted Curtius' *Histories of Alexander the Great of Macedon*, if that approximates the original title, so enigmatic is Curtius' work (see chapter 10).

Curtius was likely aboard the Roman senatorial career path (the *cursus honorum*), where training as a rhetorician was vital to success; it was not an uncommon twinning of abilities in the so-called Silver Age of Latin. But the dating of Curtius' work remains uncertain and there is no firm evidence that it was widely known or ever used by other historians before the Middle Ages, after which interest was reignited. The first two books of his monograph, in which Curtius might have identified himself more fully, have been lost. Judging by an encomium to his emperor in his tenth chapter, he would have prefaced his introduction with an imperial dedication that would have dated him nicely. Frequent gaps in the text (known as 'lacunae') appear elsewhere, and yet sufficient remains to suggest both he and Cleitarchus shared a common bond: they placed the edification of their audience above purer historiographical pursuits, with the earlier production assimilated into Curtius' Roman restaging of the play.

A 'gifted amateur', Curtius has also been termed 'a Roman who wrote for Romans', and nowhere is that more evident than when dealing with the infighting at Babylon in mid-June 323 BC.[138] Curtius' is the only surviving insight into what Cleitarchus had fulsomely documented (probably from eyewitness veterans in Alexandria) about the chaos in the days between Alexander's death and the partition of the empire following Assembly meetings of the Macedonian men-at-arms, which almost erupted into civil war.[139]

Here, the themes Curtius overlaid on events do include choice Roman themes overlaid on Cleitarchus' original detail, as if he could sense his account alone would survive. Considering the trend of his day – incorporating character declamations and comparisons between them for morality lessons – it is likely Curtius elongated Cleitarchus' speeches and suitably paired them with counter-speeches in his own sculpting of the dialogue to keep a momentum-filled hold on his audience (see Grant, *Last Will and Testament*, 2021, chapter 3).

Rome's political path influenced Curtius' retrospective view of history, and so we must appreciate the Babylonian dialogues for what they really are: thematic echoes of the originals that had been first sterilized of anti-Ptolemaic toxins by Alexandrian-based Cleitarchus, and which were now reworked by a wealthy, connected Roman noble to please an educated public readership under an unpredictable emperor.[140] As a result, the occasion on Curtius' pages was first-century Rome as much as fourth-century BC Babylon. Curtius' overlay developed what was essentially a Roman-style public debate (a *contio*), with the author presiding as the literary magistrate. The insertion of formal debates appears throughout his monograph and in the presence of varied audiences surrounding Alexander: advisers, commanders, or in front of the entire army in the manner of those attached to Roman general Scipio Africanus.[141]

It has become clear that Curtius elsewhere filled gaps in Cleitarchus' masonry with his own colourful grouting, and accessorized Alexander – and Darius III too, for that matter – with speeches from his own rhetorical wardrobe. Thus attired, the Macedonian king was paraded anew as digressions on fortune and kingship were readdressed. This was essentially the same story with a new editor and under a new literary censor, though studded with occasional unique and 'invaluable facts'.[142] Curtius justified his inclusion of less than credible episodes by explaining his journalistic dilemma: 'I report more than I believe, for while I cannot vouch for matters of which I am not certain, neither can I omit what I have heard.'[143] This was, as we now know, a familiar refrain from narrators rather than forensic historians.

If we consider that Curtius embellished Cleitarchus, who had already ornamented the agenda-laden works of Alexander's contemporaries, we appreciate how thick the sugar coating became on his bittersweet biography. Curtius' method has been described as one that frittered away priceless sources 'in the course of a tedious literary concept about the goddess Fortuna and many florid exercises in Roman rhetoric'.[144] He has been summed up as nothing more than a 'hasty irresponsible rhetorician' who was little more than a 'superior journalist', with a more barbed polemic proposing: 'He can slough the rhetoric, as a snake sloughs a dead skin. And one neglects that rhetoric at one's peril, for scattered through it, like pearls in a pig-trough, are some quite valuable facts and strange pieces of insight; the book is both repellent and fascinating.'[145]

But opinion never stands still and is now inclining towards a reinstatement of Curtius' credentials as a judicious historian; recent scholars have done much to salvage him as worthy of respect.[146] His technical descriptions are at times superior to the erratic pedantry of Arrian, even if his 'monograph remains something of a cliché of the Graeco–Roman rhetorical tradition'.[147] Another good summation reminds us: 'Scholarly research has overestimated the rhetorical and artistic contribution of Curtius while neglecting its actual relation to historical events.'[148]

The Alexander monographs by Cleitarchus and Curtius may have been one-time bids for fame, for we are not aware they authored anything but a book on the Macedonian king. Prising them apart is not an easy task, as time has firmly laminated them together. But why did Curtius' work survive when Cleitarchus' account, once so popular in Rome, did not?[149] Although Cleitarchus' book had become the perfect pizza base for new moralistic toppings, it may have been disdained by the literati with pretensions. But the most significant answer to Curtius' survival is perhaps summed up with 'Latin'.

Cleitarchus had published in Greek, the language later used by Roman intellectuals but not by the populace in general, and the effort required to translate a Greek work was greater than producing a new Latin text, so copies dwindled as Latin books proliferated in the later empire. That proliferation was especially true of books written by the politically connected, in which context it remains vexing why Curtius, likely himself a politician, is unreferenced before the Middle Ages.[150] It can be argued that Curtius wrote in the emperorship of Nero (see chapter 10), which marks the beginning of the Second Sophistic and its love of the Greek past, but Curtius' portrait was hostile and that may have sealed its fate under an emperor who idolized Alexander.[151] The owners of the relatively few manuscripts most likely had no idea of their frailty and proximity to extinction, and when Rome's own borders finally broke and libraries were burned by barbarian torches, its own Latin productions followed the Greek tragedy into the flames.

Trogus and Curtius, at the heart of the Vulgate genre, were peddling their rhetoric just as the Athenian sophists and rhetors had honed their oratory skills in the courts, where, like ships 'before a veering wind, they lay their thoughts and words first on one tack then another'. Although Diodorus considered that 'history also contributes to the power of speech', we have reason to believe it was in fact the other way around.[152]

Plutarch the Aristocratic Preacher

There is no doubting the eloquence of Plutarch, the author of the fourth surviving profiling of Alexander. He multi-sourced 'from the best to the very worst' with vigour to sculpt the expression of character he wished to display and so conformed to no particular genre, 'Court' or 'Vulgate', with elements of both incorporated to suit his cause.[153] Much of the detail that featured in his rendering of Alexander was derived from an oft-cited corpus of letters he believed to be authentic (see chapter 6), though he also implied his access to books was limited in provincial Chaeronea, a town that in his day still displayed the tree known as Alexander's Oak commemorating the battle there. But the composition of such 'open' letters was a popular template in rhetorical training and sophists' lectures, with their harsh moralizing as part of learning how to structure character declamations.[154]

Plutarch also indicated that his understanding of Latin was imperfect, and neither did the appreciation of 'the beauty and quickness of the Roman style, the figures of speech, the rhythm, and the other embellishments of the language' come easy to him. In contrast to Diodorus' more monogamous method, Plutarch's frequent changing of source partners renders any attempt to identify the authors underpinning his biographical compendiums near impossible.[155]

Often labelled a 'Middle Platonist' for his philosophical stance (where elements of Stoic and Peripatetic doctrine had been absorbed and combined), Plutarch produced a number of 'educational' works that offer auxiliary insights from a complex commentator on the nature of men and their adherence to, or divergence from, the honour code and behavioural ideals of classical Greece.[156] As a former pupil of Ammonius the Peripatetic (who may have been a Platonist) in Athens (in AD 66–67), convictions from Aristotle's *Ethics* and *Politics* frequently raise their head. These essays have been termed 'virtual history', noting that the above collection, alongside his *On the Fortune of the Romans* (also *Roman Questions* and *Greek Questions*), reflect Plutarch's political influence in both Greece and in Rome at its zenith under Trajan (emperor from AD 97–117) and Hadrian (AD 117–138), with whom he may have been personally acquainted.[157]

A senior Priest of Apollo at the oracle of Delphi, where he was employed to interpret the auguries of Delphic priestess Pythia, he maintained that gods never spoke but only gave signs, and that the divine escaped recognition if the belief was lacking.[158] Unsurprisingly, events surrounding Alexander's death (like much of his life) became a chapter more sympathetic to mysterious portents, Chaldean prophecies, diviners and superstition, as well as the liberating of the soul to higher things, for Plutarch was also a firm believer in reincarnation.[159] Thanks to sources like Aristobulus, he and Arrian a few decades after him had all the materials they needed.[160]

Plutarch had no agenda of preserving history *per se*, as he himself freely admitted; he was hunting for vices and virtues 'from a chance remark or a jest that might reveal more of a man's character than the mere feat of winning battles', and was plucking rhetorical leaves to flavour his biographical stews along the way.[161] But Plutarch was also dumping non-exploitable chapters, with something of the methodology of both Xenophon and Justin in his approach. Moreover, he was inconsistent in his methodology too, as where it suited his direction, Plutarch introduced the fabulous, and where it didn't, he was quick to scorn exaggeration.[162]

Plutarch's *Parallel Lives*, his 'cradle-to-grave' biographies in which Greeks were paired with Roman counterparts – Alexander with Julius Caesar – illustrated his own political juxtaposition of citizenship in both Greece and Rome, although perhaps his pairings were further inspired by Polybius' earlier adjacent-chapter profiling of Hannibal and Scipio.[163] Outside of the requirement for these skilled and artful comparisons, Plutarch's approach did not fuel a forensic curiosity. As for his biography of Alexander, one scholar suggested it was written late in life when 'the fire had burnt low and [Plutarch] was swamped by his much reading', though we know little of the relative chronology behind the production of his *Lives*.[164] The increasing tension between Alexander's self-control and his temper (disasters are always linked to excessive drinking in Plutarch's biography) is illustrated by 'interweaving and contrasting epic and tragic elements' throughout his biography, along with connections to the story of the god Dionysus, whence the call to drunkenness came.[165] The mighty hero Heracles, an illustrious family ancestor according to court propaganda, had also been a notoriously heavy imbiber, and Alexander was doing no less.

One scholar scathingly thought that Plutarch 'reminds us of the cookery of those continental inns ... in which a certain nondescript broth is kept constantly boiling, and copiously poured, without distinction, over every dish'.[166] It was an unfair summation that belittles Plutarch's deep curiosity about human nature, and his 'pottage' contained ingredients we find nowhere else. Along with the Vulgate historians, and like the more recent restoration of Leonardo Da Vinci's *Last Supper* painting, the faded and flaking primary pigments were retouched in brighter oils and re-rendered in vibrant tones that give us vivid moralistic portraits that are inevitably larger than the lives themselves.

Arrian the Romanized Soldier

The final surviving narrative on the life and campaigns of Alexander is Arrian's *Anabasis* (broadly 'expedition up country'), the latest of them to be written. If Plutarch was adorning Alexander with epideictic passages and Curtius was laying on rhetorical oils, then in contrast Arrian was applying paint-stripper 'to set the records straight', or so he would have us believe. The conflict and vagueness he found in earlier works irked his precise military mind, as did the fame and choral odes afforded to lesser men than Alexander; the tyrants of Sicily and Xenophon's Ten Thousand, for example, each of whom unfairly outshone his model Macedonian warrior.[167] This must explain why Arrian largely marginalized the deeds of Philip II in Greece and the Balkans, which nevertheless launched Alexander on his journey.[168]

Holding the positions of both Consul of Rome and archon of Athens through the decade of AD 130–140, Arrian was a 'public intellectual' with political influence in both peninsulas, like Plutarch and Polybius before him.[169] He challenged the 'legends' that frequented the Alexander accounts to show a judicial backbone, and Arrian appears to have been deeply religious, with the requisite soldier's superstition. His *Anabasis* ended with 'I too, have had God's help in my work', implying a favoured client relationship with the divine, and if Alexander had been a new Achilles of his age, then Arrian was to be the new Homer who immortalized him.[170] Here, Arrian was employing a more subtle rhetoric than his forerunners: that of self-promotion through the façade of truth's envoy, while his personal reflections and pedantic, though shallow, autopsy of his sources at times betrays arrogance thinly disguised as investigative fervour.[171]

As a Romanized Greek from Nicomedia in Bithynia (northern Anatolia, named Asia Minor in his day, now Turkey) and the author of a history of that region,[172] we might conjecture that Arrian credited Alexander's success with laying the foundation of Rome's Eastern Empire, thus furthering his own career. According to the *Suda*, Dio Chrysostom (*ca*. AD 40–post-112, literally 'golden mouth'), a fellow Bithynian historian, had a generation earlier written *On Alexander's Virtues* in eight books, and this must have set an influential, encomiastic tone.[173]

Close parallels between Arrian and Alexander certainly did exist: Arrian served in Trajan's war against Parthia (AD 114–117), a post that would have seen him marching south through Mesopotamia and eastern Babylonia, then down the Tigris to the Persian Gulf as Alexander once did. And as with Alexander's reality check at the Hyphasis River in India, this hard-earned Roman territory was soon lost again to the Eastern barbarian kings.[174]

Arrian may have additionally likened himself to Alexander's secretary–soldier, Eumenes of Cardia, who became a central character in Arrian's sequel, *Events After Alexander*, based on Hieronymus' account, for both were Greeks operating under a foreign regime and each was tasked with pacifying Cappadocia. In Arrian's case, this meant driving back the Alans; his treatise on the tactics used, *Deployment Against the Alans*, described his dispositions in classical Greek and Macedonian terms. He was literally walking in the footsteps of the Macedonian conquest, which had itself marched in the soleprints of Xenophon's famed Ten Thousand; appropriately, Photius termed Arrian the 'young Xenophon'.[175] Arrian's eastern experiences may explain why his first chapters read as a hurried narrative of Alexander's consolidation of Greece and the Balkans, for he was impatient for his pages to land on by-now familiar Asian soil.

When reviewing his list of 'court' sources, Arrian was drawn to Ptolemy 'the soldier's soldier', and next to Aristobulus, likely a supporting engineer, and he only drew from 'external sources' for missing detail and useful paraphrases. This did not stop him from being 'frequently warped by misunderstanding' in his narrative: geography and the sequence of events as well as names do appear erroneously.[176] Whether Arrian was genuinely inspired to use Ptolemy because he was 'a king honour-bound to avoid untruth', or he was simply being pragmatic in the face of limited sources, is debatable.[177]

Arrian was also impressed with Nearchus, whose account of the voyage from India (the *Indica*) he preserved, with giant trees, snakes and its link to the god Dionysus and all. And yet he did warn his readers, rather cynically: 'This digression can serve as a warning not to trust the accounts some writers have given of the Indians on the far side of the Hyphasis [the modern River Beas]: up to the Hyphasis those who were with Alexander on his campaign are not entirely untrustworthy.' But those whose veracity he was calling into question included the authors who documented the rest of Alexander's conquest of Asia.

One observer notes that Arrian was 'engaging in a dialogue with the great historical masters' in the style of Tacitus, another orating product of the Roman *cursus honorum* with extensive military experience.[178] Influential with the Emperor

Hadrian, Arrian opened his story with 'I have no need to write my name, for it is not at all unknown among men',[179] a self-serving introduction that recalls Livy's own.[180] Arrian went on, not without self-confidence:

> let me say this: that this book of mine is, and has been from my youth, more precious than country and kin and public advancement – indeed, for me it is these things. And that is why I venture to claim the first place in Greek literature, since Alexander, about whom I write, held first place in the profession of arms.

This self-righteousness is also somewhat reminiscent of the epilogue to Ovid's *Metamorphoses* (dating to AD 8) and rings of Polybius, who dedicated several chapters to honour the family Scipio, which nevertheless read as his own CV.

Scholarly debate is ever divided on Arrian's value as a historian. If, like Thucydides, he may have thought he was producing 'a possession forever',[181] he was ultimately an 'apologist', and 'what emerges is a powerful portrait of Alexander ... confident of the justice of his cause, careful of the legitimacy of his crusade, and pious at the moment of his triumph'.[182] But the need to combine the best qualities of a king with the worst of a tyrant would have produced a character portrait that could only have curdled on Arrian's pages, and he permitted no Vulgate agenda of moral decline to accommodate Alexander's transformation. Even the king's drinking binges were, he accepted, 'a social courtesy to his friends'. So Arrian exploited his lingering bigotry to legitimize the mass slaughter of 'barbarians', while praising the exceptional conquered tribes in condescending tones: 'Like the best of the Greeks, they claimed to know the distinction between right and wrong.'[183]

In the process, Arrian was forced to become a master of omission, like Ptolemy before him,[184] and he dismissed what could not be erased with 'then there is a story – to me quite incredible' or 'a thing one might have expected from an Oriental despot [Xerxes], but utterly uncharacteristic of Alexander'.[185] This last example was, paradoxically, expressing his disbelief in Alexander's destruction of the temple of Asclepius at Ecbatana, when he had earlier fulsomely reported Alexander's deliberate burning of the Achaemenid ceremonial capital at Persepolis.[186]

Arrian's account of India is less sanitized and probably relied on Cleitarchus when information from Ptolemy and Aristobulus was scant. Arrian littered his fifth and sixth chapters with terms associated with the carnage that followed no fewer than sixteen times from the aftermath of the Hydaspes battle with Porus, through the slaughter in Mallia, to Alexander's flotilla finally arriving at the Indus Delta: translations give us 'crushed', 'cut down', 'put to death', 'subdued', 'attacked unarmed men', 'onslaught', 'massacred', 'enslaved', 'trapped', 'stormed', 'plundered' and 'hanged'.[187] Campaigning in desert-bound Gedrosia added to the death toll, and Diodorus recorded that: 'Every spot was filled with fire and devastation and great slaughter.'[188] Remarkably, Arrian recounted this period in an easy and matter-of-fact way, despite the enemy casualties (reportedly) falling in the tens of thousands. But this was typical of Arrian's stoic principles (see below) – 'never say an action is bad' – and so the death count was simply labelled 'high'.

For all his posturing, Arrian's study of Alexander lacked creativity, as did its title, *Anabasis*, which once again emulated Xenophon's account with its eight-book length. It has been noted that of the seven surviving speeches in Arrian's book, most are once more an 'allusion to Xenophon'; it was yet another example of 'subject matter fitting the moment', rather than what had been actually said.[189] It has even been argued that Arrian's own agnomen, which appeared as Xenophon in his full name, was likewise born of the nostalgia linking him to the pupil of Socrates, rather than a genuine birth name.[190]

Arrian adopted the Ionic Greek dialect of Herodotus for his *Indica*, in which Nearchus' log and elements of the polymath–geographer Eratosthenes (*ca.* 276–194 BC) and the explorer Megasthenes (*ca.* 350–290 BC) were being blended into a formless 'discussion of Indian affairs'.[191] And yet we must recall that the nostalgia for Greek glories which permeated the Second Sophistic demanded nothing less. It was a period that saw Cassius Dio pen a Roman history in Greek in a (poor) emulation of Thucydides, and the Cynic, Dio Chrysostom (most likely his grandfather), who was banished by the emperor Domitian, depart Rome with nothing more than the lessons and speeches of Plato and Demosthenes in his bags. The period inspired Quintus of Smyrna to finally bridge the Homeric gap between the end of the *Iliad* and the start of the *Odyssey* with a fourteen-book epic, and in the view of one commentator, when the Roman Empire ceased to know Greek, its decline truly began.[192]

Arrian is himself credited with single-handedly preserving the teachings of his Greek-speaking Phrygian Stoic mentor Epictetus (*ca.* AD 55–135) with a manual written, unsurprisingly, in the style of Xenophon's records which preserved Socrates' recollections.[193] Inevitably, Epictetus' particular philosophical interpretations of kingship infiltrated Arrian's summation of the Macedonian king.[194]

If classical history was 'the circulated written works of a social elite', we have no better examples than these, for both Plutarch and Arrian enjoyed prominent political offices that provided wider publication capabilities, and thus we still read them today.[195] Although they were both educated far above the plebiscite and *hoi polloi*, Arrian and Plutarch were nonetheless shackled to the mind-set of the time. Arrian, hamstrung by a lifelong affection for his Macedonian conqueror, rarely shone a torch into the undergrowth either side of his hero's well-trodden path, except where he saw thick clods sitting on an artificial-looking turf. He added nothing truly insightful to the detail found in the Vulgate, while Plutarch was satisfied to ponder, once again, fortune's tides and fate's inevitability in stoic fashion. Polybius had frequently deferred to *tyche* (not the deity Tyche, equivalent to Rome's Fortuna, but broadly fate or providence – 'things beyond explanation'), which 'steered almost all the affairs of the world', as a final explanation,[196] and a similarly stoical Arrian chose an easy route over 'wholehearted religious or philosophical commitment' on what he read in the sources.[197]

These five extant historians, representing the 'court' tradition and the 'Vulgate' genre (Plutarch arguably had a foot in each camp with his multi-sourcing), represent almost everything coherent we have on Alexander today. The geographical treatise of Strabo and the forays into natural history by Pliny make frequent references to the Macedonian campaign in the East, but little more than that. Supplementing them for detail on the Successor Wars we have Plutarch's biographies of the generals, kings and politicians who played their part in the fate of the Diadochi, plus Polybius for their final showdown with Rome. We have fragments from anonymous epitomes and codices, such as the *Heidelberg Epitome* (so named for its discovery in the German city) with its four relevant excerpts, and while as vexatious as they are useful, they help us to build a picture of these dramatic war-torn years.[198]

The ironic result is that the *Historical Miscellany* of Aelian, a philhellene teaching rhetoric in Rome whose accomplished florid Greek earned him the title 'honey-tongued', stands as an irreplaceable goldmine of diverse historical facts and fables, anecdotes, pithy maxims and moralizing epithets that occasionally touched on Alexander's world. This, alongside Athenaeus' *Dinner Philosophers* in which some 1,250 authors and more than 2,500 works are referred to, takes on an incongruous weight in the preservation of the voices of the period.[199] Athenaeus' diversional by-product of the *Pax Romana* contains no fewer than sixteen of the thirty-six fragments we possess of Duris, the lost Samian historian, and again thanks to the *Dinner Sophists* we have more lines of verbatim Theopompus, who 'claimed the first place in rhetorical education' and is ominously credited with progress in the 'art of discourse' for the improving quality of history, than we have verbatim text for any other lost Greek historian.[200]

These cultural snapshots of the classical world, never intended to be 'histories', beside Diogenes Laertius' *Lives and Deaths of the Eminent Philosophers* ('doxographies', whose detail occasionally overlapped statements found in the *Suda*), have perhaps been mined deeply for insights more thoroughly than their authors intended. Although scholars hold a dim view of compilers like Diogenes Laertius ('the dim witted watchman who guards treasures without having a clue about their value'),[201] we are faced with the fact that 'the somewhat greasy heap of a literary rag-and-bone-picker like Athenaeus' has nevertheless been 'turned to gold by time'.[202] But anthologies and compendiums like these, the products of what some today would term 'antiquarians' rather than 'historians', caught the imagination of the reader, for anecdotal collections are usually accompanied by scandal, slanders and political intrigue: the sugar and spice that sells the bake more effectively than plain dough.[203]

Compressions Scars and Time Warps

One of the most challenging tasks facing modern historians is the synchronizing of these surviving accounts, not just in terms of factual detail (where contradictions frequently occur) but chronologically. This may be down to lost chapter sections (referred to as *lacunae*) but is principally down to the differing degree to which each episode has been compressed by each of these later sources. Most frustrating are the immediate post-Alexander years, and even the days following Alexander's passing (see Grant, *Last Will and Testament*, 2021, chapter 5). It was at this juncture that the Roman-period historians writing follow-on books had to switch sources, because their principal sources, Ptolemy and Aristobulus – and as far as we know, Nearchus and Onesicritus – stopped their accounts at Alexander's death, as did Cleitarchus a generation later. So Diodorus and Arrian (as well as Trogus, later précised by Justin) now had to unravel the scrolls of Hieronymus to obtain interlocking detail of the Successor War years.

What becomes clear from a comparison with the calculated length of Arrian's *Events After Alexander*, a précis of Hieronymus' voluminous work, is that Diodorus' compression was at times drastic.[204] Arrian needed ten books to cover the years 323–318 BC, whereas the same period occupies only Diodorus' eighteenth book.[205] The few surviving fragments of Duris' parallel work (now lost in complete form) suggest the Samian historian covered the same period at the pace of one-and-a-half to two years per book, though he appears to have sped ahead with his narrative after Eumenes' death at the close of 316 BC.[206]

Alongside this severe culling of detail, there remains the challenge of unravelling the order of events. Diodorus divided his chapters into synthetic campaign years in which little monthly or seasonal direction was provided, save his references to the hardships winter placed on operating; this was a method probably employed by Hieronymus himself, most likely following the examples of Thucydides and Xenophon before him.[207] And so the traditional divides of summer, harvest and war all merged together in a less than coherent sequence.

Diodorus additionally tried to synchronize the Roman consular year (January to January by his day) with the Athenian archon year (summer to summer) while attempting to adhere to Hieronymus' overall progression, but he filled gaps he found in that narrative – detail of affairs in Greece, for example, which Hieronymus did not personally witness – by drawing from other historians such as Diyllus.[208] In the process, Diodorus occasionally predated his entries against the eponymous archon change to more effectively introduce new subject matter, and as a result he was often six months or more off the pace. But only three of the five archon changes in the years 323–319 BC were recorded, with no reference provided at all for the years 321/320 BC and 320/319 BC.[209]

Plutarch was even less concerned about being clinical on the sequence of events so long as the resulting narrative satisfied his character development and the thematic shape. Consequently, we have a conspicuous lack of synchronicity between his and Diodorus' account, in which a lamentable text gap sits between the council of war at Triparadeisus where the empire was redivided and the battle between Eumenes and Antigonus at Orcynia,[210] while almost all of the latter half of 320 BC is 'passed over in silence'.[211]

Many scholars have dedicated lengthy studies to elucidating and solving the problem, noting that even the Triparadeisus conclave may have been wrongly dated. Modern interpretations place the gathering of generals anywhere from summer 321 BC (the 'high' chronology, as suggested imperfectly by Diodorus' text) to mid-320 BC (the 'low' chronology, suggested by what can be extracted from carvings of the *Parian Chronicle* and *Babylonian Chronicle*), though hybrid theories place events somewhere in between. If the date of Perdiccas' assassination on the Nile can be anchored down by the latter to May/June 320 BC, the meeting of generals at Triparadeisus should have logically followed soon after.[212] But the *Babylonian Chronicle* and the *Parian Chronicle* only provide chronological safe anchorages here and there, and the latter is far from reliable.[213] As has been pointed out, everything can be reinterpreted by the subtle shunting back and forward of a war council, a flotilla launch or an envoy's arrival in between.

The Dating Game; the Numbers Game

Not all the chronological slippage is down to compression of detail or the errant methodology of the Roman-period historians when knitting together the older narratives. Some of the fog is down to scribal errors in the translation and copying of decrepitated manuscripts through the ages (see chapter 9). Yet it is also clear that the earlier eyewitness writers on campaign with Alexander were inclined to falsely date formative events for sensational effect and to edit numbers no less zealously for similar reasons. Prime examples concern battles. Of course, any suspicious values could have been challenged by the Roman-period sources, but invariably they weren't.

We can start with the clash of arms at the Granicus River, the first of the three major set-piece battles against the army of Darius III, which took place close to the ruins of Troy. Alexander was being presented by ancient historians as a reborn Achilles, a role he is said to have embraced when crowning what was claimed to be Achilles' Trojan tomb.[214] As fate would have it – if Duris of Samos' calculations are correct – the confrontation in May 334 BC was fought on the very anniversary of the sack of Troy by the Greeks 1,000 years before in 1,334 BC.[215]

Alexander crossed to Asia with approximately 32,000 mixed infantry and 4,500 allied cavalry (sources are less than clinical), and these were arrayed in a strategic order.[216] It was now late in the day; the Granicus separated the armies, with the Persians on higher ground. Although the Granicus was hardly a torrent, crossing the deep-banked, rough watercourse looked precarious. Indeed, Alexander's 'best tactician', Parmenio, advised waiting in favour of a surprise attack at dawn.[217] Troops were equally reticent to fight in the month of Daesius (the moon of May), when armies traditionally did not take to the field, but Alexander convinced them to name it a 'second Artemisius' (moon of April) to remove the stigma.

At first it looked like Parmenio's advice was sage: the initial fighting was desperate, evenly matched, and could have gone either way: in the words of Plutarch, 'the enemy pressed upon them with loud shouts ... matching horse with horse.' Diodorus added that 'the Persians resisted bravely and opposed their spirit to the Macedonian valour'. Great showers of javelins descended on the Macedones, and according to Arrian they suffered badly in this first onslaught, when they were vastly outnumbered on the riverbank. The first Macedones to meet the Persian line were cut to pieces.[218]

While the reporting of the battle tactics and its progression is reasonably consistent throughout the sources, the troop numbers are conspicuously not: Diodorus reports more than 10,000 cavalry were arrayed against Alexander, with 100,000 Persian infantry lined up behind them (whether this infantry number included mercenaries is unclear; see below).[219] Arrian doubles the Persian cavalry to 20,000 and adds a similar number of 'foreign' mercenary soldiers, but gives no number for the Persian infantry contingent, though earlier he says they were 'greatly outnumbered' by Macedonian foot soldiers, leaving us a further unsolvable problem.[220] Justin provides us with an entertaining 600,000 for the total Persian force.[221]

But despite the vigour and bravery each army initially showed in evenly matched fighting élan, the Persian line eventually collapsed when the Macedones formed a bridgehead across the river and Alexander's cavalry contingents finally crossed, but it was an immense struggle to do so. With this in mind, the comparative casualty numbers are nonsensical.

Diodorus reports the Persian dead at more than 2,000 cavalry and 10,000 infantry, with 20,000 prisoners taken alive.[222] Plutarch gives us 20,000 Persian infantry losses and 2,500 cavalry, while Arrian states 1,000 cavalry died and only 2,000 of Darius' 'foreign' infantry survived, thus a loss of almost 18,000 of his stated 20,000 (principally Greek) mercenaries.[223]

The real hard-to-swallow numbers, in comparison, are Macedonian casualties, with the highest number given by Justin: a mere 120 cavalry. Arrian halved that to sixty, including twenty-five elite Companions, while Plutarch – citing Aristobulus as his source – repeats the twenty-five Companion dead. Infantry losses were even more insignificant: thirty according to Arrian and just nine according to Justin and Plutarch (from Aristobulus).[224] The press corps and eyewitness historians were less than subtle with their propaganda regarding the superhuman imbalance in numbers. Just as invidiously infiltrated was the treatment of the mercenaries.

Once the Persians forces had been routed and taken flight, the Greek mercenaries, who had stood their ground, were surrounded and asked Alexander for quarter.[225] Alexander refused and ordered them to be cut down: some 18,000 of these 'warlike and desperate' Greek mercenaries were killed at the conclusion of the engagement. Yet Plutarch claimed that 'most of the Macedones who were slain or wounded fought or fell there, since they came to close quarters with men who knew how to fight'. Clearly the engagement was bloody; Alexander's horse was impaled and killed.

Here we should ponder the scale of these claims: not many battles in the history of Ancient Greece saw 20,000 Greek mercenaries fighting side by side, or indeed an allied force of *any* coalition of city-states this large. There were only 11,000 Greeks on the plain at Marathon (490 BC) facing the Persian horde (where casualty numbers were just as suspiciously reported), and approximately 9,000 soldiers in each of the opposing armies in the biggest battle of the whole Peloponnesian War at Mantinea (418 BC). Moreover, as Plutarch reminds us, Greek mercenaries 'knew how to fight'; a force of 18,000 professional career fighters heavily armed as hoplites, and here given no quarter, would have been a formidable force to decimate by 90 per cent without a pyrrhic outcome. For this reason, modern interpretations place likely mercenary numbers at 5,000, and unsurprisingly the total Persian contingent is whittled down manyfold as well.[226] Any Greeks rounded up (Athenians, Thessalians and Thebans, who survived by 'lying unnoticed among the dead') were sent back to hard-labour camps in Macedon.[227]

If we fast-forward to the second of the great pitched battles at Issus in Cilicia in November 333 BC, where Darius III himself was present, we find something of a rerun in terms of the battle outcome. This time the Macedones were 'vastly inferior in numbers' as the Persian army now comprised some 400,000 infantry and not less than 100,000 cavalry.[228] Sources also cite 30,000 Greek mercenaries fighting alongside them, while Arrian gives a total of some 600,000 fighting men in the Persian ranks, though whether his source was Ptolemy or Aristobulus is unclear.[229] Modern estimates propose no more than 100,000 Persian combatants in total, with some suggestions of much lower numbers.

Diodorus described the ensuing melee:

> the cavalry on both sides was engaged and many were killed as the battle raged indecisively because of the evenly matched fighting qualities .... The scales inclined now one way, now another, as the lines swayed alternately forward and backward. No javelin cast or sword thrust lacked its effect as the crowded ranks offered a ready target. Many fell with wounds received as they faced the enemy and their fury held to the last breath, so that life failed them sooner than courage.[230]

The Persians additionally launched at Alexander such a shower of missiles that they collided with one another in the air.[231]

Chares, the royal usher, went as far as claiming that Alexander's thigh wound was given to him by Darius himself in hand-to-hand combat, though Alexander's own correspondence (unique to Plutarch once more, see chapter 6) never mentioned this, nor did any other source.[232]

Curtius entertains with an account of the hand-to-hand infantry fighting: 'Then the blood really flowed, for the two lines were so closely interlocked that they were striking each other's weapons with their own and driving their blades into their opponent's faces.'[233] The Persian nobles were not enough to galvanize their ranks and stem the tide of the Macedonian assault. Darius then fled in the face of Alexander's penetrating charge in his direction, despite the spirited defence of his noblemen, who were whittled down once again, forcing him to eventually abandon his chariot, shield and bow, along with his family and his harem of concubines left at Damascus.[234] Once again, the 30,000 Greek mercenaries were abandoned after attempting to breach the Macedonian line, having fought with pride, and it was here that once more many Macedones fell.[235]

Some 100,000 Persians, including (or excluding; accounts conflict) 10,000 of Darius' cavalry, were reportedly slain, though Justin claimed 61,000 infantry and 10,000 horsemen perished.[236] Varying numbers for Alexander's dead range from thirty-two to 300 infantrymen and fifty to 150 cavalry. Curtius took (what appears to be) a sarcastic swipe at the figures recorded at Issus, writing 'so the Persians were driven like cattle by a handful of men', adding that 'while not more than 1,000 horsemen were with Alexander, huge numbers of the enemy were in retreat'.[237] He stated that 504 of Alexander's men were additionally wounded, followed by the comment: 'At so small a cost was a huge victory secured.'[238] Yet all records of Macedonian losses seem remarkably small in the face of such fierce hand-to-hand fighting, the bravery of the Persian nobles and the stiff resistance of the mercenaries.

This time, some 8,000 Greek mercenaries had made good their escape in the cover of darkness.[239] Up to this point, more Greek mercenaries had fought for Darius III than in Alexander's invasion force. This was a state of affairs captured by an earlier Theban proclamation: 'Anyone who wished to join the Great King and Thebes in freeing the Greeks and destroying the tyrant of Greece [Alexander] should come over to them.'[240] Some 50,000 mercenaries might have eventually found their way into Darius' ranks – many were exiles of their city-states care of Philip's earlier campaigns – and if captured the punishment for their 'treachery' was bound to be harsh.[241]

Neither, it seems, was Alexander short on irony in victory at Issus. Following the battle, the Macedones received envoys from the freshly defeated Darius III, the 'antagonist to Alexander's genius', who were said to have spoken some Greek. With them came the offer of a huge ransom for the return of the Great King's captured family, and possibly a concession to divide the Persian Empire at the Halys River (or Euphrates – sources conflict: there may have been as many as three separate offers, spurious or real).[242] However, what appear monochrome correspondences between the kings in the campaign accounts were reborn with much colour in the *Romance* (see chapter 6).[243]

According to Diodorus (alone), Alexander hid the Great King's olive branch and replaced it with a fabricated letter containing far less benign terms so his generals would reject them.[244] If left to his Companions and the veteran Parmenio, the Macedonian war machine would most likely have settled for a truce, for under the terms of Darius III's alleged peace offer, Alexander could have shared Asia with the Great King as his son-in-law.

This particular episode does not appear in the texts of Arrian or Plutarch; if it was genuine, perhaps their 'court' sources felt the deception was best hushed-up. But according to Curtius, Alexander chose an envoy – curiously named Thersippus – to carry his terse rejection back to the Persian king from Alexander's camp at 'Marathus'.[245] We know from Plutarch, who in turn took it from the 'lost' historian Heracleides, that it was a certain Thersippus who had run to Athens after the defeat of Darius I at Marathon some 160 years before.[246] Having just defeated his namesake (Darius III), and now encamped at the like-named Marathus, Alexander allegedly chose a high-ranking man of exactly the same name to deliver his reply to the humbled Persians.[247]

The propaganda bar – for battle, prelude and its aftermath – was raised even higher for the final clash of armies at Gaugamela in northern Mesopotamia, the greatest confrontation of all.[248] With such numerical inferiority in Macedonian numbers, Parmenio again suggested a surprise attack at night, but Alexander would not hear of such cowardly underhandedness being attached to his name. It was a bold response, for the Persian infantry allegedly totalled one million men from across the breadth of the empire, with 40,000 cavalry, 200 scythed chariots and fifteen war elephants from India, according to the sober 'court source' historians, Arrian and Plutarch.[249] Curtius reported that a more restrained 200,000 infantry and 45,000 cavalry faced Alexander's army, while Justin claimed Darius himself told his troops they outnumbered the Macedones by a factor of ten to one.[250]

There was apparently no lack of Persian resolve, as according to Justin they 'were desirous to die rather than be conquered. Seldom has there been so much blood shed in a battle.'[251] Diodorus took up the theme:

> As the main bodies now neared each other and, employing bows and slings and throwing javelins, expended their missiles, they turned to hand-to-hand fighting. The cavalry first joined battle, and as the Macedones

were on the right wing, Darius, who commanded his own left, led his kinsman cavalry against them. These were men chosen for courage and for loyalty, the whole thousand included in one squadron. Knowing that the king was watching their behaviour, they cheerfully faced all of the missiles which were cast in his direction. With them were engaged the Apple Bearers, brave and numerous, and in addition to these Mardi and Cossaeans, who were admired for their strength and daring, as well as all the household troops belonging to the palace and the best fighters among the Indians. They all raised a loud battle cry and, attacking, engaged the enemy valiantly and pressed hard upon the Macedones because of their superior numbers.[252]

Darius' cavalry pressed back their Macedonian counterparts and captured Alexander's baggage train.

Nevertheless, this still wasn't enough. The battle turned into another rout when Alexander's elite cavalry regiment closed in on Darius; the king threw a spear at the Persian Great King from close quarters and impaled his chariot driver, whereupon his ranks took flight. As for the Persian losses, they were as high as 300,000 according to Arrian, while Diodorus reported 90,000 and Curtius 40,000 in total. Yet Arrian was satisfied that just 100 Macedones died that day, even though he tells us 1,000 horses died of wounds or exhaustion, some in pursuit of the Persians. Curtius believed Alexander lost 300 men and Diodorus stated 500, but added that there were very many wounded.[253]

At Gaugamela we have a further 'slippage' in reporting accuracy. Being observant of portentous signs – and having sacrificed to Phobos to bring terror to the enemy – Alexander finally slept deeply into the morning (he had to be woken) before the battle, which is dated to 1 October 331 BC. The king's apparent nonchalance may have been morale-boosting propaganda to counter the reverse effect of an ominous lunar eclipse,[254] for Curtius gave the impression that the phenomenon occurred 'right on the brink' of the final confrontation, whereas Arrian, Plutarch and tableted Babylonian observations placed the eclipse some eleven days earlier. Modern astronomical calculations point to the night of 20 September 331 BC.[255] A source (the most obvious being Cleitarchus, following Callisthenes' original propaganda) was obviously attempting to coincide the phenomenon that swallowed the 'far shining Goddess Selene' (the moon) with the final toppling of the Achaemenid Empire.[256] Alexander's Egyptian diviners managed to spin the eclipse as portentously positive, and his seer, Aristander – who rode out in front of the ranks 'wearing a white mantle and crown of gold' – pointed to a propitious eagle soaring overhead to motivate the Macedone-led army.[257]

The Persians interpreted the eclipse differently. Herodotus claimed the Magi regarded the moon as the symbol of Persia; the Great King's soldiers knew it and fear permeated their ranks. Babylonian astronomical diaries additionally recorded 'deaths and plague occurred'; two days later, a meteorite was seen 'flashing to earth' with two consecutive nights of 'falls of fire', along with an ominous reference to a dog being burned. Finally, there was 'panic in the camp', and by the time the armies faced off, there was apparently little confidence left on the Persian side of the plain.[258] This may well explain the collapse of Darius' ranks, though the eyewitness historians would hardly have mentioned that.

For each of these three battles, the narrative is extremely detailed (different compressions of the sources aside), with the rank-by-rank commanders named, the relative position of regiments given, along with the format of the battle and the identity of the notable dead, especially the Persian nobles and Macedonian Companions (or their sons), with sources broadly in agreement. This is the by-product of first-hand reporting by men who fought or were onlookers like Callisthenes. Where the credibility of these eyewitnesses suffers is in vastly exaggerated numbers and perhaps Alexander's prowess in hand-to-hand combat.

If those who witnessed the battles can be forgiven their hyperbole – after all, humbling the might of the Persian Empire was an achievement not to be belittled – should we forgive the Roman-era sources for swallowing it whole? It is difficult to fathom how, as an experienced field commander, Arrian could truly give credit to Persian troops numbers of one million at Gaugamela where the Macedones, he claimed, lost only 100 men. Arrian did, however, mention that his tally related to Companions alone; he was not about to trivialize by recalling the death of the common soldier. But did he really trust his source that far, or did he let his admiration for Alexander – clearly his career role model – cloud his forensic judgement? Of course the same could be said of many episodes and claims that had to be swallowed by Roman-era writers and their audience who preserved what we read today. Where was their journalistic curiosity and their iconoclastic zeal to peg Alexander's eyewitness historians down a notch or two?

What is the consequence of all this and how should we deal with these secondary sources? Well, what has become clear is that in the centuries between his campaigning in Asia and his refashioned form in Roman literature, Alexander was immersed in the agar of philosophical doctrine and epideictic oratory and preserved in the aspic of Graeco-Roman rhetoric, even if the authors were, at times, unconscious of the damaging effect. And yet there was also a pervading naivety to the Roman-period sources that failed to challenge what sat uncomfortably in the source scrolls. Even when they vocally spotlighted a conflict, they were loath to dissect episodes further or present alternative scenarios. So the contradictory episodes attached to Alexander's life and death – by now pockmarked with compressions scars, chapter gaps and a far-from-precise chronology – provide us at times with a unique example of historical wind over tide, leaving us wallowing in uncertainty in the choppy waters of contradiction and quasi-romance.

But if we strip away the additives that infuse his literary corpse, Alexander would become a blander tale attractive to no one. And if in the name of entertaining flavour we agree to leave them in, the health-conscious historian needs to label them with 'E numbers' for the misdirecting preservatives they are.

Chapter 6

The Greek Alexander Romance: Truth and Legend as One

the uncomfortable fact remains that the *Alexander Romance* provides
us, on occasion, with apparently genuine materials found nowhere else,
while our better-authenticated sources, *per contra*, are all too often
riddled with bias, propaganda, rhetorical special pleading or patent
falsification and suppression of evidence.[1]

Peter Green, *Alexander of Macedon*

It is often said that the Greeks were the first people to deal with the
events of the past in anything like a scientific manner ... but it is clear
that history has been far better preserved by the so-called barbarians ... .
Nevertheless, we must let those who have no regard for the truth write
as they choose, for that is what they seem to delight in.[2]

Josephus, *Against Apion* and *Jewish Antiquities*

Historical, or natural, truth has been perverted into fable by ignorance,
imagination, flattery or stupidity.[3]

Sir William Jones, *On the Gods of Hellas, Italy and India*

In 1896, historian and orientalist Sir Ernest Alfred Thompson Wallis Budge
proposed only one country could be the birthplace of Alexander's story, and that
country was Egypt.[4] Its new city – 'Alexandria-by-Egypt', as the Greeks came to
differentiate it from the conqueror's many eponymous settlements – was to become
a centre for syncretistic literature and the likely birthplace of the *Corpus Hermeticum*,
the *Sibylline Oracles*, *The Wisdom of Solomon*, the *Septuagint* – with its reputed
seventy-plus translators – and the *Alexandrian Canon* too. Much of the detail that
eventually filled the *Suda* most likely had its origins in the vibrant metropolis whose
creative environment recycled apocrypha onto papyrus in the Hellenistic Age. And
we have grounds to believe one of its earliest and most successful productions was
to eventually metamorphose into the *Greek Alexander Romance*.[5]

As antiquities adviser to the British Museum, Budge was exploring the origins of the various Ethiopic *Romance* recensions (versions descended from other or earlier text) when he stumbled on something of a basic truth: the nations humbled by Alexander, he reasoned, would not so quickly record their own downfall.[6] Only one place immediately prospered in the aftermath of the Macedonian campaigns, and that was Egypt. The propitious interpretation of Alexander's seer, Aristander, had provided a founding prophecy: the new city would feed the world.[7]

A healthy bank balance of some 8,000 talents, a legacy of over-zealous and quasi-autonomous tax collection by Alexander's appointed administrator, Cleomenes (executed by Ptolemy), probably had the greater part to play, though its fate was now underpinned by the talisman that was Alexander's body after Ptolemy redirected his funeral bier to Memphis, south of the Nile Delta.[8] Egypt's new heart, Alexandria, established to absorb the old harbour settlement of Rhacotis which had been originally settled to fend off Greek pirate attacks on the Nile Delta, was becoming something of a 'new Heraclion'; it was fostered into maturity by Ptolemy, who, within two decades of taking up his post, would proclaim himself a king.[9] The rest, as the adage goes, is 'history, or in this case 'mythistory'.

At some point in the Hellenistic period, what was arguably 'quasi-romance' – the highly embellished syncretic accounts that followed the example of Cleitarchus, who had already absorbed a number of untruths from his sources – became full-blown scrolls of fables, and eventually there emerged what is known as the *Greek Alexander Romance*.

Alexander's *Romance*, once referred to as a 'pseudo-Callisthenes' production, is in one form or another one of the most influential and widely read books of all time. It has birthed a whole literary genre on Alexander the Great and his campaigns across the Persian Empire. But where and when did it first appear and what did it originally look like? Which earlier accounts did it absorb and what is its relationship to the mainstream Alexander histories?

The Age-Old Birth of Legend

'There are many occasions in the story of Alexander when it is hard to be sure just where history ends and romance begins,' commented a scholar in his treatise on the lost historians.[10] However, much legendary material had already infiltrated biographies of the classical period in Hellas. To the Greeks, this was not particularly problematic: for them, the stories of the past *were* literally *mythoi*, and the segregation between myth, legend and the factual past was a soft border blurred by Homeric epics and Hesiod's *Theogonia* which permitted a coeval interaction between men, heroes and gods. Scholars have even pondered that 'the absence of a clear distinction between factual and fictional discourse' in the influential dialogues of Plato, 'far from being idiosyncratic, may reflect a larger feature of Greek (or ancient) thinking'.[11] What would Herodotus' *Histories* be without the embedded legends? Even the pragmatic Thucydides, who claimed to have sacrificed 'entertainment value' in order to dispense with the mythical elements, nonetheless interlaced his texts with self-constructed speeches which reintroduced just that.

Unravelling romance from sober fact is far more complex than dealing with deliberate frauds which entwined themselves around the most momentous of historical episodes, because once a deliberate deceit is discovered, the truth is more often than not revealed (see chapter 8). When an episode is adorned in the colourful robes of romance, however, we are on less firm ground, for truth and fiction may have been wedded in a ceremony that rendered them lifelong partners. To quote a historian who recently sought to trace the footsteps of Alexander: 'We are accustomed to believing that fiction can tell both truths and untruths ... poets have a (highly visible) stake in the notion, but so do historians and philosophers and scientists.' In which case it is 'misleading to contrast the so-called "historical biographies" with the legendary lives'.[12]

As for the *Greek Alexander Romance*, separating the fact from the fabulous has, indeed, proved no easy task, for material was added through a gradual 'process of accretion'.[13] Attributing the *Romance* in its earliest form to a single author or date remains impossible, but evidence suggests that both the unhistorical and the quasi-historical elements were in circulation in the century following Alexander's death, thanks largely to Alexandrian authors. The oldest text we know of today, recension 'A', is preserved in the eleventh-century Greek manuscript known as *Parisinus 1711*; the text is titled *The Life of Alexander of Macedon*, which most closely resembles a conventional historical work, though any factual narrative is just the early backbone to which other elements were attached.

Recension A, while poorly written, full of gaps and clearly a syncretic account, is nevertheless the best staging point scholars have when attempting to recreate an original (usually referred to as 'α' – alpha) dating back some 700 or 800 years (or more) before it.[14] We cannot discount an archetype that may have been written even earlier still, in the Ptolemaic era. If Alexander's official court historian, Callisthenes, was once credited with its authorship (thus 'pseudo-Callisthenes'), the prevailing belief must have been that it emerged in, or soon after, Alexander's Asian campaigns. Through the centuries that followed, the *Romance* evolved and diversified into a mythopoeic family tree whose branches foliaged with the leaves of many languages, faiths and cultures; more than eighty versions appeared in twenty-four languages.[15]

Romance offshoots were hugely influential in the Middle Ages, and were amongst the earliest texts translated into the vernacular literature that emerged in the Renaissance. Like the oil paintings of the period, they were cultural palimpsests, absorbing textual supplements and stylistic elements from other classical works as well as the iconography of their day.[16] The *Romance*-inspired poems, some obviously based on Curtius' colourful account, became so popular that they displaced the reading of ancient poets in grammar schools.[17] And through the romance genre,

Alexander's story finally infiltrated the East in a more permanent way than his own military conquest managed to.

The Hellenistic Pottage

The Hellenistic world in which the book was born, and which gravitated around the kingdom of Alexander's generals and their dynasties, saw exotic tales arriving from the fabled lands of Kush to the south of Egypt and from the distant East, carried down the Silk Road with the help of the settlements Alexander founded or simply renamed along its route. According to Strabo, who studied in Egyptian Alexandria, the 'city' of Alexandria Eschate ('the furthest') in the Fergana Valley (in Central Asia, spanning eastern Uzbekistan, southern Kyrgyzstan and northern Tajikistan) had brought the Greek settlers and the Graeco–Bactrian Kingdom into contact with the silk traders of the Han dynasty of the Seres (the Chinese) as early as the third century BC.[18]

Ptolemaic Egypt fostered trade eastward as far as India with the help of Arabs and Nabateans, and the resulting contact fertilized Hellenistic literature. Under Ptolemy II Philadelphus in the generation immediately after Alexander, Greek influence extended to Elephantine, an island in the Upper Nile that marked the boundary with Ethiopia, perhaps an early centre of the ivory trade. State-employed elephant hunters would disappear into the African interior for months at a time once the Seleucids cut the Ptolemies off from their supply of Indian war elephants, and would return with animals never before seen which became 'objects of amazement'. There were reports of snakes 100 cubits long (approximately 150ft), large enough to devour bulls and oxen and even bring elephants down.[19] A live 30–cubit-long python was delivered to Ptolemy II Philadelphus, according to Diodorus, and became a court showpiece.[20]

This was, of course, consistent with the fabulous tales that returned from India with Alexander's campaign eyewitnesses. And it was in this extravagant literary environment that the *Romance* metamorphosed into something of a book of fables that became a multicultural depository of traditions that grew up around the king.

What Made Alexander so Ripe for 'Romancing'?

Alexander had uniquely established his 'founding myth' in his own lifetime, along with a 'court mythology' which linked his genealogy to gods and heroes of the Homeric Age.[21]

Callisthenes, along with the historian Anaxarchus and the prince's tutor, Aristotle, had edited the latter's copy of Homer's *Iliad* (the aforementioned *'Recension of the Casket'*). Reliving the epic *Iliad*, in which the 'temporal boundary between the ages of myth and history is in fact a fuzzier, less distinct line than appears at first glance', was a role that suited Alexander, who took a firmly 'euhemeristic' stance (accepting legend as fact with historical substance) when tracking down his heroes. He believed he was following in the footsteps of Heracles and Dionysus, the conqueror of the Orient, and with a sense of the honour and duty which his Greek Homeric education and this homage would have bestowed.

In Plutarch's *Parallel Lives*, Alexander was juxtaposed with Julius Caesar, whose life and deeds were conspicuously *not* ripe for a romance. Both Caesar and Alexander had understood the need to lay their achievements down in writing when fresh, pliable and untarnished by partiality or the reasoned balance of hindsight. Alexander had Callisthenes and Onesicritus on the spot to do the job, whereas Caesar himself penned his own Gallic War diaries, 'incomparable models for military dispatches ... but histories they are not'.[22]

Amongst the marvels that proliferated Callisthenes' account, we hear of long-dry springs starting to flow again and the Pamphylian Sea parting to allow the Macedones to navigate a narrow rocky coastal track; presumably this report was compiled with Alexander's blessing and was later swept up by the poet Menander (*ca.* 342–290 BC), an associate of Theophrastus and Demetrius of Phalerum, his once pupil. Arrian explained the Pamphylia phenomenon in less divine terms, writing that the coastal road could only be negotiated when a north wind blew, otherwise the route would be submerged.[23] Callisthenes also reported a sacred spring, dead for 160 years, coming to life when Alexander arrived.[24]

But aquatic feats were far from original, and miraculous water-crossings were a symbol of legitimacy when attached to campaigning kings. Xenophon's *Anabasis* has the Euphrates yielding to Cyrus the Younger, who waded across its span, while Cyrus the Great enjoyed a notable revenge when diverting the River Gyndes for the impiety of swallowing his warhorse. More pertinent to Alexander's cause, we have Xerxes' triumphant (and factual) bridge across the Hellespont, which briefly joined Europe and Asia in a hubristic defiance of prevailing doctrine. Inevitably, the *Romance* gave Alexander power over dangerous water when he crossed the River Stranga when it froze every night, enabling him to meet, and then make good an escape from, Darius at Persepolis.[25]

Without the marvels developed by the fabulously inclined biographers on campaign with Alexander, a sober military treatise like Caesar's war commentaries and Ptolemy's apparently dry account would not have provided sufficient flammable tinder. 'Legends and lies about Alexander were given currency by authors who had actually seen him or accompanied his expedition: there had been no Thucydides to strangle such monsters at birth,' commented one scholar.[26] This was true. The birth of the legend required hagiographies (sanctified biographies) and panegyrics to blow on the fire, plus a death in distant Babylon, not an assassination like Caesar's on the steps of the Theatre of Pompey in a no-nonsense and fractious Rome. Strabo sensed it when he wrote of Alexander historians: 'These toy with facts, both because of the glory of Alexander and because his expedition reached the ends of Asia, far away from us.'[27]

Had Caesar wanted an enduring romance, it seems he ought to have outsourced to an author in Egypt, where a part of his story (with Cleopatra, with whom he had a son) – ultimately linking him to the line of Macedonian kings – took place. There, perhaps, a 'Vulgate' prototype of Rome's dictator would have emerged and prevailed, in much the same way that Cleitarchus' Alexander eclipsed the primary sources it subsumed. This was something of a literary Oedipus complex, when the parental work is rejected by the collusion of later sibling texts that were drawn to the story.

As it remains impossible to pinpoint the author of the *Greek Alexander Romance*, we cannot pinpoint a single reason or influence that gave the book its birth, and there were likely a number of 'pre-texts' behind the 'first edition'. But if the kaleidoscope of colourful proto-matter coalesced into focus for a moment, we would likely see Callisthenes' *Deeds of Alexander* with its apotheotic spice, the encomium on education replete with the quasi-utopian land of Musicanus and Brahmin sophistry (both in India) from the campaign historian and Cynic philosopher Onesicritus, with scrolls of the court usher Chares and Polycleitus of Larissa, and even Ctesias, physician to Artaxerxes II, in the melting-pot beside them. Much of their writing and tales had already been synthesized by Cleitarchus into an early colourful account that laid the foundations of the quasi-historical texts that added in drama and exaggeration.

Toss in the corpus of letters to and from Alexander which Plutarch believed was genuine for extra biographical seasoning,[28] and then simmer with the Indian wonders of the general and naval officer, Nearchus, before baking it in the ovens of the philosophical schools of the Cynics and the Stoics. We might further season it with the treatise *On Fortune* of the exiled peripatetic philosopher, Demetrius of Phalerum, for that linked together God, man and the mercurial nature of divine intervention.

Neither should we forget the campaign poets who, in their desire to eulogize Alexander for profit or favour, elevated his deeds a step further. The group housed the fawning camp followers whose traits Diogenes the Cynic likened to the 'worst biters' in nature, 'of wild beasts, the sycophant, and of tame animals, the flatterer'.[29] Plutarch wrote: 'So great is the power of flattery, and nowhere greater, it seems, than among the greatest people.'[30] The court poets (referred to by some scholars as 'poeasters'), including Agis of Argos, Choerilus of Iasus and Cleon of Sicily, were noteworthy amongst the sycophants who proffered Homeric comparisons to Alexander and encouraged Achaemenid-style body prostration (*proskynesis*) in front of the Macedonian king.[31] And there were more besides, those whom Curtius referred to as 'the other dregs of their various cities'.[32]

Alexander's relationship with these writers reflected the paradox within him: he recognized the utility of their artful prose for his pro-Greek press corps, and yet despised his own reliance upon them to produce a truly timeless history. If there is any truth behind the late-sourced anecdotes preserving the king's scorn of Choerilus, who was apparently paid a gold coin for each quality verse he wrote, Alexander held a dim view of their efforts. Choerilus' epic 'excremental poetry' had inevitably likened Alexander to Achilles, whose reported response to the poet was less than enthusiastic: 'By the gods, I would rather be Homer's Thersites, than your Achilles.' Thersites was the dull-witted, bow-legged fool whose 'unbridled tongue' had branded the hero a coward in the *Iliad*; he was eventually slain by Achilles for mocking his grief over Penthesilea, the dead Amazon queen.[33] The *Romance* developed this embellishment of the story in which Agamemnon took the place of the warrior.[34] In Alexander's case, however, what perhaps none of the king's entourage trailing around the Persian Empire fully appreciated was that he *did* see himself as both Agamemnon and Achilles, the king that led a flotilla to war and its most eminent warrior who fought in the foremost of the ranks.

If all these diverse elements gave us the cast and the plot, the unique cultural diversity of Alexandria, where Alexander's body eventually came to reside, tuned up a script which claimed the corpse's final resting place was apparently prompted by an oracle of the Babylonian Bel-Marduk: the god demanded his interment in Memphis, though the local priests thought otherwise.[35] So the most influential *Romance* element, more of a common denominator, *was* Egypt; the similar genre *Demotic Chronicle*, *The Dream of Nectanebo* and *Romance of Sesonchosis* (Alexander is supposed to have declared himself the 'new Sesonchosis'), and many more of the themes that were regurgitated in the *Romance*, originated here. The *Nectanebo Cycle* and the *Alexandrian Lists* were both Egyptian condiments that were ground in, and the result, a rich new Hellenistic recipe for the Macedonian king, was now not about who Alexander had been, but what Alexander meant to a world in flux.

In Hellenistic Alexandria, where Eratosthenes was to place the Prime Meridian when carving up the Earth in longitudinal lines, 'magic' was the watchword; the compressed air water pumps and musical instruments of Ctesibius (*floruit ca*. 270 BC), and later the mechanical devices of Heron (*ca*. 10–70 BC) that mysteriously opened temple doors and turned visitors into cult believers, anticipating the 'golden age of automata' by almost two millennia.[36] The *Book of Thoth* (a god paralleled to Greek Hermes) inspired *the Corpus Hermeticum*, the book of knowledge in which wisdom was fermented with alchemy, prophesy and prayer-spells. The new arts in thaumaturgy (magic), along with the influential local Jewish predilection for narrating tales, provided a suitably atmospheric set.

Josephus, the Jewish scholar, claimed that Alexander had visited Jerusalem, linking him to the Persian Empire-destroying prophecy of the *Book of Daniel*. Ptolemy I, when taking Judea in his Syrian campaigns, ferried Jewish captives (many of them willing) back to Egypt to bolster its creative population, and the Jewish Quarter in the eastern section of Alexandria, governed by an ethnarch, became almost as large as the Greek.[37] Scholars estimate that Jewish immigrants (or longstanding natives) may have comprised 10 per cent of the population of Egypt (which was perhaps five million in total), and possibly 25 per cent of the population of Alexandria, which was estimated by Diodorus to be 300,000 in his day, excluding slaves.[38]

'For a time, Alexander is lost to the practical, political and military world of the West, having been subsumed into an oriental idyll.'[39] And as a British historian of the period neatly put it: 'History commenced among the modern nations of Europe, as it had commenced among the Greeks ... in romance.'

The Oracle of Siwa

Examples of the crossover of detail from the mainstream accounts to the *Romance* are not difficult to find, but in which direction the virus of embellishment travelled is not always clear. Nevertheless, some of these paradigms and exempla stand as worthy cases in point.

We may start with the 'rebirth' of Alexander's divinity. The much-flouted lineage of the Argead (or Temenid) royal clan of Macedon was established generations before at the Pellan court with claims of it having descended from the very best pedigree of Olympian gods, the heroes born of gods from mortal mothers and the warrior class of Troy.[40] It was an illustrious start that gave Alexander cause and direction when invading the Persian Empire. His bravery was next established in the great battles at the Granicus River and Issus, his ingenuity in taking fortified cities and his tenacity at the siege of Tyre. His charisma and mercy were both confirmed with his adoption by his royal Carian 'mother', Ada, and by his treatment of Darius' captured Persian women at Damascus, while his warlord status was beyond challenge, with PR reports of incredibly small casualty numbers. Alexander's star was ascending.

But it was Egypt that sealed his apotheosis. The priests and populace welcomed him as a liberator after an era of Persian oppression. After choosing the site of his eponymous new city, Alexander had the yearning to visit the age-old desert oasis of Siwa, where an oracle linked to Zeus Ammon was to be found. The journey was unsurprising: it was Pindar, a poet Alexander demonstrably admired, who introduced Zeus-Ammon, the hybrid god, to Greece in his *Pythian Ode* 4. Pindar dedicated a cult statue in 462 BC to the sanctuary on the Cadmea (the citadel at Thebes), having seen the god being worshipped on his visit to Cyrene in Libya.[41]

It was here at Siwa that Alexander questioned the priests about both his mortal father, Philip, and a more divine parentage. We will never know if Alexander fully dismantled the stigma of parricide after Philip's death at Aegae at the wedding of his sister, where he was assassinated, but an alleged oracular reply at Siwa, which confirmed that all Philip's killers had been punished, sounds suspiciously like a contrived vote on his own innocence, though it was peculiarly exonerating to the still-at-large Persian Great King, Darius III, because Alexander claimed Persian gold was behind Philip's assassination.[42]

While the Athenians remained unlikely to have granted Alexander divine honours for facing the Persian threat, the king received the divine response he surely sought at the Ammonium here at the desert oracle of Siwa. The very public divine 'private reply', which suggested he was the son of Zeus-Ammon, was most likely crafted with Callisthenes' help, though if the priests of the sanctuary expected that Alexander would next proclaim himself pharaoh, then his immortality could hardly be denied. The outcome was an avowed confirmation of his immortal blood which readied him for the march ahead into the Asian interior.[43]

Alexander's yearning (*pothos*, an emotional 'longing' much discussed in studies of Alexander's character) to journey through the desert and consult the deity, a god now with ties with both the East and West, was less unique than Callisthenes' account might have suggested. The oracle was well known to the Greeks through their intermediaries in Cyrene. Plutarch explained that the Athenian statesman–general, Cimon, who waged incessant war on Persia a century before, had also sent messengers to the Siwan oracle to obtain answers from Zeus-Ammon, as had the Spartan commander Lysander at the end of the fifth century BC. Each was following in the windblown footsteps of Cambyses II (son of Cyrus the Great, ruled 529–522 BC), who reportedly lost a 50,000-strong army in a sandstorm (their remains were possibly discovered in 2012), and those of Heracles and Perseus before him.[44]

Guiding Alexander's entourage were, claimed Ptolemy, two talking serpents, while Aristobulus mentioned ravens and Strabo stated crows.[45] No matter; cementing the foundations of Alexander's own divine myth was the priest's allegorical slip of the tongue, which rendered '*O, Paidion*' ('O, my son') as '*O, pai Dios*' ('O, son of God', thus Zeus, or here Zeus-Ammon).

Court propaganda already held that Alexander's legendary forefather, Danaus, who settled in Argos, was in myth the son of Belus, the legendary king of Egypt, so Alexander was stepping into yet another ancestral homeland. We have no evidence of formalities to proclaim him pharaoh at this time, except claims in the *Romance*, and in any case, the more enduring epitaph was to be the founding of the city of Alexandria; Ptolemy would see to that.[46] But to quote one study of the Macedonian 'myth': 'Alexander stands at the crossroads of a Greek legend born out of the Libyan pilgrimage and the ancient Egyptian tradition of the pharaoh's divine conception.'[47]

On his PR team was his mother, Olympias, who, it seems, claimed a part in Alexander's divinity. We read in the accounts of Arrian, Plutarch and Justin that

Callisthenes accused her of spreading 'lies' about Alexander's semi-divine status when he was compiling his book on campaign.[48] After all, Heracles, Dionysus, Theseus and the consummate warrior Achilles – all Alexander's role models – were each born of gods through mortal mothers, so why not Alexander himself? He appears to have returned the favour in the hope for a 'consecration to immortality' for his mother.[49] Olympias' rejection of the mere 'mortal' Philip would have been unsurprising; many suspected she may well have been complicit in the death of her already-estranged husband, who had remarried Cleopatra (a noblewoman half her age) before he died and was producing royal 'pure-blood' heirs with her.[50]

The above reports of Siwan drama and divinities come from the 'mainstream' accounts, so the onlookers of old could be forgiven for thinking the *Romance* was a product of Callisthenes' hand. The result was that the *Romance* became proliferated with allusions to the Siwa episode, which in turn became linked to the last Egyptian Pharaoh, Nectanebo II, and supernatural claims on Alexander's paternity. Nectanebo had historically fled Egypt following the Persian conquest of 343 BC, a decade before Alexander arrived in Asia.

The *Romance* plays on this fact: foreseeing the coming invasion, Nectanebo fled to the Macedonian court, where he fell in love with Olympias. In an apparition, Olympias sees the god Ammon, who confirms he has impregnated her with a 'son who will avenge you'. Alexander, suspicious of his birth – as was his father, Philip – kills Nectanebo, who reveals all to him as he dies.[51] The allusion to what Alexander heard at Siwa in the mainstream accounts is striking, as well as possible court rumours of Olympias' infidelities and even Alexander's role in his mortal father's death. And if Nectanebo had fled, his true son, Alexander, had returned to avenge Persian occupation; this element of the *Romance* was a convenient nationalism that helped Ptolemaic Egypt's propaganda machine.

In the decades after Alexander's death, Ptolemy either invented or introduced the cult of another hybrid god, Serapis, to Egypt, where some forty-two temples to the god appeared.[52] In the *Romance*, Serapis predicts the prosperity of Alexandria (the seer Anaxarchus performs this role in the mainstream accounts), while the oracle of Ammon tells Alexander where to found the city. Alexander's posthumous coinage did carry his leonine image adorned with ram's horns, recalling Zeus-Ammon. Plutarch's biography of Alexander recorded the tradition that Philip had been warned by the Delphic oracle to hold Zeus-Ammon in special reverence, and he further claimed that Philip had lost an eye as punishment for spying upon Olympias' Orphic rituals.[53]

Whether romance or mainstream, truth or fable, or a convenient fusion of the two for the entertainment of the audience, it didn't matter. Alexander became semi-divine. This lamination of the genres *was* 'history' in this era, and it would take a very skilled surgeon today to clinically extract one from the other.

The Corpus of Court Correspondence

The careers of Plutarch, Callisthenes, Demosthenes and Aristotle, each influential to Alexander's story, have also given birth to a spurious epistolary corpus in their name. Plutarch seems to have had unique access to a folio of written exchanges to and from Alexander. So numerous were they that he commented: 'In fact it is astonishing that he [Alexander] could find time to write so many letters to his friends.'[54] He may have been quoting from other missives mentioned by older historians rather than the letters themselves, but the faith he put in them points to the latter, and no other historian seems to have had access to them. But how authentic they were remains open to speculation.

Confirmation that a written collection (not necessarily genuine) once existed, possibly collated as a book, came with the discovery of papyri in Hamburg, Florence and at Oxyrhynchus in Egypt, though suspiciously there is no trace of them before Cicero's *De Officiis* (*On Duties* or *Obligations*), which refers to a folio titled 'the Letters of Philip to Alexander, of Antipater to Cassander, and of Antigonus to Philip the Younger'. As the names suggest, there once existed a library of dispatches between Philip and Alexander, and between Antipater, Cassander and Antigonus the One-Eyed. Other references to court correspondence appear in even later sources (such as the *Suda*) and the writings of the satirist Lucian, who loved scandalous gossip, regardless of its veracity.[55]

Arrian also referred to exchanges between Alexander, Olympias and the regent Antipater, so it is likely a common source was behind the tradition.[56] Plutarch's folio was even more specific; those letters written to Alexander's mother Olympias were 'private', and only Alexander's closest friend, Hephaestion, was permitted to read them. Nevertheless, the detail we garner from them appears, in hindsight, to be fictitious. Separating deliberate imposters from these well-meaning improvisations (we might recall the predilection of ancient historians to 'make the speech fit the occasion') is not always possible.

Unsurprisingly, the authenticity of similar correspondence by the philosophers Plato, Speusippus (Plato's nephew, *ca*. 408–338 BC), Archytas (428–347 BC) and the influential rhetorician Isocrates – whose pleas for an invasion of Persia arguably motivated Philip II (and then Alexander) to launch his Asian campaign – is still debated.[57] But the composition of such letters, in emulation of the famous doers and shakers and the greatest minds of the past, was also part of the Greek classroom preparatory syllabus (termed *progymnasmata*).

Some thirty-plus letters concerning Alexander made their way into the *Greek Alexander Romance*, unique in ancient fiction in the breadth of what has been termed its epistolary 'pseudo-documentarism'.[58] Plutarch may have been unwittingly incorporating letters that had no historical foundation into his own biographies, perhaps fooled by the freehand-form of their intimacy when no stylistic baseline for comparison existed. They may have even originated, convincingly, with a court scandalmonger such as Chares, the king's chamberlain. So the argument about the 'truth' revolves around the degree of trust we place in the instincts of our 'secondary' sources and their immunity to seduction.

The Taming of Bucephalus

We ought to remember that Plutarch, by his own admission, was not writing 'history'; he was penning biographies slanted to reveal lessons on morality and behaviour codes by selecting events that revealed the essence of each man. He opened his life of Alexander with this explanation: 'Accordingly, just as painters get the likenesses in their portraits from the face and the expression of the eyes, wherein the character shows itself, but make very little account of the other parts of the body, so I must be permitted to devote myself rather to the signs of the soul in men.'[59]

A perfect character-portraying episode is Alexander's breaking of Bucephalus ('Ox-Head), the unruly Thessalian warhorse named, it was variously claimed, after its ox-head-shaped branding, a white similar-shaped colouration on its otherwise-black head or for the wide shape of the head itself.[60] Watching with rising irritation the unsuccessful efforts of Philip's horse tamers, Alexander exclaimed: 'What a horse they are losing, because, for lack of skill and courage, they cannot manage him!' Philip enquired whether his son believed he could do better, and the arrogant youth confirmed he could. Philip asked what the penalty of his rashness would be if he failed, and Alexander replied that he would pay for the horse himself.

The rendering of this story fitted the overall encomiastic portrayal of the young prince: he was being paralleled with legendary Bellerophon mounting a wild Pegasus that could only be tamed by him, and here before an incredulous Macedonian court and an elated horse-dealer, Philonicus, who was asking for a vast sum for the unruly stallion. The *Iliad* had made it clear that heroes needed to be epitheted 'breakers' or 'tamers' of horses as part of the rite of passage for a true warrior of old. Indeed, Alexander's claimed ancestor, Achilles, had been given a horse that 'excelled all others' from his father, Peleus, who had in turn received them from Poseidon, and he hitched the horse to his chariot at Troy.[61]

But on this day, Alexander had noted that Bucephalus was afraid of his own shadow, and so he calmed the horse with whispers, mounted him at a run and fully mastered the stallion he would eventually ride to India. Philip was impressed, though Plutarch captured the danger-laden foresight with which he praised him: 'My son, you need to seek out a kingdom equal to yourself; Macedon doesn't have the room.' This, of course, was a precursor to Alexander falling out with his father, entering self-imposed exile and only returning to Macedon shortly before Philip's assassination.[62]

Yet the Bucephalus episode, which 'abounds in circumstantial detail and dramatic immediacy', was preserved by Plutarch alone.[63] Did Onesicritus' encomiastic portrayal, *On the Education of Alexander* (or Marsyas' book of the same name), provide the model for the story, or had Plutarch independently, in his 'quiet naivety', found this detail in that corpus of correspondence he uniquely referred to on some thirty occasions?[64] Surely neither source was reliable. Or was the Bucephalus episode an allusion to the metaphor in Plato's dialogue, *Phaedra*, which likened the untamed horse to an unruly youth who must be broken by an education, which was itself steeped in Homeric values? In which case it is fully understandable why Bucephalus 'was born to share Alexander's fate' in the *Romance*, and even attend his death.[65] However, Bucephalus was killed in battle with the Indian raja, Porus, although accounts of the horse's ending conflict.

In the *Romance* (Ptolemy predictably features again), the 'taming' of the horse termed a 'man-eater' is an allegorical 'uncaging' of the beast, who immediately acknowledged its master; and it was Philip who had Bucephalus locked up. The oracle of Delphi predicted that whoever rode the horse though the city of Pella would rule the world, and so Alexander did just that. Philip hailed this God-given sign of his son's future with cries of joy and gave his son permission to enter the stallion in the horse chariot race at the Olympic Games. Philip had historically featured his own horses (and chariots) at Olympia, gaining notable factual victories, one of which is said to have heralded Alexander's birth in 356 BC. Indeed, Alexander's mother, Olympias, had been so named after the Olympic success (she had been variously called Myrtale, Stratonice and Polyxena in her youth).[66]

Back to the *Romance*. Arriving at Olympia, Alexander met another 'royal' athlete named Nicolaus, who boastfully proclaimed himself to be the 'king of Acarnania'. Alexander announced he would compete with him in the chariot race, whereupon Nicolaus, incredulous at Alexander's youth, mocked his reply by suggesting he was but a spectator or possibly a wrestler, or perhaps a boxer or pancratiast (an athlete of the pancratium, a discipline involving both wrestling and boxing). The two parted as enemies (apparently, Philip had killed Nicolaus' father), and the day of the race approached when Nicolaus planned to destroy the Macedonian youth. All entrants were either royal or born into nobility, and there follows a spirited description of the deadly contest. Nicolaus is thrown from his chariot and killed and Alexander finishes victorious, whereupon a prophet of Zeus predicts future successful conquests.[67]

The 'mainstream' parallel here is also exclusive to Plutarch, whose framing of his 'super-youth' seems almost close enough to be touching the *Romance*. Plutarch continues his characterization:

For it was neither every kind of fame nor fame from every source that he [Alexander] courted, as Philip did, who plumed himself like a sophist on the power of his oratory, and took care to have the victories of his chariots at Olympia engraved upon his coins; no, when those about him [Alexander] inquired whether he would be willing to contend in the foot-race at the Olympic games, since he was swift of foot, 'Yes,' said he, 'if I could have kings as my contestants.' And in general, too, Alexander appears to have been averse to the whole race of athletes ... he took no interest in offering prizes either for boxing or for the pancratium.[68]

In both accounts, Alexander scorns participating in sports which do not pit him against other royals. It is obvious that this episode was derived from a common source used by both Plutarch and the *Romance* compilers. The common denominator, once again, is that suspicious corpus of correspondence which likely provided the additional unique detail about Bucephalus. In which case we must challenge the other detail Plutarch alone supplies, including what happened next.

The Banquet of Exile

Immediately after victory at Olympia, Alexander returns to Macedon, where all is not well in the *Romance*. His mother has been rejected and Philip has taken a new bride, Cleopatra, the sister of Antalus.[69] A furious Alexander rebukes his father with: 'And when I give my mother, Olympias, in marriage to another king, I shall invite you to the wedding.'

Antalus proposes a toast at the wedding banquet to the king and his 'virtuous sister', from 'whom you shall breed legitimate children'. This was a deliberate slight on Alexander's half-Epirote bloodline, as well as fuelling rumours of Olympias' infidelity (which condoned Philip's rejection of her). When Alexander heard this, he:

hurled his goblet at Antalus, struck him on the temple and killed him. When Philip saw this, he leapt up, drew his sword and rushed at Alexander in a rage, but he tripped on the edge of his couch and fell. Alexander laughed and said to Philip, 'you are eager to conquer all Asia and destroy Europe to its foundations, yet you are unable to take a simple step.'[70]

All this detail, narrated almost identically (though Cleopatra was *niece* of the baron *Attalus*, for example), can be found in the Vulgate-style accounts of Curtius and Justin.[71] It begs the question whether Cleitarchus, who templated the Vulgate genre (likely in the late 270s or 260s BC), incorporated colourful elements from an already-circulating forerunner of the full-blown *Romance*, or whether the *Romance* compilers sucked the sensationalized life from Cleitarchus' syncretic work. The most fulsome mainstream version account is unsurprisingly provided by Plutarch:

The most open quarrel was brought on by Attalus at the marriage of Cleopatra, a maiden whom Philip was taking to wife, having fallen in love with the girl when he was past the age for it. Attalus, now, was the girl's uncle, and being in his cups, he called upon the Macedones to ask of the gods that from Philip and Cleopatra there might be born a legitimate successor to the kingdom. At this Alexander was exasperated, and with the words, 'But what of me, you wretch? Do you take me for a bastard?' threw a cup at him. Then Philip rose up against him with drawn sword, but, fortunately for both, his anger and his wine made him trip and fall. Then Alexander, mocking over him, said: 'Look now, men! Here is one who was preparing to cross from Europe into Asia; and he is upset in trying to cross from couch to couch.' After this drunken broil Alexander took Olympias and established her in Epirus, while he himself tarried in Illyria.

Scholars cannot help but conclude that this incident is redolent once more of a Homeric comparison: the famous quarrel at Troy between Achilles and the king he was loath to show loyalty to, Agamemnon, over a captive woman. This was the point at which Achilles threatened to leave the war.[72] The goddess Athena soothed Achilles' rage with the promise that the king would soon pay for his insolence with his life.[73]

In the *Romance*, Alexander made up with his father in the wake of the goblet-throwing banquet after the baron had allegedly insulted him, and he also reconciled Philip with Olympias. According to Plutarch, however, there was another major rift about to be revealed, the Pixodarus affair (see chapter 8), before father and son were indeed together again at the ancient capital of Aegae when Philip was stabbed to death.

The Naked Philosophers

Perhaps the most colourful dialogue of the whole Asian campaign involved Alexander and the philosophers known as gymnosophists ('naked sages' in Greek) in India. Onesicritus became something of a 'spokesman' for Indian affairs, and much of what we know derives from fragments of his work; in Strabo's Roman-era *Geography*, for example. In Strabo's opinion, 'all who have written about India have proved themselves, for the most part, fabricators', and those who 'begin to speak the truth' do so 'with faltering voice'. He also labelled Onesicritus the 'arch-pilot' of 'things that are incredible'.[74]

Plutarch provides a rather incredulous narrative of Alexander bullying these poor-but-venerated gymnosophists, and we might be tempted to thinking Plutarch took this from Onesicritus. But it appears he did not, because Onesicritus provides (as Strabo narrates it) a rather different dynamic between Alexander and these wise ascetics whose wisdom Alexander sought. Not wishing to burden them with travel or commend their presence, he sent Onesicritus to them, whereupon he enjoyed an enlightening and threat-free cultural and philosophical exchange, even though the straight-talking Calanus mocked the idea of clothing, possessions and power, and asked Onesicritus if he would like to take off his clothes and lay naked to learn some wisdoms.[75] Calanus was rebuked by the oldest and wisest sage, Dandamis, for being arrogant to their guest when Calanus himself was censuring the arrogance of the Macedonian conquerors.

Philosophical questions were exchanged, with curiosity displayed by all, but there is no hint of intimidation on either side in this version, a situation rendered more credible by the fact that Calanus agreed to join Alexander's expedition a short time after.[76] The whole exchange is one of the more believable narratives from Onesicritus, though steeped in pro-Cynic-school doctrine.

This was, of course, perfect stock for the soup of the *Romance* compilers who faithfully portrayed this goodwill, adding a gentle warning letter from the naked philosophers to Alexander:

> If you come to us to fight, it will do you no good. There is nothing that you can take from us. To obtain from us what we do have, you must not fight, but ask humbly, and ask it not of us but of Providence above. If you wish to know who we are – we are naked and we have devoted ourselves to the pursuit of wisdom. This we have done, not by our own decision but through the agency of Providence above. Your business is war, ours is wisdom.[77]

In the *Romance*, Alexander approaches the naked ascetics peaceably and asks them a number of philosophical questions which are clearly extracted from and inspired by Onesicritus' original account:

> Who are the greater in number, the living or the dead?
> Reply: the dead, because they no longer exist and can't be counted.
> Which is stronger, life of death?
> Reply: life, for the sun is brighter when rising and weaker when setting).
> Which is greater, earth or sea?
> Reply: earth, as the sea is surrounded by earth.
> Which is the wickedest of all creatures?
> Reply: man; look at yourself and the beasts you have with you.
> What is kingship?
> Reply: unjust power, insolence, a golden burden.
> Which came first, day or night?

Reply: night, which is dark like a mother's womb, then birth encounters day.
Which is better, right or left?
Reply: right, where the sun rises.

Dandamis then explains their sole possessions were earth, fruit, trees, daylight, sun, moon, stars and water. Alexander enquires what more he can give them. 'Immortality,' they reply in unison. The king explains that is beyond his power, being a mortal, and then goes on to justify why he wages war: it is the natural order of things that man takes and profits from others. He offers Dandamis gold, bread, wine and olive oil, so the sage would remember him. The wise old man laughs at the gesture of useless gifts and burns them on a pyre before Alexander's eyes; but not to appear too proud, he saves the olive oil. They depart amicably.

The episode is redolent not just of Strabo's retelling of Onesicritus' 'mainstream' version of the meeting, but of the exchange between Alexander and Onesicritus' philosophical master, Diogenes the Cynic, at Corinth many years before. Those details too are the lone preserve of Plutarch. Here, the almost-naked Greek philosopher, who lived in a wine urn in the city, mocked possessions, the law and institutions of men as part of his brand of cynicism (some would say 'nihilism'), though he declared himself as a 'citizen of the world'. Alexander visited the philosopher living in his famed barrel in Corinth in 334 BC, shortly after he had destroyed Thebes, and enquired if there was anything that Diogenes desired. In the famous anecdote captured by Plutarch (and others, but not the mainstream biographers), Diogenes asked Alexander to step aside as he was blocking his sun.[78] Tradition claims that this prompted the Macedonian king to confide to his companions that 'if he were not Alexander he would like to be Diogenes'.

The unlikely dialogue, probably the later output of Diogenes' Cynic school, ought to be shadowed in historical reality.[79] Superficially impressive in its hauteur as his reply was, any biography of Diogenes would not be complete without mentioning his public behaviour, which included defecation and masturbation, leading Plato to brand him (and Diogenes to brand himself, for that matter) a dog (*kynos*, the root of the word 'cynic'); it was behaviour supposed to emphasize his objection to 'regressive' civilization.[80]

A former slave captured by pirates, and one charged with debasing (or defacing) the local currency at his native city of Sinope (a charge carrying a severe penalty),[81] Diogenes had found his clay barrel (or urn) in which he slept in the Temple of Cybele. There were actually a number of traditions floating around involving Alexander and the 'dog' he so admired. Diogenes was supposedly once brought before Alexander's father, Philip II, after the Athenian defeat at Chaeronea. When questioned on his identity, Diogenes replied he was 'a spy, to spy upon your insatiability', following which his amused captor set him free. A further story, which proliferated later works, claimed Alexander found the philosopher rummaging through a pile of bones. When he asked why, Diogenes replied: 'I am looking for the bones of your father, but cannot distinguish them from those of a slave.' While no doubt allegorical too, it remains highly unlikely that the 'mad Socrates', as Plato called him, would have been worthy of Alexander's continued esteem, and if he uttered those words he may well have been killed on the spot.[82] So, here again, more hostile dialogues appeared in later doxographic material,[83] which brings us back to Plutarch's account of the gymnosophists in his Alexander 'mainstream' biography.

Plutarch painted a far more hostile and less likely encounter between Alexander and the Indian wise men. A clue to the source of this version lies in Plutarch revealing his source for the recent war with King Porus: 'Of his campaign ... he himself has given an account *in his letters*.'[84] Here is Plutarch's account:

> He captured ten of the Gymnosophists who had done most to get Sabbas [an Indian satrap) to revolt, and had made the most trouble for the Macedones. These philosophers were reputed to be clever and concise in answering questions, and Alexander therefore put difficult questions to them, declaring that he would put to death him who first made an incorrect answer, and then the rest, in an order determined in like manner; and he commanded one of them, the oldest, to be the judge in the contest. The first one, accordingly, being asked which, in his opinion, were more numerous, the living or the dead, said that the living were, since the dead no longer existed. The second, being asked whether the earth or the sea produced larger animals, said the earth did, since the sea was but a part of the earth. The third, being asked what animal was the most cunning, said: 'That which up to this time man has not discovered.' The fourth, when asked why he had induced Sabbas to revolt, replied: 'Because I wished him either to live nobly or to die nobly.' The fifth, being asked which, in his opinion, was older, day or night, replied: 'Day, by one day'; and he added, upon the king expressing amazement, that hard questions must have hard answers. Passing on, then, to the sixth, Alexander asked how a man could be most loved; 'If,' said the philosopher, 'he is most powerful, and yet does not inspire fear.' Of the three remaining, he who was asked how one might become a god instead of man, replied: 'By doing something which a man cannot do'; the one who was asked which was the stronger, life or death, answered: 'Life, since it supports so many ills.' And the last, asked how long it were well for a man to live, answered: 'Until he does not regard death as better than life.' So, then, turning to the judge, Alexander asked him for his opinion. The judge declared that they had answered one worse than another. 'Well, then,' said Alexander,

'you shall die first for giving such a verdict.' 'That cannot be, O King,' said the judge, 'unless you falsely said that you would put to death first him who answered worst.'[85]

These sages appear to have stirred up revolt and Cleitarchus accused them of the same, with 80,000 Indians slaughtered in this campaign by the Macedones.[86] But the episode is confused, because Onesicritus was specifically sent to meet a peaceful class of gymnosophists, although Plutarch states:

> Calanus very harshly and insolently bade him strip off his tunic and listen naked to what he had to say, otherwise he would not converse with him, not even if he came from Zeus; but he says that Dandamis was gentler, and that after hearing fully about Socrates, Pythagoras, and Diogenes, he remarked that the men appeared to him to have been of good natural parts but to have passed their lives in too much awe of the laws. Others, however, say that the only words uttered by Dandamis were these: "Why did Alexander make such a long journey hither?" Calanus, nevertheless, was persuaded by Taxiles to pay a visit to Alexander.

The hostility in Alexander's initial encounter is palpable; he was prepared to execute the naked philosopher who answers the questions least well. In a paradigm shift, he then showers them with gifts. But there is no suggestion in Onesicritus' formative account that Alexander visited those who offered the question-and-answer dialogue or the philosophical debate. And neither are there references to this sect stirring up rebellion; that is attributed to the Brahmins (though definitions of the sects of sages overlap in later sources). Certainly Calanus, who joined Alexander's entourage, cannot have been among the rebellious sect.

The episodes – the massacre and butchering of the Brahmins, Onesicritus meeting with the more-peaceful sect and an interpolated dialogue with Alexander which may have stemmed from a letter he sent them (genuine or not) – have become conflated for dramatic effect and intertwined forever, a typical outcome of syncretized histories which later blended sources together. So which source is closest to the truth: Strabo's long fragment of intellectual tolerance from Onesicritus' lost book, the wholly benevolent *Romance* version or Plutarch's 'mainstream' drama where Alexander becomes a threatening executioner?

We could, in fact, finger dozens more episodes in the *Romance* which appear as credible as the more-peculiar mainstream events, and conversely many 'odd' episodes in our 'trusted' sources which remind us of *Romance* chapters. Our point, illustrated from various angles, is that the dividing line between fiction and fact is subtle – if not about what actually took place, then certainly about what was actually said – and it was often muddied over by the debris of Hellenistic-era invention.

It is worth reiterating the conclusion of a pre-eminent Alexander scholar when crafting his own biography of the Macedonian king: 'the uncomfortable fact remains that the *Alexander Romance* provides us, on occasion, with apparently genuine materials found nowhere else, while our better-authenticated sources, per contra, are all too often riddled with bias, propaganda, rhetorical special pleading or patent falsification and suppression of evidence. Truth and romance make unlikely bedfellows, and yet in Alexander's story, they never slept apart.'

Chapter 7

Birth and Death: Nature's Cracked Mirror

Dying, I should willingly come back to life again for a little while,
Onesicritus, that I might learn how men read these things then. If they
praise them and admire them now, you need not be surprised; each
imagines he will gain our good will by great deceit.[1]

Lucian, *How to Write History*

Which death is preferable to every other? The Unexpected.[2]

Julius Caesar

Sadder than death itself is the manner of it.[3]

Martial, *Epitaph to Canace*

Most colourfully narrated in Classical Greece and the Hellenistic-era
biographies were the deaths of kings and tyrants and the politicians who
faced them. Their epitaphs, being posthumous commentaries by nature
and often linked to rumours of political intrigue and assassination, were all the
more easily manipulated for moralizing effect. If 'lives' were open to manipulation,
so was death itself, when the closing pages of traditional biographies were crafted
by historians and antiquarians to edify their readers.

Death has mutated into a moralistic digression too many times for us to
question its penchant for doing so. Sometimes deliberate, at other times accidental,
the metamorphosis is only magnified with time and fame. Alexander's own death
in Babylon is a notorious case in point,[4] but the spillage engulfed other giants of
the period. We take a look at the most notorious and colourful demises to help us
appreciate how 'history' metamorphosed into legend at the point of least resistance.
Many legendary figures suffered posthumous reconstructions, and from the
Homeric past through to Athens' Golden Age, colourful examples are not difficult
to find, with 'seekers of wisdom' at the forefront.

Empedocles the 'purifier', a philosopher from Sicily who put his ideas into verse
and became known as the 'wind-forbidder', is said to have jumped into the fire of

Mount Etna to ensure a legendary end. Once charged for stealing the discourses of the mathematic philosopher Pythagoras (died *ca*. 495 BC), who had clearly influenced his ideas, Empedocles was trying to arrange a heavenly disappearance after a banquet but was apparently betrayed by one of his distinctive brass-soled slippers he misplaced on the climb up. This was not the finite conclusion it suggests, for he, like Pythagoras, believed in reincarnation.[5]

With no volcano at hand, the *Romance* captured Alexander's attempt at a similar vanishing act by using the River Euphrates when he was fevered and approaching death in Babylon. Where Empedocles gained a cult, Alexander gained the ill-timed intervention of Rhoxane, his pregnant wife (see Grant, *Last Will and Testament*, 2021, chapter 8).[6] The *Romance* compilers were not so original in their imagery and most elements can be found in earlier tales, while much was regurgitated later in the biographies of the Roman emperors, for example, or more pertinently in the controversial *Scriptores Historiae Augustae*, multi-sourced accounts of the late emperors (AD 117–284) in Rome's decline and fall whose authenticity is questionable. As one critic comments: 'Theirs was an age of forgeries, interpolations, false attributions, tendentious interpretations.'[7]

These two vivid and influential Greek characters were already associated with magic by Aristotle's day. Empedocles, the founder of the Italian school of medicine, raised the dead and was said to be able to manipulate the weather. He was possibly the first philosopher to propose the existence of four divine primordial cosmic elements – earth, wind, fire and water – and his passing provides us with an early example of the 'multiple death tradition'.[8] His forerunner Pythagoras was allegedly in two places at once, sported a golden thigh and reportedly once turned a wild bear to vegetarianism, or so the legends go.

After the death of the 'father of medicine', Hippocrates, honey was found growing on his grave; unsurprisingly, it was said to have medicinal powers.[9] Hippocrates, already epitheted 'the great' according to Aristotle, had several deaths too – at the ages of 80, 90, 104 and 109. The latter numbers were apparently shared with his friend, Democritus of Abdera, so meriting a place in a book titled *The Long Lived*, the compendium of the aged (spuriously) credited to the Roman satirist Lucian.[10] Pythagoras' own numerical preoccupation concluded with the statement 'all things are numbers' and he is oddly said to have lived to 104 as well, sharing the illustrious age with Hieronymus, the Cardian historian related to Alexander's court secretary, Eumenes.[11] That may not be coincidence: as pointed out by one eminent historian, 104 – thus the 105th year – is a mystical numerical combination and the sum of the first fourteen integers.[12]

Competing stories in circulation would have us believe that Pythagoras was slain twice: he was either foiled by a bean field he refused to enter, leading to his capture and burning at the stake, or he withered away from a self-imposed starvation when philosophically pondering a world that had rejected him.[13] Yet 'any chronology constructed for his life' has been described as 'a fabric of the loosest possible weave'.[14]

The biographies of early Greek philosophers *were* apparently highly exploitable, with much material attaining legendary status, a problem facing Greek biographer Diogenes Laertius when he was writing his *Lives of Eminent Philosophers* in the Roman period. Early doxographical material was particularly susceptible to becoming 'pseudepigrapha' (falsely attributed works) because so little was known about their lives and writings, especially those who lived before Socrates ('pre-Socratics') who were already wrapped in the climbing ivy of myth. The Neo-Pythagorean scholars, for example, tended to attribute their own written treatises back to Pythagoras himself because the originators of doctrine more often than not did not write down their ideas. Prising apart the originals from the latter-day treatises demands every weapon of source that forensics can muster in stripping away the accretion. Much of this additional filler had stuck to accounts of their deaths.

Chrysippus (*ca*. 279–204 BC), the Stoic sophist who taught 'divine logic' and supposedly authored some 705 books, gave wine to his donkey and died of laughter as he watched its ungainly attempts to eat figs.[15] A different version comes from Hermippus, who reported that Chrysippus expired from the effects of unmixed wine at a sacrificial feast.[16] Zeno of Citium, the founder of Stoicism, was an austere character who nevertheless enjoyed drinking at symposia too. His experiences prompted his sober advice: 'Better to trip with the feet than with the tongue.' Diogenes Laertius reported the irony: 'When he was going out of his school, he tripped, and broke one of his toes, and striking the ground with his hand, he repeated the line out of the lost play *Niobe*, "I come: why call me so?" … he immediately strangled himself, and thus he died.'[17] Lucian, on the other hand, suggested that after his famous stumble (when entering the city assembly) he starved himself to death at home alone.[18]

Closer to home we have the death of Diogenes the Cynic, who met with Alexander with the already-mentioned surprising results.[19] Diogenes had an assortment of conflicting demises, allegedly on the very day Alexander died in Babylon, which spawned a whole literary genre. One version claimed he was seized with colic after eating a raw octopus, and another believed he was actually feeding the octopus to a group of dogs, one of which fatally bit the sinew of his foot. A variation proposed his last wish was to be thrown naked to the hungry pack. A further tradition claimed he died by voluntarily holding his breath for two days; his friends found him wrapped in his cloak, whereafter they quarrelled over the honours to bury him, despite his wish to be thrown in a ditch for nature to consume him.[20] He was reportedly aged 81, or otherwise 90.

Portentous births and mysterious deaths – life's beginning and end – were fully exploited for their instructional contents and for the symmetry philosophically likened to 'nature's mirror'; after all, 'the art of living well and the art of dying well are one'.[21] Do dying men speak, even those who have been poisoned? Well, apparently Socrates did after a shock dose of hemlock. His last recorded words were: 'Crito, I owe a cock to Asclepius; will you remember to pay the debt?'[22] It was the perfect utterance from a man at peace with himself, and possibly an allusion to life's debt to the healing god Asclepius.[23] The words were immortalized by Plato, a notable yet unlikely absentee from Socrates' final hour. Plutarch added that after Socrates had downed the fatal draught, 'he engaged in philosophy and invited his companions to do the same'.[24]

The great Athenian orator Demosthenes, so vocally opposed to Philip and Alexander, was, as we might imagine, credited with rather immortal lines for his epitaph when Archias, the assassin in the employ of the Macedonian regent, Antipater, had Demosthenes surrounded in the supposedly sacred Temple of Poseidon on the island of Calauria (Poros). Contemplating the pledges of fair treatment Antipater was delivering via his 'exile hunter', Demosthenes replied with, 'Archias, I was never convinced by your acting, and I am no more convinced by your promises', whereupon he sucked poison from his reed pen and rounded off with a speech from Sophocles' *Antigone* as the effects took hold.[25] But tradition was not content with the one recital of last moments, and Plutarch dedicated the next chapter to recording its many pluralities. The wording on the bronze statue supposedly erected by the Athenians to his memory is even questioned, and it was rumoured that Demosthenes composed the eulogy himself.[26]

Alexander's teacher, Aristotle, died soon after. In one version, he ended his life by taking a deadly dose of aconite at the age of 70 at Chalcis (Euboea) in 322 BC. A host of other sources simply claimed he died of a stomach ailment after placing 'a skin of warm oil on his stomach' to alleviate the pain.[27] Phocion, a former pupil of Plato who had since become a city military leader forty-five times (and who once turned down a 100-talent gift from Alexander), was eventually made to pay for his pro-Macedon political stance, like Aristotle; he was forced to hand over twelve drachmas to his executioner for more hemlock to be pulped ('bruised') for use.[28]

Aristophanes had described the drug's more benign symptoms in his comedy *Frogs*,[29] and Plato's *Phaedo*, which described Socrates' final hours in 399 BC, has led to the question of whether hemlock was used at all, for it was never specifically named.[30] Aristotle's protégé and successor at the Lyceum-based school, Theophrastus, helps us out with his suggestion that a cocktail of hemlock, poppy and herbs would render death more peaceful.[31] Although Plato gave Socrates some dignity in his account of his death, hemlock was unpredictable and the results not guaranteed.

No one mentioned the real effects of these life-ending poisons, in particular hemlock, the 'sin of Athens': choking, nausea, bile and convulsions. None wished to imagine Phocion, Socrates or Aristotle writhing on the floor in their own vomit. The real deaths and the actual last words of those poisoned by the city-states are lost from biographies; they were most likely full of panic-stricken, god-fearing and blood-spitting utterances that served no rhetorical purpose.

But we need to recall that all the surviving accounts of Alexander are from the Roman period. Were these secondary and further-removed historians living in an age which was any more judicious when reporting famous deaths? The answer is, emphatically, 'no'.

Re-rendering Death in Rome

Rome was no less creative with its reporting of famous exits from the stage. On the Ides of March (the 15th) 44 BC, Julius Caesar, dictator in perpetuity, managed to utter (in Greek no less) – '*Kai su, teknon*', words popularly translated as 'you too, child?', upon seeing Brutus amongst those who delivered the twenty-three stab wounds that came in thick and fast. Inevitably, portents foretold Caesar's end, just as they had Alexander's, for livers with no lobes were 'tokens of mighty upheavals' to the presiding diviners.[32] Suetonius gave us this tradition, though Plutarch was more dubious about any such lines, and these words may have carried a more accusatory and threatening tone towards Caesar's young protégé, and that is what we might expect to have come from the dictator's mouth.

It is not Caesar, however, but Cicero whose departure from life has been described as 'the most widely-evidenced of "famous deaths" in the ancient world', in which 'obfuscation, anomalies and contradictions exist, suggesting blatant manipulation of his story'.[33] It was reported by a corpus of heavyweight historians: Plutarch, Appian, Cassius Dio, Seneca, Asinius Pollio (a successful defence lawyer in accusations of poisoning) and Livy. Cicero had pointed out that all who wish death upon a man, whether they clutch the knife or not, are as guilty as one another; this was a dangerous premise to make considering Brutus, who was rumoured to be Caesar's son (from the dictator's affair with Servilia), had called for Cicero to restore the republic when plunging his dagger into Caesar.[34] In a later letter to Scribonius, another of the conspirators, Cicero began with: 'How I could wish that you had invited me to that most glorious banquet on the Ides of March.'[35]

Cicero labelled his subsequent attacks on Mark Antony in the Senate as '*Philippics*' in emulation and admiration of Demosthenes' earlier verbal assaults on Alexander's father. An unsurprising victim of the proscriptions of Antony and Octavian, Cicero is credited with six deaths, just ahead of the five credited to Alexander's own 'political conscience', Callisthenes.[36] Cicero was beheaded and had his hands chopped off, for they were the damning instruments that penned his scathing polemics against the wayward triumvir. They were nailed to the rostra, either one or both.[37] His last words are recorded as, 'There is nothing proper about what you are doing soldier but do try to kill me properly.' In yet another version, Fulvia, Antony's wife, pulled out his tongue and repeatedly stabbed it with a hairpin.[38] The popularity for oratorical declamation against Cicero's killers seems to have added new wood to the allegorical fire, and his death soon frayed into many competing strands.[39]

The Julio–Claudians emperors (Augustus to Nero) were not averse to poisons to achieve their ends. Claudius had reportedly dined on fatally seasoned mushrooms, a last meal the emperor-in-waiting Nero termed 'the food of the gods',[40] and tradition gives us a death that implicated three assassins in two different locations.[41] Nero (who murdered Claudius' son, Britannicus) had his fierce personal guard, the Phalanx of Alexander, to call upon, so any rumour of the hand of his mother, Agrippina, in Claudius' poisoning would have been dealt with harshly.

Later in his emperorship, having murdered his mother, possibly two wives as well as two literary intellectuals (Seneca and Lucan), along with countless other prominent citizens, Nero finally went mad and planned to poison the entire Senate.[42] Deserted by his bodyguard, the golden box containing his poisoner's concoctions was nowhere to be found. After a dramatic earthquake and a lightning storm accompanied his hurried flight from Rome, he had a grave dug, exclaiming: 'What an artist dies in me!' As horsemen could be heard fast approaching, Nero next recalled the *Iliad*, saying 'The thunder of galloping horses is beating against my ears', and when his pursuers finally closed in, he is said to have stabbed himself in the throat, and yet managed to utter: 'Too late! But ah, what loyalty!' This was in thanks to the centurion attending him.[43] His death fell on 9 June, or possibly on the 11th of the month (in AD 68), the latter portentously shared with the death of Alexander (11 June 323 BC).

But the artist in Nero never died; his death inspired ongoing rumours that captured the imaginations of his biographers, and the artistry began in earnest. More in keeping with Nero's reputation, an alternative version of his final hours has him smashing two invaluable Homeric crystal goblets to deny his successors their use upon hearing of the defecting legions.[44] Nero had intended to throw himself into the Tiber, and history really ought to have granted the self-proclaimed 'great tragic actor' a more extended soliloquy. Alas that would not do, as it was well known Agrippina had forbidden philosophy from his classes, just as Seneca had hidden all rhetorical works from his avowed pyromaniac pupil.

Allegorical Picture Framing

Death in itself does not sell scrolls unless the literary taxidermist has stuffed the corpse with a didactical potpourri, for the final pages of a parchment had to justify the price. And whether to eulogize or to condemn from the classical era of Greece to Rome, readerships demanded that death suitably picture-framed the life. So underlying all great exits were fitting allegorical stories that alluded to deeper meanings, sometimes subtle and often blatant.

The bean field was a foil to ridicule Pythagoras' strict vegetarian doctrine, a stance summed up by Ovid with 'what a heinous crime is committed when guts disappear inside a fellow-creature's guts',[45] as Pythagoras had warned against kidney pulses or broad beans after he noted their organ-like shape.[46] Socrates' nobility in the face of hemlock magnified Athens' sin against philosophy, though somewhat more satirical was Lucian's summation: 'Yes; and very serviceable his dissertations on Justice were to him, were they not, when he was handed over to the Eleven, and thrown into prison, and drank the hemlock? Poor man, he had not even time to sacrifice the cock he owed to Asclepius.'[47]

Because the Greek playwright Aeschylus had been branded the 'father' of the tragedians, a sense of the calamitous was required to frame his final day. Both Pliny and Aelian recorded that he perished when an eagle dropped a tortoise from a height, mistaking his bald head for a stone, a suitably sorrowful conclusion for the man who had fought bravely at Salamis and Marathon, and who humbly termed his plays 'nothing but crumbs from the rich-laden banquet of Homer'.[48]

Then we have Pyrrhus, who fought at the Battle of Ipsus in 301 BC at the tender age of 18 beside his new patron and brother-in-law, Demetrius the Besieger. He, like Alexander, was to become one of history's greatest commanders. He resembled Alexander 'in appearance, swiftness and vigorous movement' as well as in his descent from the heroes Achilles and Heracles. Plutarch wrote: 'The other kings, they said, represented Alexander with their purple robes, their body-guards, the inclination of their necks, and their louder tones in conversation; but Pyrrhus, and Pyrrhus alone, in arms and action.'[49] He went on to gain a reputation for unsustainable 'Cadmean' (today we use 'Pyrrhic') victories in Italy, and suffered four distinctly reported and different deaths.[50]

Having himself skirted with death by poison at the hand of his own cupbearer (who in fact betrayed the plot of his co-king, Neoptolemus, the son of Cleopatra, Alexander's sister), in return for all his hubris and unrelenting hostility, Pyrrhus was finally felled by a roof tile that defied the stoutness of his iconic goat-horned helmet; it was thrown down by an old woman defending her son when Pyrrhus was trapped in the narrow streets of Argos after his famous elephants had fallen and blocked the escape route out of the city's main gate.[51] Pyrrhus finally collapsed and fell from his horse by the tomb of Licymnius, an Argive warrior from Homer's texts.[52] Pyrrhus' own instruments of war had finally sealed his fate, and the grave on which he finally crumpled sang of his own sin against the city.

The Successor Wars in which Pyrrhus and Demetrius the Besieger immortalized themselves were brutal, and the penalty for speaking out inappropriately was just as harsh. The hostile Athenian orator, Hyperides, who is said to have proposed honours for Alexander's poisoner, Iollas (son of the regent, Antipater), reputedly lost his tongue on Antipater's orders; if anecdotal, it surely served as a warning to outspoken politicians and was one Demosthenes should have heeded.[53] He too was a target of Antipater in his continued stranglehold on Greece; Demosthenes' clever and pithy riposte to Antipater's assassin, Archias, recalled the opening of a prosecutor's speech worthy of the formidable speech writer.[54]

Anaxarchus, the philosopher who campaigned with Alexander and accumulated great wealth, supposedly suffered a similar fate in the post-Alexander years when Nicocreon, the Cypriot tyrant, ordered him crushed by mortar and pestle after his tongue had been non-surgically removed. This was for an indiscretion in which he had earlier suggested to Alexander following the siege of Tyre that he should serve up Nicocreon's head on a platter.[55] Diogenes Laertius recorded Anaxarchus' bold but unlikely retort: he bit off his own tongue and spat it at his tormentor. This too was a less than original epitaph, for it was one he shared with the pre-Socratic philosopher, Zeno of Elea.[56] Known in life as 'a happy one', the rendering of Anaxarchus' execution was, no doubt, a contrived lesson on careless talk and perhaps on the false tenets of 'eudaimonic' philosophy (a positive psychology which focused on personal wellbeing).[57]

Equally tragic, though from a different angle, was the death of Archimedes the geometer. He was reportedly stabbed by a Roman soldier after resisting arrest with 'do not disturb my circles', a perfect geometric epitaph. The attacking general, Marcellus, had ordered that he be taken alive, so impressed were the Romans with his defensive techniques at the siege of Syracuse that ended in 212 BC. His tomb was nevertheless left unattended and overgrown until Cicero rediscovered it in 75 BC.[58]

Finally, Cicero's humble courage sat beside a warning on political meddling, while Nero's poor theatrics recalled his destructive self-deluded life on both the political and thespian stages. As for his final exclamations, it has been pointed out that they were 'self-consciously bathetic' (framed with an unintentional anti-climax) and doused in sarcasm to highlight how far he had tumbled. 'What an artist dies in me', alluding to the loss of artistic talent, was, according to Cassius Dio, often quoted and in general use.

Birthing Legendary Men

Birth was just as exploitable as death, both in its timing and genealogy. But dating a life's beginning was not always determined by science or sources, and was often guided by the author's *floruit*, literally his 'flowering'. Without an attested birthday, standard procedure was to deduct fifty years from the production of a first masterpiece to arrive at the author's birth, and then to add on the attested lifespan to arrive at his date of death. Thus we arrive at the tenuously approximated arrivals, alongside the spurious expirations, of Thucydides, Aristophanes and Aeschylus.[59]

Suspiciously, Alexander's favourite tragedian, Euripides, was allegedly born on Salamis on the very day of the epic sea battle against Xerxes, on 23 September 480

BC, in the Euripus Strait (hence his patronymic). Though the coincidence may have been propitious, the inscription known as the *Parian Chronicle* records that Euripides arrived some years before. Socrates' birth was said to have been on day six of the month of Thargelion (supposedly an 'unlucky' month for barbarians), and the Persians were defeated at Marathon on day six of Boedromion, the late-summer month that Alexander reportedly faced Darius III at the Granicus River (which according to Duris, was to the month exactly 1,000 years since Troy fell to the Greeks), and the day (the sixth) the Macedonian king himself was said to have been born.[60]

We could, in fact, cite a host of 'coincidental' birthdays of the notable ancients that were linked to portentous signs, as well as propitious days with links to gods and heroes. Few, if any, harbour more than a modicum of truth, including the detail of Alexander's. Here is Plutarch's account:[61]

> As for the lineage of Alexander, on his father's side he was a descendant of Heracles through Caranus, and on his mother's side a descendant of Aeacus through Neoptolemus; this is accepted without any question. And we are told that Philip ... fell in love with her [Olympias] and betrothed himself to her at once... . Well, then, the night before that on which the marriage was consummated, the bride dreamed that there was a peal of thunder and that a thunderbolt fell upon her womb, and that thereby much fire was kindled, which broke into flames that travelled all about, and then was extinguished. At a later time, too, after the marriage, Philip dreamed that he was putting a seal upon his wife's womb; and the device of the seal, as he thought, was the figure of a lion. The other seers, now, were led by the vision to suspect that Philip needed to put a closer watch upon his marriage relations; but Aristander of Telmessus said that the woman was pregnant, since no seal was put upon what was empty, and pregnant of a son whose nature would be bold and lion-like. Moreover, a serpent was once seen lying stretched out by the side of Olympias as she slept, and we are told that this, more than anything else, dulled the ardour of Philip's attentions to his wife, so that he no longer came often to sleep by her side, either because he feared that some spells and enchantments might be practised upon him by her, or because he shrank from her embraces in the conviction that she was the partner of a superior being.
>
> Moreover, Olympias, as Eratosthenes says, when she sent Alexander forth upon his great expedition, told him, and him alone, the secret of his begetting, and bade him have purposes worthy of his birth... . Alexander was born early in the month Hecatombaeon ... on the sixth day of the month ... and on this day the temple of Ephesian Artemis was burnt. It was apropos of this that Hegesias the Magnesian made an utterance frigid

enough to have extinguished that great conflagration. He said, namely, it was no wonder that the temple of Artemis was burned down, since the goddess was busy bringing Alexander into the world.

But all the Magi who were then at Ephesus, looking upon the temple's disaster as a sign of further disaster, ran about beating their faces and crying aloud that woe and great calamity for Asia had that day been born. To Philip, however, who had just taken Potidaea, there came three messages at the same time: the first that Parmenio had conquered the Illyrians in a great battle, the second that his racehorse had won a victory at the Olympic games, while a third announced the birth of Alexander. These things delighted him, of course, and the seers raised his hopes still higher by declaring that the son whose birth coincided with three victories would be always victorious.

We know Plutarch was superstitious and he had to be observant of portents in his role as a priest of Apollo at Delphi. But here his art brings together a coalescence of mythical tendrils that birthed Alexander. Philip's propitious victories are altogether more credible and documented, but they certainly did not all come to pass on the very day his son was born.

Diodorus accepted Alexander's descendancy from Heracles on his father's side and from the Aeacids (thus the line of Achilles) on his mother's.[62] As popularized in the *Andromache* of Euripides, who spent his final years in Macedon, Alexander was also a descendant through the Aeacids of Hector's widow, the Trojan princess Andromache, who became Neoptolemus' concubine and gave birth to Molossus, the founder of the eponymous Epirote tribe. The ancestry thus linked Alexander to both the attackers and defenders of Troy.[63]

Arrian went further and associated Alexander with the hero Perseus, the son of Zeus and the father of both the Persian race and the Greek Dorians through Heracles.[64] Plutarch's opening lines additionally managed to trace Alexander's descent (through the Heraclid line of his father) back to the 'founding father', Caranus, who originally hailed from Argos and invaded Macedon 'with a great multitude of Greeks'.[65] This enabled Alexander to trace his lineage to the Argive Heraclids and back to Danaus and the Danaans, who shipped to Troy, the heritage Isocrates had already assigned to Philip. Other Heraclids included the kings of Sparta and the Aleuadae dynasty of Larissa in Thessaly (Heracles' supposed birthplace).[66]

In the wake of Greek victory following the Persian invasions, King Alexander I of Macedon (*ca.* 498–454 BC) had convinced the adjudicating officials of his Peloponnesian Argive roots so that he might compete in the Olympic Games. His entry resulted in victory in the furlong foot race, and soon he was epitheted 'friend of the Greeks'. From then on, the Argeads of Macedon would more legitima.⌄ıy claim Greek descent.[67]

From his own reading of Herodotus, Alexander would have been aware that King Midas, adopted by the childless Gordias and the founder of the Phrygian dynasty, was said to have emerged from a region of Macedon. Midas' legendary wealth came from mining iron ore until he was expelled by the semi-mythical Caranus, 'the founding father of Macedon' who in legend reigned *ca.* 808–778 BC. The Gardens of Midas at the foot of Mount Bermion still carried his name in Alexander's day.[68]

Of course this court propaganda was an exquisite springboard for Alexander to launch himself upon both Greece and Persia as a legitimate inheritor of power. Whether he truly believed in his descent from gods and heroes is debatable when compared to his innate pragmatism, but that same pragmatism saw him exploit his illustrious crossbreeding (he would have argued 'pure-breeding'). Backed by this useful polytheism, these heritages implied a new telegony in which their combined traits and bloodlines would converge and meet in a new demigod: Alexander himself. Perhaps the keenest blade in his Homeric arsenal was Odysseus' declaration: 'Let there be one ruler and one king!'[69]

So Alexander himself, as well as the established court PR, was responsible for his legend even in his own time. That element of the superhuman inevitably required a birth to match it, and that is what we are given in even the most sober of the surviving accounts. The same could be said of his polymorphic death in Babylon for exactly the same reasons.

Ultimately, birth and death in ancient Greece did not belong to the deceased but to those recording it, whether accompanied by a Ciceronic 'do kill me properly', a Socratic 'a cock to Asclepius' or, in Alexander's case according to the Vulgate genre, an empire left 'to the strongest'; those words, if ever said, would have been an act of 'consummate irresponsibility' (see Grant, *Last Will and Testament*, 2021).[70] But these graced the scrolls because, in Plutarch's opinion, 'certain historians felt obliged to embellish the occasion, and thus invent a tragic and moving finale to a great action'.[71]

If we can't trust the ancient historians to accurately report death, can we expect more from them in 'life'? Alexander's birth and death, then, were the legendary, romanticized and contradictory bookends upholding a life of equal manipulation between them.

Chapter 8

Illegitimate Sons, Rogue Wives, Forgotten Bastards and Courtesans

In addition to all this, he [Alexander] added concubines to his retinue in the manner of Darius, in number not less than the days of the year and outstanding in beauty as selected from all the women of Asia. Each night these paraded around the couch of the king so that he might select the one with whom he would lie that night.[1]

Diodorus, *Library of History*

But Alexander, as it would seem, considering the mastery of himself a more-kingly thing than the conquest of his enemies, neither laid hands upon these women, nor did he know any other before marriage, except Barsine ... he passed them by as though they were lifeless images for display.[2]

Plutarch, *Life of Alexander*

Yes, a son of Rhoxane or Barsine really is a fitting ruler for the Macedonian people! Even to utter his name will be offensive for Europe, since he will be mostly captive. Is that what defeating the Persians will have meant for us – being slaves to their descendants?[3]

Ptolemy speaking at Babylon; Curtius, *The History of Alexander*

Nothing exemplified Alexander's rise and fall – his early virtues and his later vices – more clearly than his treatment of the women he encountered or captured on campaign. His concurrent metaphysical affair with the Goddess Tyche, who governed fate (the equivalent of Roman Fortuna), and then her ~~ abandonment of her favourite son, adds garnish and epitomizes the ~~h to stylizing his reign. Inevitably, later admiring historians (Arrian ~~or example) attempted to cool the narrative on his sexual liaisons, ~~sensational writers, or those following Cleitarchus' lead (including ~~us and Justin), heightened the temperature of his amorous excesses, whether or not they truly believed it, possibly to sell their scrolls. As a result, the reporting of these 'affairs of state' is as contradictory and polarized as any other unfathomable campaign episode.

Royal wives and offspring – as opposed to exotic lovers and mistresses, with their greater entertainment value – suffered a more invidious fate: a whitewash from the pages. The militarized campaign historians and those at their courts were, it seems, reticent to feature these more legitimate women too prominently, along with their sons and daughters. This is unsurprising, as the Successor Wars saw many of them executed by those who penned the formative accounts or by their allies with aligned goals. Broadcasting royal blood or the sanctioned presence of these executed royals would have underpinned a legitimacy that made the crime the more heinous, so we are left scrambling for identifications that are ambiguous, manipulated and often bypassed altogether.

It is worth taking a look at some notable examples in each category: kings' wives, court concubines, campaign courtesans and the children whose very existence have been questioned. The soft-at-the-edges transmission of this biographical detail extends to the Argead royal line in both the generations before and after Alexander.

Grandmothers, Stepmothers and Dangerous Offspring

The rise and expansion of Macedon, from the reigns of Philip's parents to the warring generation after Alexander, is unparalleled in the prominence of women who featured in court politics, assassinations, war and internecine intrigue. We can start with Alexander's grandmother, Eurydice, who like all queens of the period was enveloped in scandal. Alexander's grandfather, Amyntas III (an equally intriguing and elusive figure), had two wives (that we know of), one named Gygaea by whom he had three sons, and the other Eurydice ('Eurydice' appears to be an Argead moniker suggesting the 'first lady' of the court) who produced three sons and a daughter. The three sons reigned consecutively as Kings Alexander II, Perdiccas III and finally Philip II, the father of Alexander III, the Great. This gave rise to an overly competitive pipeline of kings.

Eurydice's career proved remarkable, heralding the rise and influence of Macedonian court women. However, she is variously accused of plotting to murder her spouse, King Amyntas III, and then marrying her daughter's husband, while also credited with saving the nation through strategic alliances while educating her sons in their bid for survival.[4]

This was a period of great instability, when Macedon's very existence was under threat from a now-predominant city-state of Thebes, Thessaly, the Illyrians, Greek city-states which controlled nearby coastal towns, the Thracians to the east and a pretender to the Macedonian throne, Pausanias (of obscure royal connections).[5] As Justin tells it:

Subsequently he [Amyntas] had formidable contests with the Illyrians and Olynthians. He would have been cut off by a plot of his wife Eurydice, who, having engaged to marry her son-in-law [Ptolemy of Alorus], had undertaken to kill her husband, and to put the government into the hands of her paramour, had not her daughter betrayed the intrigue and atrocious intentions of her mother. Having escaped so many dangers, he [Amyntas] died at an advanced age, leaving the throne to Alexander [II], the eldest of his sons.[6]

According to Justin, Ptolemy of Alorus (from another branch of the Argead house) had Philip's older brother, Alexander II, assassinated and installed himself as regent with the complicit Queen Eurydice by his side, until her next oldest son, Perdiccas III, had Ptolemy murdered in 365 BC:

Not long afterwards Alexander [II] fell by a plot of his mother Eurydice, whom Amyntas, when she was convicted of a conspiracy against him, had spared for the sake of their children, little imagining that she would one day be the destroyer of them. Perdiccas [III], also, the brother of Alexander, was taken off by similar treachery. Horrible, indeed, was it, that children should have been deprived of life by a mother, to gratify her lust, whom a regard for those very children had saved from the punishment of her crimes. The murder of Perdiccas seemed the more atrocious from the circumstance that not even the prayers of his little son could procure him pity from his mother.[7]

Justin's overblown moralizing is typical of the Vulgate style and Roman-period declamations on unfettered power aimed at extinct royalty. He was also prone to confusing identities, but Eurydice suffers a wholesale character assassination (as most queens did at the hands of Latin writers).

According to Diodorus, however, Perdiccas III was killed with 4,000 men in battle against the Illyrians, with no involvement of Eurydice and no treachery mentioned.[8] This was the point at which his younger brother, Philip II, had to take control. In 359 BC, at the young age of 23, Philip was 'forced by the people to take on the kingship', as his nephew, Amyntas IV (the son of his deceased brother, Perdiccas III), was still a child. Philip, who had already administered a region of Macedon in Perdiccas' reign, may have initially acted as Amyntas' regent, as his reign is variously stated from twenty-two to twenty-five years.[9] But he soon declared himself king in his own right.

At this point the throne was still threatened on all fronts and by five potential usurpers, including his three half-brothers (the sons of his stepmother, Gygaea) and the pretender Pausanias, who was backed by the Thracian king; the fifth challenge came from an Athenian-backed claimant who had dispatched an invasion army.[10] Paeonians were pillaging in the north, while Illyrian forces occupied Upper Macedon with a history of installing puppet kings. Both Philip's father and his brother had been expelled by the Illyrians (Philip was once their hostage around the age of 12), and the still-independent upper cantons could form an alliance against him at any time, spurred on by foreign interference or funded by the Persian purse. Philip's response – a mix of brilliant campaigning, bribery, marriage diplomacy and double-dealing to buy time – was remarkable, spurring Theopompus of Chios to pick up his pen at this point and write a fifty-eight-book 'Philippic' history which Diodorus presumably used as a source.[11]

Once established, Philip went on to honour his mother with family statues in the Philippeion at Olympias (which is still partially standing today), and a statue of Eurydice was erected at Aegae (modern Vergina). The lavish tomb nearby in the so-called 'Cluster of the Queens' – known as the 'Tomb of Eurydice', whose ruins can still be seen – may well be hers (see Grant, 2019). Furthermore, in an essay titled 'On the Education of Children', which is credited to Plutarch and described as the first ever commentary on 'the parental duty of tutoring at home', there appears the dedication by Eurydice to the Muses who had aided her in learning to read and write to further educate her sons.[12]

If Philip's mother had married a usurper and conspired to kill her husband and son (Philip's father and older brother), it is remarkably unlikely that Philip would have honoured her in any way, even if her life was spared. What is clear is that the beleaguered Eurydice had to seek the intervention of the Athenian general, Iphicrates, whom Amyntas had adopted (it is said she placed her surviving sons in Iphicrates' arms and on his knee), and she was potentially also behind the summons of Theban tactical genius Pelopidas (who took Philip as hostage back to Thebes) in desperate times, but as for her domestic court scheming and accusations of planned regicide and actual filicide, these appear later scandal found only in Justin's Roman-period précis.[13]

The sum total of our knowledge on Eurydice's activity in the years leading up to Philip's kingship totals two paragraphs from Diodorus and two more from Justin, two further references in Plutarch's biography of Pelopidas, plus a few lines of a speech by the pro-Macedon Athenian orator, Aeschines. Regurgitated later fragments complete a very incoherent sketch of Eurydice's life. But the dots are loosely scattered and the picture is extremely low definition, and the same may be said of the women who followed the reign of Philip II.

Philip's Political Harem

It was this challenging environment – the previous three Macedonian kings had died in just ten years – which forced Philip to resort to 'consorting for survival' when his borders were equally pressed. He immediately commenced what would become a 'longstanding practice of fighting war through marriage'.[14] Philip was renowned for his polygamy, and was interested in young men as well. Yet we have just a single fragment in the form of a long and dense paragraph from a non-contemporary writer – now found in a Roman-period text – which actually lists his seven (known) wives. In the case of several of these queens, that brief detail – their name and the implied order in which he married them – is the sum total we know. Moreover, it appears clear to modern historians that the implied marriage order is wrong (see Grant, 2019, chapter 15).[15]

Some commentators have argued that not all the women were legitimate wives; rather, some were mistresses or consorts, though this seems unlikely considering the strategic alliances they brought with them and the valued political status of their children in the Successor Wars.[16] Again, these royal offspring were barely mentioned until a generation later when, following Alexander's death in Babylon, his halfwit half-brother, Arrhidaeus, his full-sister, Cleopatra, and his half-sister, Cynnane – with her daughter – each entered the frame with Alexander's two sons, one of whom was considered an imposter.

All of the above-mentioned royal siblings were executed over the next fifteen years, a period during which Cassander married (forcibly, it was claimed) Alexander's half-sister, Thessalonice, to legitimize his reign. She produced three 'royal' male heirs and was eventually murdered by one of them, while the other two sons were assassinated by Alexander's by-now aged successors who still had eyes on the throne of Macedon.[17] But the sum total of information we have on these seven wives and their offspring from three generations – across *all* surviving sources – could fit on a double-page spread. Only the names of Alexander's half-brother, Arrhidaeus, and his nemesis Olympias, Alexander's ruthless mother, would spill over the page as they were embroiled in the Successor War bids for survival.

Arrhidaeus the Hapless Pawn

Before Alexander's death, his half-brother, Arrhidaeus, is only briefly mentioned in the list of Philip's wives (and their children) and in Plutarch's unique narrative of what is termed the 'Pixodarus affair' some fourteen years before.[18] We don't even know whether Arrhidaeus accompanied Alexander on campaign for the eleven years in Asia or he remained at the court in Pella until the army returned from the East. His sudden appearance at Babylon suggest the latter is more likely.

Plutarch claims Arrhidaeus was a bright, vibrant child until Olympias gave him mind-destroying drugs to remove him as a threat to Alexander's path to the throne. Justin reports that his mother, Philinna of Larissa, was a harlot (but then he mistakenly terms Arrhidaeus the father of Thessalonice!), but none of these allegations likely have any substance. Philinna was probably from the royal line of

Thessaly (the Aleuadae) which gave Philip an alliance he needed, while Arrhidaeus was likely epileptic (which didn't, however, prevent Socrates or Caesar from carving out a legacy) or autistic, as one fragmentary source claims.[19]

But the most interesting episode surrounding Arrhidaeus is the Pixodarus affair, because this involved both Philip and Alexander in the very deepest court scheming and counter-scheming. Once again, this unique biographical footage comes from Plutarch alone, and potentially from the aforementioned corpus of ancient correspondence he seems to have put so much stock in.

In this vexatious episode, Arrhidaeus was being used as a pawn by his father, Philip, towards the end of his reign, in the very last year or two. If factual, it was a high-risk and almost self-defeating strategy, as it proved to be. Alexander's later reconciliation with his father, after the banquet at which the baron Attalus called in to question his legitimacy in front of the king (see chapter 6), may have not been so absolute after all. According to Plutarch, Alexander was soon conspiring behind his father's back:[20]

> But when Pixodarus, the satrap of Caria, trying by means of a tie of relationship to forge a military alliance with Philip, wished to give his eldest daughter in marriage to Arrhidaeus the son of Philip, and sent Aristocritus to Macedon on this errand, once more slanderous stories kept coming to Alexander from his friends and his mother, who said that Philip, by means of a brilliant marriage and a great connexion, was trying to settle the kingdom upon Arrhidaeus [i.e. groom him for the throne of Macedon]. Greatly disturbed by these stories, Alexander sent Thessalus, the tragic actor, to Caria, to argue with Pixodarus that he ought to ignore the bastard brother, who was also a fool, and make Alexander his relative by marriage. And this plan was vastly more pleasing to Pixodarus than the former. But Philip, becoming aware of this, went to Alexander's chamber, taking with him one of Alexander's friends and companions, Philotas the son of Parmenio [Alexander later executed them both], and upbraided Alexander severely, and bitterly reviled him as ignoble and unworthy of his high estate, in that he desired to become the son-in-law of a man who was a Carian and a slave to a barbarian king. And as for Thessalus, Philip wrote to the Corinthians that they should send him back to Macedon in chains. Moreover, of the other companions of Alexander, he banished from Macedon Harpalus and Nearchus, as well as Erigyius [brother of another boyhood friend, Laomedon] and Ptolemy, men whom Alexander afterwards remembered and held in the highest honours.[21]

In preparation for his invasion of Asia, Philip had earlier reached out to Hermias (Aristotle's father-in-law), the ruler of Atarneus (a city in coastal Anatolia opposite Lesbos), and to Pixodarus of the Carian-based Hecatomnid dynasty – the 'grandest' in the Eastern Mediterranean and influential in Lycia – to arrange a royal marriage for another alliance on the Aegean coast of the Persian Empire. Alexander had undermined the proposed pairing of his half-witted half-brother to Pixodarus' daughter by offering himself instead; it was Parmenio's son, Philotas, who possibly revealed the plot to Philip, and Philotas appears to have been a marked man thereafter.

Some have interpreted this episode as showing that Alexander already had plans to lead the invasion of Asia in his father's stead. His recent impetuous founding of the 'city' of Alexandropolis in 340 BC (when Philip was busy besieging Byzantium) after campaigning in Thrace at the age of just 16 was a testament to the prince's growing ambition. It may have left his father wary, despite Plutarch's claim that Philip 'was excessively fond of his son, so that he even rejoiced to hear the Macedones call Alexander their king, but Philip their general'.[22]

Justin painted a more hostile picture of court affairs: after the initial rift with Philip at the banquet with Attalus, Olympias urged her brother, Alexander Molossus, now the Epirote king, to declare war on her estranged husband; it would have been an opportune moment, with Philip's most effective generals, Parmenio and Attalus (Cleopatra's uncle), absent in Asia with a significant part of the royal army, which was establishing a bridgehead for the Persian invasion. At this point Alexander's envoy, Thessalus, was to be found in Corinth, potentially seeking military Greek support for the prince. Only the diplomacy of Demaratus of Corinth managed to reconcile father and son. Astute as ever in a political crisis, Philip paired Alexander's sister, also named Cleopatra, to Olympias' brother (so, Cleopatra's uncle) to stave off any Epirote threat; he 'disarmed him as a son-in-law', as Justin put it.[23]

Arrian did refer to a credible exile of Alexander's friends (which Plutarch links to the Pixodarus episode) but associates that back to the family hostility from Philip's rejection of Olympias.[24] The absence of the whole Pixodarus incident from other sources leads scholars to surmise that if the episode ever played out it must have been when Alexander was in that self-imposed exile (which either commenced after the ill-fated banquet attended by Attalus or the Pixodarus affair). But we must ask ourselves if Philip would have really sent his halfwit son to the powerful dynast in Caria with whom he hoped to forge a military alliance (a dynast who had most likely, until that time, opposed Philip's military operations and city sieges at the Hellespont on behalf of the Persian Great King)?[25]

Arrhidaeus' incapacity for any regal function is clear, accounting for his exploitation post-Babylon, so Philip's strategy would have surely backfired. And why would Alexander have objected to the convenient plan to side-line his mentally defective brother to Asia which cleared the path in Macedon for himself? If left in Pella, others could have used the halfwit in a bid for power should Philip die or in Alexander's campaigning absence – in the very way they did at Alexander's death, when Arrhidaeus was thrust into the limelight in Babylon (see Grant, *Last Will and Testament*, 2021, chapter 3). Furthermore, if Philip needed a strategic base of operations in Asia, why not propose a marriage-tie with his more-impressive son, with whom he could combine forces in Asia? Philip's upbraiding of Alexander as 'ignoble and unworthy of his high estate, in that he desired to become the son-in-law of a man who was a Carian and a slave to a barbarian king', seems to answer the question, but this dialogue also undermines the credibility of the entire Pixodarus episode.

Modern scholars remain vexed, and yet the episode has its followers, with one eminent historian commenting: 'It is too odd a tale to invent and no plausible reason for inventing it occurs.'[26] Odd it is, but more suspicious still is that such an important intrigue, which displayed Philip's covert plans for his halfwit son and Alexander's ambition in the context of what came next with Philip's assassination, remained unknown by all other sources except Plutarch. It would surely have featured in Cleitarchus' radar for court intrigue and scandal, and thus the Roman Vulgate.

The Pixodarus affair also remains absent from the mainstream accounts' coverage of the period in which Alexander *did* finally take Caria, home of the Hecatombid dynasty and its impressive stronghold at Halicarnassus – modern Bodrum – where Mausolus, the brother of Pixodarus, had built the famous Mausoleum, one of the Seven Wonders of the ancient world. Equally illogical is Alexander's reinstatement of Queen Ada, Pixodarus' deposed sister, who then 'adopted' Alexander as her son, an unlikely outcome if he had once reached out to form an alliance with her scheming brother who relegated Ada to the inland fortress of Alinda.[27]

Is this another example of Plutarch naïvely accepting the authenticity of correspondence which propelled the halfwit Arrhidaeus into international affairs more than a decade before his presence at Babylon? Was this perhaps more hostile propaganda erupting in the Successors Wars designed to underline Alexander while soliciting sympathy for Arrhidaeus, who was murdered by Olympias? This is a political stance that would have been very much in tune with Cassander's political objectives, supporting as he did Arrhidaeus (now King Philip III Arrhidaeus) and his new young queen (Adea Eurydice) against the faction of Olympias in the Successor Wars.[28]

At Babylon in 323 BC, events are even less decipherable. As mentioned, we don't know if Arrhidaeus was a campaign fixture or whether he was brought out to Babylon just before Alexander's death, when Cassander arrived, for example, and was allegedly assaulted by Alexander (perhaps more Cassander-originating propaganda).[29] Curtius claimed Arrhidaeus had already become Alexander's 'associate in ceremonies and sacrifices', which suggests the king trusted his half-brother not to shame him and the gods before a crowd. In contrast, Curtius' rendering of the gathering of the Assembly at Arms in the days following Alexander's death paints Arrhidaeus as a cowering and terrified pawn used by the infantry generals (see Grant, *Last Will and Testament*, 2021, chapter 3).[30]

But here Curtius was crafting a dialogue for a Roman audience, and historians have noted the similarity of its portrayal to the equally cowed (but eloquent) Claudius found hiding behind curtains at Caligula's death.[31] To please his readers, it seems, Curtius provides Arrhidaeus with an impossibly noble address in which he entreated his troops to 'choose a better man than me' if an agreement on the kingship could not be reached.[32] The imbecile Assembly pawn apparently never uttered a coherent word again until his death six years or so later, except for some incoherent babble when he became incensed and almost ran through an Athenian ambassador.[33]

Alexander's Court Courtesans

Like Philip (who was aged 22 or 23 when he became king),[34] Alexander had ascended to the throne when relatively young (20), although previous events had proven he was way ahead of his years. But *unlike* his father, he was disinterested in women and showed little inclination to establish his own lineage. Indeed, worrying about his indifference to the opposite sex (when his male boyhood companion, Hephaestion, was reportedly commanding his affections), Philip and Olympias presented him with a beautiful courtesan (a *hetaira*) named Callixeina from Larissa in Thessaly. Yet only after the repeated entreaties of his parents did she reputedly become one of the first sexual encounters Alexander ever had (with women, at least).[35] This detail is presented in the Roman-period text of Athenaeus, whose primary source this time was Theophrastus, Aristotle's successor at the Lyceum.

Athenaeus' (broad) contemporary in Rome, Aelian, describes a similar but more positive encounter with another courtesan from Larissa named Pancaste, who is listed as the 'first woman Alexander slept with'.[36] This was allegedly an ongoing affair which led to the prince commissioning a nude painting of her by the famous artist, Apelles. The painter was so overcome with her beauty that he fell in love with his subject, resulting in Alexander presenting him with Pancaste as a gift.[37]

These women may have been confused by the sources (as the Larissa connection suggests). Knowing that Theophrastus was the source of detail on Callixeina leads historians to ponder whether this negative propaganda was to undermine Alexander's morals, for the Peripatetics (the philosophical school of Aristotle, headed by Theophrastus after him) became hostile to the king's memory. Alexander did, after all, execute Callisthenes, Aristotle's relative and school pupil, and Theophrastus is known to have written an epitaph in Callisthenes' honour, *On Grief*, which may have questioned Alexander's behaviour in a period when Cassander controlled Athens. Cassander, we recall, had wiped out Alexander's direct line and was politically astute enough to have been spreading his own court propaganda.[38]

Alexander's encounters with these women appear to have been the object of manipulation and the women likely confused; Athenaeus and Aelian, both teachers of rhetoric, were set to entertain and gathered their golden nuggets of moralizing epithets and philosophical maxims wherever they could without questioning their authenticity. But there were males of exploitable interest as well.

Alexander's Conquests on Campaign

The mainstream Alexander accounts, which scholars like to imagine were based on eyewitness 'court' sources, make it clear that the king's generals were concerned at his continued reticence to take a Macedonian bride. Consequently, they pleaded with the young king to produce a legitimate heir before they departed for Asia.[39]

Stories of Alexander's proclivity for male youths whom he 'loved to distraction', besides Hephaestion's youthful charm,[40] manifested itself in a number of episodes on campaign (homosexuality was commonplace at court; Philip's assassination was linked to his affair with a youthful male court lover). These include Alexander's ongoing relationship with the beautiful eunuch Bagoas (a former catamite of Darius III), whom he kissed at public events,[41] as well as reports of several profferings of boys of unsurpassed beauty by members of his entourage attempting to curry favour. These stories may be anecdotal and are almost certainly *not* from eyewitnesses, as the moralizing flavour underpinning them once again suggests spurious non-contemporary origins.

Unsurprisingly, Plutarch (potentially from his unique corpus of letters once more) is behind several of these episodes, while Athenaeus reports another; both come from the Roman period. In each case, Alexander is apparently incensed at the offers to provide him with male youths and voiced his anger aloud at the disgraceful proposals, so the king's honour remained intact.[42] The hubris is overdone and smacks of posthumous scandal, while Plutarch appears keen to defend the king, who had 'the most complete mastery over his appetite'.[43] The admiring Arrian followed a similar line: Alexander was 'most temperate in pleasures of the body, his passion was for glory only'.[44] But then we know Arrian's sources: the equally sanitizing Ptolemy and Aristobulus. As one historian noted, 'whereas Ptolemy had been content to pass over the less pleasant aspects of Alexander's character, Aristobulus' book seems to have had a distinctly "apologetic" character which earned him in antiquity the soubriquet of "flatterer".'[45]

On campaign in Asia, Alexander's superhuman self-control – in the early years at least – reportedly led to an impressive sexual restraint, with Plutarch claiming that Alexander consorted with no woman except his mistress, Barsine (captured after the Battle of Issus when he was aged 23) before his marriage to Rhoxane some six years later.[46] As far as Darius' captured wife and his equally beautiful daughters are concerned, they were 'guarded as though in sacred and inviolable virgins' chambers, instead of in an enemy's camp, apart from the speech and sight of men'.[47]

In contrast, the Vulgate sources paint a rather different picture, with Alexander choosing a girl each night from Darius' captured harem, which numbered some 360 women. Apart from the courtesans he knew back home, Alexander allegedly had an affair with an 'Amazon-styled' queen, Thalestris, most likely from a Scythian tribe.[48] After being wed to Rhoxane, he married a daughter of Darius (named either Stateira or Barsine, see below), as well as a daughter of former Achaemenid Great King Artaxerxes III Ochus who was named Parysatis.[49] However, in *this* particular style of 'legitimizing' polygamous approach to regional diplomacy, Alexander was doing no more than following in the footsteps of his father.

What we can be sure of, however, is that mistresses and courtesans *were* certainly a part of campaign life, with Arrian claiming over 10,000 of the Macedonian troops had children by Asiatic camp followers, captives or wives along the way. Alexander's most prominent officers were wed to Persian nobility in the mass weddings at Susa in 324 BC, and it seems the king truly understood the need for a next-generation hybrid aristocracy for the successful governance of the vast Asian provinces now under Macedonian control. Alexander also forbade these offspring from returning to Macedon with his returning veterans, foreseeing the upheaval it would cause in the conservative home state.[50] Instead, he compensated their fathers and promised to fund the education, maintenance and arms of their children in Asia, and if orphaned they would receive their father's pay.[51]

We may wonder what became of the myriad half-Asiatic children sired by Alexander's soldiers and born in the wake of the decade-long campaign. Some may have served in Successor War armies, in the Antigonid and Seleucid ranks in particular. They must have had an estate claim or two in the name of their fathers, and surely this is one of the reasons why Alexander forbade their repatriation.

One of the more prominent camp mistresses was the aforementioned Thais (see chapter 4), a courtesan from Athens, whom we imagine was educated and cultured as professional Greek ladies of companionship were.[52] Thais allegedly 'knew' Alexander before she was passed to Ptolemy and eventually gave the dynast of Egypt-to-be three children, while Athenaeus claimed he eventually married her, thereby legitimizing the offspring. But there were other mistresses associated with Alexander by whom 'mystery' bastards were allegedly sired; some appear in the mainstream accounts and others reappear in some parallel form in the *Romance*. The first of them is Cleophis.

Affairs Lost in Romance

According to the Vulgate genre (here Curtius and Justin), Cleophis was the mother of the Indian dynast Assacenus, and her robust defence of Massaga (today's Swat region of Pakistan) brought her to Alexander's attention. Latin tradition (from the Roman period, not earlier) portrayed the king as impressed with her beauty, with Justin going as far as claiming he fathered a son (named Alexander), Cleophis retaining her position through ongoing sexual favours: she ransomed her captured citadel by sleeping with the king. The name 'Cleophis' is once more unique to Latin sources and might have been 'invented in the Augustan age as a play on the name of the Cleopatra', who gave Rome a run for its money.[53]

The historicity of the story is clouded by reports from Diodorus, Plutarch and Arrian of Alexander's massacre of the mercenary contingent of Massaga which 'stained his career'.[54] If, on the other hand, this dishonourable conclusion was Roman-era scandal, and recalling Cleopatra's similar seduction of Julius Caesar and Mark Antony, the Cleophis affair may well have inspired the legend behind Alexander's liaison with Candace of Meroe (in the kingdom of Kush, today's Sudan) in the *Romance*.[55]

Candace (in Greek, Kandake), the legendary Queen of Nubia, was, it seems, derived from *ktke* or *kdke* in the Meriotic language of Meroe, meaning 'queen mother', and the name was used for all Ethiopian female sovereigns.[56] A parallel moniker with similar meaning is perhaps the name which appears frequently in sources dealing with Achaemenid Persia: Semiramis. This is actually a Greek derivative of the Sumerian *sammuramat*, 'woman of the palace', perhaps the official consort of the Great King and a title variously attributed to Assyrian queens of repute and monuments strewn across the western Persian Empire.[57]

In the *Romance*, it is the palace of Semiramis which is inhabited by Candace, who is eventually visited by Alexander in disguise after exchanging correspondence featuring the oracle of Ammon. Alexander shelters her son, Candaules, from an attack on the way to an annual Amazon festival. Notably, Ptolemy appears in the episode and takes the throne with Alexander's blessing in a change-of-identity charade, with Alexander pretending to be his own bodyguard, Antigonus. Together in the subterfuge, Alexander and Ptolemy rescue Candace from the abductor who raped her with a night attack, following which her son takes Alexander (still playing the subordinate role of his own messenger) to the palace with all its wonders on their way (recalling the mainstream colourful descriptions of India) to the Dwellings of the Gods.

The awe-inspiring and 'above-normal-human size' Candace (who reminds Alexander of his mother, Olympias) becomes wise to Alexander's disguise (she had her Greek court painter secretly capture his likeness on canvas before), and so has him outwitted. Sensing he is trapped (after she shows him his portrait), Alexander contemplates stabbing himself and Candace with his sword. After all, the wife of Candace's younger son, Thoas, was the daughter of King Porus, whom Alexander killed in battle. Thoas now wishes to kill the Macedon king and his messenger, Antigonus, while her other son, Candaules, wishes to set him free.

Candace, who had not revealed his true identity, now beseeches Alexander to intervene in the feud between her two sons, who were preparing themselves for a duel. To appease them, Alexander (still disguised as Antigonus) promises the sons he will cunningly lure 'King Alexander' to their city with the promise of gifts, and Candace, impressed with his cleverness, sends Alexander off with a bodyguard escort to the place where the gods dwell.

Here, Pharaoh Sesonchosis (an attested name from Egyptian prehistory, also see chapter 6) reveals himself – with light flashing out of his eyes – as Lord of the World, and though now diminished in reputation, he predicts favour for Alexander for founding the city of Alexandria. Seated on the throne is the omnipotent and ever-present god Serapis. With this promise of knowledge, Alexander asks how long he has to live. The reply advises against the question but confirms: 'the city you have founded will be famous throughout the world. Many kings will come to destroy it. But you will dwell in it, dead and yet not dead; the city you founded will be your tomb.'

This last paragraph is steeped in the mainstream accounts of Alexander's visit to the oracle of Siwa, his mysterious death in Babylon (where Serapis is consulted), Ptolemy's redirection of Alexander's body (bound for Macedon) to Egypt and his final tomb built in Alexandria. This favourable treatment of the Ptolemaic dynasty of Egypt anchors the birth of the *Romance*, as is the promotion of Ptolemy's hybrid deity, Serapis.

How much of the mainstream Candace affair is truth or downright brazen invention, and how much of what we read in the *Romance* is based on actual characters and events? How much was contemporary propaganda for Alexander in his lifetime from 'excretal' poets and fawning courtiers, and how much posthumous for the benefit of his successors? Did the ancient readership really care? Judging by the popularity of the *Romance*, the answer to the latter is 'no', but perhaps they too were unable to differentiate fact from fable.

Alexander and the Amazons

Some of the *Romance* letters describe Alexander's visit to legendary female warriors, the aforementioned Amazons. He not only met them in person, but there were written exchanges, after which Alexander relayed the reports back to Olympias in Epirus.[58] We may be tempted to credit these episodes to romancing alone, but that would be a mistake.

The Amazons had fascinated the Greeks for centuries. Homer's texts portrayed them as women 'equal to men', and the mighty Achilles slayed their queen, Penthesilea, at Troy.[59] In legend, the founder of Athens, Theseus, had abducted the Amazon Antiope, and Heracles all but wiped them out after being tasked with winning the girdle of Antiope's sister, Queen Hippolyta. Amazonomachy (art depicting Greeks fighting Amazons, often equipped with light battle-axes), much of it based on Heracles' 'Ninth Labour', adorned everything from the Parthenon to the Painted Stoa and the Temple of Zeus at Olympia.[60]

Herodotus' *Histories* explain how the Amazons interbred with a Scythian tribe which inhabited the lands north of the Black Sea. The vast Scythian homelands spread from here eastwards across the northern reaches of the Persian Empire, where these semi-nomadic tribes were known as the 'Saka'. The excavation of Scythian graves has confirmed that as many as 25 per cent of their fighters may have been females (see Grant, 2019, chapter 6).

Unsurprisingly, given their reputation for confronting the great warriors of Greek prehistory, tales of the Amazons entered the campaign of Alexander, who had immersed himself in the ancient texts as part of his classical Greek education. Alexander came across 300 of the fabled warriors and their queen, Thalestris, in the region of Hyrcania ('Wolf Land') south of the Caspian Sea. According to the Vulgate-genre sources (Curtius, Diodorus and Justin, as well as the multi-sourcing Plutarch), Alexander satisfied her desire to beget a 'kingly' child for thirteen days (and presumably nights).[61]

Plutarch was always creative when dealing with a scandal. He named fourteen different sources that either confirmed or repudiated Alexander's affair with Thalestris. Superficially, the incident is quaint and much developed in the *Romance*, and is a tutorial on the grey matter between the black and white. Of those sources cited, five declared for the meeting, while nine, according to Plutarch, maintained it was a fiction. Notably, one of the five authenticators was Onesicritus, a supposed eyewitness to the event. Another was Cleitarchus, who likely followed Onesicritus' lead. Surprisingly, scandalmongering royal usher Chares was among the nine doubters; Ptolemy and Aristobulus also came down on the side of invention.[62]

Plutarch named six historians who are little known or unique to this passage, and their responses, it seems, confirmed it either happened or did not. But we need to tread carefully here, for in the same passage, Plutarch confirmed Alexander *did* write to Macedonia reporting a meeting with a Scythian king who offered him his daughter. Moreover, the Macedones *were* indeed close to the lands associated with 'Amazons' – the relevant part of southern Scythia attached to the legend popular since the *Iliad*. Arrian recorded the presence of embassies from various Scythian tribes as Alexander progressed through Asia. Although Plutarch saw the presence of the Scythian king as a vindication of the doubters, it nevertheless confirmed that an event that broadly approximated the reports could have in fact taken place.

Here, the reputation of Onesicritus is smudged by an alleged quip from Lysimachus when he ruled Thrace. As Plutarch tells it: 'And the story is told that many years afterwards Onesicritus was reading aloud to Lysimachus, who was now king, the fourth book of his history, in which was the tale of the Amazon, at which Lysimachus smiled gently and said: "And where was I at the time?"' The retort, however, may have been targeted at the tryst with Thalestris and not at the meeting itself.[63] So can we blame Onesicritus for what may amount to a modest embellishment of truth inspired by a remarkable meeting of Macedones and Scythian women who did historically form part of the warrior ranks in their tribes (see Grant, 2019, chapter 9)?

In a separate episode in the mainstream accounts, the governor of Media, Atropates, sent 100 women dressed as Amazons – in gender-obscuring britches tucked into leather boots and distinctive pointed hats – to the Macedonian king. Atropates obviously knew of Alexander's urge to emulate the destiny of Homeric heroes. Even the sober soldier Arrian was romanced into stating: 'I cannot believe that this race of women never existed at all, when so many authorities have celebrated them.'[64]

Regardless of the historicity of the Amazons, if Alexander was presenting himself as a new Achilles, as sources appear to confirm, then the hero needed an encounter with his own 'Penthesilea'. The fact that Alexander seduced an Amazon where Achilles slayed her instead (though he did fall on love with her in the throes of her death) did not lessen the romantic parallel. At this point, Alexander still had his campaign historians and poets on hand to fuse the accounts together.

Barsine and Heracles; King's Mistress and Bastard Son

But perhaps the affair which best captures all the uncertainty of eyewitness writers' reporting and the agenda-driven embellishment of those later looking on was Alexander's relationship with his mistress, Barsine, the mother of his first son, Heracles.

A read through the accounts of the Successor War years suggests it was the veteran of Alexander's campaigns and the former regent of Macedon, Polyperchon (who was nominated by Antipater on his death bed, much to Cassander's disgust), who alone recalled the existence of Alexander's oldest son, Heracles, a figure so obscure that many historians have dubbed him a fraud.[65] The boy did not feature at all in the main biographical narratives of Alexander; Curtius, and thus we suppose Cleitarchus, first brought him into the debate during the Assembly at Babylon after the king's death. Yet Heracles and his mother featured briefly, though significantly, in Diodorus' later books, when we may reasonably assume he was still following Hieronymus' narrative of events. Yet at the point of Alexander's death, even Diodorus failed to mention them: 'Alexander the king had died without issue, and a great contention arose over the leadership'; this was an extraordinary statement to have made.[66]

After Cassander executed Olympias sometime in 315 BC, the barometer dropped on the Antipatrids and a new Polyperchon–Antigonus alliance was cobbled together against him in the Peloponnese. Duplicities followed which saw sons turned and then assassinated in the next five years, in which Polyperchon's power and credibility was whittled away; he faded into a relative obscurity that bordered on 'retirement', and the peace treaty of 311 BC in which he didn't feature essentially isolated Polyperchon from any wider role.[67] His last bid for power was to bring Heracles, and so himself, out of that obscurity in 310/309 BC.

By then Polyperchon was past 70 and without the support of his own son, Alexander, who had been murdered in 314 BC, and he also lacked the support of his son's remarkable wife, Cratesipolis (literally 'conqueror of cities'), a renowned beauty who had held the leaderless army together.[68] Yet Polyperchon managed to extract Heracles from Pergamum and raise an army of 20,000 infantry (including Antigonus' allies, the Aetolians), with 1,000 cavalry, to launch an invasion of Pella from his native canton of Tymphaea in Upper Macedon. None of this could have been possible, as commentators have since concluded, without the support of Antigonus, who was once again attempting to undermine Cassander and his allies (Ptolemy, Lysimachus and Seleucus) in the wake of the failed peace of 311 BC.[69]

Heracles was most likely around 17 by 310/309 BC, so he had been born *ca.* 327/326 BC when Alexander had been campaigning in the upper satrapies or planning to enter India.[70] When Polyperchon tried to promote the youth, 'the Macedones regarded the restoration of the king without disfavour'.[71] The terms Diodorus associated with this episode – 'ancestral throne' and 'regal title' – suggest his source, Hieronymus, recognized the legitimacy of the boy, or at least the legitimacy others attached to him. One scholar has argued that because Hieronymus published in the rule of Antigonus II Gonatas, he never revealed the role of his king's grandfather (Antigonus the One-Eyed) in the venture; moreover, this is why Hieronymus omitted to mention that Pergamum, where Heracles had been installed years before, was under Antigonus' control.[72]

We may speculate whether Cassander, who had implored his father 'not to get too far away from the kings' after the conference at Triparadeisus in 320 BC in the wake of Perdiccas' death, was also thinking of the danger that Heracles posed in hostile hands, otherwise the warning is vexing, for Diodorus made it clear that Antipater kept the infant Alexander IV and the half-witted Philip III with him on his way back to Pella. The one short time Antipater *might* have deposited these two in temporary custody with Antigonus was during what reads in the *Gothenburg Palimpsest* as a humiliating campaign against Eumenes.[73]

The doubting scholar further suggested that Hieronymus knew full well that Alexander had no second son, implying that any mention of Heracles at Babylon was part of a later fabrication.[74] Other historians have effectively turned the 'intruder' arguments back on themselves, and surely it would have been foolhardy for someone of Polyperchon's standing (and that of Antigonus behind him) to try to dupe the remaining Diadochi with a late-entry pretender, for all would have been familiar with Alexander's past liaisons and presumably with their results.[75] Cassander was clearly unsettled by the move, and now that rumours (or open knowledge) of his recent execution of Alexander IV and Rhoxane were circulating, he could not trust Macedonian sentiment.

With promises of reinstatement as his general in the Peloponnese with a share in power, Cassander convinced Polyperchon to turn from supporting Antigonus and murder the boy, rather than grasping the opportunity to expose the teenager as a fraud himself, which, as one scholar has argued, is an argument for Heracles' legitimacy.[76] The conclusion to the sad affair, like all character-exposing outcomes, provided useful epideictic material for Plutarch's moralistic reflections.[77]

But Heracles' story began some twenty-four years earlier and in far less tragic times for Macedon. Following the Persian defeat at Issus in November 333 BC, the royal family of Darius III was captured, including his wife (Stateira), his mother (Sisygambis), two adolescent virgins (his daughters, Stateira and Drypetis) and a 'not yet past his sixth year' son (Ochus).[78] Immediately after Issus, Parmenio captured other notable Persian women at Damascus, including the wife and three 'maiden' daughters of the former Great King known as Artaxerxes III Ochus, whose son (Arses, Artaxerxes IV) Darius had deposed with the help of the eunuch Bagoas. We may assume one of these daughters was Parysatis, Alexander's future bride at Susa, though the other two daughters remain anonymous. Also listed in this set of captives was the daughter (probably Amastris) of Oxyathres, the brother of Darius III. To the tally of captured women we need to add the Great King's concubines, allegedly 360 in number.[79]

Also apprehended were the wife and son of Pharnabazus (the son of Artabazus), who had been given supreme Persian command of the Aegean coast by the new Great King, Darius III, along with the three unnamed daughters of Mentor, the some-years-dead Rhodian mercenary who had fought both against and for Artaxerxes III. Next were listed the 'wife and son of the renowned general Memnon'; he was Mentor's brother and Alexander's most talented opponent in Asia Minor, who had died of illness much more recently. We are led to believe that this captured wife, Barsine, became Alexander's mistress.

Barsine, we are told, was a daughter of Artabazus, the 'chief of courtiers' and former Persian satrap of Hellespontine Phrygia (grandson of Artaxerxes II and nephew of Artaxerxes III). Artabazus' son (Ilioneus) and wife were also in the group; she was possibly the Rhodian sister of Mentor and Memnon who had borne to Artabazus eleven sons and ten daughters, that is if a later bride was not being referred to here, as might be suggested by Ilioneus' immaturity. Alongside this royal haul at Damascus, hostile Spartans and Athenians had been rounded up, and a useful cache of 2,600 talents of coined money, 500lb of wrought silver and 7,000 loaded pack animals.[80]

Artabazus had initially refused to recognize his uncle, Artaxerxes III, whose pogrom wiped out his brothers' rival lines (when eighty of Sisygambis' brothers by various concubines were killed in a single day) as he ascended the throne in 358 BC. The new Great King then issued a royal edict that the mercenary armies of the satraps were to be disbanded. Although assisted by his Rhodian brothers-in-law in the so-called 'Great Revolt of the Satraps', Artabazus was finally defeated and took refuge with his family at the court of Philip II in Macedon in 349/348 BC, along with Memnon.[81] So he, along with his large clutch of offspring and his talented son-in-law, were well known to (the then young) Alexander.[82] Artabazus' 'honourable' surrender to the Macedones in Hyrcania some three years after Issus, and the reported warmth between him and his captor, stemmed from this former 'guest exile', whereupon Alexander appointed Artabazus as his new satrap in Bactria. Memnon had fared worse; he had died when still in opposition to the Macedonian invasion of Asia.[83]

The dense and intertwined branches of the line of Artabazus with the two Rhodian brothers and sister, the inter-related Achaemenids and the captive lists from Issus and Damascus with their anonymous females, were bound to provide latitude for confusion to historians.[84] For here we have three daughters of Artaxerxes III Ochus, three of Mentor, two of Darius and ten of Artabazus; most were unnamed and all of them could be referred to as 'royal'.[85] To add further scope for misidentification, while Justin described the allure of these regal women, 'He [Alexander] fell in love with his captive Barsine for her beauty, by whom he had afterwards a son that he called Heracles', Justin later linked Heracles to Rhoxane in his careless epitomizing form and Porphyry erroneously stated Rhoxane was the daughter of Darius, as did the *Romance* compilers.[86] But it seems that all prominent royal women were described as visually prepossessing: Darius III's two daughters were also complimented this way, while his wife was voted 'the most beautiful woman in all Asia', with Rhoxane a runner-up. Plutarch additionally stated that Darius' daughters resembled their handsome parents.[87]

Plutarch's rundown of Barsine's qualities included her 'agreeable disposition', and thus 'Alexander determined (at Parmenio's instigation, claimed Aristobulus) to attach himself to a woman of such high birth and beauty'.[88] But once again, this description could fit the now-captive daughters of both Great Kings, and in particular the daughter of Darius, who was curiously named 'Barsine' by Arrian.[89] It has been convincingly argued that the 'beautiful captive' Parmenio urged Alexander to marry *was* one of Darius' two daughters, for that would clearly provide the legitimacy the Macedonian king sought in Asia.[90] Darius *had* reportedly proffered his daughter to Alexander previously, along with a portion of his empire, and Parmenio urged him to accept the olive branch.[91]

The bold rejection we read of might not in truth have been so confidently drafted, as the marriage would have been attractive to a man who had conquered the western satrapies of the Persian Empire and now sought legitimacy in the East. Alexander allegedly replied with: 'That which was offered was already his.' The result was that he had Darius III's daughters with him for perhaps two years after Issus and may have come to know them well, despite Plutarch's claim that the women continued to live 'as though guarded in sacred and inviolable virgins' chambers'.[92] Leaving them at Susa in 331 BC, Alexander ordered that the princesses be given a Greek education, which in itself suggests he had unique future plans for the girls: he and Hephaestion married them when they returned to Susa some seven years later.[93]

It was Plutarch (uniquely it seems) who claimed Heracles' mother was one of the daughters of Artabazus, who was already in his late 60s when Barsine was captured post-Issus in 333 BC (though Curtius implied he was around 90).[94] To truly entangle matters, Plutarch stated that Barsine had been the wife of Memnon, but Arrian wrote that Barsine had a daughter by Mentor; this would suggest that Barsine had married her dead husband's brother, unless Arrian, or later scribes, were confused by their similar names (Strabo may have made the same mistake). Plutarch's statement reads:

> But Alexander, as it would seem, considering the mastery of himself a more-kingly thing than the conquest of his enemies, neither laid hands upon these women, nor did he know any other before marriage, except Barsine. This woman, Memnon's widow, was taken prisoner at Damascus. And since she had received a Greek education, and was of an agreeable disposition, and since her father, Artabazus, was son of a king's daughter.[95]

Here, the Greek education rears its head again. Plutarch believed Barsine was the *only* woman Alexander had consorted with before his marriage to Rhoxane in 327 BC. This is a romantic but highly unlikely proposition, all the more so if we give any credence to Diodorus' claim that Alexander consorted with concubines from Darius' harem.[96] There is no further evidence that the widowed Barsine remarried Memnon; only a nameless 'widow' of that Rhodian commander was mentioned in the captive list by Curtius and Diodorus.[97] Perhaps because Mentor's wife was not listed, Plutarch (or his source) concluded Memnon was caring for his brother's three orphaned daughters and thus he had married Barsine for the practical application of that. This may have further led Plutarch to conclude Memnon's young son was born from the new union.[98]

Clearly, judging by these associations, Barsine already had a number of children by the time she was captured. Taking this into account, one dubious scholar quite reasonably concluded she was a woman of a different (older) generation to Alexander, who was 23 when he captured her. The reasoning is further supported by evidence that a son of Mentor (if Barsine was his mother too) may have been mature enough for battle in 327/326 BC. Memnon also had sons fighting beside him at the Granicus River in 334 BC, though Plutarch must have assumed these were from a previous marriage (if indeed his above text originally referred to 'Memnon' and not 'Mentor').[99] Moreover, there is no mention that this Barsine accompanied Alexander for the next six years, or longer, until 327/326 BC, the time Heracles would have been born.[100] We also know from Arrian, who stated that he was taking some of his detail from Aristobulus at this point (and probably from Ptolemy too), that one of Barsine's daughters had attained marriageable age by 325 BC at the Susa weddings:[101]

> to Ptolemy the Bodyguard and Eumenes the Royal Secretary he gave two daughters of Artabazus, Artacama to Ptolemy and Artonis to Eumenes; to Nearchus the daughter of Barsine and Mentor.[102]

The inference given by Plutarch, however, when describing the same Susa weddings was that the Barsine who consorted with Alexander had *only* two sisters, and not two of ten, if this is not a misleading translation:

> For Barsine the daughter of Artabazus, the first woman whom Alexander knew in Asia, and by whom he had a son, Heracles, had two sisters; of these Alexander gave one, Apame, to Ptolemy, and the other, also called Barsine, to Eumenes.[103]

The names Plutarch provided for the brides of Ptolemy and Eumenes (Apame and Barsine) are different from those given by Arrian (Artacama and Artonis), and it is unlikely (though not impossible) that Artabazus named two daughters 'Barsine'. 'Apame', however, was a well-established Achaemenid name, and one also attached to Seleucus' bride.[104] How could such confusion arise when eyewitness historians presumably passed down their identities? Ptolemy was a bridegroom at Susa, and Aristobulus may well have been. The scholar doubting Heracles' identity, and who paradoxically concluded Ptolemy's detail came from the Eumenes-compiled court *Journal*, simply quipped: 'One may suppose that they knew their wives' names.'[105]

Identifications within the interwoven royal lines of Persia *are* perilous; a read of Plutarch's *Artaxerxes* (III) reveals the recurring use through the generations (though not for two coeval daughters) of these traditional Achaemenid names, including Oxyathres, Apame, Stateira and Parysatis. Darius III himself had married a 'Stateira', his second wife, who was in fact his sister (or half-sister).[106] He had been previously married to a sister of Pharnaces (*possibly* related to Artabazus), the Persian commander who died in battle at the Granicus River, and he probably had a daughter by her.[107] As has been pointed out, when considering wives beside concubines, Darius III could have had many more than the three children who were named, and his mother, Sisygambis, may have had as many as seven children herself.

A seemingly unexploited conclusion surrounding the identity of Barsine is that we are dealing with sisters from more than one generation of Artabazus' line, with the confusion surely arising from what were ambiguous original references to 'nieces', 'sisters-in-law', 'aunts' and 'uncles', and probably 'cousins' too. For if Mentor had married a daughter of Artabazus, and recalling that Artabazus had in turn married Mentor's Rhodian sister, then Mentor married his niece. This exhibits a true strategic bonding of the two families, and judging by the attested children from both sides it had proved a highly successfully union.

This dynastic interweaving would make it quite probable that Memnon had also married another of Artabazus' ten daughters. Furthermore, Mentor's own three daughters by Barsine would have also been termed Memnon's 'nieces', and vice versa, as well as them being the nieces of Artabazus' wife (their sister). Barsine's three daughters (assuming Mentor's girls were by her) were additionally nieces to the remaining nine of Artabazus' girls, whose own daughters (not mentioned but surely existing) were in turn the nieces of Barsine. In fact, the two unnamed daughters of Artaxerxes III Ochus (Parysatis was the third) were cousins of Artabazus.

The potential age ranges of the captives, both the youngest daughters of Artabazus and the oldest of his granddaughters, could well have made them suitable for intimacy with their captors between Damascus in 333 BC and Susa in 325 BC. Moreover, marriages between mature men and far younger women were commonplace then.[108] It seems doubtful in this environment that Alexander would have chosen an older woman who was already the mother of numerous children as his mistress when far younger, equally royal and illustrious 'maidens' were available to him.[109]

It is quite reasonable to assume that more of Artabazus' ten daughters, who now depended upon Alexander for their wellbeing in the new Macedon-ruled empire, were present at the Susa weddings. If 'Barsine' was a traditional family name or title, it could have proliferated through their offspring. A credible explanation for two same-named girls is to conclude that one of the three daughters by Barsine and Mentor was named after her mother, in which case she is a more credible candidate as the mother of Heracles. Considering the many corruptions that crept into manuscript transmission over two millennia or more, could a single archetypal sentence, stripped of its precision, have led to the different names given by Arrian and Plutarch? Well, the wording below, unpunctuated to highlight its potential ambiguity, could (along with other permutations) achieve j ust that:

> to Ptolemy the Bodyguard and Eumenes the Royal Secretary he
> gave sisters of Barsine the daughter of Artabazus and to Nearchus

> Alexander gave a daughter of Mentor and Barsine who had two sisters including Alexander's mistress also named Barsine to Eumenes Artonis Artacama to Ptolemy Apame to Seleucus the daughter of Spitamenes.[110]

Without punctuation, the double references to Eumenes and Ptolemy look awkward, but inserting a comma or break after the second mention of 'Barsine who had two sisters' would suggest the source was proceeding to name the aforementioned anonymous women, here the daughters of Barsine. This wording would justify Plutarch's belief that Heracles' mother had two sisters (accounting for the three daughters of Mentor, one named Barsine after her mother) and overcomes the objection that 'these women all belonged to an older generation'. It would explain the presence of two Barsines, and the corruption (or loss) of punctuation would also explain how both Nearchus and Eumenes were linked to a Barsine. Plutarch would then have believed the 'stranded' names of Artonis and Artacama were the remaining two (non-paired) sisters of Nearchus' wife.

The same ambiguity could additionally indicate how Ptolemy and Seleucus were linked in marriage to Apame, and also explain why Strabo thought Apame was a daughter of Artabazus, where Arrian believed Seleucus' unnamed wife was the daughter of Spitamenes.[111] Strabo frequently used Aristobulus as a source, and Aristobulus was the only source named by Arrian for detail of the Susa weddings, so perhaps it was he who provided the original unifying (though misinterpreted) text.

In this nexus of Persians, progeny and 'beautiful' prisoners, it seems a spurious bridge or two was built, with the mother of Heracles sitting somewhere in its span. What *does* appear to have happened, through marriages to either the daughters or granddaughters of Artabazus, is that Ptolemy, Nearchus and Eumenes became related through Heracles. Unfortunately, as events made clear, they thought little of its significance. Nearchus' alleged speech at the Assembly in Babylon, in which he made a case for Heracles, certainly supports the connection, if it was not a back-construct of Cleitarchus. Eumenes also appears to have gained family loyalty, for Pharnabazus (brother of Barsine, or more likely her uncle) fought for him in 321/320 BC against Craterus.[112]

The claim that Heracles was based at Pergamum in 323 BC, rather than Susa, for example, further supports his descent from Artabazus, for the family estates did reside in Hellespontine Phrygia, with its southern border falling just to the north of the city.[113] The family *condottieri*, Mentor and Memnon, had also been granted substantial estates in the Troad, probably for helping Artabazus to reclaim his father's lands from Autophradates.[114] And we can assume that following Artabazus' voluntary retirement from service under Alexander, he and his family returned to their lands. It is tempting to credit his retirement, and Barsine's departure from the court and the king's bed, to Alexander's marriage to Rhoxane, for according to Curtius, Rhoxane's father, Oxyartes, was granted the governance of Bactria, the very satrapy Alexander had previously bestowed on Artabazus. But this appears to have taken place a little later, though much chronological confusion exists at this point in the extant texts.[115]

It is universally assumed that Alexander never married his mistress Barsine, so Heracles remained an unrecognized bastard son, which would of course go some way to explaining his rejection at Babylon. But at Susa, Alexander was demonstrably 'marriage-minded' in the face of whatever objections Rhoxane may have thrown up or the fears she harboured, for there he took the hand of Stateira, the daughter of Darius III, and Parysatis, the daughter of Artaxerxes III Ochus.[116] If Heracles' mother was descended from an Achaemenid line, there remains the question of why he did not legitimize his (then) only son.[117] We cannot in fact be sure he did not, for a slight amendment to Arrian's statement (or Aristobulus' before him) changes the context of the marriages altogether and explains why Arrian named Darius' daughter 'Barsine' when the Vulgate texts gave us the more convincing 'Stateira'. Consider the text as it stands relating to the weddings at Susa:

> He [Alexander] himself married Darius' eldest daughter Barsine, and according to Aristobulus, another wife as well, Parysatis, the youngest daughter of Ochus (he was already married to Rhoxane, the daughter of Oxyartes of Bactria).

Although this represents a modern translation descended from Arrian's Greek, it once again requires no more than a punctuation change, with a comma or break to be placed after 'Darius' oldest daughter' to suggest that *three* marriages took place, including one to Barsine, whose identity had already been established in texts above relating to the marriages of Alexander's court friends.[118] The loss of punctuation (or spacing) led to Arrian's confusion. When dealing with this grand event, whether Aristobulus was the sole source for Plutarch, Arrian and Cleitarchus before them, or simply an *auxiliary* source for extra detail (as the above text could imply), we have shown that a single archetypal statement *could* in fact have provided the different conclusions we read.

It is possible that Ptolemy avoided commentary at this point, as he did not wish to boost either the profiles of his Successor War opponents or the status of Alexander's children and their politicking guardians. Ptolemy's alleged Babylon speeches and his rejection of Asiatic unions could support that conclusion; after Alexander died, Ptolemy married solely Greek and Macedonian wives, despite his attempts to integrate his kingship into the Egyptian dynastic mode.

Other solutions have been proffered to explain Arrian's 'slip', one of which supposes that because his source, Aristobulus, wrote late in life he was by then confused on names.[119] But this seems extremely unlikely; if the Cassandrean engineer–cum–historian was lucid enough to pull together a history of the campaign, then the detail as momentous as the Macedonian king's brides would have surely remained unsullied in his mind. If he was that unreliable, Arrian would surely have highlighted many more obvious discrepancies and probably questioned his veracity in his opening rundown of his sources.

A second solution, backed by recent studies of Persian tradition, suggests Darius' daughters may have been referred to under different titles at different stages of their lives: formal court monikers and informal family names.[120] Thus, a daughter of Darius, referred to as 'Barsine' in early life, could have assumed the royal title 'Stateira' (or vice versa) once proclaimed a queen, either of which could have more generally denoted 'royal daughter' or 'queen to be'.[121] We recall that Adea became 'Eurydice', a name by then synonymous with Macedonian queens; Audata, Philip's first Illyrian wife, his mother and possibly Cleopatra, his last wife, had assumed the title too.[122] Alexander's mother, Olympias, had in her youth been called 'Polyxena' (named after a Trojan heroine), after marriage (or as a girl) 'Myrtale' (perhaps from Myrtle, *Myrtos*, the sacred plant of Aphrodite) and later in life was known as both 'Olympias' (after Philip's victory at the Olympic Games at the time Alexander was born) and 'Stratonice'; presumably she was never given the title 'Eurydice' herself as Audata (now Eurydice) was still residing at the Pellan court when she married Philip.[123]

Heracles' maternal identity aside, could a true son of Alexander have really been ignored for so long? This was a bone of contention that persuaded the doubting scholar to conclude the boy was a pretender. But Heracles may not have been 'forgotten' at all, either at Babylon as evidenced by Nearchus' speech (and its rejection) or by Perdiccas and Rhoxane; no doubt Eumenes and Olympias pondered his part, or removal, in their developing plans. It was simply Hieronymus' later literary silence on Antigonus' tenure of the boy at Pergamum that made Heracles' re-emergence appear 'sudden'.

But what of Heracles' fate in any succession instructions Alexander may have given or contemplated?[124] As the outcome of Rhoxane's pregnancy was unknown in summer 323 BC, Alexander would have recognized his existing son. If he was to have two boys, the immortal Vulgate lines 'to the strongest' or 'to the most worthy', if ever truly uttered, were perhaps an answer to the question posed to a dying king on which son he wished to eventually take the diadem when of throne age. Justin concluded his narrative of the Babylon settlement with: 'A portion of the empire was reserved for Alexander's son, if a son should be born.' This clearly referred to Rhoxane's child, and supposedly to the compromise reached, but two sons raised at Pella would have been a recipe for more Macedonian fratricide and would have pitted their guardians against one another. In Asia, the sons also had hereditary claims in different regions, Alexander IV with hereditary residencies in Bactria (or Sogdia) and Heracles in Hellespontine Phrygia. It was an arrangement that was never going to work without Alexander himself (see Grant, *Last Will and Testament*, 2021, chapter 9).

The digression on legitimate and illegitimate women and children, Barsine and Heracles in particular, serves to remind us that even the most prominent queens and mistresses and their offspring were wrongly named, shamed and dealt with uncertainly by the secondary and further-removed sources, who could not fathom why the eyewitness historians themselves were at odds on their identities. It appears once again that the power of the pen on papyrus was a more enduring victory than any on the battlefield in the Successor Wars.

Chapter 9

Forgery, Philology and Meddlesome Morphology: Battle on Papyrus

We can claim to have learnt reasonably well how to detect forgeries of ancient texts made either in the Middle Ages or in the Renaissance or later … . On the other hand, it would be fatuous to maintain that we can readily expose a forgery when the forgery was made in Antiquity. Indeed in this case the name of forgery becomes a problem. What we are tempted to label as a forgery, may, on closer examination, be a perfectly honest work attributed to the wrong author.[1]

Arnaldo Momigliano, *Studies in Historiography*

But one thing the facts cry out, and it can be clear, as they say, even to a blind man, that often through the translator's clumsiness or inattention the Greek has been wrongly rendered; often the true and genuine reading has been corrupted by ignorant scribes, which we see happen every day, or altered by scribes who are half-asleep.[2]

Erasmus, *Epistle 337*

Not all the loss of definition in Alexander's story, with the uncertainty of names and the conflicts in numbers, is down to the politics and propaganda of the primary sources. The 2,340-odd years since Alexander died have seen the loss of classical libraries, the format and materials of books change dramatically, and time has witnessed the emergence of religions and philosophies that tugged at the consciences of those who decided which of them would survive. Adding to these challenges was the gradual metamorphosis of the classical and vernacular languages into which texts had to be translated, and this provided further latitude for interpolation and corruption, well-meaning or otherwise. Perhaps most troublesome of all was the sad fact that the evolving classical library additionally gave rise to an industry of damaging imitations and outright fakes; the authenticity of some of the books we read today is still open to question.

It is worth reviewing the precarious path of the book, from its origins in Egyptian papyrus to the Renaissance and the age of the printing press, to appreciate how far the Alexander 'pages' may now lie from the eyewitness authors' original message and intent. But 'forgery and philology fell and rose together in the Renaissance, as in Hellenistic Alexandria';[3] it is an observation that gives this book much of its momentum, for Alexander's eponymous city *was* a key ingredient in the birth of his story, which, with some justification, we could term his 'legend'.

The sobering truth behind our library of classics is a stark one: we have nothing more than a very narrow cross-section of the literary output of the creative minds of antiquity. We might ponder what remained after Caliph Omar (AD 579–644) allegedly burned the 'infidel' Library at Alexandria (*ca.* AD 641) and fuelled the 4,000 furnaces heating the city's bathhouses for over six months from the contents, though the historicity of the infamous destruction cannot be confirmed.[4]

The Ancient Identity Crisis

Aware as we are that no primary source material survives on Alexander – that is, 'books' written by the eyewitnesses to Alexander's campaigns and the era of the Diadochi – we need to further appreciate that neither do the original scrolls and codices of the secondary and tertiary historians who preserved them. Although manuscripts credited to these Hellenistic and Roman-era historians sat in medieval libraries across Europe, they were more often than not poor translations of much earlier vellums and papyri that had themselves been survivors of an earlier discriminatory process.

At the Library in Alexandria, either founded by Alexander's former general Ptolemy I or his son, Philadelphus (sources are at odds; Ptolemy II may have finished it), *kritikoi* (literary adjudicators) had been employed to oversee the process of separation and judgment (the *krisis*) which decided what scrolls were to be copied and have a chance of survival as a result. So the antiquated books we enjoy today are the survivors of a selection process that commenced far earlier in our story, one that was itself at times judicious, occasionally malicious and more often grossly negligent too. The lucky manuscripts became the 'admitted few' which, if they were fortunate enough, were copied from papyrus to parchment and eventually into industrial print. This was a perilous journey that shaped the canon of what we read today.

The establishment of the two great public libraries at Alexandria and Pergamum (modern Bergama in western Turkey) in the Hellenistic era created a massive demand for the works of famous authors. Galen (*ca.* AD 130–200), the Greek self-titled 'doctor–philosopher' who cut his teeth patching up gladiators in Pergamum, reported that 'the recklessness of forging books and titles began' when the kings of Egypt and the Attalids sought to outdo one another in the number of scrolls on their competing library shelves, 'for there were those who, to increase the price of their books, attached the names of great authors to them and then sold them to nobility'.[5]

It was Library scholar Callimachus (*ca.* 310/305–240 BC) and his *Pinakes* (literally 'tables'), the 120-volume list of the genuine against the 'pseudos', which brought some kind of order to the growing corpus of works being catalogued and copied in Alexandria.[6] The Ptolemies, voracious collectors, confiscated original books from the incoming vessels and marked them 'from the ships', compensating the owners with a new scriptorium copy.[7] Ptolemy III Euergetes later swindled the Athenians out of many of their originals, forfeiting a 15-talent bond. Financial rewards were offered for the more valuable texts, and in consequence many imitations of ancient works were passed off as genuine, especially those of Alexander's teacher, Aristotle, a prized catch according to Ammonius Saccas, the third-century AD Alexandrian philosopher.[8]

Galen, prodigious in writing, indignantly described how both his own medical works and the writings of Hippocrates had been corrupted by the interpolations of unscrupulous and careless editors, which prompted him to publish *On His Own Books* to help identify the works truly his. This may have assisted Diogenes Laertius when gathering the doxographies for his *Lives and Opinions of Eminent Philosophers*. Though the collection remains a rich biographical potpourri, we must assume much misattribution occurred, a suspicion reinforced by Diogenes himself, who pointed to the frequent contradictions in his sources.[9] Winding up his *Life of Aristotle*, Diogenes commented: 'There are, also, a great many other works attributed to him, and a number of apophthegms which he never committed to paper.'[10]

The Christian historian and polemicist Eusebius (*ca.* AD 260–340) and his *Preparation for the Gospel* later recalled the objections of Apollonius 'The Grammarian' (amongst others) to the plagiarism of the historians Theopompus and Ephorus, and he also brought to our attention the books with telling titles: Latinus' six books *On the Books of Menander that were Not by Him* and Philostratus' treatise *On the Plagiarisms (or Thefts) of Sophocles*.[11] Some misattribution was of course innocent, and later writers repeatedly misidentified authors of the same name; as many as twenty writers named Dionysius or Ptolemy are known to us, a situation which prompted Demetrius of Magnesia, a tutor to Cicero, to publish *Of Poets and Writers of the Same Names*, which sought to differentiate them.

The real identities of the Pseudo-Callisthenes attached to the *Romance* and Curtius who biographed Alexander remain just as obscure; both may prove to be classic cases of mistaken identity (see chapter 10). But these are not unique; the Byzantine encyclopaedia we know today as the *Suda*, possibly deriving from the Greek *souda* meaning 'fortress' or 'stronghold', was thought by Eustathius (*ca.* 1110–1198), the Archbishop of Thessalonica, to be named after its compiler, Suidas. This is a worrying state of affairs as Eustathius presented himself as a scholar on things Homeric.[12] In truth, we don't know its etymology. Although Strabo mentioned a Suidas as author of a separate work on Thessaly, the tenth-century lexicon, with its 30,000 entries, remains essentially orphaned.

Even the venerable tales of Homer and the Epic Cycle (poems from Greece's Dark Age linked to the story of the Trojan War) were surrounded by confusion and were not beyond early exploitation. From the fall of Troy to the Persian Wars, Greek history was 'covered with an obscurity broken only by dim and scattered gleams of truth'.[13] It was an environment bound to give birth to legends, lies and folklore. As for the view of Plato on the matter, he wrote: 'Hesiod and Homer and the other poets ... composed false stories which they told people and are still telling them.'[14] Although his pupil, Aristotle, concluded that 'It is not the poet's function to describe what has actually happened, but the kinds of thing that *might* happen',[15] the pre-Socratic philosopher, Heraclitus of Ephesus (*ca.* 535–475 BC), declared: 'Homer deserved to be expelled from the contests and flogged.' Herodotus argued that Homer exaggerated because he was a 'poet' when Herodotus' father had been an epic poet too; even Thucydides couldn't resist taking a stab at Homer.[16]

Despite these criticisms, or perhaps *because* of their underlying allegations, newly manipulated accounts of the war at Troy had surfaced by two supposed participants. The anonymous composers, the 'charlatans [who] cloak their non-existence with names well-tailored to their roles in the accounts of dramatic historians', were apparently exercising their rhetorical skills through the eyewitness accounts of Dares of Phrygia, a Trojan ally, and Dictys of Knossos on Crete, who arrived with the invading Greeks.[17] The diary of Dictys, written in Punic, was ferried from Crete back to the philhellene emperor Nero, who enthusiastically commissioned a translation into Greek.[18]

Paralleling Dictys' tale, and supposedly unearthed when an earthquake revealed his tomb, was *The History of the Destruction of Troy* of Dares, which contained an absurd precision of detail: the war for Troy lasted ten years, six months and twelve days, with 676,000 defenders and 886,000 Hellenic invaders taking part. Yet it fooled the influential Augustan-era historian Cornelius Nepos, and even duped the sapient Cicero. Nepos wrote to his lettered friend Sallust explaining that he 'delighted' at finding a 'history written in Dares' own hand', continuing: 'Thus my readers ... can judge for themselves whether Dares the Phrygian or Homer wrote the more truthfully; Dares, who lived and fought at the time the Greeks stormed Troy, or Homer, who was born long after the War was over.'[19]

These newly found accounts were, however, more accessible than the originals of Homer, whose *Odyssey* had been translated into Latin as early as *ca.* 250 BC by the Roman poet, Livius Andronicus. Once translated into Latin by Nepos, the easy-to-read diaries of Dictys and Dares, with elaborate prefatory letters giving the precise circumstances of their discovery, were immortalized into the romances of the Middle Ages, for example in the form of Benoit de Sainte-Maure's *Le Roman de Troie* and other Trojan-inspired poems such as Chaucer's *Troilus and Criseyde*.[20] Elements of Dares and Dictys even entered a French edition of the *Iliad* by

Jean Samxon in 1530.[21] Their continued popularity reflected their monopoly on information concerning the Trojan War.

Rome also fell for what we might translate as *The Battle of Frogs and Mice*, a parody of the *Iliad* with probable Hellenistic origins but regarded as a genuine Homer work. Plutarch was less convinced and pinned the epic poem on Pigres of Halicarnassus, who was of Carian royalty and thus an ally of the Great King Xerxes, and surely this better explained its blatant Trojan irreverence.[22] Alexander once described a clash fought at Megalopolis between his regent, Antipater, and a Sparta-led Greek coalition as a 'battle of mice'; we may ponder whether the origins of the *The Battle of Frogs and Mice* were earlier still.[23]

Further evidence of manipulation of the Homeric epics comes from Strabo in his *Geography*. He proposed that a verse supporting Athens' claim to the island of Salamis had been inserted into the *Iliad* by the Athenian 'law-giver' Solon or the tyrant Peisistratus.[24] According to Herodotus, and somewhat suspiciously, Onomacritus, the friend and counsellor of Peisistratus, had been banished from Athens after it had been proven that he added his own material when editing the *Oracles of Musaeus*, the sixth-century BC mystic seer, predicting the islands off Lemnos would disappear into the sea.[25]

Tampering with text was not the exclusive territory of historians and antiquarians. Legislation passed by Lycurgus, the Athenian speech writer and one of the so-named Ten Attic Orators, suggests creative interpolation had been damagingly interwoven into Greek drama. The new law demanded that actors should not deviate from the 'official' scripts as part of a move to preserve the integrity of the original plays of Aeschylus, Sophocles and Euripides. So liberated from the originals had the thespians' lines become that actors were threatened with losing their performing licences if embellishment was detected.

But a precedent had already been set; some two centuries earlier, Solon had berated Thespis (sixth century BC), the first actor to perform on stage as a character from a tragedy, for telling blatant lies. Thespis predictably replied that there was nothing wrong with lying in a play.[26] Many of the new deviations were no doubt justified under the banner of 'freedom of speech' and were later picked up by scholiasts in the Library at Alexandria, proving Lycurgus' attempts were not altogether successful. But theatre was particularly susceptible to manipulation and misattribution; in Rome, the prolific Varro judged 109 of 130 plays credited to Plautus to be falsely assigned, while the remaining twenty-one were termed 'Varronian' or 'Plautines' in recognition of the forensic success in identifying the genuine.[27]

The Painful Path from Papyrus to the Modern Codex

We tend to refer to 'books' with a liberal definition, though their formats have changed dramatically. The history of the 'written word' commenced in Egypt, the home of papyrus used in scrolls, with the earliest extant specimens dating to *ca.* 3,500 BC.[28] Their preparation was lucidly described by the inquisitive Pliny in his *Natural History*, but drawing from Theophrastus' earlier *Enquiry into Plants*.[29]

The inner rind, *biblos*, which gave us the word 'bible', was cross-braided and bound with glue before being pressed and dried. Like modern textured paper, papyrus had a front and reverse, with one receptive to ink and the other coarser and less readily written on. This observation is helping modern researchers unravel the life cycles of newly found palimpsests. In one case, what was once considered the 'original text' recording a funeral oration that we now frequently refer to as (the remarkably eloquent) *Hyperides over Leosthenes and his Comrades in the Lamian War* – written in 322 BC, the year following Alexander's death – has now been subordinated in terms of date of the original papyrus use to a horoscope from AD 95, for this occupied the 'right side' of the scroll.[30]

Papyri were best preserved rolled up and housed in jars, a state described by the Latin *volumen*, which gives us our 'volumes'. In Rome, first-quality papyrus was once termed 'Augustan', second-quality 'Livian' (after the emperor's wife), and the 'hieratic' grade used for administrative records came in third.[31] Formats continued to evolve as texts were copied to parchments, finely pressed animal skins, which included vellum, from the Latin *vitulinum* (skin 'from the calf'). These were more hardwearing and had the added advantage of being scratchable for erasing mistakes. They were more expensive as well, but their emergence had been necessitated by the restrictions the Ptolemies placed on papyrus exports to hamstring their dynastic rivals. In response to the squeeze, Eumenes II, the king of Pergamum – where a competing library emerged – had the old art of parchment preparation perfected; they became known as *membrana* (or *charta*) *pergamena* in Latin.[32] Parchment was expensive, and therefore copyists were fewer and more carefully chosen.

By Arrian's day, the codex had arrived, the new book format that had developed from the old practice of stringing wooden writing tablets together. The codex was first described by the poet Martial in *ca.* AD 85/86, when it began the gradual process of replacing the scroll.[33] A standard papyrus roll was made from twenty sheets glued together and was some 15–20ft long when fully unravelled. Papyri of major works often ran to unwieldy lengths – 30ft or more; the last two books of the *Iliad* alone ran to 25ft.[34] The codices, representing the modern book format, were much more compact, as both sides of each leaf could be read in succession, giving us *recto* (right or 'front') and *verso* (left or 'back') pages. The works of Homer, previously housed in fifteen thick scrolls, could be compressed to a practical size, and additionally, specific lines and middle chapters could be more easily accessed. Martial's amazement at the result is recorded: 'How small a tablet contains immense Virgil!'

We might speculate that more compressed accounts were largely responsible for the extinction of the far longer originals they précised, despite the codex format.

The first known epitome of another's books was Theopompus' compression of Herodotus' *Histories*, a unique production for its time.[35] Thankfully, the original (though many versions circulated) survived the summary, but in Rome the opposite was more often the case. Once Justin had boiled down Trogus' 'Philippic' history to a fraction of its original size, the writing was, so to speak, on the wall for the forty-four volumes painstakingly compiled by the learned Romanized Gaul, while over 200 of Justin's manuscripts survive today.[36]

Perhaps the Romans had simply had enough of the extended moralizing and rhetorically filled texts. But it was more likely that economic pressure and production practicality determined the need for the epitome. Diodorus' *Library of History*, some forty books in length and without which we would know far less of the Successor Wars, was itself a huge compression of its sources, and it too may have helped to push the originals out of circulation. Yet Diodorus remains our central link to our knowledge of the lost histories of Hecataeus, Ctesias, Poseidonius, Agatharchides, Megasthenes, Ephorus and Hieronymus, amongst others. One modern scholar proposed an epitaph that 'They faced the sentence of oblivion or the fate of being pickled' in Diodorus' volumes.[37]

But even the compact codices produced before the turbulence that followed the last of the Severan emperors (Alexander Severus, ruled AD 222–235), which resulted in a division that produced the Eastern and Western Roman Empires as well as the rise of the Sassanids, were not guaranteed to survive into the Byzantine era. Today, only several of the oldest codices of Virgil survive, and just one copy of Homer. Primary materials that did survive through the fourth and fifth centuries had a better chance for further longevity if they were already 'codexed', as these books had the protection of leather covers, whereas scrolled papyri did not. Works that had been hidden, or particularly well prepared, fared better.

The parchment skins of many of the Dead Sea Scrolls, for example, are still almost white rather than a faded yellow; it is thought they were treated with salt and flour to remove the hair, and then tanned with a gallnut liquid brushed on both surfaces. But the inks of this period were generally still charcoal-based, so were too easily erased by accident or were mendaciously amended. Reed pens gave way to quills in the sixth century, by which time the previously vulnerable ink of soot, gum and water had evolved into a more permanent mix of gum, gallic acid and iron sulphate. This latter formula was used as early as the Herculaneum Scrolls, a collection of carbonized papyri unearthed in 1752 under the volcanic mud of Vesuvius and a find that has been described as the 'only intact library from antiquity'.

The Fate and Fall of the Classical Library

If political turmoil was often the catalyst behind a historian picking up a pen, sadly it was often also the reason for the irrevocable loss of his output. In a sense, libraries were both the saviour and the nemesis of literature, for though their collecting and copying provided some order and safety to the few ancient texts in circulation, the delicate literary eggs were then all in one easily targeted basket. Libraries were prizes of war: Xerxes ferried Peisistratus' public library (the first in Athens) back to Persia before putting Athens to the torch in 480 BC; King Perseus' Macedonian library at Pella went back to Rome with the Roman general Aemilius Paullus after victory at Pydna in 168 BC; and Mark Antony gifted the entire contents of the Pergamum library (some 200,000 scrolls) to Cleopatra, in the process ending the literary legacy of the Attalids.[38] What was most likely a more modest library at Antioch founded by the Seleucids (certainly by the reign of Antiochus III, 222–187 BC) probably disappeared when Pompey the Great annexed Syria in 64 BC.

Although more robust parchments were creeping into the ancient scriptoriums, a voluminous world history would have been prohibitively costly for a provincial library to procure on vellum, despite the advent of awkward opisthographs, scrolls written on both sides to save space and materials before the codex arrived.[39] Cheaper but more frail papyrus remained the copyists' principal medium well past the arrival of skins, especially in Egypt.[40] This meant that the condition of the major Greek works demanded by the Roman literati was already poor. Neleus of Scepsis, to whom Theophrastus bequeathed his own library in his will – some 232,808 lines of text, which include Aristotle's collection gifted with his school, the Lyceum – absconded sometime around 287 BC with the scrolls, though as a foreign resident in Athens, Aristotle was not technically able to 'own' the Peripatus nor bequeath its contents in his will.

The fate of the collection thereafter is uncertain: Neleus' heirs either had the scrolls hidden in a basement to prevent the princes of Pergamum from appropriating them, or as Athenaeus alternatively claimed, he sold them to Ptolemy II Philadelphus, who imported the collection to the Alexandrian Library.[41] According to Strabo, however, the mildewed and worm-eaten remnants of Neleus' library were sold around 100 BC to Apellicon of Teos, a minor Athenian military leader and lover of books. Apellicon, who had fled Athens after stealing a number of rare works to enrich his own shelves, tried to restore the volumes himself.[42] He only succeeded in damaging them further when inserting 'incorrect corrections' for missing fragments of pages, and otherwise poorly editing the works.[43]

When Sulla, the Roman consul and dictator, 'liberated' the library to Rome, it needed much salvaging by Tyrannio, whom Cicero later employed alongside a full staff to renovate his own private collection.[44] These works had already been subjected to editing by Andronicus of Rhodes (writing *ca.* 60 BC), the head of the Peripatetic school who organized Aristotle's work into the chapter and book divisions that survive today.[45] Although Diodorus confirmed the goldmine of resurrected sources when he arrived in Rome from Sicily, the damaging patching-up had already been done.[46]

Like so much associated with Rome, the admirable resided beside the lamentable. When Sulla died, he dedicated his own memoirs to Lucius Licinius Lucullus, the book collector and patron of the arts as well as praetor and great general of the East, along with the guardianship of Faustus, Sulla's wayward son.[47] Despite that, Faustus sold his father's collection, including the library of Apellicon, to pay off his gambling debts. Caesar's fire at Alexandria probably sealed the fate of many of the remaining manuscripts.[48] If they survived that, then Aurelian's fire in the AD 270s, the revolts that Diocletian suppressed in AD 272 and 295, the earthquake beneath Crete that caused a tsunami to strike Alexandria in AD 365, Bishop Theophilus' conflagration of the Serapeum in AD 390/391 and the Muslim conquest from AD 642 onwards surely finished them off.[49]

Julius Caesar never mentioned the burning of the famous Alexandrian Library in his memoirs. He did admit to setting the fleet alight in the harbour for his own safety, and stated that some arsenals were also burnt down, a claim that appears to be backed up by Cassius Dio, but many books were stored in harbour warehouses.[50] Caesar's additional comment, 'for Alexandria is in a manner secure from fire, because the houses are all built without joists or wood, and are all vaulted, and roofed with tile or pavement', has the hallmark of a guilt-ridden defence when considering that Lucan's *On the Civil War* claimed that fire 'ran over the roofs like meteors through the sky'.[51] That lingering sense of culpability might be why Caesar entrusted Varro with the establishment of a new library in Rome in 47 BC,[52] though the proscriptions of Mark Antony were to soon deprive Varro of his books.[53]

But was the Alexandrian commentary truly Caesar's own? For the authorship of *The Alexandrine War* is heavily disputed; Suetonius, writing less than two centuries after the dictator's death, told us no one knew who wrote up Caesar's memoirs of the Spanish, African or Egyptian campaigns. The contenders are his legate, Aulus Hirtius (*ca.* 90–43 BC), or perhaps his friend, Gaius Oppius, and no doubt both would have written under Caesar's direction. The quality of its construction was praised, especially by Hirtius, but that might have been a discreet vote of self-confidence.[54]

But time has taken its toll on the great dictator's legacy: in all copies of Suetonius' *Lives of the Twelve Caesars*, the beginning of the *Life of Julius* is lost. This, along with colophons, excerpts and cataloguing data, enables us to assume that all these copies go back to a lost *Codex Fuldensis* (which formed part of a library at Fulda in *ca.* AD 844), a singular draft stemming from an earlier lost archetype.[55] Suetonius had himself questioned the authenticity of speeches later attributed to Julius Caesar.[56]

Historians are at odds over the scale of the Library at Alexandria and even argue its origins, for there is no actual report of its founding. Aulus Gellius and Ammianus Marcellinus reported that at its height it contained 700,000 'books', whereas Seneca the Younger claimed 400,000 perished in the fire Caesar started, with other sources divided on the total number housed.[57] The Seneca manuscript from Monte Cassino actually mentions 40,000, though this is an example of a 'composite scroll' that contained multiple works and so the numbers may be corrupted. A further 42,800 books are said to have been stored in a separate library (the Serapeiana) in the Temple of Serapis. What is clear is that Callimachus' *Pinakes*, in 120 volumes, could not have credibly systematically listed the larger numbers of works cited, and many papyri must have been so-called 'mixed rolls' that contained several works.[58] As a postscript to the library's fate, Athenaeus mourned: 'and concerning the number of books and the establishment of libraries and the collection in the Hall of the Muses, why need I even speak when they are all in men's memory?'[59]

We cannot forget that Rome burned the library at Carthage, which had housed a reported 500,000 volumes. It would have been a fascinating collection of Punic and barbarian works and their opposing views. Scipio Aemilianus, who later earned the agnomen 'Africanus the Younger', was there to oversee its final destruction in 146 BC. He is said to have shed a tear for the fate decreed by the Roman Senate while quoting Homer's *Iliad* to Polybius, the historian standing beside him: 'A day shall come when sacred Troy shall perish and King Priam and his warriors with him.'[60] Scipio apparently foresaw the collapse of Rome itself.

Modern wars have, of course, added to the loss of books. The parental tenth-century *Metz Epitome* manuscript (*Codex Mettensis* 500 D), which detailed Alexander's campaign on the Upper Satrapies, was destroyed in an Allied bombing raid in 1944, so we now rely on two editions from 1886 and 1900.[61]

Common Greek and Vulgar Latin

While the written book format was changing in response to supply and demand, and to the price of raw materials, language was also evolving, which played its part in the destiny of books.

The Hellenic root languages were under scrutiny in the earliest scriptoriums, as they were themselves shifting and occasionally clashing head-on. Zenodotus, the first head of the Alexandrian Library (*ca.* 280s BC), inherited materials in archaic Attic script and had to transliterate them into the new Ionian alphabet adopted by Athens in 403 BC. Archaic Greek texts were often written boustrophedonically (the direction and orientation of letters was reversed on alternate lines; imagine an ox ploughing a field back and forth), which inevitably slowed the process, as presumably would have acrostics, which would be senseless after translation.[62] Orthographic decisions (on the conventions of writing a language) were complicated by three 'E' and three 'O' sounds that were not distinguished in the original alphabet.

The victory songs of Pindar, written between 498 and 446 BC, suffered from this dilemma, and Zenodotus' imperfect understanding of the poet's rhythms ('a torrent rushing down rain-swollen from the mountains', thought Horace) violated the metrical scheme, chopping up his stanzas into irregular lines. Callimachus was confronted with the violations when he was later arranging the poems, and the results were further 'disorganized' by Aristophanes of Byzantium (*ca*. 257–180 BC), the head librarian from *ca*. 194 BC.[63]

Zenodotus did, however, provide some standardization to the Homeric epics in the reign of Ptolemy II Philadelphus, while Apollonius of Rhodes, the librarian's successor, supplied further organizational commentaries so that some order finally fell upon the heroes of Troy.[64] He restricted Homer to the *Iliad* and *Odyssey* alone, though some 'Homerists' still believe the *Odyssey* is a product of a number of authors who gave it its final shape.[65]

Homer's *Iliad* contained Bronze-Age words in Mycenaean dialect that had been preserved from the earliest oral tradition against a later Ionic linguistic background;[66] the antiquity of the battles being fought is apparent in that spears and arrowheads are being spoken of in bronze rather than iron.[67] Moreover, in Homer's day, the Phoenician alphabet – initially termed *phoinikia grammata* by the Greeks – was starting to fill the void left when Mycenaean Linear B ended centuries before. How, then, were the epic Homeric tales to bridge the Greek Dark Age (broadly 1200–750 BC) if not through oral recitation?[68]

The Hellenistic grammarian, Dionysius Thrax ('Thrax' – of Thracian descent, *ca*. 170–90 BC), produced a work titled *Art of Grammar* in a further attempt at rationalization. He was a pupil of Aristarchus of Samothrace, another librarian working under the Ptolemies, whose harsh literary criticism gave rise to the term 'aristarch' to describe a severely judgmental commentator. True to Alexandrian tradition, his grammatical work appears syncretic (later layers of text added or interpolated), and it is doubtful that the technical content we have represents Thrax's original.[69]

The focus of Thrax's treatise was to finally facilitate the translation, with some systematic order, of Attic Greek (which became known as 'Alexandrian Greek') into Hellenistic *koine* ('common') Greek, which was still a spoken dialect only; yet it was too late to salvage the earlier works that had undergone operations at the hands of lesser surgeons. Soon, from the first century AD, Egyptian itself (though hieroglyphics before) was being written in Coptic script, an adaptation of the Greek alphabet that included signs from the demotic script to accommodate Egyptian sounds not represented in Greek, though its use in literature was principally confined to the output of priests.

Thrax, who in turn encouraged the learning of classical Greek, went on to teach rhetoric in Rhodes and Rome, perhaps in the process even inspiring a young Apollonius Molon, the orator employed by Caesar and Cicero to improve their method. The adoption of *koine* into literature would later prompt Phyrnichus Arabius, a second-century AD Bithynian rhetorician, to compile a Greek lexicon of solecisms or grammatical deviations from the Old Attic standard that had taken place over the previous 600 years.[70]

In Alexander's day, the eyewitness historians had a further translation challenge. Much of what they heard or extracted en route in Asia came from the myriad of races absorbed by the Persian Empire; it was a linguistic rainbow, even though the administration of the Great Kings was conducted most widely in Aramaic and Parsi (and formerly in Old Persian).[71] Strabo preserved Onesicritus' meetings with the Indian gymnosophists, commenting that they translated their respective philosophical ideas through interpreters who 'knew no more than the rabble'. Consequently, expecting clarity on doctrines was 'like expecting clean water to flow through mud'. As one scholar pointed out, the Macedones most likely arrived at their Indian translations through Bactrian or Sogdian interpreters, from which point a second polyglot would have turned this into Persian, with a third then rendering it into Greek.[72] The opportunity for misunderstanding and oversimplifying, or perhaps 'Hellenizing' an alien concept, precept or word, was thus ever present.

In Rome, Latin was evolving too. Polybius remarked that he had difficulty in translating an account of the first official treaty between Rome and Carthage, which dated back to some twenty-eight years before Xerxes invaded Greece (thus *ca.* 508 BC):

> I give below as accurate a translation as I can of this treaty, but the modern language has developed so many differences from the ancient Roman tongue that the best scholars among the Romans themselves have great difficulty in interpreting certain points, even after much study.[73]

In the late Roman Republic, the literati were conscious of the progression in Greek and Latin prose style and aware of the resulting translation challenges. The first translation we know of from Greek to Latin was of the *Odyssey* by the aforementioned Livius Andronicus, and this was only a 'partly successful' attempt.[74] Cicero, who had already created something of a philosophical vocabulary when coining the terms *humanitas*, *qualitas* and *essentia* as he introduced Rome to concepts he had learned in Greece under Philo of Larissa and Poseidonius the prominent Stoic, took a practical line on textual transmission. He advocated a 'sense for sense' approach over a 'word for word' translation of Greek into Latin, considering that this better preserved the intent of the original author. His methodology placed an emphasis on what we would term today 'communication equivalence'.

Roman poet Horace, on the other hand, gave priority to methods that created 'impact' on the target language; thus a dynamic re-rendering of a text became the norm and literal fidelity suffered as a result, that is, if what we read is genuine.[75] Suetonius was dubious; in his *Life of Horace*, he explained: 'There have come into my possession some elegies attributed to his pen and a letter in prose, supposed to be a recommendation of himself to Maecenas [imperial friend and patron of the arts], but I think that both are spurious.'[76] The fine line between tight transmission and a total rewrite was often tested when translators wished their labour to acquire a literary status of its own. This explains the widening gap between the grammatical structure of the 'linguistic arts' – poetry, history, oratory and rhetorical pursuits – and the language of the business, diplomatic and legal worlds where there was no latitude for literary licence. That gap remains markedly visible today.

As the Alexandrian scholars had noted two millennia before, the expansion of the Graeco–Macedonian and Roman Empires homogenized linguistic identity, though at the expense of classical linguistic purity, which is agreed by modern philological studies interrogating the sources. The classical Latin once spoken by the 'good' and noble families, the *sermo familiaris* ('speech of good families') and *sermo nobilis* ('noble speech'), disintegrated to Vulgar Latin and then into the early Romance languages as the Roman Empire expanded and fragmented. As with Hellenistic *koine* Greek, *sermo vulgaris* was first spoken by soldiers, dispossessed townsfolk and slaves across the empire, resulting in marked differences between the spoken and written forms. Letters took on new sounds through palatalization, a process that produced the phonetic splits we read and hear in the romance languages of today. The loss of nasal inflection resulted in the dissimilation of voiceless consonants, and thus Platon became Plato.

The Greek 'K', which had become a 'C' in Latin though still pronounced as *kappa*, graduated to a soft 'S' before the vowels 'I' and 'E'. Cicero, originally pronounced 'Kikero' (we believe), and Caesar, pronounced 'Kaisar', took on the pronunciations we are more familiar with in English. In Hellenistic Greece, 'Y' and 'OI' were often written as a 'U', and later the distinction in vowel length was lost as part of a wider monopthongization (when diphthongs become monophthongs). Double consonants were reduced to single and aspirated voiceless stops were changed to fricatives by the fourth century AD. By the Byzantine period, sounds and their corresponding letters were further simplified, when, for example, 'H' and 'EI' became 'I'. These processes played their part in textual infidelity as new translations were made.

The early Latin-from-Greek manuscripts, perhaps already incorporating corruptions from these linguistic challenges, went through further transmission processes as Western scripts developed. The latitude for confusion widened still further when Latin texts were translated into 'modern' languages that were not rooted in Latin (the Germanic branch, for example). When use of the capital and uncial scripts of the fourth and fifth centuries came to an end with what Petrarch (1304–1374) termed another 'Dark Age', Christian copying of pagan literature halted for almost three centuries, so few manuscripts of this period survived. The so-called Carolingian Renaissance (late eighth to ninth century) saw a resurgence, when monks once more started copying the oldest texts available to them into

Carolingian miniscule. This lower-case script, developed under the patronage of Charlemagne (never fully literate himself), had the advantage of spaces and punctuation, so liberating Latin from the confusing continuous flow of capitals in uncial texts.

Besides scriptorium transmission errors, further loss of chronological precision resulted from the fluidity of the calendar year (in Greece especially), the loss of intercalary months (inserted to realign calendars with moon phases) and the awkward synchronization of archon years with consul elections; all troublesome detail for copyists trying to make sense of the order of events.[77] Additional slippage arose from the word-denoted and numeral-based counting systems of Greece and Rome, which lacked the numeric dexterity to efficiently deal with large numbers, fractions and percentages. As a result, these were awkwardly presented as long sequences of letters and acrophonies, which must partly explain the disparity in the treasury figures and troop and casualty numbers we encounter in the battles of Alexander and his successors.

The 'plus', 'minus' and 'equals' symbols were still a millennium-and-a-half away, and the concept of 'zero' as a placeholder still eluded mathematicians. It was not until *ca*. AD 250 (an uncertain and debated date) in Alexandria that Diophantus, 'the father of algebra', in his *Arithmetica* gave us an abbreviation for (and for powers of) the unknowns and a shorter means of expressing equations. But the use of true numbers in maths with succinct algebraic notation and symbolism – instead of long sentences of letters and words that Diophantus still employed – made its way west later (in the eighth and ninth centuries AD as a refinement of the Hindu–Arabic system), and only then did it establish a useful and easily transmitted system to deal with and reproduce complex numbers.

Alongside the problems presented by complex numbers, an ignorance of how to separate continuous script led to nominative cases being confused with genitive and dative cases, and singulars with plurals, especially where the letters 'a' and 'e' and diphthongs were concerned.[78] Add to this the mistaking of proper names with verbs, plus the faulty extraction of numbers from uncial text, and we have some idea of the task facing scribes. Mistakes may have been innocent and well-intended, but 'they were rich in the germs of future corruptions'.[79]

Paper was first imported into Europe around the tenth century and was manufactured in the West from the twelfth century onwards, with watermarks soon following. Until the development of the printing press and oil-based inks, which led to the production of the 'first editions' to exist outside of handwritten codices *manu scripti* – which gave us our term 'manuscript' – all written pieces of historical evidence, whether a voluminous 'library of world history' or a short pamphlet of anecdotes, 'were exposed to all the chances and imperfections which attend the scribe and pen'.[80] New Latin transcriptions made during the eleventh, twelfth and thirteenth centuries attempted to restore some sense and order to already corrupted passages, but this, more often than not, further damaged the original prose.

Renaissance Dilemmas

After a millennium of neglect, it was during the Renaissance that what *did* survive from the classical world and texts on Alexander was extracted once more from moth-eaten scrolls and decrepitated manuscripts that had been hidden in 'leaky rat-ridden monastery attics'. But the scholars of the day faced a huge challenge with these time-ravaged books which, according to the collector Poggio Bracciolini (1380–1459), were 'looking up at him for help' like 'friends in a hospital or a prison'. Following in Bracciolini's footsteps, Erasmus (1466–1536), a Dutch theologian, manuscript collector and so-called 'prince of the humanists', was so irked by the manuscript work of 'clumsy translators' that he mastered 'pure' Latin, a skill he employed to unify the parallel Greek and Latin traditions of the *New Testament* which was dedicated to Pope Leo X and 'rushed' into print in 1516. The new edition stabilized (Erasmus said 'purified') the Greek, Byzantine and Vulgate biblical texts in the same way the Alexandrian librarians had fifteen centuries ago anchored down the fluid Homeric epics and other erratic texts in circulation in the Hellenistic world.[81] Through his correspondence with numerous influential scholars of his day, Erasmus had seen first-hand the damage being done to ancient manuscripts at the scriptoriums across Europe.

A pertinent example of what he found involves a comparison of two manuscripts containing Livy's *History of Rome* – the fifth-century *Codex Puteanus* and the ninth-century copy known as the *Codex Reginensis 762* – and illustrates further scriptorium challenges.[82] The *Reginensis* transcription was undertaken by eight separate scribes, each given a different section to work on. We even know the copyists' names, as their signatures appear at the end of each quaternion, the manuscript unit of four double leaves. They were also of more than one nationality, as evidenced by the repeated nature of the blunders they make and their non-identical ink types. Earlier divergent processes had already been at work on Livy; all manuscripts of the first ten books stem from the single recension commissioned by Quintus Aurelius Symmachus, a Roman consul, in AD 391. Moreover, the emendation of the editor would have produced this version by selecting what was considered the best of the then extant earlier editions. Epigraphists have detected the hands, once again, of a number of scribes in the recensions that followed, one branch of which is known as the *Nichomachean* after the named scribes.[83]

Fortunately, it is possible to determine if early book sections have been pieced together by different copyists and whether pages have been lost by studying the parchment on consecutive sheets, as the hair side of the skin is distinct from the flesh side and the double folding of the quaternion ought to produce matching textures. In the nineteenth century, a German scholar employed the techniques of codicology to highlight such discrepancies when describing the *Codex Sinaiticus*, believing that four separate scribes worked on the manuscript, with five 'correctors' amending the text at different times.[84] Recent palaeographical studies of the codex do indeed confirm numerous scribes were employed.

The multiple-copyist methodology was, nevertheless, typical pre-Renaissance when a work encapsulating centuries of history had been either originally released by the author in 'packets' (as in the case of Livy's volumes, see chapter 4) or packeted in later editions, when they were often separated into decade or pentad divisions that might be a wholly contrived new arrangement. Understandably, Livy's 142 books were a challenge to read through without some kind of break; moreover, he had drifted into loquaciousness and repetitions, which Horace declared 'are not well received'.[85] As one classicist supposed, 'the declining quality of Livy's later books was the cause of their loss; they were considered less worthy of copying'.[86] The result is that only thirty-five books remain in reasonably complete form.

Supervisors or 'correctors' had been on hand in the scriptorium to immediately edit the quaternions as they were completed, but this was an ink-upon-ink process and the inevitable dittographies, haplographies and parablepses, the scribal errors of repetition and omission, crept in.[87] If the corruptions manifested themselves in clear conflicts between what should have been identical manuscripts, we are at least alerted, but when multiple texts are divided, we are on softer ground. For example, in Plutarch's *Life of Demosthenes*, the anti-Macedonian orator and statesman, we cannot be sure if it is Theopompus or Theophrastus who refused to incriminate him, as various manuscripts cite both.[88] One scholar tackling the dilemma suggested a 'meddlesome' scribe made the error; he is no doubt correct, but which name should we amend?[89] Oratorical imitation was part of the classical education syllabus, so the orators were vulnerable to having the speeches debased. We have six surviving letters supposedly written by Demosthenes; new analyses of an old debate suggest four are genuine and two are fakes, while roughly one-third of his extant speeches appear to be less than genuine too.[90]

So manuscript corruptions were, more often than not, due to the simple blind incompetency and lawlessness of ill-trained scribes. Erasmus' linguistic skills highlighted many, and he pertinently coined the adage 'in the land of the blind, the one-eyed man is king'.[91] But it was Petrarch, born in exile at the close of the High Middle Ages (or High Medieval Period, *ca.* 1000–1300), who was 'the first man since antiquity to make a systematic collection of Latin classical manuscripts'. In his attempt 'not to fashion fables but to retell history', he opened the pages of antiquity once more as his fascination took hold, though in the case of Alexander, Petrarch thought he died in Babylon 'effeminate' and 'transformed into some kind of monster'.[92] Although the knowledge of Latin had improved, with much of its purity preserved by the Church, scholars' dexterity with classical Greek lagged far behind; there was once a time when the *Bible* was *only* available in Greek, but at the beginning of the Renaissance, almost no Greek versions existed.[93]

As the works that had not been translated into Latin were in less demand in the Middle Ages, the Greek texts of Homer, Herodotus and Thucydides were largely bypassed until Petrarch was able to acquire a 'very wooden' Latin translation of a genuine Homer manuscript from Constantinople in the 1360s. Remarkably, the West had been blind to original Homer for almost 1,000 years.[94] The case for the resuscitation of Herodotus was further challenged by the criticism heaped upon him in the texts that had been translated. As a result, it is estimated that there are just eight surviving manuscripts of Herodotus' *Histories*, while the extant manuscripts of Thucydides only date to some 1,300 years after his original.

It was not until 1448–1452 that Laurentius Valla (1406–1457) produced a Latin edition of both the 'awe-inspiring' Thucydides and the 'radiant' Herodotus (1452–1457), who was finally exhumed from his classical slashing with Stephanus' *Apology to Herodotus* published in 1566. It was not an easy task, as Valla explained in his preface dedicated to Pope Nicholas V:

> as everybody admits, Thucydides is steep and rocky, especially in the speeches, in which his books abound. This is clear from what Cicero, whom men of his time called 'the Greek', says in his *de Oratore*: Those speeches have many over-subtle thoughts that can scarcely be understood.

Valla added: 'There you see, highest Pope, what Thucydides is like in Greek, and if you decide that in my translation he keeps this same dignity, I shall be oblivious of my labour.'

Petrarch admitted that similar linguistic shortcomings with Greek had hampered his own translation efforts, lamenting of a rare Homer manuscript that had been presented to him: 'Alas! Either Homer is dumb or I am deaf, nor is it within my power to enjoy the beauty I possess.'[95] Although Petrarch's attempt to learn more than the rudiments of Greek from a Calabrian monk came too late in his own life to be completely successful, his younger friend, Giovanni Boccaccio (1313–1375), did master the classical language before his reconversion to Church doctrine, and he saw to it that one Leontios Pilatos (died 1366) became the first professor of the neglected tongue in Western Europe by 1360, though this too inclined to Byzantine Greek.[96]

A new generation of 'Graeco–Romans' was being born, despite the diversion of wars, Crusades and the Black Death of 1348, which indiscriminately took scholar and pauper with it. In the re-educational process, the European languages were enriched with Greek and Latin loan words and attached phraseology, because the 'poorer' vernacular languages had previously evolved around purely practical, though rarely intellectual, vocabulary. This, in turn, broadened the translator's style as the new literary devices and linguistic structures entered the target language through 'positive paganism' at last.[97] English was to benefit through the well-travelled Chaucer (*ca*. 1343–1400) and his translations.

The *Bible* went through similar transmutations into English once the outcome of the Reformation finally permitted publication of Greek gospels and Latin sermons into the modern languages. The Renaissance additionally saw a 'humanist' enlightenment that returned the individual to the centre stage as Hellenistic philosophies came under scrutiny with their templates of personal virtue and vice. Erasmus inspired fellow Dutchman Jeroen de Busleyden to found the Collegium Trilingue to promote the teaching of Greek, Latin and Hebrew to better arm scholars resuscitating ancient texts. This was not for purely esoteric purposes; as one historian put it, men emerging from the 'ruins of a feudal system' were anxious to get 'all the advice they could' when searching for new 'political and military machinery' from the classical thinkers.[98] Enlightened Europeans knew they needed the lessons from the past to plot the path of a learned future.

But scholarship was still weighted down by the religious intolerances of the Holy Roman Empire and the threat of Ottoman invasion, so religious works dominated the scriptoriums located at abbeys and monasteries at the expense of the 'heathen' classics that preceded Christianity. Original Greek and Christian texts were ferried westwards as Byzantium (Constantinople) threatened to fall, and then were chaperoned to safety by private collectors such as Cosimo de' Medici (1389–1464), Erasmus, Bracciolini and Boccaccio, who burst into tears at seeing the state of the library at Monte Cassino.[99] The likes of Valla and Niccolò Machiavelli (1469–1527), nevertheless, revived a wider philosophical curiosity that was inspired by these classical manuscripts, and finally universities and new libraries emerged, including the Vatican Library founded by Pope Nicholas V (reigned 1447–1455), whose eight years in office saw 5,000 volumes emerge from the hands of copyists and scholars.[100]

Diodorus' *Library of History* survived intact in the imperial palace in Constantinople until the early Renaissance. The 1453 sack of the city by the Ottomans has left us with just fifteen relatively intact books. Fifty-nine medieval manuscripts remain, and they variously contain books 1–5 and 11–20. Of the former, four 'prototypes' can be identified of the twenty-eight remaining manuscripts (containing books 1–5), but they are all corrupted to some degree.

The task of stocking a library anew was soon revolutionized with the arrival of codices *impressi*, the printed books that emerged in 1439 with Gutenberg's mechanical press and which immediately reduced the room for future transmission errors. Until 1500 (so convention has it), the *incunabula*, the books printed using wood blocks or moveable metal typographic sets, were laid out to replicate the manuscript format, complete with the diverse typefaces, abbreviated sentences, columns, margin notes and rubrications (red ink emphases); with them were reproduced the decorative and much-enlarged chapter-opening letters.[101] Although a print-press defect was an error immortalized in every future run, manuscripts were at least now 'crystallized' and could not decrepitate further. Mark Twain later weighed up the merits of the device that lay behind the literary reinvigoration of the Renaissance:

> What the world is today, good and bad, it owes to Gutenberg. Everything can be traced to this source, but we are bound to bring him homage … for the bad that his colossal invention has brought about is overshadowed a thousand times by the good with which mankind has been favoured.[102]

The momentum behind Renaissance 'enlightenment' had led to a rising demand for previously neglected manuscripts from the classical past, and ironically this led to the start of a new industry in politically opportune and profitable forgeries. Pope Leo X was paying handsomely for new Greek and Latin texts, and Maffeo Vegio (1407–1458) wrote a thirteenth book to the *Aeneid* at the tender age of 21, unsatisfied as he was with the original conclusion of Virgil. Bishop Gavin Douglas used Vegio's homespun edition when first translating the *Aeneid* to Scots in 1553, and he was followed by Thomas Twyne and his English edition published in 1584. In 1583, another unsatisfied scholar, Carlo Sigonio, declared he had discovered a complete copy of Cicero's *On Grief*; when challenged on its authenticity, he indignantly replied that if not genuine, it was at least *worthy* of Cicero.

The authenticity of Tacitus' *Annals* was soon called into question and Poggio Bracciolini was accused of being their fabricator. It was Bracciolini 'who rose to high posts in public affairs and won imperishable fame in letters' after he had fortuitously stumbled upon a genuine hoard of lost Latin texts some fifty years before, including (amongst others) the masterpieces of Cicero, Quintilian and Vitruvius, the Roman civil engineer.[103] Debate on whether we have the fully genuine article for Tacitus' books 1–6 and 11–16 still has an audience, though one scholar in an 1878 treatise on the matter was in no doubt:

> I give a detailed history of the forgery, from its conception to its completion, the sum that was paid for it, the abbey where it was transcribed, and other such convincing minutiae taken from a correspondence that Poggio carried on with a familiar friend who resided in Florence.

He went on to explain why not all agreed with his conclusion: 'The cause is obvious: the forger fabricated with the decided determination of defying detection.'[104] Bracciolini was not against using bribery to obtain the manuscripts he wanted or attacking his contemporaries with compositions that led to a decade of invectives with contemporary scholars. Whether the accusations are founded or not we may never know, but his sale of a Livy manuscript in 1434 enabled him to build a villa and adorn it with fine antiques.

Forgery and Historiography Intertwined

This brings us to the career of Johannes Annius of Viterbo (*ca.* 1432–1502), one of the 'great crop of forgers bred of the dark earth'. Although Annius' story is far removed from the death of Alexander, it remains potently pertinent too,[105] for his is a tale of contemporaneous historical forgery and creative historiographical method rolled into one. It raises the obvious question: has the history of Alexander survived with any more or less integrity? Documentary fakes and political frauds have changed the course of history, and many, we must speculate, remain undetected. Furthermore, these historical traditions now have inertias that make them difficult to reconsider any other way, and so they remain unchallenged. Given a following wind and with less-talented philologists in circulation, Annius may well have become a hero of Italian Renaissance historiography, and for a while he was. Instead, the man who claimed to read Etruscan is remembered today as a fraud.[106]

Annius was a Dominican preaching monk as well as an archaeologist and meddler in antiquity, who held an apocalyptic view of the struggle between Christianity, Islam and Judaism. He perceived the worlds of Europe and Asia as historically irreconcilable and as culturally opposed as Alexander had once found them some 2,000 years before him, though some scholars romantically maintain that Alexander was attempting to change just that as the first 'citizen of the world'. In the late 1490s, Annius faked a number of Etruscan inscriptions, giving 'pseudoarchaeology' a new birth, and his *magnum opus* was an anthology of seventeen classical manuscripts he claimed to have 'unearthed' at Mantua.

Annius was probably inspired by Poggio Bracciolini, so another hoard of new 'finds', all written by Annius himself, were published as *Commentaries on the Works of Various Authors Discussing Antiquity*. His attendant explanation notes, which first saw light in Rome in 1498, lent a fine verisimilitude to the whole affair, and the collection soon became famous as the *Antiquities of Annius*, which had Europe talking for a century or more.[107]

Annius' elaborate fabrications, which supposedly stemmed from ancient narratives leading back to the biblical Creation, were falsely attributed to Berossus, the Chaldean priest of Babylonian Bel-Marduk a generation after Alexander, to a Persian named Metasthenes and the Egyptian priest Manetho (third century BC), alongside fragments from Xenophon and Cato the Elder; in other words, writers whose influential accounts shaped our knowledge of the classical world. Along the way, Annius placed his home town of Viterbo on the site of Fanum Vultumnae, and thus as the capital of the Etruscan Golden Age.

For good measure, Annius proposed the Roman emperor Augustus had founded Florence, thereby enhancing the state ideology of the Medici.[108] This was a civic elevation synonymous with earlier classical claims by the Greek historian, Ephorus, who proposed that Cyme, his home city in Aeolis (modern Nemrut in Turkey), was the birthplace of Homer and Hesiod.[109] Although he was eventually exposed, Annius' deceits were initially influential and he dedicated them to Ferdinand V and Isabella of Spain with a bold preface assuring the reader that as a theologian he had a particular duty to respect the truth; it was a 'denunciation of mendacity' that gave his 'discoveries' an 'air of moral as well as factual superiority'.[110]

In the fraudulent process, Annius' work paradoxically gave us the valuable concept of primary, secondary and tertiary sources, the foundation of the methodology that distinguishes 'eyewitnesses' from those who drew from their testimonia, while relegating to 'tertiary' the writers even further removed from events. As has been pointed out, though devoted entirely to fakes, his categorization is the earliest extant Renaissance epigraphic treatise.[111] Annius' emphasis on chronology and inscriptions, and his rules of historical evidence alongside his linguistic theories, were all adopted in some form in later historiographical methods, the disciplines that ironically sealed his own fate.

Contemporary with Annius was Abbot Johannes Trithemius, a theologian, moralist and antiquarian born in 1462. Trithemius concocted a history of the Franks from the fall of Troy up to King Clovis (*ca.* AD 466–511), who first united them, claiming ancient Frankish manuscripts as his unimpeachable source. He managed to 'trace' the Habsburg House back to Noah, enabling Emperor Maximilian I, with whom he was on good terms, to follow his illustrious line back to Theodoric and King Arthur.[112] As Trithemius noted, 'everyone was trying to find himself a Trojan ancestor', as Alexander himself had.[113]

But philologists like Erasmus were hot on the heels of duplicity. He set a tone of enlightenment when exposing the apocryphal correspondence known as the *Epistles of St Paul*;[114] it was long overdue according to one modern scholar, who noted that the letters between the apostle and Seneca were written in atrocious Latin when perhaps more convincingly Greek would have been used (most educated Romans had mastered Greek)![115] But there is an irony in implicating Seneca in the correspondence, for the stoic philosopher had stated of historians in general: 'Some are deluded, some delighted, by falsehood ... the whole clan of them have this in common; they fancy their work cannot merit approval and become popular unless they freely interlard it with lies.'[116]

Annius' fall from grace finally came in the form of Johannes Goropius Becanus (1519–1572) and Joseph Scaliger (1540–1609), who brought their deep knowledge of classical Greek and Latin to bear on his *Antiquities*. Their philological autopsies were capitalizing on developments in Renaissance historiography and laying the foundations of modern source analysis.[117] But these developing historiographical processes did not kill the industry of falsification; they simply sharpened the wits of future pretenders peddling their wares. As more deceptions and fakes fell out of the closet, some occasionally fell in. Laurentius Valla had already exposed the *Donation of Constantine*, a forged decree that placed a good deal of the Western Roman Empire under the authority of the Pope.[118] The 'donation' enjoyed a long legacy: it helped legitimize the 'returning' of lands by the Frankish king, Pepin the Short, to papal control in AD 756 and was not acknowledged by the Church as spurious until 1440. It nevertheless took the Catholic fathers almost 500 years to 're-donate' the Papal States back to Italy in 1929, the year the Lateran Accords recognized the Vatican as an independent state.

Scaliger, the son of an Italian scholar portentously christened Julius Caesar, was the first person to scientifically identify Indo-European linguistic groupings. He is remembered for his appreciation that classical historiography should include the Persian, Babylonian, Jewish and Ancient Egyptian records, beside the Greek and Roman accounts that dominated Western interpretations of the classical age.[119]

Somewhat inevitably, the 'barbarian' finds of Annius – those credited to Berossus, Metasthenes and Manetho, for example – eventually came under scrutiny. These 'rediscovered' historians were broadly contemporary with Alexander, if we accept that Megasthenes the Greek travelographer, rather than the otherwise unattested 'Metasthenes', was Annius' intended reincarnation. Perhaps this was a correction supposed to reinforce his pedantic philological zeal, for 'to throw together the real and the fictitious is an old device of verisimilitude and deceit', and it may explain Annius' own contention: 'Authors can both deceive and be deceived but an imposed name cannot.'[120]

Aristotle's *On the Universe*, once thought to be a dedication to Alexander, fell apart under the Renaissance scrutiny of Daniel Heinsius (1580–1655), Scaliger's gifted pupil, and Isaac Casaubon, a regular correspondent with the by-now-famous philologist who provided the attendant commentaries.

As for the fate of Annius, he was (it is claimed) finally – and philologists might deem fittingly – poisoned by Cesare Borgia. Cesare's alleged father, Rodrigo Borgia, had already furnished the living quarters in the Vatican with images of the great Macedonian conqueror; indeed, when elected Pope in August 1492, he assumed the name 'Alexander VI'.[121] Annius had placed an importance on onomastics, the derivation of proper names in the historical framework that provided him with his 'irrefutable arguments'.[122] He had etched-on with his own hand many of the Etruscan inscriptions he claimed to have found, and so we may reflectively deem them 'primary fabrications' of pseudoarchaeology. His real name was Giovanni Nanni, though he had adopted a title more reminiscent of the Roman golden age. Like Alexander, he was attempting to fuse his own imagery with another heroic past.

In the Name of the Lord

Annius' own deceits unwittingly set in motion the wheels of historiographical method and provided us with 'an organon for arriving at historical truth'. Although the later proponents of source forensics have done much for historiographic methodology, even if they exhibited bias when doing so,[123] its operators have not, and it was the heavy hand of religious doctrine that played the weightiest role in the loss of what once graced the library shelves.

Much of the polemical noise emerging in the Renaissance was also piously motivated, for the new age of rational analysis still fought a stubborn tradition of faith, so the 'enlightenment' was not seen as a universally popular movement.[124] Even Scaliger felt the backlash of his own autopsies when the Jesuits attacked him for exposing the authenticity of their *New Testament* compilations and their associated chronologies. There commenced a literary battle with his former friend and Church defender, Gasparus Scioppius, who published a retort in which polemics and refutations were hurled back and forth.[125]

In October 1623, Digory Whear dedicated a treatise, which broadly translates from the Latin as *On the Plan and Method for Reading Histories*, to fellow historian William Camden.[126] Summing up the extant accounts, and mentioning Annius' deceits, Whear's 'plan and method' cited Roman antiquarians Varro and Censorinus (third century AD), who proposed three distinct epochs had existed: the Creation to the flood, which they named 'the unclear'; the flood to the first Greek Olympiad, termed 'the mythical'; and the first Olympiad down to the Roman Caesars, which they sensibly proposed was 'the historical'.

Whear saw the first epoch as 'clearer than the noonday sun', citing the first six chapters of 'Genesis' as an impeccable source of these 1,656 years. He next argued away the mythical, suggesting the holy secretaries, Moses and the prophets, had provided a 'sufficiently ample history' of that period. Ironically, Whear then challenged the integrity of the final 'historical' epoch, admitting, however, that it was 'distinguished by exact dates'. He rounded off with: 'All of these are to be read after biblical history, which is the oldest of all, and the truest.'

The damaging trend of précising history had also reared its head again. Jean Bodin's 1566 *Method to Facilitate the Knowledge of History* attempted to provide a method of easy absorption and comprehension in which the epitome was often recommended above the parental work itself. Whear subsequently advised: 'If our reader wishes to remain engaged longer and more capaciously in universal history, [the epitome of] Justin can be read.' The dedication in Bodin's book (surely taken from Justin too) stated that 'one should cull flowers from History to gather there of the sweetest fruits', and so history *was* indeed culled.

Whear would have been mortified to hear that 'arguably the most distinctive feature of early Christian literature is the degree to which it was forged', for 'orthodoxy and its faithful follower, persecution, encouraged literary dishonesty'.[127] This is a contention that explains why publications like Speyer's 300-page *Literary Forgery in Pagan and Christian Antiquity* were needed to keep track of them.[128] Speyer was able to identify twenty-six Greek linguistic terms, with Latin parallels such as *adultere, configure, falsare* and *supponere*, each associated with the act of forgery, suggesting a fraudulent tradition had already proliferated the classical world.[129]

The Christian Church, or rather religion per se, had a legacy of 'pious fraud', a term first used by English historian Edward Gibbon (died 1794; he penned the famed and voluminous *The History of the Decline and Fall of the Roman Empire*), to protect the potency of its proprietary texts and the continued loyalty (and donations) of its congregation. It explains the fervour with which Scioppius defended Catholicism and the zeal with which the Church issued the *List of Prohibited Books*, the papal list of banned works first issued in 1559 under the directorship of Pope Paul IV. From spurious reincarnations of biblical scrolls, the *Sibylline Oracles* and *Gnostic Gospels*, elements of *The Apostolic Constitutions*, the aforementioned epistolary corpus between St Paul and Seneca and the *Decretals of Pseudo-Isidore*, religious falsification spurred a literary genre of erudite pious defence and attack. Much of that corpus took the form of forgery and counter-forgery too.[130] Some stretched back to spurious 'originals' dating to the Hellenistic and Roman periods.

Eusebius, whose lost *Chronicle* (a universal history from Abraham to the reign of Constantine in his day) was diligently reconstructed by Joseph Scaliger, had added to the problem long before. In his *Ecclesiastical History* (*ca*. AD 312), Eusebius had declared: 'We shall introduce to this history, in general, only those events, which may be useful first to ourselves and after to prosperity.'[131] Edward Gibbon attacked Eusebius for proposing that falsifications were a lawful and necessary 'medicine' for historians.[132]

Eusebius claimed that a document had appeared early in the fourth century purporting to be the *Pagan Acts of Pilate*, filled with slanders against the character of Jesus. The author, possibly Theotecnus, a violent persecutor of the Church at Antioch, issued an edict that schoolmasters should have their pupils study and memorize the contents.[133] There were, however, many '*Acts of Pilate*' entering circulation, including those which came to be known as the *Gospel of Nicodemus*, and they were collected by von Tischendorf in his 1853 *Evangelical Apocrypha*. Eusebius, once again setting out to undermine paganism, found use for a regurgitation of the already semi-fictional work named *Phoenician History* by Philo of Byblos (*ca*. AD 64–141); he slanted it with his own evangelical agenda, leaving us wondering whether Philo's source, a certain Sanchuniathon, really existed or not.[134]

In the Hellenistic era, and then later in the twilight years of the Roman Empire, new philosophies were fighting for recognition and old ones for survival; religions too were fighting for the souls of kings, tyrants and emperors.[135] One of the bolder attempts at self-promotion came in the form of the so-called *Letter of Aristeas*, a sophisticated subterfuge explaining the origins behind the translation of the *Pentateuch*, the first five books of the *Septuagint*, the Hebrew *Bible*. It was written in the *koine* ('common') Greek, now the *lingua franca* of the Eastern Mediterranean. Seeking to promote Jewish interests in Alexandria, the letter – supposedly written by a gentile, Aristeas, to his brother, Philocrates – detailed the role of its seventy-two translators (six from each of the twelve tribes of Israel) with their deep philosophical knowledge.

Central to the *Letter of Aristeas* is an ingenious documentary dialogue between Demetrius of Phalerum and Ptolemy II Philadelphus in the Successor War years, in which the former sought to acquire Jewish texts for the Alexandrian Library in an attempt to elevate their significance.[136] Demetrius allegedly advised his king: 'It is important that these books, duly corrected, should find a place in your library, because this legislation, in as much as it is divine, is of philosophical importance and of innate integrity.'[137] Over twenty manuscripts of the letters survived, the first mentioned in Josephus' *Jewish Antiquities*, and though it has now been convincingly exposed (after 1522), the *Letter of Aristeas* remains the oldest surviving document attesting to the existence of the great Alexandrian Library within the museum founded by the Ptolemies.[138]

So, for a host of reasons, manuscripts were, as Digory Whear observed in 1623, 'interpolated by the hands of smatterers, and most basely handled'.[139] Petrarch bemoaned: 'What would Cicero, or Livy, or the other great men of the past, Pliny above all, think if they could return to life and read their own works?'[140] Here, Petrarch was referring to the sad condition of the 'treasure house' of Pliny's *Natural History* that he had purchased in Mantua in 1350; some seven intact manuscripts survived, though none of them are earlier than AD 850 (older examples were either incomplete or survived as palimpsests). For all his efforts in educating scholars to collect ancient texts with reverence, when Petrarch died, as his will made no reference to his library of manuscripts, the collection was subsequently seized by the Lords of Padua and scattered across Europe.[141]

What the copyists in churches and monasteries of Late Antiquity and the Middle Ages did give us in return for their intolerance were the bold and striking illuminations, the manuscript decorations in gold (gilding), silver and vibrant inks. These were ubiquitous in the Gothic period (principally the thirteenth and fourteenth centuries), but they had been produced from the fall of the Roman Empire through to the Renaissance. The border artistry often cramped texts, the two battling for territory on the pages, until a more disciplined approach placed the texts first and adornment only where gaps permitted. Rubricators who fashioned chapter headings and paragraph openings, usually in red ink, added further textual impact, and so an ornate and expensively illuminated book was inevitably treated with more reverence than a plainly bound sibling. As demand increased in the

Renaissance, professional illuminators and freelance painters finally created the first early Italian 'mass' production lines.

Despite a book's immediate impact, or the quality of the illuminations and the contemporary influence of their author, it still needed a well-connected admirer to be preserved, copied and ultimately printed. Plato had Augustine of Hippo, but others were not so fortunate. Another example of the waxing and waning of literary favour is Pliny's massive *Natural History*, one of the very first printed works. It was published fifteen times between the initial 'distinctly imperfect' translation of 1469 and 1500, when it was clearly in vogue in the inquiring spirit of the Renaissance.[142] In contrast, the twentieth century saw less than half that number of new editions.[143] As for Pausanias' *Guide to Greece*, there is no evidence it was read widely in classical times at all, possibly because its 'antiquarian sentiment' highlighted how far Greece had fallen from its glory.[144] A single reference to the work comes from the sixth century AD and several others from the Middle Ages; one single manuscript seems to have survived in the hands of Niccolo Niccoli (1364–1437) in 1418, and it was lost again by 1500. Three further copies survived, but they are full of lacunae and errors, each loosely dated to the fifteenth century. It was not until Heinrich Schliemann was guided to the royal tombs at Mycenae by Pausanias' descriptions that classicists began to consider the work reliable. Finally, after some 1,600 years and with his credibility reinstated, its publication widened.[145]

The Art of the Linguistic Sacrifice

Commercial publication pressures eventually demanded that translations from Greek and Latin into vernacular languages were more readily available. If Aristotle had captured something of the essence of modern grammatical theory in his *On Interpretation*, neither he, nor Cicero and Horace – who had been conscious of their methodology when undertaking translations – could have anticipated the shifting linguistic sands that would give rise to an industry of translation controversy. As the celebrated translator and Poet Laureate, John Dryden, eloquently put it:

> the Words; when they appear (which is but seldom) literally graceful, it were an injury to the Author that they should be chang'd: But since every Language is so full of its own properties, that what is Beautiful in one, is often Barbarous, nay sometimes Nonsense, in another, it would be unreasonable to limit a Translator to the narrow compass of his Author's Words: 'tis enough if he chuse out some Expression which does not vitiate the Sense.[146]

Dryden penned an illuminating preface to Ovid's *Epistles* in 1680. In it he 'reduced all translation to three heads': metaphrasing (word by word), paraphrasing (translation with 'latitude') and imitation ('the liberty to forsake' both 'words and sense'), a necessary means with which Dryden planned to tackle Latin texts: 'Tis almost impossible to Translate verbally, and well, at the same time; for the Latin (a most Severe and Compendious Language) often expresses that in one word, which either the Barbarity, or the narrowness of modern Tongues cannot supply in more.' Ovid had wound up his *Metamorphoses* with a bold claim about the immortal nature of the work 'that nothing can destroy ... not Jupiter's wrath, nor fire nor sword, nor devouring time'.[147] But Ovid had not factored in the challenges of translation.

Dryden's edition of Virgil (published 1697) and Alexander Pope's Homer (the *Iliad* was published between 1715 and 1720 and the *Odyssey* in 1726) became the authoritative and representative English classical texts of their era. Yet the classical scholar, Richard Bentley, scoffed at Pope's efforts: 'It is a pretty poem Mr Pope, but you must not call it Homer.'[148] Dryden's translation of Virgil too was termed nothing less than 'alchemy'; in the words of Sir Walter Scott, Dryden managed to explain the 'sense ... with the eloquence in his own tongue, though he understands not the nice turns of the original'. In Scott's view, Dryden 'cared not if minute elegancies were lost, or the beauties of accurate proportion destroyed, or a dubious interpretation hastily adopted on the credit of a scholium'.[149] He nevertheless concluded generously:

> many passages that are faulty, many indifferently understood, many imperfectly translated, some in which dignity is lost, others in which bombast is substituted in its stead. But the unabated vigour and spirit of the version more than overbalances these and all its other deficiencies.

The meddling tendency to 'modernize' or 'clarify', 'abbreviate' and 'embellish', or as Dryden put it in the seventeenth century, 'lop off the superfluous branches', has never departed the hand of the historian, antiquarian or copyist.[150]

In the age of Dryden and Pope, the rhyming couplet was the standard choice for reconstruction of Homeric hexameter, whereas a six-beat line or 'iambic decasyllabic' structure is employed in more modern translations, though any rigid adherence to method requires necessary liberties with structure to avoid what the Greeks termed 'pedestrian wording', where the spirit of the original gets lost.[151] Archaic poetry remains a conundrum because its metre may simply not exist in the target language, and perhaps this is why almost all Greek and Roman lyric poetry disappeared in the Dark Ages.

A recent translator of the Homeric Hymns commented on early hexameter verse: 'As the Greek language operates very differently from English using a system in which the function of a word is generally signalled by its ending, rather than by its position in the sentence, a strict literal translation is often impossible or unsatisfactory.'[152] The result, as with the case of the Alexandrian attempts to modernize the poems of Pindar, is that the lilt, flow and formula, and ultimately the very essence and mood of the hymn in the mind's ear, is interrupted by the need to reposition the words.

Dryden had himself compared the translation of a classical work to a 'drawing after life', and yet one that should nevertheless retain recognizable facial features. He further proposed a middle methodological ground in translation, shunning both 'word for word' and 'imitation'. John Denham had already proposed a similar approach in his 1656 preface to the *Destruction of Troy*, though neither scholar's method was well defined. Dryden went on to admit: 'I am ready to acknowledge that I have transgress'd the Rules which I have given; and taken more liberty than a just Translation will allow.'[153] In contrast, Bardon's approach to reproducing Curtius has been described as 'misguided conservatism' in that it maintained corrupted Latin even when it made little sense.[154]

Any scholar who has read parallel translations of the classics can understand the challenge, and especially so in the case of Tacitus. As a modern linguist candidly explained of his translation of Tacitus' *Annals*: 'The more prudent translators preface their efforts by apologetic reminders that Tacitus has never been translated and probably never will be.'[155] The translators were, and always are, faced with what has been termed 'the art of the correct sacrifice'.[156] This is itself a moveable feast, as classical Latin was on the move and had visibly developed in style from Republican to Imperial Rome.

Classifying Classical Latin

The term 'classical' entered modern English in the sixteenth century, and by 1870 Wilhelm Siegmund Teuffel (1820–1878) had developed his philological classifications, which included the so-called Golden and Silver Ages of Latin: 80 BC–AD 14 and AD 14–117 respectively. Like all 'new' linguistic ideas, these built upon earlier less systematic models incorporating faulty systems of categorization based upon political events rather than pure prose style.[157] In 1877, Charles Cruttwell refined the groupings by focusing on the progression of Roman literature through the Republican and Imperial periods, in which it evolved from an 'immaturity of art and language' to 'ill-disciplined imitation of Greek poetic models', and finally to 'clear and fluent strength'.[158]

The Silver Age (broadly) witnessed the end of the true Roman Republic, so Diodorus, Trogus, Curtius, Plutarch and Arrian were publishing under successive Roman dictators and emperors. Despite that 'clear and fluent strength', Teuffel gave a scathing opinion on the loss of free speech through much of this period, particularly in the Julio–Claudian era (Augustus to Nero, 27 BC–AD 68); it was a period of 'continued apprehension' when natural composition was subordinated to the desire to appear 'brilliant', 'hence it was dressed up with abundant tinsel of epigrams, rhetorical figures and poetical terms'. He continued: 'Mannerisms supplanted style, and bombastic pathos took the place of quiet power.'[159] Freedom of expression was apparently not the cure, for Teuffel labelled the literature of the 'happier' second century that followed as nothing less than a scandalous 'imitation'.

Able to appreciate the textual markers defined by these eras, modern scholars developed the tools of linguistic 'archaeology' to help decode the past and even gene-tag individual historians. Narratologists note that the classical writer had a literary pace, gait or shuffle. In 1889, Dessau concluded that the *Scriptores Historiae Augustae* (see chapter 7) were written in the time of Theodosius rather than Diocletian or Constantine – as the manuscripts claimed – noting 'the uniformity in phraseology and stylistic devices' which pointed to a single author, not six.[160] We can similarly identify where texts noticeably stride ahead or stumble from that uniformity, revealing what may be a historian's non-seamless switch between sources. When analyzing texts dealing with Alexander, for example, one expert on the sources on ancient Macedon pointed to Plutarch's change from 'florid' structures to 'restrained and artistic' prose, and especially to clues in his rhythm, identifying 'iambic and spondaic runs and occasional tribrachs'.[161] He also observed Arrian's switches from narrative tenses when a new source was introduced, whereas the profiler of the lost Alexander historians saw 'Asianic rhythms' that betrayed the presence of genuine fragments of Cleitarchus.[162]

More recently, the linguistic studies of classicist Sir Ronald Syme concluded that Curtius' style was 'sub-Livian and pre-Tacitan', while elements within the *Metz Epitome* place its authorship in the fourth or fifth century AD. Only Curtius and the *Metz Epitome* employed the word *testudo* (tortoise) to describe the Greek shield formation.[163] The term didn't exist in Alexander's day or in Greek military history (aside from a mention of something similar in Xenophon's *Hellenica*), so Curtius was delving into his own Latin vocabulary to describe an earlier, but now familiar, shield-locking tactic.[164] Using similar observations, linguists determined that Carlo Sigonio's fragment of Cicero's *On Grief* was a fake, as it employed terminology Cicero could not yet have himself been familiar with. Linguistic progression remains just as visible today; anyone reading the biographies of Alexander by Wheeler or Mahaffy cannot help chewing with difficulty on the prose laid down just a century ago, and Rooke's 1814 second volume of Arrian's *Anabasis* has already been described as 'archaic'.[165]

Mass Graves of Micro Production

Not everyone shared the enthusiasm for rekindling the past. In a posthumously written historical review of 1847, English archaeologist Sir William Gell commented on the tedious job of copying newly found manuscripts and the Herculaneum Scrolls: 'If Omar, according to the tale, burned the library of Alexandria, we have doubts whether he ought not to be honoured as a benefactor of our race.' Gell followed with: 'The palimpsests so laboriously deciphered, have given us scarcely anything that is either of interest or value.'[166]

So, for one reason or another, time has lost more of Alexander and his literary heroes and biographers than it has preserved, along with the linguistic challenges that renders what we have somewhat less than precisely worded. Considering that it required thousands of hours for a skilled scribe to make a single copy of a set of papyri scrolls that constituted a modern book, the number of editions of the scrolls of Callisthenes, Onesicritus, Nearchus, Aristobulus and Ptolemy would have been initially limited to library commissions, state archives and wealthy private collectors, and from there into the damp basement of a wealthy senator to suffer the degenerative fate of Apellicon's worm-eaten collection. Duplicates were usually only made on demand, not as part of a production line. So we might question how many copies would have been made of Alexander's Royal Diaries (see Grant, *Last Will and Testament*, 2021, chapter 6), that enigmatic and hotly debated collection of mapmakers' charts and measurements (via the *stathmoi*, 'stages'), ordnance accounts, troop movements, requisitions and satrapal appointments which must have originally existed in some organized form. In the case of the genuine campaign diaries, the answer is probably none; it would have been a hugely laborious task with no commercial or didactic result.

Arrian's *Anabasis* has become almost the sole guardian of the very existence of the primary histories of Ptolemy and Aristobulus; some forty manuscript copies seem to have made it through, though none dating to earlier than *ca*. AD 1200. All of them stemmed from the *Codex Vindobonensis* (Vienna, Nationalbibliotek hist. gr. 4), so each has a lacuna in chapter eight, the 'Indica', the account of Nearchus' voyage from the Indus delta to the Persian Gulf. What we consider to be Arrian's original wording therefore emanates from the hands of the copyist(s) behind that single manuscript. It is a wonder that we still have a corpus of Aristotle's 'student notes' via the five ancient manuscripts that were copied some 1,400 years after the polymath had died, and which preserve thirty-one of the 200 treatises he wrote; Diogenes Laertius calculated they once amounted to 445,270 lines.

In comparison, we are left with nothing but rare fragments of the writing of Demetrius of Phalerum, his prolific school student.[167] Plato was unique; for a time it seemed that Thrasyllus, a friend of the emperor Tiberius and collector of the Platonist canon, had overdone it and assigned spurious works to the authentic, so providing Plato with a 100 per cent-plus survival rate.[168] The apocryphal were later thrown out, and yet the tide is once again turning to reinstatement, reminding us that when analyzing fragments the pendulum of opinion is never still.

The weighty volumes titled *Philippica*, *Hellenica* and *Macedonica* are lost to us.[169] Sicilian historian Philistus, termed by Cicero 'the miniature Thucydides', has vanished without a trace even though admired by Alexander himself, possibly because Philistus had died in an epic sea battle; for all we know, the Pellan court had procured the very last copy.[170] Of Theopompus' seventy books comprising his Greek and Macedonian epics, scholars have managed to collect 115 threadbare fragments, many from Athenaeus; Diodorus was clear that five of the fifty-eight books comprising the *Philippica* had already been lost by his day.[171]

Euripides was estimated to have written ninety-plus works, yet only eighteen authenticated plays survive, an 80 per cent loss despite Lycurgus' advice to have them copied. Some won awards at the festivals of the Dionysia ('peep-shows for fools', according to the cynical Diogenes) and at the Panathenaea, held at the Odeon situated dramatically at the foot of the Athenian Acropolis.[172] A more impressive credential is Plutarch's claim that after the military disaster at Syracuse, any Athenian captives able to quote Euripides had their liberty restored.[173]

Menander, whose comic drama and character portrayals Rome so loved, and who counted Theophrastus, Demetrius of Phalerum and Ptolemy I amongst his acquaintances, has a legacy of one play surviving (discovered in Egypt in 1957) against 100 or more lost.[174] We are left with just three tragedians (four if *Prometheus Bound* can be pinned on Euphorion, Aeschylus' son), one comedian in Aristophanes (in eleven plays) and one lyric poet, Pindar (along with Sappho's complete *Hymn to Aphrodite*), and only seven of Aeschylus' ninety plays survive in complete form. The fickleness of micro-production is clear for even the ivy-wreathed playwright. In the case of Aristophanes, he might have sealed his own obscurity, for he was liberal in the accreditation of his works: his first three plays were staged in the names of Philonides and Callistratus, and two of his last were credited to his son, Ararus, to ensure a favourable public reception.[175]

Here the generosities appear to have been an open secret, yet in Rome a poet or playwright would lose all rights to his work once they had been accepted and paid for by the commissioner, which often resulted in the complete loss of the author's name. An inordinate number of anonymous works were thus floating around, possibly explaining why Varro doubted that 109 of the 130 comedies attributed to Plautus were genuinely his.[176] Varro's own work suffered; his *Imagines* is said to have contained 700 illustrations of the famous men he biographed, each provided with 'suitable epigrams'. The work was later epitomized but without the sketches, no doubt due to the labour required in their reproduction.[177]

Almost a century-and-a-half ago (found in 1879 and published in 1880), the sands of Egypt delivered to us what appeared to be Aristotle's lost *Constitution of the Athenians*, a copy evidently prepared by four different scribes and now in the British Library. It revealed a less than objective and rather prejudiced Peripatetic polymath.[178] And despite being referred to as 'the Attic bee because of the sweetness of diction', the reputation of Xenophon has declined since some 900 lines of the superior *Hellenica* of a fourth-century historian known today as 'p' (for 'papyrus') were discovered at Oxyrhynchus in 1906, with further fragments published in

1946.[179] Similarly, Claudius' lucid *Letters to the Alexandrians* has reappeared, further regenerating his intellectual reputation. New finds are still possible. More recently, an unearthed Archimedes palimpsest revealed a further ten pages of Hyperides' speeches under the new multi-spectral imaging techniques which are being brought to bear on previously illegible *Herculaneum Scrolls*.[180] An exhumed Egyptian mummy was even found wrapped in the entire collected works of the Macedonian poet, Poseidippus.

Supplementing Alexander

If texts became threadbare and lacunose (if not entirely lost) over the past two millennia, the reverse has also taken place, with 'supplementary' texts inserted by scribes attempting to recreate the lost section, with no–less–damaging results. Curtius' history of Alexander provides an educational example.

Curtius provides us with the most comprehensive detail of events at Babylon immediately following Alexander's death, though his final chapter is riddled with lost paragraphs. We have 123 codices of his work, all deriving from a single incomplete archetype dating back to the ninth century.[181] Notes from the colophons – literally the 'finishing strokes' at the end of a manuscript in which the copyist detailed his work – inform us that the earliest of them, referred to as the *Codex Parisinus 5716*, was written in the Carolingian period by a scribe named Haimo. This dates to the second half of the ninth century in the vicinity of the Loire in France.[182] Unfortunately, Curtius' florid style had gained him early Middle Ages meddling, whereas the drier pedantic Arrian was virtually forgotten until the more disciplined Renaissance had provided a better methodology for textual recovery and transmission. The 'base handling' of the textual revisers (known as diaskeuasts, broadly 'interpolators of texts') of this earlier period was less easily deciphered, when artful rather than informed filler damaged already wounded manuscripts.

Five of the Curtian manuscripts provided the basis of all modern translations, like Hedicke's influential 1867 edition, one of a number of informed copies to emerge.[183] All of the manuscripts were corrupted and most of poor quality, and as a result the *Codex Parisinus* is in places significantly different from the other four (*Bernensis, Florentinus, Leidensis* and *Vossianus*), giving us two textual traditions. Large lacunae existed in books 5, 6 and 10, and the first two chapters are missing completely, so the single and now lost archetype must have been similarly mutilated. We are still not sure how Curtius divided his work, and editions have been variously split into anything from eight to twelve chapters.[184] Whereas conscientious scribes were vigilant to the missing texts – *Codex 'P'* (Paris B N Lat. 14629) was, for example, translated by a scribe aware of the major lacuna between books 5 and 6 – others misleadingly ran the books together, often with a margin comment on 'some missing words', in this case creating a new edition with only nine books.[185]

No library in the Renaissance was considered well equipped unless a copy of Curtius sat on its shelves. The first translation from Latin to a modern language took place in 1483 by Pier Candido Decembrio in Milan, and it existed in manuscript form until 1470/71, when the first edition of *Vindelinus Spirensis* appeared in Florence (or Venice), often with spurious resurrections of the first two lost chapters.[186] Unfortunately, this became a trend: Decembrio called upon his knowledge of Arrian, Justin and Plutarch to propose a reconstruction of the missing text. One scholar recently warned: 'Poets, antiquarians and historians drew on heroic narrative patterns to plug these gaps, places in the tale where objects or figures disappear from events.'[187]

Other scholars did adopt a more disciplined approach when supplementing lost texts, and informed us when they did so. The first recorded *auctor supplementorum* was Christopher Bruno, whose edition was printed at Basel in 1545; certainly the *scholia* – the explanatory margin notes – were informative to the followers of a growing 'Curtiana'.[188] Analysis of a Curtius manuscript at Oxford's Corpus Christi College (O 82) revealed textual supplements that appear to have originated in France along with the redactions that preserved them. Here we find a patchwork of clear emulations of Seneca, Cicero, Josephus, Horace and Virgil, alongside elements of Julius Valerius' *Romance* translation, to name but a few. In this particular case, margin notes *were* included, identifying the inspirational inserts. This was a 'transparent' attempt at *compilatio*. But the Curtius manuscripts, more often than not, became partnered by a process of 'anonymous fluidity', which, for example, absorbed elements of the *Roman d'Alexandre* by the twelfth-century poet Albéric de Pisançon.[189] Where margin notes are absent, we are left with an ever-present danger of assuming the style was Curtius' own or an example of *his* emulation of the great literary stylists of the age.

Middle Ages romance transmission was an even more difficult client itself, for its artistry was by definition anything but literal. Curtius was influential to both the romance genre and to the speculum literature of the Middle Ages, when alchemy rather than erudition walked the centre stage. The *Mirror of History* of Vincent de Beauvais was a monumental encyclopaedia that attempted to embrace the sum of all knowledge. It had relied on the similarly ambitious *Chronicon* of Helinand of Froidmont, written sometime in the early thirteenth century, for its references to Alexander, replicating all the mistakes therein, including extracts from the supplements of the Corpus Christi manuscript.[190] The popular edition of Johannes Freinsheim (1608–1660), which came with textual supplements and voluminous explanatory notes, was in fact reprinted up until the twentieth century. His infills 'were so successful that we almost cease to lament the loss of the original'.[191] Efforts were finally made to standardize Curtius' text and highlight these interpolations: Zacher (1867), Thomas (1880) and Dosson (1887) published commentaries on these earlier manuscripts as the disciplines of source analysis began to establish themselves.

Taking these examples of decrepitated Curtius manuscripts into account, what chance is there that Arrian, Diodorus and Plutarch accurately captured the intent of their earlier sources, no matter how well (or ill) meaning their attempts? How faithfully did Cleitarchus transmit the essence of his eyewitness sources, and how successfully did Curtius convert Cleitarchus' Greek construction and the underlying thought processes into Latin?

We may equally ponder how accurately their interpretations have been preserved in the centuries since, with the attenuation of time, for a subtlety unappreciated, an inflection misused, and sarcasms and witticisms taken too literally each diffuse the focus and nuances of the original. Moreover, 'fiction, true, false or free-falling, is intimately bound up with figures of discourse such as metaphor and irony, and with speculation and hypothesis', all the elements vulnerable in translation.[192] Alongside them we find deep-lurking lacunae, scribal cut-and-pastes, scriptorium pastiches and the text-amending prejudices of pious distaste, and each – or any – one of them may have changed our very interpretation of history.

The above digression on Curtius highlights the 'precarious path of Pergamum and papyrus' though the ages. But the biggest challenge Curtius presents is identifying the author himself.

Chapter 10

Mystery Historian, Mystery Agenda

Nothing is known about Quintus Curtius Rufus. To us he is only a name
at the head of the book … : he is never mentioned anywhere, and no
other writing of his is known or even referred to: possibly the name was
not even the author's real name. He presents a mass of problems, and the
first is, why his book was ever written.[1]

W.W. Tarn, *Alexander the Great, Volume II, Sources and Studies*

If the content of our ancient eyewitness Alexander sources must be called into
question at the most crucial junctures of his story, we can also query the very
identity of those who transmitted this detail, for some of them remain totally
obscure, even among the five surviving accounts which give us 'Alexander'. The
most debated of all is Curtius.

Although Curtius' campaign account is stock to the mainstream Vulgate genre,
his life remains a mystery. Like the Roman epitomizer Justin, we have no biographical
details at all, only clues which have long been picked over. We have not much more
on Diodorus, for that matter. But Curtius' text has been particularly influential,
especially to the Middle Ages romance and poetical genre. Who was this Roman
author we know as 'Quintus Curtius Rufus', when did he write and what political
and imperial pressures were influencing the direction of his profiling of Alexander?

'There is an unwritten law that the volume of scholarship on a subject is in
inverse proportion to the evidence available', or so commented one modern-day
historian on the elusive Alexandria-based Cleitarchus.[2] The observation holds true
for the identity of Curtius Rufus, for Tarn's chapter-heading remark – that we know
nothing for sure about Curtius – is accurate and remarkable considering what has
been distilled from the clues. Curtius' book is an extremely detailed monograph
and remains the richest account of events at Babylon surrounding Alexander's
death. So it is equally vexing that 'no ancient reference is known to his account or
to a Q. Curtius Rufus as the author of such a work'.[3] If he is not quite as obscure
as the 'Pseudo-Callisthenes' behind the *Greek Alexander Romance*, or even the
identification of 'Suda' (or Suidas) as an individual compiler of the otherwise-
anonymous Byzantine lexicon, we may nevertheless have been sidetracked on
Curtius' name.

'Lost historians' from the Hellenistic Age and the Silver Age (see chapter 4) of Roman literature are, paradoxically, not difficult to find, and they left legacies. Although little or nothing remains of their own works, fragments often proliferated in later accounts, usually with a commentary on their style, whether laudatory or more commonly derogatory. The most relevant example is of course Cleitarchus, Curtius' principal (so convention has it) but not exclusive source, and about whom little is known.[4] Nevertheless, Cleitarchus was sufficiently influential in Rome for Strabo, Quintilian, Cicero, Athenaeus, Aelian – and Curtius himself – to reference him directly. Curtius, on the other hand, represents a 'found historian' in terms of his text but with a lost literary genesis. The intrigue has inspired forensic attempts to salvage him from that anonymity, analyze his style and method, contemplate his other sources, assess how influential he might have been to other writers of the day and finally to ponder what day that might have been.

The identification of his full name as 'Quintus Curtius Rufus' appears one of a later age (in Hedicke's 1867 manuscript edition, for example, see chapter 8), for the praenomen 'Quintus' did not appear against the title of the earliest surviving manuscripts, but in the colophons, the copyist's endnotes. These were generally written in the first person and usually included the copyist's name, the title of the work, the date and place of the transcription and the patron ordering the edition. Amongst the five most intact texts, manuscript 'V' also omitted 'Quintus', leaving us with simply 'Curtius Rufus'. Alongside this dubiety, we cannot say the name of his book with any certainty.

The 123 surviving manuscripts (see chapter 8) are variously titled in Latin *Historiae*, *Historiae Magni Macedonis Alexandri* or *Historiae Alexandri Magni Macedonis*, with older scripts including *De rebus gestis Alexandri Magni libri* and *Cvrti Rvfi de rebvs ab Alexandro magno gestis*.[5] If this suggests a lack of clarity on the name from an early date, we should recall that Arrian's *Anabasis* (see chapter 4) and Livy's *Ab urbe condita libri* (*History of Rome*, see chapter 4) are as fluidly rendered in translations today.[6]

The uncertainty of the original book titles is certainly not unique. Somewhat relevant to arguments on Curtius' identity (more below) is an attribution made by Cassius Dio to what he termed the *Apocolocyntosis of the divine Claudius* (literally 'pumpkinification'), a play on the word 'apotheosis' in a 'pungent satire' at Claudius' expense, and it is attributed to Seneca, who had been banished by Claudius to Corsica between AD 41 and 49. The title suggests the deification of a 'pumpkin-head', though extant texts don't support that,[7] and surviving anonymous manuscripts are variously titled *Ludus de morte Divi Claudii* (the *Play on the death of Divine Claudius*) and *Divi Claudii Apotheosis per saturum* or *Satira de Claudio Caesare* (derivatives of the above), though nothing in the text alluded to the better-known title we use today. In fact, its connection to Seneca is even questioned. His nephew, Lucan, wrote an account of civil war between Julius Caesar and Pompey,

On the Civil War, but that is now better known as *Pharsalia* (after the location – Pharsalus in Thessaly, Greece – of the decisive battle between Caesar and Pompey).

But vexing as titles are, the greatest challenge with the Alexander monograph is to identify Curtius himself.

A Possible Political Identity

The vigorous century-and-a-half-old debate on Curtius' dating and identification remains hugely inconclusive.[8] Although the subject matter has become 'a fine field for critical and uncritical revelry', it is generally agreed that the language and style of Curtius' prose places him in the first three centuries of the Roman Empire.[9] Studies have variously promoted publication dates as early as the emperorship of Augustus (27 BC–AD 14) and as late as Constantine (emperor AD 306–337), while more recent opinions incline to Claudius (emperor AD 41–54) and Vespasian (emperor AD 69–79).[10]

A superficially attractive identification is the senator named Curtius Rufus referred to by Pliny in his *Epistles* and by Tacitus in his *Annals*, in which case the biography of Alexander must have been published sometime between AD 31 and 53, potentially in Claudius' emperorship.[11] This Curtius had been a suffect consul under Claudius, a quaestor (supervising public affairs, finances, army and officers), and then a senator and attaining a praetorship (magistracy, or in times of war a military command) under Tiberius, who appears to have described him as a 'self-made' man, whether this was well-meaning or otherwise.[12]

After administrating Germania Superior, the aforementioned Curtius Rufus made it to the prestigious governorship of Africa around AD 53 when apparently in old age. He died shortly after, possibly early in the emperorship of Nero. Could this be our man? He might otherwise have been the rhetorician, Q. Curtius Rufus, referred to by Suetonius in the index to his *On Grammarians and Rhetoricians* (*De Grammaticis et Rhetoribus*), and if so, it reconciles that career path with a later senatorial post.[13] If the list of rhetors is arranged in chronological order, a Claudian dating does work. Rhetoric was a necessary device on the Roman political road (the *cursus honorum*) from tribune to consul, as Suetonius himself made eminently clear and as Cicero had so eloquently proven. Yet neither identification fits the Alexander historian sufficiently well.[14]

By Augustus' day, a senatorial career demanded upwards of one million Roman sesterces (possibly equivalent to US$3.5 million), and despite the fact that the currency had been demoted from silver to a large brass coin, this was still a fortune and restricted who could aspire to the path.[15] The true magnitude of the financial requirement for such a political career becomes apparent when compared to the salary of a first-century Roman legionary: around 900 sesterces per annum, half of which would have been deducted at source for maintenance and equipment.

The low-interest and interest-free loans we see provided by the wealthy Brutus, Crassus and Caesar once in power (800,000 sesterces to Cicero, for example) illustrate the requisite political alliances behind such funding, though other loans could be procured more expensively (and potentially without political strings) from professional moneylenders.[16]

The rubric for establishing the 'before' and 'after' date terminuses when Curtius could have (or must have) published (referred to by scholars as the *termini anti* or *post quem*) has been to analyze references within his rather conspicuous eulogy (here a paragraph of praise) to his emperor in his final chapter. This sits out of context within his narrative of army infighting and the uneasy settlement reached at Babylon following Alexander's death (see Grant, *Last Will and Testament*, 2021, chapter 5). The eulogy reads:

> But already by the Fates civil wars were being forced upon the Macedonian nation; for royal power desires no associate and was being sought by many. First therefore they brought their forces into collision, then separated them; and when they had weighted the body with more than it could carry, the limbs also began to give out, and an empire that might have endured under one man fell in ruins while it was being upheld by many. Therefore the Roman people rightly and deservedly, asserts that it owes its safety to its *princeps*, who in the night which was almost our last shone forth like a new star. The rising of this star, by Heaven! rather than that of the sun, restored light to the world in darkness, since lacking their head the limbs were thrown into disorder. How many firebrands did it extinguish! How many swords did it sheath! How great a tempest did it dispel with sudden prosperity! Therefore our empire not only lives afresh but even flourishes. Provided that only the divine jealousy be absent, the posterity of that same house will continue the good times of this our age, it is to be hoped forever.

Here Curtius refers to an unnamed *princeps* ('foremost' or 'most eminent' person, here an emperor), who may well have been identified at the beginning of Curtius' first book ('books' 1 and 2 have been lost; there are ten 'books', more like chapters, within his Alexander history), along with a preface and potentially a self-identification, all of which would have dovetailed neatly with the imperial laudation.

Such self-identification, along with praise of the present imperium, was common practice: Tacitus, for example, identified himself in the opening of his book with a clear date reference (by naming the current consuls), and Pliny identified his *princeps*, Titus the son of Vespasian, with: 'This treatise, *Natural History*, a novel work in Roman literature, which I have just completed, I have taken the liberty to dedicate to you, most gracious Emperor.'[17] Pliny went on to further praise both

Titus (he termed him 'friend') and Vespasian for their respective patronage of the arts. His entry ended with a rundown of his methodology and contained a list of his sources, the latter a unique acknowledgement, as he himself observed. A further example is Ovid's *Apotheosis of Julius Caesar*, in which he prudently framed his emperor Augustus as something of a demi-god.[18]

Curtius' self-identification is lost, but he also made contemporary references to the powerful Parthian Empire. Nevertheless, this, along with the aforementioned encomium, only acknowledges that his work was written between 27 BC – when a *princeps* first appeared (when Octavian became 'Augustus') – and AD 224 – when the Arsacid Parthian Empire ended, after which the Sassanids ascended. However, if the theory of one scholar is correct – that the consul–poet Silius Italicus (died *ca.* AD 101) knew of Curtius' work and drew inspiration from it for his *Punica* (an epic poem about the Second Punic War between Hannibal and the Roman general, Scipio Africanus) – then that corridor is significantly narrowed.[19]

Additional dating clues come from Curtius' references to the Phoenician city of Tyre, described as enjoying 'tranquillity under the merciful protection of Rome', and from the terminology he used to describe military units.[20] But these, along with references to archers and archery, as well as to *cataphracti* (heavy-mailed cavalry), all remain inconclusively dissected, as does the allusion to a 'civil war' that appears to have been averted by the emperor being eulogized.[21] But deeper textual themes of the Roman political arena permeate Curtius' work, as does a linguistic style that displays notable similarities to the historians of the Gold and Silver Latin ages, as scholars have noted. This in itself isn't helpful, as establishing who emulated who, and whether they were influenced through an intermediary, remains problematic.

The Julio–Claudian age (Augustus to Nero, so from 27 BC–AD 68), which is the strongest contender for Curtius' publication date, arrived with additional historiographical challenges: 'The gradual concentration of political power within a smaller and smaller group, together with the secrecy and mystery which resulted, could not but affect the task of recording Roman history.'[22] If those holding the stylus were from privileged backgrounds (as was almost always the case), then the opening of Tacitus' *Annals* captured a dilemma that began with Augustus:

> Many historians ... dealing with the Republic they have written with equal eloquence and freedom. But after the battle of Actium, when the interests of peace required that all power should be concentrated in the hands of one man, writers of like ability disappeared; and at the same time historical truth was impaired in many ways: first, because men were ignorant of politics as being not any concern of theirs; later, because of their passionate desire to flatter; or again, because of their hatred of their masters. So between the hostility of the one class and the servility of the other, posterity was disregarded.[23]

Tacitus added: 'Opposition there was none: the boldest spirits had succumbed on stricken fields or by proscription-lists while the rest of the nobility found a cheerful acceptance of slavery the smoothest road to wealth and office.'[24] This looks like a template for one of Plutarch's later polemics, and Cassius Dio's after him.[25] But setting out one's virtuous stall, as Tacitus did, and sitting on it, as Tacitus did not always do, are very different matters.[26]

An independent literary spirit was not impossible under the Julio–Claudians, as evidenced by the not-always-compliant writing of Aulus Cremutius Cordus under Tiberius, and Aufidius Bassus under Claudius, but imperial criticism was dangerous and more often than not was fatal.[27] Lucan, once a favourite of Nero, published the benign first three books of his *On the Civil War* without initial repercussions, though his (now lost) *Praises of Nero*, read out at the first Greek-styled celebration of the quinquennial Neronia of AD 60 (with contests of music, gymnastics and riding), had clearly helped, for Lucan was crowned and appointed to the city augurate soon after (see chapter 4).

But as Lucan's *On the Civil War* advanced, the poem, influenced by Livy's republican nostalgia, increasingly appeared to attack the tyrannical excesses of Nero, which alongside Lucan's brazenly vocalized critiques, saw the young prodigy dead at 25 in the wake of the Pisonian plot against Nero exposed in April AD 65. Another example of the imperial danger was Claudius' early literary career, which had been cut short for being too critical of his emperor, Augustus; when he resumed his writing, now himself holding an imperial pen, he avoided altogether the Triumvirate Wars in which Octavian had risen to power.[28]

If Curtius was, indeed, aboard the political *cursus honorum*, then the expediency of his imperial sycophancy becomes clear: it was a simple necessity for survival, if not the genuine admiration of an emperor.

Celestial Guides

Curtius' laudation of his emperor, though it was typically thematic of the day, contains some further noteworthy pointers. He compared his emperor's arrival to a 'new star' (*novum sidus*), and one that shone in the night.[29] The 'star' seems to have become a commonplace theme (a *topos*) in panegyrics of the Julio–Claudian dynasty, and one possibly continued through to Vespasian; in his *Satires*, Horace suggested its continued use was even being mocked.[30] It was an expedient term of endearment apparently used at Caligula's accession and again by Seneca to describe Claudius in AD 43, while Pliny the Younger employed the symbolism for the dynasty of Trajan.[31] Lucan's *On the Civil War* even described Alexander the Great as an 'evil star of humanity' that brought disaster to mankind, whereas Curtius himself referred to Alexander as 'a star of Macedon', with similar phraseology appearing in Livy and Virgil.[32] More strikingly, Tacitus attached the motif (here 'ill-starred') to the final consulate of Galba which heralded in the 'year of the four emperors' (AD 69).[33]

If references to a 'star' were a rhetorical ubiquity, we might wish to take the stellar observation more literally and less metaphorically in the case of Curtius' imperial panegyric, for its luminous attachment to 'shining in a darkened world' suggests a further specificity. The same could be said of the reference to the 'putting-out of torches'; what could they be?

The classical world maintained a fascination with the night sky. It was viewed with an awe evoked by the scientifically unexplained and by prevailing superstitions; moreover, the celestial clarity from a lack of light pollution and emissions only enhanced the spectacle. The wonder and dread of moving stars (in Greek, *planetai*, 'wanderers'), the Milky Way (from the Greek *galaxias kyklos*, 'milky circle') and a comet in particular (*kometes* in Greek, *crinitas* in Latin – a 'hairy' star), is well recorded; the astronomical theories of Pythagoras, Anaxagoras and Democritus had been well summarized in Aristotle's treatise *Meteorology*. Rome was equally curious about the phenomena, as evidenced by Seneca's *On Comets* in his *Natural Questions*, and by Pliny's frequent references in book 2 of his *Natural History*.[34] The most portentous celestial episode of all took place in Constantine's rule in the twilight of the Roman Empire, when, according to Eusebius, in AD 312 'a most marvellous sign appeared to him from heaven': what was witnessed by the emperor and his army was reportedly a cross in the sky, which might have redirected the religious doctrine of the empire.[35]

In Curtius' eulogy, a 'new star' and dark nights could also be references to comets and eclipses, for they satisfy both. Linking the 'new star' to a comet has already been pondered and such arguments could point to, as just one example, the birth of the emperor Alexander Severus in October AD 208.[36] However, it seems the imperial attachment has not been fully exploited. Although a clearly developed encomiastic device, 'new star' is conspicuous in its attachment to emperors whose imperial tenancy was linked to stars rising and to comets as well as eclipses; the appearance of the latter was considered biographically portentous, usually as a harbinger of death and the end of an administration, so they were often exploited by the successor, or a historian wishing to remind his audience of such.

Pertinent to the era under scrutiny, a comet appeared shortly after Julius Caesar's death in 44 BC, while Virgil claimed of Caesar's assassination: 'Never fell more lightning from a cloudless sky; never was comet's alarming glare so often seen.'[37] That cataclysmic scene begged a salvation by Augustus, to whom he dedicated a prayer early in the chapter. Possibly more relevant still, both Suetonius and Cassius Dio reported a comet sighting four months prior to Claudius' death in AD 54, thus heralding Nero's imperium: 'the principal omens of his death were the following: the rise of a longhaired star, commonly called a comet.'[38]

Seneca, Calpurnius Siculus and Tacitus mentioned a further comet which 'blazed into view' in AD 60 and was visible for a full six months, with the latter historian commenting on its portent: 'The general belief is that a comet means a change of emperor. So people speculated on Nero's successor as though Nero were already dethroned.' However, in this case they were to be some eight years out (Nero died in AD 68).[39] Another was seen in late AD 64, the year of the great fire in Rome, and was visible from July to September, with Tacitus commenting that it was 'a phenomenon to which Nero always made atonement in noble blood', for the emperor massacred selected nobility to appease the obviously angry gods.[40]

Suetonius recorded the presence of a comet, possibly Halley's, in AD 66 (visible in January), and another graced the Jerusalem night and might have preceded the capture of the historian Josephus following the battle and siege at Jotapata in the Jewish Revolt in AD 67; the comet appeared 'like a sword' hanging over Jerusalem. The fact that it was allegedly visible for a whole year has made scholars question whether it was in fact Halley's Comet of three years earlier used for rhetorical effect.[41]

According to Suetonius, the end of Nero's ill-starred time in power was once more marked by celestial portents:

> Those outside his family he [Nero] assailed with no less cruelty. It chanced that a comet had begun to appear on several successive nights, a thing which is commonly believed to portend the death of great rulers. Worried by this, and learning from the astrologer Balbillus that kings usually averted such omens by the death of some distinguished man, thus turning them from themselves upon the heads of the nobles, he resolved on the death of all the eminent men of the State.[42]

After Nero, then the 'year of the four emperors' (AD 69), some stability arrived with Vespasian and the Flavian Dynasty, but the night sky was just as troubled. A brilliant comet was visible for forty days in AD 72, the year that followed Vespasian's accession, and a further sighting occurred in AD 73, the year he expelled philosophers from Rome. One followed in AD 75 when Vespasian made a dedication to peace at the temple in which he housed the works of art he had dubiously amassed during his term.[43] Then in AD 79, Vespasian is recorded as having declared, 'the "hairy star" is an omen not for me, but for the Parthian king, for he had long hair where I am bald'; portents are littered across Suetonius' biography of Vespasian.[44]

Solar eclipses carried similar predictive gloom as comets, and with them came a verifiably 'darkened world'. They could cause panic in the ranks, as one did with Darius III's troops at Gaugamela (see chapter 8), and provoked the sapient Sulpicius Galus to explain the phenomenon to the shaken Roman army amassed against the Macedones at the Battle of Pydna in 168 BC. So in Curtius' praise of his emperor, an eclipse potentially brought the 'last night' with it. According to Pliny, a protracted eclipse also occurred shortly after Julius Caesar's death in 44 BC, though modern calculations suggest none was visible from Europe until AD 49, which has led some scholars to question the whole chronology of the Julio–Claudian era. A further solar eclipse was described by Cassius Dio as one of the portents of Augustus' death, though this too cannot be substantiated by modern calculations.

Cassius Dio also recorded a partial eclipse of the sun in AD 26 and a further event in Claudius' rule prompting the emperor to enquire of his astronomers the date of the next occurrence. It actually coincided with his birthday on 1 August (AD 45), and to forestall panic, Claudius issued a proclamation detailing the time and duration of the darkness, with a full scientific, though non-heliocentric, explanation.[45] Dio detailed a lunar eclipse that accompanied a comet before Vitellius' short emperorship in AD 69. Although two lunar eclipses would have been visible from Rome on 25 April and 18 October, modern reckoning dates the unusual double-event (eclipse and comet) to the summer of AD 54, and once again this broadly coincided with the death of Claudius and the beginning of Nero's term. It has been further speculated, in the case of Curtius' encomium, that the use of the term 'darkened' (*caliganti* in Latin) was a deliberate pun on 'Caligula', whose rule had ended in AD 41, still recent enough to have the desired literary effect for a writer who might have published in the colourful imperium of Nero.[46]

So does Curtius' dual reference to 'new star' and 'darkened world' give us a more specific date? We should appreciate that encomia of this nature were two-dimensional at best, here relating to the breadth of an emperor's achievement and the height of their exulted standing. We can hardly expect the author to embody any literal 'length' – the more useful chronological dimension – within a few lines. Thus, civil war, dark nights, peace and prosperity were rolled into a few sentences in which a decade of colour might be compressed to this paragraph-long sycophancy. So where does this leave us?

Arguments for Curtius Publishing under Nero

> And in our own age, about the time when Claudius Caesar was poisoned and left the Empire to Domitius Nero, and afterwards, while the latter was Emperor, there was one [comet] which was almost constantly seen and was very frightful.[47]

Referring to the above extract from Pliny, modern calculations confirm a comet would indeed have been visible at the accession of Nero in autumn AD 54 (Nero succeeded Claudius on 13 October). Both Suetonius and Cassius Dio recorded the noteworthy sighting that 'lasted for a long time', while Pliny termed it 'frightful'.[48]

Tacitus mentioned two further comets ('omens of impending misfortune'), and a lacuna in the *Annals* would surely have included the Halley's Comet sighting in January AD 66.[49] No one became more firmly associated with the night sky, stars, the sun god Apollo and Helios the Charioteer streaking across the firmament than Nero, in what has been termed his 'solar monarchy'.[50] Nowhere is this more evident than in the aforementioned *Apocolocyntosis* that eulogized him, which suggests his Stoic teacher Seneca (if this can be attributed to him) once held high hopes for his new 'radiant-faced' Nero. One extract reads:

> He brings glad days, to muted law a tongue,
> As the Morning Star, setting the stars to flight,
> As the shining sun, when his chariot moves first from the line,
> So Caesar comes, so Nero appears to Rome,
> His bright face glowing with gentle radiance,
> His neck all beauty under his flowing hair.[51]

Comparisons with elements of Curtius' laudation are unavoidable, despite varied liberal translations. The dawn of Nero heralded an imperium that required new obeisance, for the dangerous 'actor–emperor' managed thirteen years and eight months in the purple-bordered robe despite his bankrupting of the empire.[52] As Erasmus later noted, Dawn was a friend of the Muses, whom Nero believed could not rival his own sweet voice, and it is difficult to avoid the conclusion that one encomium drew inspiration (if not a strictly parallel wording) from the other.[53] But which came first?

The issue is complicated by the suggestion that this extract from the *Apolococyntosis* was a later addition to an original draft that had been published soon after Nero's succession in AD 54, perhaps by Seneca himself or by an anonymous compiler writing with the hindsight of events, possibly as late as AD 59 (or early AD 60). Laudation of Nero would still have been relevant at this time, as it was only later in that year that Nero's true colours began to emerge following the death of his mother, the universally hated Agrippina (murdered in March AD 59), the great-granddaughter of Augustus who had previously manipulated her way to becoming Claudius' fourth wife.[54] It was Agrippina who had Seneca recalled from exile, for she saw the value of his educating and counselling her impressionable son.

Nero *had* distinguished himself in the first five years of his rule (AD 54–59), taking an interest in civic affairs: taxes were reduced, legal fees capped, he empowered freedmen and had corrupt officials arrested. Seneca's own reference to the comet of AD 60 (six years into Nero's emperorship) was still accompanied by 'in the happy principate of Nero'.[55] Striking likenesses were captured on coinage by the emperor's engravers and struck at the new mint at Lugdunum (Lyons), and though much of the 'happy' spin stemmed from his obsession with popularity,

Trajan appears to have later commended Nero's early years too, while Otho (second emperor in the 'year of the four emperors') used 'Nero' as a surname to boost his appeal.[56] Dio Chrysostom recalled the nostalgia with which the populace, especially that in the East, mourned his eventual death in AD 68.

Seneca's poem (if it *was* Seneca's), possibly written with genuine optimism, appears elegant, with a completeness that suggests a smooth original composition and not one awkwardly absorbing a forerunner's prose.[57] If that is the case, Curtius' encomium (assuming one of the texts was inspired by the other) was published after. It is notable that Curtius' description of a state with limbs lacking a head contains striking similarities to Seneca's *Of Clemency* published in AD 56.[58] Further, as one scholar notes, Seneca and Curtius employed identical phraseology to describe Alexander's devastation 'of peoples so remote as to be unfamiliar with even their neighbours'; this is wording that does not appear anywhere else in literature.[59]

But what of the 'extinguishing of torches'? If we are associating Curtius' encomium with the term of Nero, we arrive inevitably at 'fire'. Butt fires were common, noteworthy conflagrations destroying parts of the city under both Titus and Trajan. Yet the Great Fire of Rome of July AD 64 was exceptional, and so was Nero's part in it. On the night of 19 July, while the city burned, we have the popular image of Nero playing the fiddle, an instrument that was only developed some 1,500 years later; Nero was in fact a player of the cithara (lyre), and a bad one according to Vindex, his rebellious governor in Gaul.[60] Although Suetonius and Cassius Dio claimed Nero was the arsonist who sang *The Sack of Ilium* while the fire spread (thus paving the way for his new-planned city, 'Neropolis'), Tacitus asserted that Nero organized a relief effort and paid for it himself. He even opened his palace grounds to shelter the homeless and followed up with stringent fire codes governing new construction.[61]

Conflicting reports have the conflagration raging for anywhere from five to nine days, despite the 7,000-strong city fire brigade officers who were armed with two-handled water pumps, a fire-suppressing vinegar mix and fire-smothering patchwork quilts. The destruction recognized no class: starting close to the Circus Maximus, the blaze spread down the Triumphal Way to the Forum, decimating the finest villas and temples as well as the vulnerable crowded slum, the Suburra.[62]

The great fire heralded the most ambitious civil construction project ever undertaken in the city, and one that included a financially ruinous colossus of Nero in the new Domus Aurea. Nero's immediate financial fix was to rob the temples of their votive offerings. After his death, the statue's face was modified to represent Sol Invictus, the unconquered god, and moved by Hadrian – with the help of twenty-four elephants – to a new home beside the Flavian Amphitheatre which became known as the Colosseum.[63]

Curtius' encomium additionally called for a 'long life' for the 'same house', a clear reference to the emperor's line. Pertinent to his final chapter on the

Macedonian king, Curtius knew from his sources how short-lived the reign of Alexander's half-brother, King Philip III Arrhidaeus, had proved to be after the settlement at Babylon in 323 BC. Recalling the fate of Olympias and Alexander's sons soon after, Curtius was therefore obliquely beseeching the gods for a better destiny for his Roman emperor.

Like Caligula and Claudius before him, Nero was of the line of the much-loved Germanicus (his grandfather), whose suspicious death was still greatly lamented in Rome, despite the damage Caligula had done to the reputation of the so-called Julio–Claudians.[64] While Curtius' phraseology suggested a new line of imperial hope, it was again a general motif that heralded each new princeps. Nevertheless, he would have been unlikely to pin such hopes on emperors who were disinclined, or obviously unable, to produce heirs. Excluding female issue and adopted sons, that would rule out Galba (who was in his early 70s at the close of Nero's rule) and possibly Otho too, for both were rumoured to prefer males as partners. In Otho's case that meant Nero, perhaps with a similar affiliation to Caligula before him, though we must recall that Otho had two (now dead) sons, so while procreation was not impossible, his short tenure as emperor makes him a rather unlikely candidate for Curtius' wording. Notably, each of the 'five good emperors', comprising the Nervan–Antonian dynasty from Trajan to Marcus Aurelius, were no more than adopted sons.[65]

Interestingly, this state of affairs, partly stemming from infertility, has been recently blamed on poisoning from the lead-lined aqueducts and water pipes in Rome (*plumbum*, lead, is the root of 'plumbing'), as well as from lead acetate that was used to sweeten wine, and from defrutum, a food preserving must-reduction often boiled in lead pots. Despite a warning from the Roman architect Vitruvius and from Pliny, who knew the risks of *morbi metallici* (as the fatal 'disease' was known), recent tests of lead isotopes from the River Tiber confirmed huge concentrations when compared to the spring water of the region.[66]

More relevant to Curtius' dynastic hope, Nero's second wife, the 'proud whore' Poppea Sabina, was pregnant in AD 65 with their second child, that is until Nero is recorded to have kicked her to death.[67] Poppea had been previously married to Otho, who subsequently became emperor himself in AD 69 for three months until he killed himself after the Battle of Bedriacum at which the historian, Suetonius, earned his equestrian spurs. Obsessed with Poppea Sabina, Nero had taken her first as mistress and then, when he became emperor, he removed Otho from Rome by appointing him governor of Lusitania, a region more or less equivalent to modern Portugal.

Tacitus suggested that Poppea deserved her fate for the intrigues that led to the death of Agrippina and Nero's first wife, the childless Claudia Octavia. Although Tacitus, Cassius Dio and Suetonius each recorded versions of Poppea's violent death, their accounts might be nothing more than a polemical tradition, for fatal miscarriages were not uncommon. Nero mourned her lavishly; he embalmed her body in the fashion of the royalty of Egypt and had it incarcerated in the mausoleum of Augustus. Their first child, Claudia Augusta, had lived just four months. Nero was again childless, and hopes for the continuation of his line now had particular relevance.

But what of the encomium's reference to the sheathing of swords? If truly a reference to civil war, it would narrow the contending emperors down further to Augustus, Claudius, Galba, Vespasian, Nerva and Septimus Severus. But it has been noted that the use of the verb *trepidare*, 'to tremble in anticipation', suggests a world on the brink and one waiting for something calamitous to happen, not a world that had already been torn apart; here the parallel 'brink' is the civil war averted by the eventual settlement at Babylon.[68] So the sheathing of swords could simply be a celebration of Nero's peaceful accession, in contrast to the Praetorian bloodletting accompanying the new reign of the unwitting Claudius. Perhaps more relevant was Nero's unravelling of the Pisonian plot to kill him in April AD 65.

Gaius Calpernius Piso, literary benefactor and statesman, had rounded up support for Nero's assassination amongst prominent senators and the joint-prefect of the Praetorian Guard. Yet support for Nero was far from extinct, especially amongst the equestrians who enjoyed his favour; if Piso had been successful, there would have been collateral damage and recriminatory bloodletting.[69] Swords were certainly sheathed, most notably the emperor's, which struck down the captured conspirators. The aftermath saw Lucan, Seneca and the satirist, Petronius, summarily forced to commit suicide. After being denied tablets on which to write a will, Seneca's last alleged words to his friends were: 'Who knew not Nero's cruelty? After a mother's and a brother's murder, nothing remains but to add the destruction of a guardian and a tutor.'[70]

Nero's behaviour is something of an irony against the cultural background, because the Second Sophistic, with its love of Greek culture and expressive freedom, is reckoned to have commenced with his emperorship. Josephus saw the retrospective problem when 'aiming for the truth':

Many historians have written the story of Nero, of whom some, because they were well treated by him, have out of gratitude been careless with the truth, while others from hatred and enmity towards him have so shamelessly and recklessly revelled in falsehoods as to merit censure.[71]

What we now refer to as the *End of Illustrious Men*, a compendium written by Titinius Capito containing the names of those banished or killed by Nero, and the *Deaths of those Killed or Exiled*, a parallel work by Gaius Fannius, were read by Pliny the Younger, who coined the former name.[72] If published sufficiently early (its dating is uncertain), Tacitus might have used this material for his depiction of Seneca's death.

The 'sheathing of swords' was phraseology also used by Seneca in his *Of Clemency*, once again suggesting Curtius could have drawn from his template; in fact Seneca 'communed' with Nero to restrain himself in his use of swords throughout book 1 in favour of the more merciful behaviour he was advocating, and it rather suggests that Seneca had seen the writing on the wall, even though *Of Clemency* was composed just two years into Nero's emperorship.[73]

The above extract from Seneca's *Apocolocyntosis* alluded to his emperor as a 'charioteer' who was moving 'first from the line'. If a literal link, it could refer to Nero's attested participation in the sport. He appeared in AD 65 at the Circus Maximus, an event that heralded his tour of Greece, and so it is likely that he was seen practising or participating in games and festivals in Rome before he had Seneca kill himself. Nero repeated his chariot performances at the Olympic Games of AD 67, advancing them a full year to fit in with his travel plans. Inevitably, he was awarded a crown, despite falling from his ten-horsed carriage; we should note that Alexander was himself portrayed as a charioteer in the *Romance*.[74] Nero went on to become an 'all conquering champion' on the circuit of games as well as a guaranteed 'victor' who paid judges to adjudicate 'wisely'.[75] He returned to a triumph through a breach in Rome's wall, reportedly on the chariot Octavian had used a century before, and the crowd now hailed their emperor as 'Nero Apollo'.[76]

As for Curtius' references to Parthia, Nero responded vigorously to Parthian incursions into Armenia in the wars of AD 58–63, and so a fascination in Rome with the East and the former Macedonian Empire was inevitable at that time. Curtius' reference to the widespread skill of archery fits here as well, for Nero's general, Gnaeus Domitius Corbulo, faced formidable Parthian mounted bowmen and had to enlist auxiliary archers himself. No doubt when preparing for the campaign, the city was keenly aware of this requirement and we imagine training was being given to the Roman counterparts.[77] Nero was possibly encouraged to campaign in Asia by the early books of Lucan's *On the Civil War* published from AD 61–64, and which recalled Alexander's legacy in the East with a nostalgia that embodied something of a challenge:

> Yet he [Alexander] fell in Babylon and Parthia feared him.
> Shame on us! That they dreaded more the sarissa
> Of Macedon than they do now the Roman javelin.[78]

As one commentator points out, Lucan's *On the Civil War* also mentioned the frequent shipwrecking activities of the Nasamonians (a North African tribe), a detail Curtius also included in his geographical digression of Africa, and which may further point to a relevant date after which it must have been published.[79]

Nero's Parthian campaign was eventually successful, but it is possible that at the time Curtius was writing, the 'fates' still waited for Nero to subjugate the East, and Curtius' repeated references to Parthian power were magnifying the task facing his young emperor. He was as a result potentially comparing his 'new star' to a young Alexander. To cement Roman influence in the East, Armenian ruler Tiridates was invited to Rome and crowned (client) king by Nero in AD 66. A Zoroastrian priest and founder of the Arsacid dynasty, Tiridates arrived with a grand entourage and much fanfare. It was a huge propaganda success, and he too publicly worshipped Nero as the Sun – thus as Apollo or Helius.[80]

Despite the public obeisance, however, Tiridates was reportedly disgusted at seeing Nero playing the lyre when entering the city. Nero was, as Cassius Dio stated, 'ushering in his own career of disgrace'.[81] There are again clear overtones of Alexander's Eastern victories here, and Nero was just as attached to the heroic imagery of the past as Alexander had been: his thespian activities reinforced Homeric themes, and his paean to Troy as Rome burned, whether true or invented, was equally emblematic of that. Indeed, Virgil's *Aeneid* had vividly set the scene with his references to the 'last night' of Troy that saw Priam's city burned.[82]

The comparison with the Macedonian conqueror did not end there. The declamations and rhetorical essays from Seneca and Lucan which warned of the trappings of excessive power – which emerged after the happier early years of Nero's rule – as well as being badly veiled assaults on their present emperor were also hostile to Alexander. Curtius' explicit correction of claims that Alexander had caged Lysimachus with a lion (see chapter 4) appears a further link to Seneca, for the allegation appeared most vividly in his *On Anger* as well as *On Clemency*.[83] Many of Curtius' moral reflections, which permeated his book, also have parallels in Cicero's writings (such as the moralizing content in his *Letters to Friends*) as well as Seneca's declamations, for these were themes almost impossible to avoid when Alexander's imperial excesses begged all the rhetorical devices of the day. Motifs were recycled and declamatory exercises rolled out, retreading the familiar literary highway with a vocabulary that standardized biographical themes in Roman monographs. This is presumably why few scholars have associated Nero with the subject of Curtius' imperial laudation.

But if Curtius' paragraph of sycophancy can be pinned on Nero, and contemplating how precarious was his own fate in the wake of Nero's court-demanded suicides, Curtius' encomium was conspicuously reconstructed with due imperial care. He knew any implied comparison with Alexander had to be conspicuously Nero-friendly, with any criticism directed at behaviour Nero did *not* adopt: Alexander's orientalization, for example, and his massacres in the upper satrapy and in India, when, in contrast, Nero was developing friendly client-king relations in the East. So where Seneca and Lucan saw the Macedonian taking 'weapons all over the world' and 'plunging his sword through all peoples', in

Curtius' account it was the 'best of Alexander' that Nero was supposed to see in himself. It was an exercise that anticipated Dio Chrysostom's dissections of Philip and Alexander in his *Kingship Orations* for *his* emperor, Trajan.[84]

Any unavoidable behavioural overlaps were defended in the character post-mortem Curtius provided for Alexander a few pages before the imperial encomium, for much of its content and direction would have been equally valid for the young Nero, whose mental energy could not be denied. Curtius philosophically wrote of the Macedonian conqueror, 'And, by Heaven! To those who judge the king fairly it is clear that his good qualities were natural, his faults due to his fortune or to his youth.'[85]

Curtius followed with a further *apologia* that pardoned Alexander for his lust for glory by taking into account his 'youth and achievements'. Virtues highlighted by Curtius included Alexander's devotion to his parents, his mental energy, ingenuity and magnanimity 'barely possible at his age'. Notably, he also praised Alexander's sexual restraint. Fortuna is blamed for his assumption of divine honours and for Alexander giving credence to oracles. Curtius interlaced Alexander's irascibility and a love of wine with his clemency, benevolence and forgiveness, where the faults were again credited to youth alone.[86] Curtius' obituary to Alexander ended with: 'the fates waited for him to complete the subjugation of the East and reach the Ocean, achieving everything of which a mortal was capable.'[87]

Nero had become emperor when he was just 17, and he was only 22 when he murdered Agrippina. Everyone, including Curtius, would have known of Nero's attachment to, and emulation of, Alexander, who also played the cithara. Although Trajan's admiration of the conqueror is often cited as the turning point in the reception Alexander's memory received in Rome, it appears it was earlier, at the imperial level at least; thus the beginnings of the so-called 'Second Sophistic' and its nostalgia for Classical Greece commenced with Nero and his interest in the Macedonian king.[88] Nero formed a bodyguard which he named The Phalanx of Alexander (which became the First Italica legion), and the obituary in Curtius' final chapter could have fed that nostalgia. We should further recall that an 'Alexander of Aegae' was allegedly employed as one of Nero's tutors.[89] Curtius may even have written his history specifically as a gift to an emperor so enamoured.

On his Greek tour in AD 67, Nero visited the Pythia at Delphi to request information on his fate, just as Alexander once had, and Suetonius claimed he was warned to 'beware the seventy-third year'. Nero, then aged 30, rejoiced at forty-three more years of imperium and rewarded her with 400,000 *sestertii*. Less benign though unverifiable traditions exist, the darkest of which claimed he 'abolished the oracle, after slaying some people and throwing them into the fissure from which the sacred vapour arose', either because the god made 'unpleasant predictions' or the Pythia had reproached him for his matricide. Pausanias more credibly reported that Nero couldn't resist ferrying 500 bronze statues from the sacred precinct back to

Rome to grace his Golden House.[90] Prophetically, two years later, Galba, then in his seventy-third year, attained the emperorship.

Other Pointers to the Unnamed Emperor

In his fourth chapter, Curtius made a vexing reference to the city of Tyre and its tranquillity under Roman rule in his day. The city was definitely on Nero's list of banks to loot, as its lucrative murex industry provided the purple dye associated with Roman imperial dress. Nero took to wearing exclusively purple robes to reinforce his status, decreeing that any other person doing so would be executed. If the comparison with Tyrian resurgence after its destruction by Alexander in 332 BC was the underlying political message, the sentiment might even be traced back to Cleitarchus, as the city's trade was rekindled by the new harbour and naval requirements of the successors in the decades following Alexander's siege. By 315 BC, Tyre was even able to sustain the fifteen-month siege of Antigonus the One-Eyed.

But the allusion to its more recent regained prosperity on the back of that, as well as its 'protection' by Rome, could have applied to any time period after Pompey's conquest of Judaea and its occupation in 63 BC; the Syrian-born Ammianus Marcellinus referred to a flourishing Tyre when Pompey annexed the Levant.[91] Nero minted a new portrait coin, the Neronian Sela, at Antioch, and possibly at Tyre as well. The currency was most likely forced upon the population, which until that time had used the Tyrian shekel. If the move proved unpopular, then Curtius' intimation that the city enjoyed new prosperity was indeed more antique spin to smother a financial controversy. Inland from Tyre, the lush settlement of Caesarea Philippi was certainly named 'Neronia' in honour of the emperor by Agrippa II, the Rome-supported king of the region who commenced new palace construction, so the allusion to prosperity is explicable.[92] Judaea did, nevertheless, rebel in AD 66, expelling the Roman legions, whereafter the Jewish population minted their own silver currency until Vespasian and his son, Titus, quelled the uprising. Following that, the Roman emperors adorned the obverse of the new coins, though familiar Tyrian motifs of Melquart and the Eagle of Egypt were still stamped on the reverse to partially appease the Phoenician population.

Finally, we have possible dating evidence in the undercurrent of Roman affairs that were expressed more generally through Curtius' narrative.[93] There was the aforementioned profiling of the halfwit king, Philip III Arrhidaeus, for example, a possible comparison with Claudius, and Perdiccas' behaviour at the Assembly in Babylon, which amounted to a 'Tiberian farce' (see Grant, *Last Will and Testament*, 2021, chapter 3). Tiberius' laggard behaviour apparently justified the deathbed quip from Augustus: 'Alas for the Roman people, to be ground by jaws that crunch so slowly!'[94] No doubt Tiberius' behaviour was recounted in Nero's day. In Curtius' portrayal of Alexander's trial and execution of Philotas (see Grant, *Last Will and Testament*, 2019, chapter 3) for his alleged part in a regicidal plot in 330 BC, Craterus' incrimination of the arraigned son of Parmenio displayed visible Roman themes; the sham trial was depicted as a *fait accompli*, which recalls the infamous trial of Asiaticus in AD 47 by Claudius and his ruthless wife, Messalina: clapped in chains without a Senate hearing, Asiaticus was essentially denied a defence.[95]

All this may provide a chronological triangulation of some relevance and with a date after which Curtius' imperial laudation could have been published – at the end of Claudius' rule, when the almost simultaneous comet and eclipse provided a uniquely exploitable portent. The Great Fire of AD 64, a foiled plot in AD 65, Halley's Comet in AD 66 and perhaps allusions to the successful Parthian War (the 'safety of Rome' and a 'tempest dispelled') might all be found in Curtius' encomium. Moreover, we have the manifest emulation of Alexander that cannot have gone unnoticed by historians attempting to please Nero.

If we *were* to attach Curtius' encomium to Nero – and if the 'sheathing of swords' did not, in fact, allude to the new peace in the East – the book's publishing would fall somewhere between the Pisonian plot of spring AD 65 and the brewing of the Vindex rebellion in late AD 67 or early 68, which finished Nero off. The statement from Curtius that preceded his eulogy – 'a throne is not be shared and several men were aspiring to it' – would have captured Nero's early suspicions of M. Junius Silanus, Rubellius Plautus and Faustus Sulla, all of whom he was to eventually 'remove'. The expression would have been equally relevant to Nero's fear of those already supporting the causes of the four emperors who came to power in the year that followed his death.[96] If this timing is correct, then Curtius clearly knew the intimacies of political affairs in Rome.

Of course, much of the chronology debate can be explained away as simple encomiastic plagiarism; the textual similarities between Seneca, Lucan and Curtius' history of Alexander have been well explored.[97] The histories of Tacitus and Pliny can be similarly connected as imperial ideograms were rehashed. Their careers, and those of Josephus, Pliny the Younger and Suetonius, followed on from one another in close succession and with significant thematic overlaps. Each was an accomplished rhetorician and each lived in, or immediately after, Nero's emperorship.[98]

Here, the allegation that a gradual concentration of political power (and we might add politically backed *literary* power) resided within an ever-smaller group appears justified.[99] Somewhere in the middle most likely lay our Curtius Rufus; we recall Sir Ronald Syme concluded that his style was sub-Livian and pre-Tacitan (see chapter 9). Livy published in Augustus' administration (27 BC–AD 14) and Tacitus' works appeared towards the end of the first century AD.[100] It appears that much of Curtius' style and imagery was adopted from Livy, with frequent use of the same modes of expression – some reused almost verbatim – so that today 'nobody doubts Curtius studied Livy'.[101]

A prime example appears to be a direct Curtian extraction from a Livian text that pondered Rome's ability to deal with the Macedonian sarissa. Livy mused that if Alexander had faced Rome, 'he would often have been tempted to wish that Persians and Indians and effeminate Asiatics were his foes' instead. Curtius similarly described how, at his death, Alexander of Epirus (Alexander's uncle and brother-in-law) reflected that where he had faced real soldiers in Italy, Alexander had fought women in Asia; this was a theme curiously reiterated by Arrian.[102] Curtius' comparison was attached to the accusations emanating from an ill-fated speech made by Alexander's general and companion Black Cleitus, which saw the king run him through, though this is hardly credible as an original utterance for such an occasion as it would have undermined Cleitus' own argument that Alexander's men (and father) were responsible for a great deal of his hard-fought success.[103] But the reading of Livy's epic on the founding of Rome (and Virgil's as well) was compulsory reading for anyone on the Roman political road, so Curtius, showing due respect, was following their lead.[104]

There may well be one final – and perhaps the most relevant – clue to a publication under Nero, for Curtius made a noteworthy denial that Alexander left succession instructions before he died in Babylon: 'some have believed that the provinces were distributed by Alexander in his Will, but I (or 'we') have ascertained that this report, though handed down by some authorities, was false' (see Grant, *Last Will and Testament*, 2021, chapter 3).[105] Curtius was attempting to suppress any further debate on the matter with his emphatic wording, and the relevance of this stems from the lingering rumour that Nero had poisoned Claudius, with Agrippina dispensing with the will that would have publicly reconfirmed as his successor the 14-year-old Britannicus, Claudius' son by his former wife, Messalina.[106] Moreover, as one historian points out: 'Both Alexander and Nero had domineering mothers, both of whom were suspected of complicity in the deaths of the two fathers and accessions of the sons.'[107] Curtius' idiomatic will denial seems aggressively penned in the context of distant Alexander, when he could have simply stated he knew of the tradition, just as Arrian had dismissively referred to the claims of conspiracy to poison Alexander. But Curtius' emphatic and clearly targeted forensic denial would have resonated loudly as a rumour-buster, or at least a suppressant, for allegations still pointing at Nero. And if it did not, it would still have earned Curtius imperial points.

Problems Identifying Curtius with Tacitus' Senator of the Same Name

If these parallels assist a dating, they also argue for a familiarity between the historian and his emperor. Curtius' description of 'the night that was almost our last' could suggest more than observer status, and potentially to personal political involvement. To suppose that the senatorial Curtius Rufus identified by Tacitus (see above) might find himself in imperial company is reasonable, but he appears to have died of old age in Africa late in Claudius' rule, or very early in Nero's. He becomes an even less adequate candidate when we consider that: 'It has long been recognised that there are many verbal similarities between Tacitus and Quintus Curtius Rufus.'[108] Indeed, some 600 examples have been identified, which suggest one historian repeatedly borrowed from the other, and if widely held dating contentions are correct, Tacitus was obviously plagiarizing Curtius.[109] Walter saw further textual parallels between Curtius' obituary for Alexander and Tacitus' summation of Germanicus' qualities, as well as similarities detailing the mourning following their respective deaths.[110] This emulation of Curtius perhaps justifies one summary of Tacitus' embellished style: 'He tells a fine story finely, but he cannot tell a plain story plainly.'[111]

As a recent study concluded, this provides no more than a date 'before which' Curtius could have published, for Tacitus commenced his own literary career with publications in AD 98, with his *Histories* and *Annals* following in AD 105 and 117. This would also indicate that Tacitus held Curtius in high esteem, or at least worthy of emulation. If we can agree with one scholarly opinion of Curtius – 'he can make epigrams which might pass for Tacitus on a day when Tacitus was feeling not quite at his best' – then Tacitus not only borrowed from Curtius, but on the whole he bettered him by far.[112]

Here we encounter the major problem with the aforementioned Curtius Rufus, for the senator who died in Africa around AD 55 was rather vilified by Tacitus, who afforded him the following: 'As to the origin of Curtius Rufus, whom some have described as the son of a gladiator, I would not promulgate a falsehood and I am ashamed to investigate the truth.'[113] In the previous paragraph, Tacitus recounted the omen that foretold Curtius' praetorship in Africa, his career under Tiberius and his unsuccessful mining activities that led his men to secretly petition the emperor to grant *advance* triumphal distinctions *ahead* of their toil. This cast a shadow on Curtius' overzealous activity in dangerous subterranean conditions. Tacitus summed up his career with:

> Afterwards, long of life and sullenly cringing to his betters, arrogant to his inferiors, unaccommodating among his equals, he held consular office, the insignia of triumph, and finally Africa; and by dying there fulfilled the destiny foreshadowed.[114]

Reiterating the poignant observation in a parallel source autopsy, would a literary 'mountain' like Tacitus have been moved by a relative 'molehill', and one he seems to have afforded such little respect?[115] Moreover, Tacitus' narrative gave no hint of *this* Curtius Rufus having a literary career, and neither did the index to Suetonius' *On*

Grammarians and Rhetoricians link the similarly named rhetorician to any historical monograph; he was listed as a '*rhetores*' but not as a '*grammatici*'.

If these individuals are to be discounted, do we have alternative historians who might fit the bill and who *were* respected by Tacitus, recalling that the forename (the Latin *praenomen*), Quintus, is absent from early manuscript headings? Tacitus cited two historians who provided detail for his *Annals*, the work that covered the Julio–Claudian emperors: Fabius Rusticus, 'an angry outsider', and more interestingly a Cluvius Rufus, a 'dispassionate insider'.[116] Both were of equestrian rank and both were intimately involved in the politics of the day.

Arguments for a Flavian Publication Date

Before we argue for an alternative identity for the historian we know as 'Curtius', we should take a look at the Flavian dynasty, for Vespasian's rule includes many of the ingredients to challenge Nero's as the most likely publication period, though it conspicuously lacks some too. But we should also consider the probability that Curtius' *History of Alexander the Great* (assuming this approximates the original title) was the product of many years' work, potentially spanning the terms of *more than one* emperor, and that for all we know, the final chapter might have been redrafted numerous times to 'fit the occasion' before finally being published.

After Nero and the 'year of the four emperors', Vespasian came to power for ten years, bringing the first true political calm since Tiberius' death over thirty years before. The intervening years had witnessed the intrigues associated with Caligula, Claudius, Nero, Galba, Otho and Vitellius. On 20 December AD 69, Vitellius was defeated and Vespasian, already proclaimed emperor by his troops in Egypt and Judaea that July, could now enter Rome and end the civil war. So here we find a good home for Curtius' 'sheathing of swords'.[117] The chaotic advance of Vespasian's troops under the command of Antonius Primus did result in a fire that again destroyed much of Rome, though no doubt the conflagration was easily attributed to retreating forces. Calm was restored, so 'torches' were metaphorically doused. To quote Suetonius, Rome was 'given stability by the Flavian family'.[118] But as some commentators remind us, the use of the verb *trepidare* ('to tremble in anticipation'), along with a 'rhetoric' that is 'too tame' for the structure, suggest an event *yet to happen*, and that seems to rule out Vespasian.[119]

However, a 'flourishing empire' did follow, in which much of the capital was rebuilt without the Neronian excesses, including a Temple of Peace.[120] Coinage was minted with the slogan *Roma resurgens* ('Rome rises again'), and Vespasian was remarkably 'down to earth' compared to the imperium of the previous decades. Much of the rustic virtue of former pre-Principate days resurfaced in him, minus the Republican zeal. Vespasian had suffered his own humiliations: Caligula had once filled his aedile toga with mud.[121] Furthermore, he is recorded as being tolerant of criticism and supportive of the literati and the arts, providing salaries from the Privy Purse to poets and teachers of rhetoric, including Quintilian who was soon elevated to consul.[122] Vespasian even had a sense of humour; his alleged last words – 'Oh dear, I think I am turning into a god!' – epitomized what was purportedly an extremely dry wit.[123]

Benign historians such as Josephus flourished; he was one of only two survivors of forty fighters besieged at the hillside town of Jotapata (Yodfat) in Judaea in AD 67, a siege in which Vespasian himself almost lost his life.[124] As the walls fell to the Roman ballistae and battering rams on the forty-seventh day of the siege, the last survivors drew lots as part of a collective suicide pact. The last lot fell to Josephus, who, after talking the second-to-last man out of death, was presented to Vespasian and then offered his services, predicting his captor would someday become emperor at Rome. It was prophetic, and Josephus, a renowned academic and prodigy from an early age, began his new career under the Flavians with free imperial lodging and an income as a Roman citizen.[125]

Vespasian is likely to have fostered an environment in which an imperial history might be published, if it sidestepped the complex web of intrigues of the recent civil wars.[126] Thus an account of Alexander could have been circulated then. Philosophers were not so fortunate, and Helvidius Priscus, outspokenly pro-republic, was put to death, though according to Suetonius it was reluctantly called for by the emperor.[127] Curtius' hopes for the longevity of 'the line of this house' would equally relate to the Flavians. Moreover, Curtius' prayer for a 'long duration' hinted at an exacerbation born of recent turbulence that immediately preceded Vespasian's term. Tacitus' own introduction to AD 69 suggested it was almost the last year for Rome, thus the 'last night' finds its place comfortably.

Taken at face value, the prosperity of Tyre remains a problem, for the Jewish Wars brought upheaval to the region, even if the thirteen references to the city in Josephus' account never mention Tyre's part. The Phoenician city remained neutral, or arguably loyal to Rome, perhaps for the commercial benefit that came from supplying the legions.[128] But as we noted, Curtius' was an encomium constructed when the need to mollify outweighed the literal truths, and when a *Pax Romana* could be invoked in a largely rhetorical sense.[129] Josephus confirmed that Vespasian had visited the region in AD 67 in the company of Agrippa II, king of the adjacent provinces.[130] If this later Flavian publication date can be successfully argued for, then the Curtius Rufus who died in Africa around AD 55 can once again be discounted as our historian.[131]

A Possible New Identity

Numerous scholars credit much of the material Tacitus used for his biographical detail of Caligula, Claudius, Nero and the 'year of the four emperors' to the much-admired Cluvius Rufus, a historian whose name appeared again in the accounts of Plutarch, Pliny, Suetonius, Cassius Dio and most likely Josephus; the citations made it clear that he was their source as well as, significantly, their subject matter.[132]

Josephus' coverage of the death of Caligula (which occupied three-quarters of his nineteenth book) and the Claudian coup is certainly the most detailed surviving account in the absence of Tacitus' books 7–10. It was penned with the confidence of a historian drawing on at least one impeccable 'inside source', and is replete with the dialogue of conspirators reproduced in a verbatim and non-rhetorical style. As early as 1870, one scholar proposed Cluvius Rufus was the 'inside source' who provided this detail. Josephus – whose forename, incidentally, also remains unknown – professed the importance of 'exactness' in his preface.[133] Assuming he adhered to his own methodology (never a safe assumption), then his choice of source would have mirrored that requirement; if Cluvius Rufus *was* the inside source, then Josephus also held him in high esteem.

Cluvius Rufus was also most likely the archetype for Suetonius' detail for the assassinations of Caligula, Claudius and Nero, and he provided detail for Plutarch's biographies of Galba and Otho, that is assuming Plutarch did not simply extract from Tacitus.[134] Suetonius had initially been well placed to access the court archives when he was given the freedom of the imperial library under Trajan, then holding the office of secretary under Hadrian. However, his verbal indiscretion, or physical affair, with the empress Vibia Sabina lost him imperial favour, so Suetonius must thereafter have resorted to using testimony from earlier historians such as Cluvius Rufus.[135]

The unnamed common source was clearly an eyewitness to events and we know that Cluvius Rufus had been an intimate of Nero and at the centre of the post-Nero intrigues of Galba, swiftly moving his allegiance to Otho and Vitellius after him. He needed to reassure the latter of his innocence in the charges brought against him, and what was obviously an eloquent defence resulted in a new imperial post. Cluvius was once again in imperial favour: he was one of two witnesses (with Silius Italicus) party to the surrender pact being discussed by Vitellius and Flavius Sabinus, the prefect of Rome and the city's cohorts (he was actually the brother of Vespasian), when surrounded by Vespasian's forces in late AD 69.[136]

It would be specious to create a link to the author of Alexander's history through the similarity in name alone, but other parallels do exist. Cluvius is a 'lost historian' in that none of his works survive and his forename is also uncertain.[137] His identification with the senators referred to by Suetonius and Tacitus confirmed he too followed the political road in the Julio–Claudian era as a political *nobilis*.[138] He was born as late as AD 8 and was an ex-consul by AD 65 (and as early as AD 41 if a 'Cluitus' mentioned by Josephus actually refers to Cluvius), possibly acting variously as a suffect consul under Caligula, then as a senator and later as a governor appointed in AD 68 by Galba (if not Nero himself before his death) to Hispania Tarraconensis, the province Galba had previously governed under Nero.[139]

This lucrative region of northern Spain was an expansion of the former province of Hispania Citerior, the mines of which were so lucidly described by Pliny, who became Procurator of the region during the 'gold rush' of AD 73.[140] And it seems that Cluvius did take some part in Caligula's assassination, if an episode recorded by Josephus is accurate and if the same Rufus is being referred to. If so, he was a careful operator. When questioned on rumours of political change by a senator sitting beside him – who then confided in him that 'the programme for today will include the assassination of a tyrant' – Cluvius denied any knowledge of it and quoted a line from Homer: 'Quiet, lest one of the Achaeans should hear your word.'[141]

Although his work is lost, we do know that Cluvius Rufus published historical accounts; Plutarch's *Roman Questions* cited him as the source for an answer on Dionysiac origins, so he appears something of an antiquarian. In this case, his knowledge stretched back to a plague of 361 BC, the time of Alexander's father's reign.[142] Pliny preserved a dialogue between Cluvius and the veteran governor of Germania Superior, curiously named Lucius Verginius Rufus, who had quelled the Vindex rebellion of AD 68 for Nero. Cluvius made an insincere-looking *apologia* pertaining to elements of his book that the governor might disapprove of:[143]

> You know, Verginius, how binding is objectivity in writing; thus, if in my *Histories* you happen to read anything not to your liking, I ask that you forgive me. And he to him, 'Why don't you know Cluvius, that what I did I did only that you may be free to write what you deem right?'[144]

The dialogue has spawned many different interpretations, each involving the intrigues behind Nero's fall and the calamitous year that followed.[145] Late in Nero's term, Verginius' legions had twice attempted to elevate him to the emperorship, and he had twice declined the role, so his riposte underpins his philosophical position on the usurpation of power. It seems the two men in the dialogue were central to those intrigues.

Pliny later described Verginius' 'double-vocation of history', saying he was 'one who outlived his moment of glory by thirty good years: he read poems and histories about himself and became a member of his own posterity'.[146] Cluvius' reference to his own *Histories* suggested he published more than one account, or at least biographed more than a single emperor or period. His care with imperial issues suggests these were unlikely to have been accounts of those *then* in power.[147] It also raises a further question: were Lucius Verginius Rufus and Cluvius Rufus related?

The gens Cluvii were situated in Capua in the third century BC and moved to Puteoli in Campania (a region now centred on Naples) a century later, enjoying a long history of commerce with Greeks and political success as praetors, senators, consuls and governors.[148] Virginius Rufus is attested as hailing from Mediolanum, modern Milan in northern Italy, so if they were related it would have been a 'new' family attachment. But name alone is an uncertain prosopographic method of establishing blood ties. The traditional naming convention, the *tria nomina* (*praenomen, nomen* and *cognomen*), evolved as ambitions widened, and when – to reinforce status or ancestry – new naming conventions were used. Genealogies were further clouded by adoption within the aristocratic classes and the confusion between the clan name (*nomon gentile*) and *cognomen* (the line within the gens) in later manuscripts.

Uncertainty aside, the careers of Verginius Rufus and Cluvius Rufus bear remarkable resemblances to one another through this period. Both were political survivors *par excellence*. Verginius Rufus, regarded as a *novus homo*, a 'new man' in Rome, came from humble origins: *equestri familia, ignoto patre* – a 'mere equestrian family, and a father unknown to fame' – according to Tacitus.[149] He was honoured with a consulship by Otho and elevated again thirty years later by Nerva (AD 30–98), the consul then beside him. Verginius penned poetry from the literary salon of his villa at Alsium in between, and enjoyed intimate friendship with (and guardianship of) Pliny the Younger, whose letter, *To Voconius Romanus*, eulogized him; an admiring Tacitus eventually delivered his funeral oration.

As for Cluvius Rufus' career, Tacitus stated that he received the following treatment from Stoic philosopher Heldivius Priscus: 'So he began his speech by praising Cluvius Rufus, who, he said, though just as rich and just as fine an orator as Marcellus, had never impeached a single individual in Nero's time.'[150] If Cluvius evidently blew with the political wind, or rather set his sails to gybe past the squalls that whipped through those years, his oratory must have been politically neutral too, perhaps in the style of Quintilian's *Institutes of Oratory*, which also sidestepped the traditional polemics on tyrants, dictators and trappings of absolute power. But that would not have prevented Cluvius profiling Alexander, with the aforementioned discretion and care attached to any imperial comparisons.

Priscus' praise, if it was praise and not a slight, suggests that although Cluvius' tact prevailed through Nero's emperorship, it did not exclude him from the odd declamation thereafter. The delayed polemic could be backed up by a further explanation from Tacitus on the source challenge behind his Annals:

> But, while the glories and disasters of the old Roman commonwealth have been chronicled by famous pens, and intellects of distinction were not lacking to tell the tale of the Augustan age, until the rising tide of sycophancy deterred them, the histories of Tiberius and Caligula, of Claudius and Nero, were falsified through cowardice while they flourished, and composed, when they fell, under the influence of still rankling hatreds.[151]

Though by now these are quite familiar themes, they were acutely relevant here.

A 1960 study proposes that the frequent use of Greek in Suetonius' biographies of the Caesars could be traced to Cluvius Rufus, passages conspicuous in that they 'attribute the worst excesses to the main characters'.[152] Campania was the most Hellenized part of Italy, and it is possible that Cluvius was a philhellene himself with his attested Greek ties. If correct, this suggests he *was* prepared to become a 'sensational and polemical writer' when the political climate permitted.[153] This *scandaleuse*, based around the court secrets he was privileged to, does not, as has been pointed out, preclude the lurid and scandalous being true.[154]

However, it is just as likely, or perhaps more probable, that Cluvius was the source of Tacitus' more lenient treatment of Nero, displaying the tact, not sensationalism, which Priscus attached to him. Cluvius was, indeed, maintaining the 'golden mean'.[155] In which case the source of Suetonius' Greek is more likely Pliny (also from the Como–Milan region), who tagged Nero an 'enemy of mankind'.[156] Pliny used Greek extensively, both isolated words and longer phraseology, because there were often no direct Latin equivalents for the subtle undertones of many Greek words and terms he found in his sources.[157] But sprinkling Greek onto Latin prose was a running theme through the Silver Age, providing texts with an archaic charm, especially using extracts from poetry, to impress an educated audience. It may also have been a necessary means of implication and innuendo when simple straight talk was not always possible.[158]

Moreover, Cluvius Rufus had been part of Nero's inner circle, acting as the emperor's herald or master of ceremonies at the new Greek-style artistic contests, the Neronia, where he announced the emperor would be singing the story from *Niobe*.[159] And he accompanied Nero on his artistic tour of Greece in AD 66–67, probably when Cluvius was in his 50s.[160] Notably, the future emperor, Vespasian, accompanied them too, falling out of favour with Nero for the apathy he showed towards his performances.[161] Cluvius was unlikely to have later published a biography that painted Nero as the monster Suetonius portrayed, for this would have called into question his own close association. His account was indeed most likely another quarantined affair. Tacitus was clear that Cluvius, possibly as an eyewitness, credited Agrippina with incestuous behaviour towards her son (possibly when she sensed she was losing authority over him), while others claimed the roles had been the reverse.[162] Although Claudius' suspicious death from the 'food of the gods' became a popular comical theme in Rome, it remains an allegorical episode and one Tacitus (possibly influenced by Cluvius' account) curiously refused to endorse.[163]

In complete contrast to his treatment of the governor of Africa, Tacitus, whose style was also visibly influenced by Sallust and Virgil, referred to Cluvius Rufus as 'an eloquent man'. Cluvius appears to have capably bottled essences from the Golden Age of Latin in his *Histories*; 'eloquent' was a term afforded to Tacitus himself by Pliny the Younger.[164] We don't know when Cluvius Rufus died. AD 70 has been suggested because Tacitus stated Spain was left vacant by his absence, but this does not require his death, only his retirement from the region.[165] We have four fragments and one anecdote of Cluvius' work.[166] Nonetheless, 'Cluvius has been recognised more and more as a literary artist', which is consistent with the style, or the attempted eloquence, we read in Curtius' history of Alexander.[167]

Oratory was, as we know from Cicero, a close cousin of history, so Cluvius was well placed to litter a non-contemporary account with epideictic speeches. The 'striving for rhetorical *tour de force*' is evident in a number of speeches found in Josephus' coverage of the downfall of Caligula and accession of Claudius.[168] If Josephus' vivid recounting of the aftermath and the plight of the people is truly based on Cluvius' style and vocabulary, and if Suetonius' description of Nero's last hours was likewise sourced, then we have further evidence of a technique reminiscent of that narrating the chaos at Babylon in the wake of Alexander's death.

A Case for Confusion

If Cluvius Rufus is a candidate for the authorship of the Alexander monograph, how could the confusion with a 'Curtius Rufus' have originally arisen? Well, firstly, the career similarity with the widely favoured candidate is striking. The Q. Curtius Rufus referred to in the index to Suetonius' *On Rhetoricians* was an eloquent rhetor, and Tacitus' African governor was a well-connected politician. Cluvius Rufus was both, it seems, and he was without doubt a historian as well.[169]

The Latin alphabet then had twenty-three capital characters. The letters 'J', 'U' and 'W' were added in the Middle Ages (or later) to facilitate use of the Roman alphabet in languages other than Latin, and 'U' sounds would have previously been written as 'V'. Hence Curtius Rufus would have appeared as CVRTII RVFI when pertaining to ownership of the manuscript title; we still see this in the 1623 *Cvrtii Rvfi de rebvs ab Alexandro magno gestis* manuscript from Mattaus Rader in Germany, for example. 'Cluvius' Rufus, appearing as CLVVII RVFI in similar circumstances, resided as close then to 'Curtius' as it does today, and possibly with more scope for confusion, as would CVRTIVS and CLVVIVS written as standalone names.

We still don't know when an uncorrupted Curtius manuscript was last available for reference, but certainly it was some time before the ninth-century *Codex Parisinus 5716* was produced. Neither do we know when 'Quintus' first appeared in the colophons. However, if a medieval scribe or his overseer was attempting to link the author to a historical figure, and one known to be a high-ranking equestrian from the Claudian age with a rhetor's eloquence, then the Curtius Rufus so conspicuously investigated by Tacitus and appearing in Suetonius' *On Rhetoricians* was an obvious choice, with the 'Q' (most obviously 'Quintus') for his *praenomen* being erroneously attached following the latter.

Other misidentifications in the biographing of Alexander are not difficult to pinpoint, and we might even have another example of the corruption of Cluvius. The aforementioned and otherwise unattested 'Cluitus' was cited in Josephus' *Jewish Antiquities* in a text concerning the murder of Gaius, the emperor better known by his *agnomen*, Caligula. Mommsen argued that the identity in Josephus' original Greek manuscripts should be corrected to 'Cluvius', recalling the historian's own advice to a praetor that he keep quiet on the planned treason.[170] Again, the arguments are not conclusive and were rejected by some later scholars, but the parallels are striking.[171]

The poet Martial curiously suggested that a colourful writer named Canius Rufus had covered the lives of Claudius and Nero:[172]

> Tell me, Muse, what my Canius Rufus is doing: is he putting on paper the acts of Claudian times for posterity to read, or the deeds which a mendacious writer ascribed to Nero? Or does he emulate the fables of rascal Phaedrus?[173]

Canius Rufus was cited as a 'poet and historian from Gades', modern Cadiz. Martial himself came from Hispania Tarraconensis, north-east Spain, and it is tempting to link Canius Rufus to Cluvius once more due to his Spanish presence, though in the northern region and not Gades. Yet the cognomen was common; Martial mentioned the name 'Rufus' thirty-three times in his *Epigrams*, while Cicero, a century earlier, wrote to his young protégé, Marcus Caelius Rufus, who appears to have even been an avid reader of Cleitarchus, Curtius' principal source. Caelius was the talented author of some of the more prominent letters in Cicero's epistolary *Letters to Friends*.[174] Catullus may have been referring to him in his *Rufus*, and if so, the references support a controversial figure that needed Cicero's defence: the *Pro Caelio*.[175]

Yet the addition of the poet from Gades places us in a position in which we must accept, if names have indeed been transmitted intact (and Josephus' 'Cluitus' aside), that both a Cluvius Rufus and a Canius Rufus – each well connected and linked to regions of Spain – penned accounts of Claudius and Nero, while the clues in Curtius Rufus' imperial encomium arguably fit Nero's emperorship. Additionally, the works of all three have either disappeared or exist without any background to the historian.

Interestingly, the 'Phaedrus' referred to in Martial's *Epigrams* is likely Gaius Julius Phaedrus, a Romanized Macedonian contemporary who wrote sometime between AD 43 and 70, and who Latinized the books of Aesop's fables. His largest collection bears the name *Romulus*, and a prose manuscript dating to the tenth century is addressed *Aesopos ad Rufum*, suggesting a dedication by the compiler to a 'Rufus'.[176] Was that to Canius Rufus, with whom Phaedrus might have been acquainted?

The fact remains that there is no evidence that Cluvius Rufus published a book on Alexander. This would be troublesome if much else was known about his work, but save his own reference to the *Histories*, nothing is. His subject matter is not described, only implied by the citations in the sources, and neither was he mentioned in Quintilian's list of the literati who appeared in his *Institutes of Oratory*, yet this remained incomplete as Quintilian himself admitted; neither Pliny the Younger nor other writers mentioned by Tacitus featured in his famous line-up.[177] As one scholar has remarked, surviving detail on historians publishing in the long interval between Livy and Tacitus is sparse.[178]

We do not even know where, or when, Tacitus, the mighty Roman annalist, was born, or in fact his *praenomen*: only books 1–4 of Tacitus' fourteen-book *Histories* are preserved complete. The first half of his *Annals* survived in a single copy of a manuscript from Corvey Abbey, and books 11–16 (and what remained of his *Histories*) are reproduced from a single manuscript found in the Benedictine Abbey at Monte Cassino – a 'barbarous script', commented Poggio Bracciolini. The latter, the *Codex Mediceus II* written in the Langobard script of the mid–eleventh century (though evidence suggests it derives from fifth–century Rustic Capitals manuscript, possibly through an intermediary),[179] gave Tacitus' *praenomen* as 'Publius', whereas Apollinaris Sidonius (*ca.* AD 430–489), a learned Gallo–Roman aristocrat, named him 'Gaius.'[180]

The paucity of Tacitus' material likely reflects the disfavour of both the late Caesars and the Church fathers, for he was openly contemptuous of the 'new' religion as well as the tyranny of the early emperors. We may also question whether his last annalistic work was to be titled *Annals*, for he actually named the former *Books of History from the Death of the Divine Augustus* (*Ab excessu divi Augusti*). We do not even know if it was designed to be distinct from what we call his *Histories*, though the temporal divide between past and contemporary history did likely separate them.

In the view of one eminent historian, Cluvius Rufus was not just a source, he was the *principal* source for Tacitus' own *Histories* and for much of his *Annals*, and hence concluded: 'The surviving books of Tacitus' *Annals* are the most conspicuous example of a great work of history written with the minimum amount of independent research.'[181] If, as has recently been argued, the textual similarities suggest that Tacitus drew from Curtius' history of Alexander, we should give credence to the fact that Curtius and Cluvius are one and the same author. If not, then the evidence requires we accept that Tacitus, the 'Roman Thucydides', took detail and style from *both* a Cluvius Rufus and a Curtius Rufus.

To reiterate: what this identity excursion on Curtius illustrates is that not only is much of the content for the surviving sources on Alexander – all from the Roman period – suspicious and conflicting, but we cannot even identify with any certainty several of the extant historians. What makes the separating of possible writers almost impossible is their plagiarism of style and content, lack of investigative creativity, their blind adherence to the rhetorical devices of the day and the requirement to mollify not just the audience but the imperial authority presiding over them. While Livy raised the question of whether Alexander's army could have defeated the legions of Rome, there is no doubt at all that the politics of Rome had the final word on the conqueror himself.

Chapter 11

Through the Cyclical Looking Glass

One should not look for thoughtful, or even consistent,
characterisations any more than one looks for sincerity or accuracy ...
the mistake has commonly been made of trying to divide Alexander's
historians into two classes, favourable and unfavourable.[1]

Lionel Pearson, *The Lost Histories of Alexander the Great*

A history in which every particular incident may be true may on
the whole be false.[2]

T.B. Macaulay, *History*

According to Aristotle, the tenets of Zoroastrianism and the Magi of the East believed there are two 'first principles' in the world: 'A good spirit and an evil essence; the name of the first is Zeus or Ahura Mazda, and the other Hades or Ahriman.' This dualism could have featured in any introduction to the life of Alexander, so divergent is his character portrayal within the Vulgate genre.[3]

Written in vastly different times, two books became required reading for the American founding fathers as a lesson and warning on the nature of governance, Machiavelli's *The Prince* and Xenophon's *On the Education of Cyrus*, copies of which remain today in the US Congress Library. Like the Magi's opposed spirits, they represent the two faces of man, one promoting rule by fear and the other by benign enlightenment, and each book had its place in the evolving profile of the Macedonian king.

One of the leitmotifs of Alexander's story is his belief in his own divine and heroic origins. Yet he also had mortals to emulate, and one of them was Cyrus the Great. Two centuries before him – tradition suggests 29 October 539 BC – Cyrus stood on the steps of the ziggurat of Etemenanki, the 'Cornerstone of the Universe', and made a dedication to the god Marduk in his newly conquered Babylon.[4] Rejecting the slavery and loot which was his by 'victor's justice', he purportedly made an address which is widely regarded as the first charter of human rights. In 1879, a clay cylinder was unearthed at Babylon that recorded the complete address, previously known to us only from the biblical references in the first chapter of the *Book of*

Ezra. A copy of the so-called Cyrus Cylinder now sits in the halls of the United Nations Secretariat Building in New York.[5]

Portrayed as politically astute, in the first years of the campaign at least, Alexander III chose to emulate Cyrus when in 333 BC he too first entered Babylon via the ancient Processional Way, having just defeated Darius III at the Battle of Gaugamela. He respected personal freedoms as well as local religious rights, and surviving cuneiform inscriptions found in the city's astronomical diaries captured a part of the declaration: 'Into your houses I shall not enter.'[6] Alexander even sought to repair the Esagila Temple, whose golden statue had been melted down by Xerxes upon his hasty return from Greece following defeat at Plataea in 479 BC.[7] This, along with the adoption of Persian customs and his inheriting a still largely unified Persian Empire, had led some modern commentators to even refer to Alexander as 'the last of the Achaemenids'.[8]

Whether Alexander displayed a genuine Graeco–Oriental spirit unique for his time or simple political expediency is perennially debated, but few men in history have been subjected to so many post-mortems through the ages. His body of literature was bruised by, or benefited from, the ebbs and flows of the philosophical movements and social tides that washed back and forth across the 'universal Comparandum', as Alexander has been termed.[9] Yet few men from our classical past have been so variously summed-up and decanted; Alexander remains, as one commentator aptly put it, 'a bottle which could be filled with any wine'.[10]

In Western eyes, Alexander metamorphosed first through the Hellenistic Age and the rise and fall of Rome, then through the so-called European Dark Ages and the Renaissance that rediscovered Hellenistic philosophies.

Renaissance France of the sixteenth and seventeenth centuries reviled Alexander, and much of the polemical tone was surely inspired by the darker episodes in Curtius' account, for the National Library of France had printed ten editions of his texts before 1550.[11] Nicolas de Soulfour proposed: 'Alexander, in order to acquire the title "Great", ceased to be just and did not hesitate to appropriate the empires of the others or lay unjust hands on the treasures of all the world, to increase his own glory.'[12] And though King Karl XII of Sweden (ruled 1697–1718) thought he *was* Alexander reborn when campaigning brilliantly in his Great Northern War in the Baltic, Nicolas Beauzée, in 1781, suggested Alexander 'had no other motive than his own vanity, no right on his side other than that he could seize with his sword, no rule other than that dictated by his passions'.[13] Durante degli Alighieri (*ca.* 1265–1321), whom we refer to mononymously as simply 'Dante', ultimately consigned Alexander to the inferno.[14]

But the popes – Alexander VI in particular and the Borgia line especially – had inclined to the opposite view, decorating the Vatican with his likeness and charging their contemporaries to 'behave like Alexander, in dealing with the kings of the East'.[15] Louis XIV, the 'Sun King' (1683–1715), fashioned himself on the conqueror, commissioning paintings and a set of prints named *Battles of Alexander*. Even Mehmet II, who ended the Byzantine Empire when conquering Constantinople, adopted the iconography of the Macedone.[16] The political philosopher, Montesquieu, saw an enlightened policy of infrastructure improvement and racial integration in Alexander's maritime plans and his Graeco–Persian intermarriages.[17]

Whereas Gustav Droysen saw a 'Bismarck' in Alexander in the 1870s,[18] classical scholar William Woodthorpe Tarn, born into privilege in 1869 and writing on the subject through to 1948 in the heyday of the League of Nations, represented Alexander's campaign somewhat differently: he saw in him that 'utopian' mission to bring unity or 'brotherhood to mankind'.[19] Fritz Schachermeyr published in 1949, and as a result saw the 'mixing of cultures' as a dangerous 'chaos of blood', rejecting Tarn's ideals completely.[20] As one commentator proposed, Tarn's thematic approach 'has tended to cow originality into silence, because of the mass of erudition underlying that study'. Ernst Badian, writing in 1958 in the aftermath of Jewish persecution, considered Alexander a ruthless totalitarian tyrant, while Peter Green, who published his brilliant but cynical account in the liberal 1970s, was simply disillusioned and failed to see any higher ideals at all.[21] And yet it has been said that the studies of 'Droysen, Berve, Tarn, Schachermeyr and Badian have both added to our understanding and multiplied uncertainties' attached to the Macedonian king.[22]

In contrast, Robin Lane Fox's charismatic 1973 biography has been labelled a 'last great gasp' of the Alexander 'romance'. Yet that persisting romantic stream has always existed when summing up his military achievements.[23] Even Polybius allowed Alexander some divinity when recognizing his soul had, 'as all admit, something of the superhuman in it'; and Peter Green conceded that Alexander was 'perhaps, taken all in all, the most incomparable general the world has ever seen'.[24] More recently still, Hammond's influential source studies were branded as: 'A misguided attempt to turn back the clock of Alexander studies to the time when W.W. Tarn dismissively rejected the fruitful work of German *Quellenforschung* [systematic source analysis] in an attempt to lay the foundations for his Alexander, the "Nice".'[25]

Alexander's character and mindset remain elusive, despite the best attempts of modern source forensics to unmask the man behind the rhetorical veil. Modern historians soon discovered they lacked the vocabulary to cope with him, and hybrid words like *verschmelzungspolitik* appeared in a German dissection to describe what some have romantically believed was his 'policy of racial fusion'.[26] So we are looking through yet another biographical-warping lens when assessing the Macedonian king through modern studies.

But to attempt to attach to Alexander the simplistic and polarized behavioural notions of 'good' or 'bad', or to label him 'benevolent' or 'evil', would be as anachronistic as concluding that Demosthenes, or any one of the Ten Attic Orators, was (in our sense of the word) a democrat or republican, a monarchist or anarchist, on the basis of the few speeches ascribed to them and in the context of the still not-fully-understood Athenian political system. While the Vulgate-genre authors would immerse us in the tale of a great king turned evil and abandoned by fortune, Alexander *had* surely changed in the decade on the march, but not in the absolute manner we read.

There can be no doubt that Alexander was, on the whole, incomprehensible to the average man of his age; simply put, he was a maverick. But we seek absolute definitions for Alexander's mercurial character when there was clearly an evolution. Can we reconcile the king who paired eighty officers with Asiatic brides at the Susa mass weddings with the campaigner who forbade them to take their half-caste offspring back to Macedon? Can we explain why Persepolis was burned when Cyrus' tomb and the Esagila Temple were repaired? And can the Alexander who ran through Black Cleitus with a spear be the same tyrant who let the ever-hostile Demosthenes outlive him?[27] The clean-cut and abstemious prince of age 18 who fought with his father at Chaeronea could hardly be the king who enjoyed nightly court banquets (which often descended into drinking binges) at Babylon, dressing variously as Ammon, Artemis and Hermes, a point even Alexander-admiring scholars reluctantly conceded.[28] Friedrich Nietzsche apparently took philosophical delight in discovering that at his death, the solemn Plato was found to be reading the light-hearted Aristophanes. He concluded that the philosopher had a sphinx-like nature; isn't it just possible Alexander did too?[29]

It remains difficult to establish just who or what Alexander had become when the historians of old, like the media of today, exaggerate peaks and troughs and sensationalize to sell. Besides, 'the original author of the myth was often Alexander himself'.[30] So the task of any modern historian is to strip back the layers of social, political, rhetorical and philosophical debris that cling to the extant accounts. Somewhere below that exoskeleton lies the bare-boned truth. To many historians, however, the icon of Alexander is not so much about who he was or even what he did; it is about what he came to represent in their particular era. And therein lies the flaw.

Aristotle warned that 'men are duped through certain likenesses between the genuine and the sham'.[31] His caution can be applied well to the primary witnesses to events of his day who blueprinted the Macedonian king. So along with those agenda-laden primary historians and those who later came under their sway, and beside the philosophers and rhetoricians who wished to add their brushstrokes to the art, it is their iconograph, and not Alexander's, that has been hanging in history's gallery. And in the pages of his books. *Caveat emptor*: buyer beware!

Bibliography

The English titles of ancient works are often the result of a very liberal translation process. I have used the most popular and accepted names.

ABBREVIATIONS – ANCIENT AUTHORS

Aelian, *Historical Miscellany*
Ammianus Marcellinus, *Historical Events*
Arrian, *The Campaign of Alexander*
Athenaeus, *The Dinner Philosophers*
Aulus Gellius, *Attic Nights*
Cassius Dio, *Roman History*
Curtius, *History of Alexander the Great*
Dexippus, précis by Photius of Dexippus' epitome of Arrian's *Events After Alexander*
Diodorus, *Library of World History*
Diogenes Laertius, *Lives and Opinions of Eminent Philosophers*
Eusebius, *Ecclesiastical History*
Herodian, *History of the Empire From the Death of Marcus Aurelius*
Herodotus, *The Histories*
Josephus, *Jewish Antiquities*
Justin, *Epitome of the Philippic History of Pompeius Trogus*
Juvenal, *Satires*
Livy, *The Early History of Rome*
Nepos, *Eumenes; Lives of Eminent Commanders*
Ovid, *Transformations*
Pausanias, *Guide to Ancient Greece*
Pliny, *Natural History*
Plutarch, *The Life of Alexander from his Parallel Lives*
Polyaenus, *Stratagems of War*
Polybius, *Histories*
Quintilian, *Institutes of Oratory*
Romance, *The Greek Alexander Romance*
Strabo, *Geography*
Suetonius, *About the Life of the Caesars*

Tacitus, *Annals*
Thucydides, *History of The Peloponnesian War*
Valerius Maximus, *Nine Books of Memorable Deeds and Sayings*
Xenophon, *The Education of Cyrus*

MODERN ABBREVIATIONS

FGrH, *Fragmente der griechischen Historiker*, F. Jacoby (Leiden, 1926–1958).

MODERN BIBLIOGRAPHY

For clarity, only the publication being referred to in the book is italicized, though convention would also italicize the journal or publication in which the article appeared.

Alonso-Núñez, J.M. (1987), *An Augustan World History: The Historiae Philippicae of Pompeius Trogus*, Greece and Rome, Second Series, 34, pp.56–72.

Anson, E.M. (1977), *The Siege of Nora: A Source Conflict*, Greek, Roman and Byzantine Studies, 18, pp.251–256.

Anson, E.M. (1980), *Discrimination and Eumenes of Cardia*, The Ancient World 3, pp.55–59.

Anson, E.M. (1984), *The Meaning of the Term Makedones*, The Ancient World 10, pp.67–68.

Anson, E.M. (1985), *The Hypaspists: Macedonia's Professional Citizen-Soldiers*, Historia 34, pp.246–248.

Anson, E.M. (1986), *Diodorus and the Dating of Triparadeisus*, The American Journal of Philology 107, no. 2,, pp.208–217.

Anson, E.M. (1988), *Hypaspists and Argyraspids after 323 BCE*, The Ancient History Bulletin 2, no. 6, pp.131–133.

Anson, E.M. (1988), *Antigonus, the Satrap of Phrygia*, Historia: Zeitschrift für Alte Geschichte 37, no. 4, pp.471–477.

Anson, E.M., *The Evolution of the Macedonian Army Assembly (330–315 BC)*, Historia: Zeitschrift für Alte Geschichte 40, no. 2, pp.230–247.

Anson, E.M. (1992), *Craterus and the Prostasia*, Classical Philology 87, January 1992, pp.38–43.

Anson, E.M. (1996), *The 'Ephemerides' of Alexander the Great*, Historia: Zeitschrift für Alte Geschichte 45, no. 4, pp.501–504.

Anson, E.M. (2003), *The Dating of Perdiccas' Death and the Assembly at Triparadeisus*, Greek, Roman and Byzantine Studies 43, pp.373–390.

Anson, E.M. (2004), *Eumenes of Cardia: A Greek amongst Macedonians* (Brill).

Anson, E.M. (2013), *Alexander the Great, Themes and Issues* (Bloomsbury).

Anson, E.M. (2014), *Alexander's Heirs, the Age of the Successors* (Wiley Blackwell).

Arthur-Montagne, J. (2014), *Persuasion, Emotion, and the Letters of the Alexander Romance*, Ancient Narrative 11, pp.159–189.

Atkinson, J.E. (1963), *Primary Sources and the Alexanderreich*, Acta Classica 6, pp.125–137.

Atkinson, J.E. (1994), *A Commentary on Q. Curtius Rufus' Historiae Alexandri Magni*, Books 5 to 7.2, Acta Classica, Supplementum 1.

Atkinson, J.E. (1996), review of A.B. Bosworth, *Alexander and the East: the Tragedy of Triumph* (Clarendon Press).

Atkinson, J.E. (1997), *Q. Curtius Rufus' Historiae Alexandri Magni*, Aufstieg und Niedergang der römischen Welt II, no. 34.4, pp.3447–3483.

Atkinson, J.E. (2009), *Alexander's Last Days: Malaria and Mind Games*, Acta Classica 52, pp.23–46.

Atkinson, J.E. & Yardley, J.C. (trans.) (2009), *Curtius Rufus, Histories of Alexander the Great, Book 10* (Oxford University Press).

Attridge, H.W. & Oden, R.A. (1981), *Philo of Byblos: Phoenician History, Introduction, Critical Text, Translation, Notes*, Catholic Biblical Quarterly Monograph Series 9.

Avcio lu, N. (2011), *Turquerie and the Politics of Representation 1728–1876* (Ashgate Publishing Company).

Badian, E. (1958), *Alexander the Great and the Unity of Mankind*, Historia: Zeitschrift für Alte Geschichte 7, no. 4, October 1958, pp.425–444.

Badian, E. (1963), *The Death of Philip II*, Phoenix 17, pp.244–250.

Badian, E. (1964), *Alexander the Great and the Loneliness of Power*, in Studies in Greek and Roman History (Blackwell), pp.192–205.

Badian, E. (1968), *A King's Notebooks*, Harvard Studies in Classical Philology 72, pp.183–204.

Badian, E. (1975), *Nearchus the Cretan*, Yale Classical Studies 24, pp.147–170.

Bagnall, R.S. (1976), *The Administration of the Ptolemaic Possessions outside Egypt* (Leiden).

Bagnall, R.S. (2002), *Alexandria: Library of Dreams*, American Philosophical Society 146, no. 4, December 2002, pp.348–362.

Bagnall, R.S. & Derow, P. (eds) (2004), *The Hellenistic Period, Historical Sources in Translation* (Blackwell).

Baker, M. & Saldanha, G. (eds) (2009), *Routledge Encyclopedia of Translation Studies* (Routledge).

Balme, M. (2001), *Menander, The Plays and Fragments* (Oxford University Press).

Balot, R.K. (2001), *Greed and Injustice in Classical Athens* (Princeton University Press).

Barber, G.L. (1993), *The Historian Ephorus* (Ares Publishers).

Barnes, J. (2000), *Aristotle, A Very Short Introduction* (Oxford University Press).

Barrett, A.A. (1978), *Observations of Comets in Greek and Roman Sources Before AD 410*, Journal of the Royal Astronomical Society of Canada 72, pp.81–105.

Bartlett, J.R. (1985), *Jews in the Hellenistic World, Josephus, Aristeas, The Sybilline Oracles, Eupolemus* (Cambridge University Press).

Baynes, N.H. (1926), *The Historia Augusta. Its Date and Purpose* (Oxford University Press).

Baynham, E.J. (1995), *An Introduction to the Metz Epitome: its Tradition and Value*, Antichthon 29, pp.60–77.

Baynham, E.J. (1995), *Bucephalus, Various Versions of Alexander's Taming of his Horse*, Ancient History Bulletin 9, no.1, pp.1–13.

Baynham, E.J. (1998), *Alexander the Great, The Unique History of Quintus Curtius* (University of Michigan Press, 2004 edition).

Bentley, R. (1697), *Dissertation upon the epistles of Phalaris, Volumes 1 and 2* (Dyce, 1836 edition).

Berry, P. (1999), *Correspondence between Paul and Seneca, A.D. 61–65* (Edwin Mellen Press).

Berthold, R.M. (1984), *Rhodes in the Hellenistic Age* (Cornell University Press).

Berve, H. (1926), *Das Alexandererreich auf prosopographischer Grundlage* (CH Beck).

Berzunza, J. (1941), *Preliminary Notes of the Three Italian Versions of Quintus Curtius Rufus' Historiae Alexandri Magni*, Italica 18, no. 3, pp.133–137.

Bevan, E.R. (1902), *The House of Seleucus* (Ares Publishers, 1985 edition).

Bevan, E.R. (1913), *Stoics and Sceptics* (Clarendon Press).

Bevan, E.R. (1927), *The House of Ptolemy: A History of Egypt under the Ptolemaic Dynasty* (Ares Publishers, 1968 edition).

Billows, R.A. (1990), *Antigonus the One-Eyed and the Creation of the Hellenistic State* (University of California Press, 1997 edition).

Bishop, M. (1983), *Petrarch and his World* (Indiana University Press).

Blackburn, S. (2006), *Plato's Republic, A Biography* (Atlantic Books).

Blackwell, C.W. (1999), *In the Absence of Alexander, Harpalus and the Failure of Macedonian Authority* (Peter Lang Publishing).

Boardman, J. (1964), *The Greeks Overseas, Their Early Colonies and Trade* (Thames and Hudson, 1999 edition).

Boardman, J., Griffin, J. & Murray, O. (1986), *The Oxford History of Greece and The Hellenistic World* (Oxford University Press).

Borchardt, F.L. (1986), *Forgery, False Attribution, and Fiction: Early modern German History and Literature*, Studi Umanistici Piceni 6, pp.27–35.

Borza, E.N. (1995), *Makedonika*, Essays by Eugene N. Borza (Regina Books).

Borza, E.N. & Palagia, O. (2007), *The Chronology of the Macedonian Royal Tombs at Vergina*, Jahrbuch des Deutschen Archäologisches Instituts 122, pp.81–125.

Bosworth, A.B. (1971), *The Death of Alexander the Great: Rumour and Propaganda*, Classical Quarterly, New Series 21, no. 1, pp.111–136.

Bosworth, A.B. (1976), *Errors in Arrian*, Classical Quarterly, New Series 26, no. 1, pp.117–139.

Bosworth, A.B. (1978), *Eumenes, Neoptolemus and PSI XII 1284* (University of Western Australia).

Bosworth, A.B. (1981), *A Missing Year in the History of Alexander the Great*, The Journal of Hellenic Studies 101, pp.17–39.

Bosworth, A.B. (1983), *History and Rhetoric in Curtius Rufus, A Commentary on Q. Curtius Rufus' 'Historiae Alexandri Magni', Books 3 and 4 by J.E. Atkinson*, review in Classical Philology 78, no. 2, April 1983, pp.150–161.

Bosworth, A.B. (1988), *From Arrian to Alexander: Studies in Historical Interpretation* (Clarendon Press).

Bosworth, A.B. (1988), *Conquest and Empire, The Reign of Alexander The Great* (Cambridge University Press).

Bosworth, A.B. (1992), *Philip III Arrhidaeus and the Chronology of the Successors*, Chiron 22, pp.55–81.

Bosworth, A.B. (1993), *Perdiccas and the Kings*, Classical Quarterly 63, pp.420–427.

Bosworth, A.B. (2002), *The Legacy of Alexander, Politics, Warfare and Propaganda under the Successors* (Oxford University Press).

Bosworth, A.B. (2004), *Mountain and Molehill? Cornelius Tacitus and Quintus Curtius*, Classical Quarterly, December 2004, pp.551–567.

Bosworth, A.B. & Baynham, E.J. (2000), *Alexander the Great in Fact and Fiction* (Oxford University Press).

Boyer, C.B. (1991), *Euclid of Alexandria, a History of Mathematics* (J. Wiley and Sons).

Briant, P. (1974), *Alexander the Great and his Empire, A Short Introduction* (Princeton University Press, 2012 edition).

Brickhouse, T.C. & Smith, N.D. (2001), *The Trial and Execution of Socrates* (Oxford University Press).

Brosius, M. (1996), *Women in Ancient Persia (559–331 BC)* (Oxford University Press).

Brown, T.S. (1947), *Hieronymus of Cardia*, The American Historical Review 52, no. 4, pp.684–696.

Brown, T.S. (1949), *Onesicritus: A Study in Hellenistic Historiography* (Ares Publishers, 1981 edition).

Brown, T.S. (1950), *Clitarchus*, The American Journal of Philology 71, no. 2, pp.134–155.

Brown, T.S. (1959), *Timaeus and the Aeneid*, The Vergilian Society 6, 1959–fall 1960, pp.4–12.

Brown, T.S. (1962), *The Greek Sense of Time in History as Suggested by Their Accounts of Egypt*, Historia: Zeitschrift für Alte Geschichte 11, no. 3, July 1962, pp.257–270.

Brunt, P.A. (1975), *Alexander, Barsine and Heracles*, Rivista di Filologia di Instruzione Classica 103, pp.22–34.

Brunt, P.A. (1974), *Notes on Aristobulos of Cassandria*, Classical Quarterly 24, pp.65–69.

Brunt, P.A. (1980), *On Historical Fragments and Epitomes*, Classical Quarterly, New Series 30, no. 2, pp.477–494.

Carney, E.D. (2006), *Olympias, Mother of Alexander the Great* (Routledge).

Carney, E.D. & Ogden, D. (eds) (2010), *Philip II and Alexander the Great, Father and Son, Lives and Afterlives* (Oxford University Press).

Casson, L. (1971), *Ships and Seamanship in the Ancient World* (Princeton University Press, 1995 edition).

Casson, L. (2001), *Everyday Life in Ancient Egypt* (The Johns Hopkins University Press, expanded edition from the original published in 1975 as The Horizon Book of Daily Life in Egypt).

Casson, L. (2001), *Libraries in the Ancient World* (Yale University Press).

Champion, C. (2000), *Romans as BAPBAPOI: Three Polybian Speeches and the Politics of Cultural Indeterminacy*, Classical Philology 95, no. 4, October 2000, pp.425–444.

Champion, J. (2014), *Antigonus the One-Eyed, Greatest of the Successors* (Pen & Sword Military).

Champlin, E. (2003), *Nero* (The Belknap Press of Harvard University Press).

Chroust, A.H. (1964), *Aristotle and the Philosophies of the East*, The Review of Metaphysics 18, no. 3, March 1964, pp.572–580.

Chroust, A.H. (1970), *Estate Planning in Hellenic Antiquity: Aristotle's Last Will and Testament*, Notre Dame Lawyer 45, pp.629–662.

Chugg, A.M. (2009), *The Death of Alexander the Great, a Reconstruction of Cleitarchus* (AMC Publications, 2010 edition).

Collins, D. (2008), *Magic in the Ancient Greek World* (Blackwell Publishing).

Cook, B.L. (2000), *Theopompus not Theophrastus: correcting an Attribution in Plutarch Demosthenes 14.4*, The American Journal of Philology 121, no. 4, winter 2000, pp.537–547.

Copenhaver, B.P. (ed.) (1992), *Hermetica: The Greek Corpus Hermeticum and the Latin Asclepius in a New English Translation* (Cambridge University Press).

Cornell, T.J. (2013), *The Fragments of the Roman Historians* (Oxford University Press).

Crake, J.E.A. (1940), *The Annales of the Pontifex Maximus*, Classical Philology 35, no. 4, October 1940, pp.375–386.

Cruttwell, C.T. (1877), *A History of Roman Literature from the Earliest Period to the Death of Marcus Aurelius* (Charles Griffin & Co).

Dalley, S. (2013), *The Mystery of the Hanging Garden of Babylon: an Elusive World Wonder Traced* (Oxford University Press).

Deane, S.N. (1918), *Greek in Pliny's Letters*, The Classical Weekly 12, no. 6, pp.41–44.

de Polignac, F. (1999), *From the Mediterranean to Universality? The Myth of Alexander, Yesterday and Today*, Mediterranean Historical Review 14, no. 1, pp.1–17.

Drews, R. (1975), *The Babylonian Chronicles and Berossus*, Iraq 37, no. 1, spring 1975, pp.39–55.

Droysen, J.G. (1877), *Geschichte des Hellenismus I, Geschichte Alexanders des Grossen* (Gotha).

Ehrman, B.D. (2014), *Forgery and Counterforgery; The Use of Literary Deceit in Early Christian Polemics* (Oxford University Press).

Ellis, W.M. (1994), *Ptolemy of Egypt* (Routledge).

Engels, D.W. (1978), *Alexander the Great and the Logistics of the Macedonian Army* (University of California Press).

Errington, R.M. (1969), *Bias in Ptolemy's History of Alexander*, Classical Quarterly, New Series 19, pp.233–242.

Errington, R.M. (1970), *From Babylon to Triparadeisus: 323–320 BC*, Journal of Hellenic Studies 90, pp.49–77.

Erskine, A. (2002), *Life After Death: Alexandria and the Body of Alexander*, Greece and Rome 49, no. 2, October 2002, pp.163–179.

Fears, J.R. (1976), *Silius Italicus, Cataphracti, and the Date of Quintus Curtius Rufus*, Classical Philology 71, no. 3, pp.214–223.

Fears, J.R. (1976), *The Solar Monarchy of Nero and the Imperial Panegyric of Q. Curtius Rufus*, Historia: Zeitschrift für Alte Geschichte 25, no. 4, 4th quarter 1976, pp.494–496.

Feldman, L.H. (1996), *Studies in Hellenistic Judaism* (Brill).

Finlay, M.I. (1973), *The Ancient Economy* (University of California Press, second edition, 1985).

Fitzgerald, R. (trans.) (1998), *Homer, The Odyssey* (Farrar, Straus and Giroux).

Flower, M.A. (1994), *Theopompus of Chios, History and Rhetoric in the Fourth Century BC* (Clarendon Press).

Fortenbaugh, W. & Schütrumpf, E. (eds) (2000), *Demetrius of Phalerum* (Transaction Publishers).

Foster, B.O. (1874), *Livy* (Trollope Press, 2008 edition).

Fraser, P.M. (1996), *Cities of Alexander the Great* (Clarendon Press).

Frier, B.W. (1979), *Libri Annales Pontificum Maximorum: The Origins of the Annalistic Tradition* (University of Michigan, 1999 edition).

Frolov, R.M. (2013), *Public Meetings in Ancient Rome: Definitions of the Contiones in the Sources*, Graeco-Latina Brunenesia 18, no. 1, pp.75–84.

Fubini, R. (1996), *Humanism and Truth: Valla Writes Against the Donation of Constantine*, Journal of the History of Ideas 57. no. 1, January 1996, pp.79–86.

Fuhrmann, H. (1972–1973), *Einfluß und Verbreitung der pseudoisidorischen Fälschungen*, 3 vols, Schriften der Monumenta Germaniae Historica 24, nos 1–3.

Geller, M.J. (1990), *Astronomical Diaries and Corrections of Diodorus*, Bulletin of the School of Oriental and African Studies, University of London 53, no. 1, pp.1–7.

Gibbon, E. (1776–1789), *History of the Decline and Fall of the Roman Empire* (Penguin, 1996 edition; originally published as vol. I, 1776; vols II, III, 1781; vols IV, V, VI, 1788–1789).

Gibson, T. (1998), *The Platonic Canon*, the APA Newsletter 98, no. 1.

Gill, C. & Wiseman, T.P. (eds) (1993), *Lies and Fiction in the Ancient World* (University of Exeter Press).

Goralski, J. (1989), *Arrian's Events after Alexander, Summary of Photius and Selected Fragments*, The Ancient World 19, nos 3–4, pp.81–108.

Gottschalk, H.B. (1980), *Heraclitus of Pontus* (Oxford University Press).

Goukowski, P. (1978), *Essai sur les origins du mythe d'Alexandre, vol 1* (Publications de l'Universite de Nancy).

Grafton, A. (1975), *Joseph Scaliger and Historical Chronology*, History and Theory 14, pp.156–185.

Grafton, A. (1983), *Joseph Scaliger: A Study in the History of Classical Scholarship*, 2 volumes (Oxford University Press).

Grafton, A. (1990), *Forgers and Critics: Creativity and Duplicity in Western Scholarship* (Princeton University Press).

Grafton, A. & Blair, A. (eds) (1998), *The Transmission of Culture in Early Modern Europe*, Shelby Cullom Davis Center for Historical Studies series (University of Pennsylvania Press).

Grafton, A., Most, G.W. & Settis, S. (2010), *The Classical Tradition* (Harvard University Press).

Grant, M. (trans.) (1956), *The Annals of Cornelius Tacitus* (Penguin).

Grant, M. (1995), *Greek and Roman Historians, information and misinformation* (Routledge).

Grant, D. (2017), *In Search of the Lost Testament of Alexander the Great* (Matador Press).

Grant, D. (2019), *Unearthing the Family of Alexander the Great, the Remarkable Discovery of the Royal Tombs of Macedon* (Pen & Sword History Press).

Grant, D. (2021), *The Last Will and Testament of Alexander the Great, an Empire Left to the Strongest* (Pen & Sword History Press).

Graves, R. (1955), *The Greek Myths* (Penguin, 1992 edition).

Gray, V. (1987), *Mimesis in Greek Historical Theory*, The American Journal of Philology 108, no. 3, autumn 1987, pp.467–486.

Green, P.M. (1970), *Alexander the Great* (Book Club Associates, 1973 edition).

Green, P.M. (1974), *Alexander of Macedon, 356–323 BC: A Historical Biography* (University of California Press, 1991 edition).

Green, P.M. (1990), *Alexander to Actium: The Historical Evolution of the Hellenistic Age* (University of California Press).

Green, P.M. (2007), *The Hellenistic Age: A Short History* (Random House).

Greenwalt, W. (1985), *The Introduction of Caranus into the Argead King List* (The University of Santa Clara).

Gregory, C.G. (1886), *The Quires in Greek Manuscripts*, The American Journal of Philology 7, no. 1 (The Johns Hopkins University Press).

Griffin, M. (1986), *Philosophy, Cato and Roman Suicide*, Greece and Rome 33, no. 2, October 1986, pp.192–202.

Griffith, G.T. (1935), *The Mercenaries of the Hellenistic World* (Ares Publishers, 1984 edition).

Grmek, M.D. (1989), *Diseases in the Ancient Greek World* (The Johns Hopkins University Press, 1989).

Gudeman, A. (1894), *Literary Fraud Amongst the Greeks*, in Classical Studies in Honour of Henry Drisler (Macmillan), pp.52–74.

Gudeman, A. (1894), *Literary Fraud Amongst the Romans*, Transactions of the American Philological Association 25, pp.140–164.

Guthrie, W.K.C. (1971), *The Sophists* (Cambridge University Press).

Hadjinicolaou, N. (1997), T*he Disputes about Alexander and his Glorification in the Visual Arts*, in N. Hadjinicolaou (ed.) catalogue of the exhibition Alexander the Great in European Art, Thessaloniki, 22 September 1997 to 11 January 1998.

Hadley, R.A. (1969), *Hieronymus of Cardia and Early Seleucid Mythology*, Historia 18, pp.142–152.

Hadley, R.A. (2001), *A Possible Lost Source for the Career of Eumenes of Kardia*, Historia: Zeitschrift für Alte Geschichte 50, no. 1,1st quarter 2001, pp.3–33.

Hall, F.W. (1913), *A Companion to Classical Texts* (Clarendon Press).

Hamilton, J.R. (1961), *Cleitarchus and Aristobulus*, Historia 10, pp.448–458.

Hamilton, J.R. (1971), introduction to *Arrian, The Campaigns of Alexander* (Penguin).

Hamilton, J.R. (1988), *The Date of Quintus Curtius Rufus*, Historia: Zeitschrift für Alte Geschichte 37.

Hammond, N.G.L. (1991), *The Miracle that was Macedonia* (Sidgwick & Jackson).

Hammond, N.G.L. (1993), *Sources for Alexander the Great: An Analysis of Plutarch's Life and Arrian's Anabasis Alexandrou* (Cambridge University Press).

Hammond, N.G.L. (1994), *Collected Studies III, Alexander and his Successors in Macedonia* (Adolf M. Hakkert).

Hammond, N.G.L. (1994), *Philip of Macedon* (Duckworth, 2002 edition).

Hammond, N.G.L. (1996), *The Early History of Macedonia*, The Ancient World 27, no. 1, pp.67–71.

Hammond, N.G.L. (1998), *Portents, Prophesies and Dreams in Diodorus books 14–17*, Roman and Byzantine Studies 39, no. 4, pp.407–428.

Hammond, M. (trans.) & Atkinson, J. (introduction & notes) (2013), *Alexander the Great, The Anabasis and the Indica* (Oxford University Press).

Hannah, R. (2005), *Greek and Roman Calendars, Constructions of Time on the Classical World* (Gerald Duckworth and Company).

Hanson, V.D. (ed.) (1991), *Hoplites, The Classical Greek Battle Experience* (Routledge).

Harris, M.H. (1999), *History of Libraries in the Western World*, 4th edition (Rowman and Littlefield Publishers Inc).

Hauben, H. (1977), *The First War of the Successors (321BC): Chronological and Historical Problems*, Ancient Society 8, pp.85–120.

Heckel, W. (1984), *Introduction to Quintus Curtius Rufus, The History of Alexander* (Penguin).

Heckel, W. (1987), *Fifty-Two Anonymae in the History of Alexander*, Historia: Zeitschrift für Alte Geschichte 36, no. 1, 1st quarter 1987, pp.114–119.

Heckel, W. (1993), review of N.G.L. Hammond, *Sources for Alexander the Great: An Analysis of Plutarchs' Life and Arrian's Anabasis Alexandrou* (Cambridge University Press), in the Bryn Mawr Classical Review 97.4.8.

Heckel, W. (2006), *Who's Who in the Age of Alexander the Great* (Blackwell Publishing).

Heckel, W. & Yardley, J.C. (1997), *Justin, Epitome of the Philippic History of Pompeius Trogus, Volume 1, Books 11–12* (Clarendon Press).

Heckel, W. & Yardley, J.C. (2004), *Alexander the Great: Historical Sources in Translation* (Blackwell Publishing).

Hedrick, C.W. (2000), *History and Silence; Purge and Rehabilitation of Memory in Late Antiquity* (University of Texas Press).

Hegel, G.W.F. (1837), *Lectures on The Philosophy of History*, originally delivered as lectures at the University of Berlin, 1821, 1824, 1827, 1831. First published by Eduard Gans in 1837 and by Karl Hegel in 1840; first full English edition by H.B. Nisbet (Cambridge University Press, 1974).

Heller-Roazen, D. (2002), *Tradition's Destruction: On the Library of Alexandria*, October 100, Obsolescence, spring 2002, pp.133–153.

Herm, G. (1975), *The Phoenicians, The Purple Empire of the Ancient World* (William Morrow and Company).

Higbie, C. (2003), *The Lindian Chronicle and the Greek Creation of Their Past* (Oxford University Press).

Highet, G. (1949), *The Classical Tradition, Greek and Roman Influences on Western Literature* (Oxford University Press).

Hochart, P. (1889), *De l'Authenticite des Annales et des Histoires de Tacite* (G Gounouilhou).

Hornblower, J. (1981), *Hieronymus of Cardia* (Oxford University Press).

Huffman, C. (1993), *Philolaus of Croton Pythagorean and Presocratic: A Commentary on the Fragments and Testimonia with Interpretive Essays* (Cambridge University Press).

Iossif, P.P., Chankowski, A.S. & Lorber, C.C. (eds) (2007), *More than Men, Less than Gods, Studies on Royal Cult And Imperial Worship*, Studia Hellenistica 51, Proceedings of the International Colloqium Organised by the Belgian School at Athens (1–2 November 2007).

Jacoby, F. (1923–1958), *Die Fragmente der griechischen Historiker I-II* (FGrHist, Berlin).

Jaeger, W. (1939), *Paideia, The Ideals of Greek Culture* (Oxford University Press, 1965 edition).

Jobes, K. & Silva, M. (2001), *Invitations to the Septuagint* (Paternoster Press).

Jones, W.H.S. (1868), *Hippocrates Collected Works I* (Harvard University Press).

Jones, Sir W. (1783), *On the Gods of Hellas, Italy and India*, extracted from Asiatic Researches (1788), pp.221–275.

Kagan, D. (ed.) (1965), *The Great Dialogue: A History of Greek Political Thought from Homer to Polybius* (The Free Press).

Kebric, R.B. (1977), *In the Shadow of Macedon: Duris of Samos* (Franz Steiner Verlag GMBH).

Kenyon, G. (1899), *The Paleography of Greek Papyri* (Ares Publishers, 1998 edition).

Ker, J. (2009), *The Death of Seneca* (Oxford University Press).

Kotrc, R.F. & Walters, K.R. (1979), *A bibliography of the Galenic Corpus. A newly researched list and arrangement of the titles of the treatises extant in Greek, Latin, and Arabic*, Transactions and Studies of the College of Physicians of Philadelphia 1, no. 4, December 1979, pp.256–304.

Kraus, C.S. (ed.) (1994), *Ab Urbe Condita Book VI* (Cambridge University Press).

Kuhrt, A. (1983), *The Cyrus Cylinder and Archaemenid Imperial Policy*, Journal of Studies of the Old Testament 25, pp.83–97.

Lane Fox, R. (1973), *Alexander the Great* (Penguin, 1986 edition).

Lane Fox, R. (1980), *The Search for Alexander* (Little, Brown and Company).

Lattimore, R. (1953), introduction to *Aeschylus Orestia* (The University of Chicago Press).

Levick, B., *L. Verginius Rufus and the Four Emperors*, Rheinisches Museum für Philologie 128, pp.318–346.

Levine, M.J. (1991), *The Battle of the Books: History and Literature in the Augustan Age* (Cornell University Press, 1994 edition).

Ligota, C.R. (1987), *Annius of Viterbo and Historical Method*, Journal of the Warburg and Courtauld Institutes 50, pp.44–56.

Lincoln, B. (2002), *Isaac Newton and Oriental Jones on Myth, Ancient History and the Relative Prestige of Peoples*, History of Religions 42, no. 1, August 2002, pp.1–18.

Macaulay, T.B. (1828), *History* (a review of H. Neele's *The Romance of History*), first published in the Edinburgh Review, May 1828, p.361, reproduced by H. Neele (1889), *The Miscellaneous Writings and Speeches of Lord Macaulay* (Longmans, Green and Company).

Madan, F. (1893), *Books in Manuscript* (Kegan Paul, Trench, Trubner and Company).

Mahaffy, J.P. (1888), *Alexander's Empire* (T. Fisher Unwin).

Mallory, J.P. (1989), *In Search of the Indo-Europeans: Language, Archeology and Myth* (Thames and Hudson).

Malthus, T. (1798), *An Essay on the Principle of Population* (originally published anonymously and printed for J. Johnson in St Paul's Churchyard).

Marasco, G. (ed.) (2011), *Autobiographies and Memoirs in Antiquity* (Brill).

Marchesi, I. (2008), *The art of Pliny's letters: a poetics of allusion in the private correspondence* (Cambridge University Press).

Margotta, R. (1968), *The Story of Medicine* (Golden Press).

Marmodoro, A. & Hill, J. (eds) (2013), *The Author's Voice in Classical and Late Antiquity* (Oxford University Press).

Martinez, J. (2011), *Fakes and Forgers of Classical Literature* (Alfonso Martinez Diez).

Mayor, A. (2014), *The Amazons, Lives and Legends of Warrior Women across the Ancient World* (Princeton University Press).

McGing, B. (2010), *Polybius' Histories* (Oxford University Press).

McKechnie, P. (1999), *Manipulation of Themes in Quintus Curtius Rufus Book 10*, Historia Zeitschrift für Alte Geschichte 48, no. 1, pp.44–60.

McInerney, J. (2007), *Arrian and the Greek Alexander Romance*, The Classical World 100, no. 4, summer 2007, pp.424–430.

McKitrerick, R. (2004), *History and Memory in the Carolingian World* (Cambridge University Press).

Metzger, B.M. (1972), *Literary Forgeries and Canonical Pseudepigrapha*, Journal of Biblical Literature 91, no. 1, pp.3–24.

Metzger, B.M. (1992), *The Text of the New Testament. Its Transmission, Corruption and Restoration* (Oxford University Press).

Milns, R.D. (1966), *The Date of Curtius Rufus and the 'Historiae Alexandri'*, Latomus 25, no. 3, July–Sept 1966, pp.490–507.

Momigliano, A.D. (1954), *An Unsolved problem of Historical Forgery: The Scriptores Historiae Augustae*, Journal of the Warburg and Courtauld Institutes 17, nos 1–2, pp.22–46.

Momigliano, A.D. (1966), *Studies in Historiography* (Harper Torchbooks).

Momigliano, A.D. (1977), *Essays in Ancient and Modern Historiography* (Blackwell).

Mommsen, C.M.T. (1870), *Cornelius Tacitus und Cluvius Rufus*, Hermes 4, pp.320–322 (republished in Gesammelte Schriften 7, 1909, pp.210–215).

Monophthalmus (1978), *Asthippoi*, Classical Quarterly 29, no. 1, pp.128–135.

Morford, M. (1973), *The Neronian Literary Revolution*, The Classical Journal 68, no. 3, pp.210–215.

Mossman, J.M. (1988), *Tragedy and Epic in Plutarch's Alexander*, The Journal of Hellenic Studies 108, pp.83–93.

Mylonas, G. (1964), *Priam's Troy and the Date of its Fall*, Hesperia 33, pp.52–380.

Nauta, R.R., van Dam, H.J. & Smolenars, J.J.L. (2006), *Flavian Poetry*, Mnemosyne Supplementum 270, pp.315–328 (Brill).

Needham, P. (1979), *Twelve Centuries of Bookbindings 400–1600* (The Pierpont Library, Oxford University Press).

Nolan, B. (1992), *Chaucer and the Tradition of the Roman Antique* (Cambridge University Press).

Niebuhr, B.G. (1844), *The History of Rome*, Volume III (Lea and Blanchard).

Nietzsche, F. (1974), *The Gay Science*(Vintage Books).

Nisetich, F.J. (1980), *Pindar's Victory Songs* (The Johns Hopkins University Press).

Oakley, S.P. (2005), *A Commentary on Livy VI–X: Volume 3, Book 9* (Clarendon Press).

Olbrycht, M.J. (2008), *Curtius Rufus, The Macedonian Mutiny at Opis and Alexander's Iranian Policy in 324 BC*, in Jakub Pigón (ed.), *The Children of Herodotus: Greek and Roman Historiography and Related Genres* (Cambridge Scholars Publishing), pp.231–252.

Ormerod, H.A. (1997), *Piracy in the Ancient World*, (The Johns Hopkins University Press).

Pagels, E. (1979), *The Gnostic Gospels* (Random House).

Parke, H.W. (1933), *Greek Mercenary Soldiers* (Ares Publishers).

Parke, H.W. (1985), *The Massacre of the Branchidae*, The Journal of Hellenic Studies 105, pp.59–68.

Pearson, L. (1955), *The Diary and Letters of Alexander the Great*, Historia: Zeitschrift für Alte Geschichte 3, no. 4, pp.429–455.

Pearson, L. (1960), *The Lost Histories of Alexander the Great* (The American Philological Association).

Pernot, L. (2000), *Rhetoric in Antiquity* (The Catholic University of America Press, 2005 edition).

Pitcher, L. (2009), *Writing Ancient History* (I.B. Tauris).

Polcaro, V.F., Valsecchi, G.B. & Verderame, L. (2008), *The Gaugamela Battle Eclipse, An Archeoastronomical Anaylsis*, Mediterranean Archaeology and Archaeometry 8, no. 2, pp.55–64.

Polo, F.P. (2011), *The Consul at Rome, The Civil Functions of the Consuls in the Roman Republic* (Cambridge University Press).

Potter, D.S.A. (2006), *Companion to the Roman Empire* (Blackwell Publishing).

Powell, J.E. (1939), *The sources of Plutarch's Alexander*, Journal of Hellenic Studies 59, pp.229–240.

Reeve, C.D.C. (2001), *Introduction to The Basic Works of Aristotle* (The Modern Library).

Renault, M. (1975), *The Nature of Alexander* (Pantheon Books).

Robbins, M. (2001), *The Collapse of the Bronze Age, The Story of Greece, Troy, Israel, Egypt and the People of the Sea* (Authors Choice Press).

Robinson, C.A. (1953), *The History of Alexander the Great: a Translation of the Extant Fragments and the Ephemerides of Alexander's Expedition* (Ares Publishers).

Roisman, J. (1994), *Ptolemy and his Rivals in the History of Alexander*, Classical Quarterly 34, pp.373–385.

Roisman, J. (2012), *Alexander's Veterans and the Early Wars of the Successors* (University of Texas Press).

Roisman, J. & Worthington, I. (eds) (2010), *A Companion to Ancient Macedonia* (Wiley-Blackwell).

Rolfe, J.C. (1913), *Suetonius and His Biographies*, Proceedings of the American Philosophical Society 52, no. 209, April 1913, pp.206–225.

Roller, L.E. (1981), *Funeral Games in Greek Art*, American Journal of Archaeology 85, no. 2, pp.107–119.

Roller, M.B. (1997), *Color-Blindness: Cicero's Death, Declamation, and the Production of History*, Classical Philology 92, no. 2, April 1997, pp.109–130.

Romane, J.P. (1987), *Alexander's Siege of Tyre*, The Ancient World 16, nos 3–4, pp.79–90.

Ross, J.W. (1878), *Tacitus and Bracciolini, The Annals Forged in the XVth Century* (originally self-published in London in 1878, now available from Project Gutenberg EBook at http://www.dominiopublico.gov.br/download/gu009098. pdf).

Rozen, K. (1967), *Political Documents on Hieronymus of Cardia (323–302 BC)*, Acta Classica 10, pp.41–94.

Russell, B. (1946), *History of Western Philosophy* (Routledge, 2004 edition).

Sachs, A. & Hunger, H. (1988), *Astronomical diaries and related texts from Babylon 1*, Verlag der Osterreichischen Akademie der Wissenschaften.

Samuel, A.E. (1986), *The Earliest Elements in the Alexander Romance*, Historia: Zeitschrift für Alte Geschichte 35, no. 4, 4th quarter 1986, pp.427–437.

Sandy, J.E. (1921), *A Companion to Latin Studies edited for the Syndics of the University Press (3rd edition)* (Cambridge University Press).

Schachermeyr, F. (1949), *Alexander der Grosse: Ingenium und Macht* (Pustet).

Scramuzza, V. (1940), *The Emperor Claudius* (Harvard University Press).

Seeley, J.R. (1881), *Livy, Book 1, with introduction, Historical Examination and Notes*, 3rd edition (Clarendon Press).

Seltman, C.T. (1938), *Diogenes of Sinope, Son of the Banker Hikesias*, Transactions of the International Numismatic. Congress 1936, London.

Shelmerdine, S.C. (1995), *The Homeric Hymns* (Focus Publishing, R. Pullins and Company).

Shilleto, R. (1874), *Demosthenis De Falsa Legatione* (Deighton, Bell and Company).

Shipley, F.W. (1903), *Certain Sources of Corruption in Latin Manuscripts: A Study Based upon Two Manuscripts of Livy: Codes Puteanus (Fifth Century), and its Copy, Codex Reginensis 762 (Ninth Century)*, American Journal of Archeology 7, no. 1, January–March 1903, pp.1–25.

Shipley, G. (2000), *The Greek World After Alexander 323–30BC* (Routledge).

Shipley, G. (2011), *Pseudo-Skylax's Periplous: the Circumnavigation of the Inhabited World* (Phoenix Press).

Shorter, D.C.A. (1967), *Tacitus and Verginius Rufus*, Classical Quarterly, New Series 17, no. 2, November 1967, pp.370–381.

Shrimpton, G.S. (1991), *Theopompus the Historian* (McGill-Queen's University Press).

Simpson, R.H. (1959), *Abbreviation of Hieronymus in Diodorus*, The American Journal of Philology 80, no. 4, pp.370–379.

Smith, L.C. (1981), *The Chronology of Books XVIII–XX of Diodorus Siculus*, American Journal of Philology 32, pp.283–290.

Smits, E.R. (1987), *A Medieval Supplement to the Beginning of Curtius Rufus's Historia Alexandri: An Edition with Introduction*, Viator 18, pp.89–124.

Spencer, D. (2002), *The Roman Alexander* (University of Exeter Press).

Speyer, W. (1971), *Die literarische Fälschung im heidnischen und christlichen Altertum* (CH Beck).

Sprague de Camp, L. (1972), *Great Cities of the Ancient World* (Dorset Press).

Stadter, P.A. (1967), *Flavius Arrianus: The New Xenophon*, Greek, Roman and Byzantine Studies 8, pp.155–161.

Steele, R.B. (1915), *Quintus Curtius Rufus*, The American Journal of Philology 36, no. 4, pp.402–423.

Stewart, A. (1993), *Faces of Power, Alexander's Image and Hellenistic Politics* (University of California Press).

Stoneman, R. (1991), *The Greek Alexander Romance* (Penguin).

Sullivan, J.P. (1966), *Seneca: The Deification of Claudius the Clod*, Arion: A Journal of Humanities and the Classics 5, no. 3, autumn 1966, pp.376–399.

Sundberg, A.C. (1958), *The Old Testament of the Early Church (A Study in Canon)*, The Harvard Theological Review 51, no. 4, pp.205–226.

Syme, R. (1964), *The Historian Servilius Nonianus*, Hermes 92, no. 4, pp.408–424.

Syme, R. (1971), *Emperors and Biography: Studies in the Historia Augusta* (Oxford University Press).

Tarbell, F.B. (1920), *Centauromachy and Amazonomachy in Greek Art: The Reasons for Their Popularity*, American Journal of Archeology 24, no. 3, July–September 1920, pp.226–231.

Tarn, W.W. (1921), *Heracles Son of Barsine*, Journal of Hellenic Studies 41, pp.18–28.

Tarn, W.W. (1948), *Alexander The Great, Volume II, Sources and Studies* (Cambridge University Press, 1979 edition).

Temple, N. (2002), *Heritage and Forgery: Annio da Viterbo and the Quest for the Authentic*, Public Archaeology 2, no. 3, pp.151–162.

Teuffel, W.S. & Schwabe, L. (1892), *Teuffel's History of Roman Literature Revised and Enlarged, Volume II, The Imperial Period* (Deighton, Bell & Company).

Thomas, C.L. (1963), review of *Incerti auctoris epitoma rerum Gestarum Alexandri Magni cum libro de morte testamentoque Alexandri*, Classical Philology 58, no. 2, April 1963, pp.129–131.

Thomas, C.G. (2007), *Alexander the Great in his World* (Blackwell Publishing).

Timpanaro, S. & Most, G.W. (2005), *The Genesis of Lachman's Method* (University of Chicago Press).

Todd, M.N. (ed.) (1985), *Greek Historical Inscriptions* (Ares Publishers).

Townend, G.B. (1960), *The Sources of the Greek in Suetonius*, Hermes 88, pp.98–100.

Townend, G.B. (1964), *Cluvius Rufus in the Histories of Tacitus*, The American Journal of Philology 85, pp.337–377.

Townsend, D. (trans.) (1996), *The Alexandreis of Walter of Chatillon, A Twelfth Century Epic* (University of Pennsylvania Press).

Verbrugghe, G.P. & Wickersham, J.M. (2000), *Berossus and Manetho Introduced and Translated: Native Traditions in Ancient Mesopotamia and Egypt* (University of Michigan Press).

Vrettos, T. (2001), *Alexandria, City of the Western Mind* (The Free Press).

Walbank, F.W. (1962), *Polemic in Polybius*, The Journal of Roman Studies 52, nos 1 and 2, pp.1–12.

Walbank, F.W. (1981), *The Hellenistic World* (Harvard University Press, 1993 edition).

Wallis Budge, E.A. (1896), *The Life and Exploits of Alexander the Great: being a Series of Translations of the Ethiopic Histories of Alexander by the Pseudo Callisthenes and Other Writers* (J. Clay and Sons).

Wardle, D. (1992), *Cluvius Rufus and Suetonius*, Hermes 12, no. 4, pp.466–482.

Wardle, D. (2005), *Valerius Maximus on Alexander the Great*, Acta Classica 48, pp.141–161.

Wardy, R. (1996), *The Birth of Rhetoric: Gorgias, Plato and Their Successors* (Routledge).

Warner, R. (trans.) (1966), *Xenophon, A History of My Times* (Penguin).

Watson, J.S. & Miller, M.C.J. (eds) (1992), *M. Junianus Justinus, Epitoma Historiarum Philippicarum, Books VII–XII Excerpta de Historia Macedonia* (Ares Publishers).

Weiss, R. (1962), *An Unknown Epigraphic Tract by Annius of Viterbo*, in C.P. Brand (ed.), Italian Studies presented to E.R. Vincent (Heffer, 1992 edition), pp.101–120.

West, M.L. trans.) (2008), *Hesiod, Theogeny and Works and Days* (Oxford World's Classics).

Wheatley, P.V. (1995), *Ptolemy Soter's Annexation of Syria 320 B.C.*, Classical Quarterly, New Series 45, no. 2, pp.433–440.

Wheatley, P.V. (1998), *The Date of Polyperchon's Invasion of Macedonia and Murder of Heracles*, Antichthon 32, pp.12–23.

Wheeler, I.H. (1902), *Alexander The Great, The Merging of East and West in Universal History* (G.P. Putnam's Sons).

Whitmarsh, T. (2002), *Alexander's Hellenism and Plutarch's Textualism*, Classical Quarterly 52, no. 1, pp.174–192.

Wilkes, J. (1972), *The Julio-Claudian Historians*, The Classical World 65, no. 6, pp.177–192, 197–203.

Williams, C.A. (trans. & commentary) (2004), *Martial, Epigrams Book II* (Oxford University Press).

Wiseman, T.P. (1991), *Death of an Emperor, Flavius Josephus*, Exeter Studies of History no. 30 (University of Exeter Press).

Worthington, I. (ed.) (2000), *Demosthenes: Statesman and Orator* (Routledge).

Worthington, I. (ed.) (2007), *A Companion to Greek Rhetoric* (Blackwell Publishing).

Wright, A. (1995), T*he Death of Cicero: Rhetorical Invention in Ancient Historiography*, Humanities Research Centre, Australian National University, 12–14 July 1995.

Yardley, J. (2003), *Justin and Pompeius Trogus* (University of Toronto Press).

Notes

Chapter 1: Introduction: 'Study the Historian before you Study the History'

1. Lane Fox (1973), Preface, p.11.
2. Plutarch, *Pericles* 15, translation by J. Dryden (1683).
3. Philip's reign is variously stated as twenty-three or twenty-five years, but an early regency or throne guardianship for his nephew Amyntas Perdicca confuses things; see Grant (2019) p.226 for discussion. The post-Alexander period is twenty-three years from Alexander's death in 323 BC to the aftermath of the Battle of Ipsus in 301 BC.
4. For the numbers of fragments and writers, see Wilken (1967) and quoting from the Introduction by E. Borza, p.XXV.
5. A statement credited to both Voltaire and André Gide: *Croyez ceux qui cherchent la vérité, doutez de ceux qui la trouvent.*
6. The first recorded use of the epithet 'Great' came from the Roman playwright Plautus in the *Mostelleria* 775 in *ca.* 200 BC. It may of course have been in use before, but Greek literature did not employ it and was somewhat more hostile to his memory.

Chapter 2: Primary Sources: Eyewitnesses at War

1. Arrian 4.14.3, translation by A. de Selincourt (Penguin Classics edition, 1958); his jibe was aimed at Ptolemy and Aristobulus, and specifically at their reporting of Callisthenes' death.
2. Plutarch 53.1 for Callisthenes' motives, and Justin 8.3.9–11 for the Olynthian intrigue. Philip had already executed a third half-brother, and the other two by Gygaea, his stepmother, and Amyntas, his father, were destined for the same.
3. Diogenes Laertius *Aristotle* 6 for both his and Callisthenes' petitions to Philip.
4. Strabo 13.1.27 and Plutarch 8.2; Plutarch, *Moralia* 327f and Pliny 7.29.108 for the casket *Iliad*.
5. Atkinson (1963) pp.125–126 for discussion of Callisthenes' political role.
6. Pearson (1960) pp.25–27 for discussion of the fragments of Callisthenes' works. The *Suda* also accredited him with a *Persica*. Barber (1993) p.133 for the quality of Callisthenes' work. Robinson (1953) pp.45–77 for other possible publications, including a *History of Thrace* and a *Macedonica* that may or may not be distinct from the *Hellenica*. Diodorus 14.117.8, 16.14.4 stated Callisthenes' ten-book Greek history ended in the fourth year of the 105th Olympiad, the year in which Philomelus the Phocian despoiled the temple at Delphi. Following Flower (1994) p.40 for the multi-genre trend.

7. *Gnomologium Vaticanum* 367 for Callisthenes' riposte. The fragments that attest to Callisthenes' caging collected in Robinson (1953) pp.52–53; citations came from Ovid, Plutarch and Strabo as well as eyewitness historians. Pearson (1960) p.33 for discussion on the title of Callisthenes' work.

8. Curtius 3.10 and Justin 11.9.3–6 cited Alexander's multinational encouragement to his allied force. Plutarch 33.1 mentioned Callisthenes 'seeking to win the favour of the Hellenes'. The 'pan-Hellenic set piece' quotes Bosworth-Baynham (2000) p.112.

9. Pearson (1960) p.31 for discussion quoting the *Vatican Gnomologos* 367. Full citation in Robinson (1953) p.54.

10. Cicero, *On the Orator* 2.58; full text in Robinson (1953) p.55. Quoting Pearson (1960) p.250 for the merging of 'rhetorical history and antiquarian scholarship'. Polybius 12.12.b and 17–22.

11. The collected fragments can be found in Robinson (1953) pp.45–77. For examples of the treatment of Parmenio, see Tarn (1921) p.24; this appears to have infiltrated the Vulgate, examples at Curtius 4.9.14–15, 4.13.4 and 4.7–9; also Arrian 3.10.1–2 and Plutarch 31.11–12.

12. Arrian 4.14 suggested both Aristobulus and Ptolemy deliberately implicated Callisthenes in their texts. Certainly they were not apologetic. Curtius 8.6.22 suggested Ptolemy brought Callisthenes' involvement to Alexander's attention.

13. Aristotle was reportedly aware of the danger of Callisthenes' outspokenness in front of Alexander; Diogenes Laertius 5.4–5. Diodorus 17.80.4 and Polyaenus 4.3.19 for the censoring of letters.

14. Arrian 4.10.1–2.

15. Oscar Wilde, *The Critic as Artist* Part 1 (1891).

16. Robinson (1953) p.46 for the fragment relating to Aristotle's purported joke on wit and common sense.

17. At Plutarch 33, Callisthenes is mentioned twice; Plutarch, *Aristeides* 27.2 mentioned Callisthenes as a source but this is clearly not from his account of Alexander; Pearson (1960) pp.72–74.

18. Stoneman (1991) p.28 for discussion of the possible more sober archetype of the *Romance* texts. Also Fraser (1996) pp.210–226 for the earliest form of the *Romance*.

19. For Callisthenes' alleged part in the pages' conspiracy, see Plutarch 55.3–5, Arrian 4.12.7, 4.13.3–4, 14.1 and 8.6.24–25, Curtius 8.7.10, 8.6.8 and 8.8.21, Justin 12.7.2. There are five conflicting reports of how he died.

20. Plutarch 55 claimed letters were circulating to Craterus, Attalus and Alcetas in which Alexander stated the pages had no accomplices, a contention supported by Arrian 4.14.1.

21. The underlying themes and speeches surrounding the Hermolaus affair discussed by S. Müller in Carney-Ogden (2010) pp.26–27.

22. Arrian 4.141–4 for the reporting disunity of the eyewitness sources. Lane Fox (1980) p.307.

23. Diogenes Laertius, *Theophrastus* 1.5.44. Atkinson (1996) p.135 for citation on fortune. However, the treatise may not have been about Callisthenes, just dedicated to him.

24. Pearson (1960) p.25 for discussion of his being referenced as a 'sophist'. Plutarch 53.2 for the quote and Callisthenes' superior sophistry that earned him the hatred of the Macedones.

25. Onesicritus' family may have been from Aegina, according to Diogenes Laertius 6.84. Heckel (2006) p.183 assumes he was with the campaign earlier, citing Diogenes Laertius, *Onesicritus*. However, this remains uncertain as this text simply suggested 'he accompanied Alexander' with no dating reference. It does not confirm Onesicritus 'set out' with Alexander. For discussion, see Heckel (2006) p.183 and Pearson (1960) p.85, and in depth in Brown (1949) pp.1 ff, 4, 24.

26. Diogenes Laertius, *Onesicritus* 6.75–76, Plutarch 65.2, Plutarch, *Moralia* 331e, Strabo 15.1.65. *Metz Epitome* 331 for Onesicritus' association with Diogenes the Cynic.

27. Tarn 1 (1948) p.82 and Tarn (1948) p.97 for discussion of the Peripatetic treatment of Alexander. The hostile tradition to Alexander from the Peripatetics is challenged by Badian; see Borza (1995) pp.179–182 and Milns (1966) p.499, as there is little evidence to prove this. Aristotle founded the Lyceum in Athens in 335/334 BC. It took its name from Apollo-Lyceus, the god incarnated as a wolf, and was initially a gymnasium and meeting place. The building had colonnades, *peripatoi*, through which Aristotle would walk while teaching, earning him the title *peripatetikos*, hence peripatetic. While the link is attractive, the term *peripatetikos*, of walking, was likely already in use; Diogenes Laertius, *Aristotle* 4 for the origins of the name.

28. Robinson, *The Ephemerides of Alexander's Expedition* (1953). The missing year discussed in full in Bosworth (1981) relating to the lack of synchronicity through 329/328 and 328/327 BC.

29. Conflicts best summarized in Heckel (2006) p.187 for Oxyartes and p.250 for Sisimithres, where the possible meeting with Rhoxane took place after the capture of the Rock of Chorienes, or after the siege of the Rock of Sogdia. The sons that Curtius attributed to Oxyartes, Rhoxane's father, appear in fact to belong to Chorienes. Even Oxyartes' governorship and territorial claims are uncertain. Also Bosworth (1981) pp.29–32 for discussion of conflicting reports from this period. *Metz Epitome* 70 recorded that Rhoxane bore a child who died in infancy; its narrative runs, broadly, from July 330 to July 325 BC.

30. Heckel (2006) pp.76–77 for a summary of Callisthenes' conflicting deaths recorded by Curtius, Arrian, Chares, Aristobulus and Ptolemy and references to either Bactria or Bactra (the regional capital, modern Balkh) in Zariaspa.

31. For the dating of Callisthenes' death and the termination of his writing, see Robinson (1953) Preface pp.viii–xi.

32. Robinson, *The Ephemerides of Alexander's Expedition* (1953) Introduction pp.11, 70–71. Fragments of Onesicritus' work do relate the curiosities of Sogdia and Bactria, though this could be hearsay and does not prove he was there. For the relevant fragments, see Robinson (1953) pp.152–153. Likewise, the Amazon affair was probably considered 'essential' reporting though Onesicritus might have arrived after the event; Plutarch 46 for Onesicritus' version.

33. Brown (1949) p.7 for the fragments relating to India. Brown (1949) p.89 for the reporting on cotton; Herodotus had more vaguely referred to the plant's 'wool' as a fruit, and p.7 for the surviving fragments of Onesicritus in Strabo 15.1.63–65.

34.   Strabo and Pliny for Onesicritus' claims; see Robinson (1953) p.153 ff for translations of fragments.

35.   The 'philosopher in arms' is distilled from Onesicritus' own narrative preserved by Strabo 15.1.58–66. Various other texts, including most notably Plutarch 64–65, described dialogues between Alexander and the sages. Onesicritus referred to India as 'a third part of the world', suggesting his view that it was a distinct continent, possibly as a PR move to help explain Alexander's decision to turn back west at this point. Discussion in Pearson (1960) p.95.

36.   Strabo 15.1.28 discussed by Pearson (1960) pp.83–111 and p.98 for Onesicritus' place in the *Romance*, referring to Strabo 15.1.58–66 and the description of the Indian wise men or gymnosophists and the philosophical dialogues.

37.   Brown (1949) p.108 for discussion of Pliny preserving Onesicritus' account of the coastal voyage.

38.   Xenophon's legacy discussed in Flower (1994) p.42.

39.   Discussion on the reference to Xenophon's lack of introduction in McGing (2010) p.61. Xenophon, *Hellenica* 4.8.1. Compare with Arrian Preface 1.1–2.

40.   For Onesicritus' reputation as a purveyor of marvels, see discussion in Pearson (1960) p.86, citing Aulus Gellius 9.4.1–3.

41.   There are four references to Onesicritus, two that indicate he was the original source of detail; see Robinson (1953) pp.149–166.

42.   Arrian 6.2.3. In contrast the *Suda* N117 claimed it was Nearchus who lied about his role of admiral of the fleet.

43.   Plutarch 46.4–5 for the episode involving Onesicritus and Lysimachus; see the chapter on the *Greek Alexander Romance* for further detail.

44.   Pearson (1960) pp.84–87 for discussion; other third-party references can be found in Diogenes Laertius, *Onesicritus* 6.84–85; Aulus Gellius 9.4; Strabo 2.1.9; Arrian 6.2.3–4, 7.5.6 and 7.20.9; these are pro-Nearchus, suggesting they came from Nearchus' own account. Quoting Diogenes Laertius, *Onesicritus* 6.84.

45.   For Onesicritus' fear, see *Metz Epitome* 97. The theme of 'fearful historians' is reiterated in the Vulgate texts at Curtius 10.10.18–19, Diodorus 17.118.2, Justin 12.13.10. Grant, *Last Will and Testament* (2021) for full discussion.

46.   Arrian 3.6.5 for confirmation of his exile and Plutarch 10.1–4 and Arrian 3.6.5–6 for the alleged Pixodarus affair that led to Philip banishing them. Hammond Philip (1994) pp.173–174 suggests the whole affair was the 'malicious fiction' of Satyrus' *Life of Philip*. However, for a different interpretation see Carney-Ogden (2010) pp.4–11.

47.   Ormerod (1997) pp.14, 108 for Cilician piracy. Piracy was still rife and Alexander had tasked his admiral Amphoterus with clearing the seas of them; Curtius 4.8.15. *The Hymn to Apollo* 452–5 from the anonymous *Homeric Hymns* mentioned the hazards of pirates. Thucydides 1.5 also described their plundering. Demosthenes 17 explained how the Athenian fleet needed a further 100 ships to escort Athens' grain fleet; Blackwell (1999) pp.95–96 for discussion.

48.   Following the arguments cited in Pearson (1960) pp.114–115 surrounding Nearchus' naval expertise.

49. For Nearchus' role commanding mercenaries and light-armed troops, see Arrian 4.7.1 and 4.30.5–6. For his role at the Hydaspes–Indus, see Arrian, *Indica* 18.1–11. Trierarchies were expensive and often didn't return capital to those obligated under the Athenian system of 'liturgy'. It came with the obligation to fit out and provision a naval ship.

50. 1,700 miles according to Pliny 6.96–100. Apparently Nearchus and Onesicritus concurred on the distance. Arrian, *Indica* 18.10 and 18.14 for Nearchus' role on the Indus. The Erythrean Sea is literally the 'Red Sea', though the Greeks loosely extended its use for the Persian Gulf and Indian Ocean. Curtius 8.9.14 and 10.1.13–14 claimed the name 'Red' came from King Erythrus, who also featured in Strabo 16.3.5, Pliny 6.13.28, 19.1.2, Arrian, *Indica* 37.3. Engels (1978) p.13 for the calculation of the length of Nearchus' voyage. Pearson (1960) p.15 for Nearchus' observations for crossing the tropics and equator.

51. Pearson (1960) p.83 for discussion on the nautical conflict. Other titles for his work are suggested by Pliny and Strabo; full discussion in Badian (1975) pp.157–159. Arrian 6.2.3 suggested Onesicritus lied about his and Nearchus' relative authority and at 7.20.9 outlined a disagreement. There is evidence Nearchus slandered Onesicritus, as evidenced in Arrian's *Indica*. See discussion in Heckel (2006) p.183. For discussion of their titles, see Berthold (1984) p.44.

52. Arrian penned his *Indica* in Ionian dialect, which suggests Nearchus had too. Pearson (1960) pp.112–149 for discussion of Nearchus' emulation of Herodotus, the *Odyssey* and even Pseudo-Scylax's *Periplous*. Herodotus 4.44 claimed Scylax ventured down the Indus and west to the Persian Gulf.

53. Arrian 7.19.3–6 for Nearchus' warning, Plutarch 73, Diodorus 17.112.3; discussed in Pearson (1960) p.116.

54. Closely following Badian (1975) p.148.

55. Discussion in Badian (1975) pp.147–148 quoting C.F. Lehman-Haupt.

56. Arrian, *Indica* 18.1–11 for the list of trierarchs and Homer, *Iliad* 2.494–759 for the catalogue of ships. Tarn 1 (1948) p.101 for the ethnic breakdown.

57. Strabo 2.1.9. For examples of the fables, see Badian (1975) p.148. Others mentioned were Deimachus and Megasthenes, a successor at the Mauryan court in India.

58. Quoting Pearson (1960) p.135 for 'epic adornment' and Shipley (2011) for a 'philosophical geography', referring to Pseudo-Scylax' *Periplous*. The *Periplous* was attributed to a 'Pseudo-Scylax' for it was supposedly compiled by the sixth-century BC Greek navigator mentioned at Herodotus 4.44, and yet its knowledge base appears to be that of a much later age, perhaps the mid-330s BC, and with direct connections to Athenian teaching.

59. Arrian 7.5.6 recorded that all the Bodyguards were crowned as well, with the addition of Onesicritus.

60. Diodorus 19.85.1 for the death of 'most of Demetrius' friends'. Peithon son of Agenor is cited as the most distinguished of them, which may suggest Nearchus may have survived. Heckel (2006) p.171 for discussion of Nearchus' birth date. Nearchus' whereabouts from Babylon to his re-emergence working under Antigonus some four or five years later are unknown. An episode in Polyaenus 5.35 is undated (possibly 318 BC)

though he was operating under Antigonus by 317/316 BC, as suggested by Diodorus 19.19.4–5. Plutarch 76.3 portrays Alexander listening to Nearchus' account of the sea voyage; it hints, but does not necessarily prove, he might have already completed a written account. See Flower (1994) p.34 for a possible reference (in Strabo 1.2.35) to the authors of an *Indica* by Theopompus, who is reckoned to have died *ca.* 320 BC.

61. See Grant, *Last Will and Testament* (2021) for discussion of conflicting claims of Alexander's death, and in particular this pamphlet.

62. The lion monument at Amphipolis was originally thought to sit above the tomb which held the remains of Nearchus, Laomedon or Androsthenes, each born or resident at some point. Recent excavations suggest a grander tomb than first thought, leading some historians to ponder whether Rhoxane and Alexander IV were entombed in Amphipolis after their murder by Cassander. Archaeologists now conclude the lion was too heavy and adorned another nearby tomb. It has long been thought that Tomb III at Vergina, possibly constructed by Cassander, held the remains of Alexander IV; Carney-Ogden (2010) pp.118–119.

63. Quoting Heckel (2006) p.235 for Arsinoe's possible royal roots. For the rumour of parentage, see Curtius 9.8.22 and Pausanias 1.6.2, but it is rendered unlikely by the claim in Pseudo-Lucian, *The Long Lived* 12 that Ptolemy was 84 when he died, thus born in 367 BC when Philip II was only 16. Also see discussion in Heckel (1992) p.222. The authorship of the *The Long Lived* is, however, disputed and other commentators variously assigned it to a 'pseudo' compiler.

64. Photius reported that Ptolemy wished Theopompus dead; discussion in Flower (1994) p.12.

65. Arrian 3.27.5. Heckel (2006) p.351 pointed out that the term *Somatophylakes* is occasionally used in the general sense and hypaspists were at times being referred to, i.e. the king's personal infantry corps. Diodorus 17.61.3, Curtius 4.16.32, Arrian 3.15.2 for references to Hephaestion commanding the undefined bodyguard corps. We restrict its usage to the Bodyguards alone. Also discussion in Chugg (2009) pp.14–18 citing specific examples where the term was more broadly used, and Tarn (1948) p.138. Heckel Somatophylakes (1978) p.224 for the Latin derivatives.

66. Curtius 9.5.21. Bosworth (1983) p.157 noted the similarity with Livy 34.159 and Tacitus 11.11.3.

67. Heckel (1992) p.222 and Marasco (2011) p.59 for the thirty-five fragments. Quoting G. Shipley's review of Heckel (1992) in *The Classical Review*, New Series 49, no. 2 (1999), pp.480–482, on his prosopography.

68. Quoting G. Cawkwell in Warner (1966) p.43.

69. Discussion of the military slant in Ptolemy's account in Pearson (1960) p.196. Pearson (1955) p.436 for lack of interest in Ptolemy's book in Rome.

70. Citing Roisman (1994) pp.373–374; bias in Ptolemy's history is well covered by Errington (1969) and also by Pearson (1960) pp.188–211. For the reference by Badian, see Roisman (1994) p.374, who sees less propaganda than some others in Ptolemy's history.

71. Citation from J. March, D.F. Kennedy, J. Salmon, T. Wiedemann, B.A. Sparkes, P. Walcot, *Greece and Rome*, 2nd Series, Vol. 41, No. 2 (1994) pp.220–255 and also Ellis (1994) p.60: private letters of Professor Peter Green to W.M. Ellis.

72. Pearson (1960) p.154. Lucian, *The Long Lived* 22 for his ages.
73. Pearson (1960) p.151 for his technical roles and examples on p.161; his account of the siege of Tyre was praised by Menander, *Oration* 27.6 ff; Brunt (1974) p.66 for discussion.
74. Pearson (1960) p.186 for divine intervention, including the Siwa episode. For the journey to Siwa, see Diodorus 17.49.2–52.7, Arrian 3.4–5, Curtius 4.7.8–4.89, Plutarch 26.3–27.11, Justin 11.11.1–13, Strabo 17.1.43, *Itinerary of Alexander* 48–50.
75. Arrian 2.3.1 for the acropolis location and Justin 11.7.3–4 for the dedication. 'Fate's silent riddle' as it was described in the *Alexandreis* of Gautier de Chatillon 2.99. The waggon or chariot was fastened to its yoke by the bark of the cornel tree. See Plutarch 18, Arrian 2.3, Curtius 3.1.14, Justin 11.7.3 for biographical sources narrating the episode.
76. Justin 11.7.16.
77. Quoting Pearson (1960) p.157.
78. Quoting Graves (1955) p.282
79. Lucian, *How to Write History* 12. See Pearson (1960) p.150, who rejects the veracity of Lucian's reference.
80. Lucian, *How to Write History* 40–41.
81. See discussion in Pearson (1960) pp.150–151 for discussion on Aristobulus' flattery and pp.156–157 for discussion of his possibly sanitized reporting of the Gordian Knot episode. Following Pearson (1960) p.263 for the conclusion that Aristobulus fell into no obvious category.
82. The various accounts of the siege of Tyre are a good example where engineers were mentioned, and Hephaestion's death for mention of architects, for example.
83. See Robinson (1953) pp.205–243 for fragments citing Cassandrea. Tarn argues Kos; discussion in Pearson (1960) p.106 and Pearson (1960) p.151. Plutarch, *Demosthenes* 23.6 cited him as a Cassandrean. See full career discussion in Pearson (1960) pp.150–187. Arrian 6.29.4–6.30 for his engineering role suggested by the task of restoring Cyrus' tomb. Heckel (2006) p.46 assumes Aristobulus returned to Europe, but there is little evidence.
84. Cassander's brother Alexarchus founded the city of Uranopolis at the same time; Athenaeus 3.98d–e.
85. Theocritus, *The Festival of Adonis* 15.6, cited in Erskine (2002) p.165.
86. The letter from Antigonus to Scepsis for the reference to an Aristobulus who appears to have been a representative of Ptolemy in the so-called 'Peace of the Dynasts'. See citations by Bosworth-Baynham (2000) pp.231–232 and Heckel (2006) p.46. A late publication date for Aristobulus' work is supported by Arrian's detailing of the divination of Pythagoras the seer in which Aristobulus is mentioned as the source, and it suggests the engineer–historian published after the Battle of Ipsus in 301 BC, for Arrian also recounted the fate of Antigonus the One-Eyed who perished at the battle; it is inconclusive as Arrian used Hieronymus for this period.
87. Diodorus 19.52.1–3 for the founding of Cassandrea.
88. Arrian 7.26.3. The interpretation of the Greek has been debated, but it seems clear the Journal had nothing more to say about events after Alexander's death.

89. Grant, *Last Will and Testament* (2021) for detailed discussion.
90. Heckel (2006) p.46.
91. Grant, *Last Will and Testament* (2021) for discussion of royal diaries, and in particular chapter 6.
92. Plutarch, *Eumenes* 2.3.
93. He was awarded a golden crown at Susa, see Arrian 7.5.6. Arrian, *Indica* 18.7 for the trierarch role.
94. For a full account of Eumenes' career, see Grant, *Last Will and Testament* (2021), chapters 6 and 7 in particular.
95. See Robinson (1953) pp.77–86 for translations of the assembled fragments.
96. Until the Battle of Ipsus in 301 BC, Lesbos was most prominently under the control of Antigonus or his supporters. Thereafter the Ptolemies assumed control.
97. Robinson (1960) p.86 for Ephippus' accounts of the symposia that led to the downfall of Hephaestion and Alexander.
98. Suda M 227 and Plutarch, *Moralia* 182c for Marsyas' relations to Antigonus, and Diodorus 20.50.4 for his command at Salamis; Robinson (1953) p.166 for the fragments. Pearson (1960) pp.253–254 and Kebric (1997) pp.43–44 for discussion of Marsyas' career and work. The reference to thirteen possible historians that wrote histories of Macedon is taken from Roisman-Worthington (2010) p.7.
99. Roisman-Worthington (2010) p.24 for full citation from Borza's *Before Alexander: Constructing Early Macedonia* (1999, Claremont) p.5. The title of Antipater's book in FGrH 114 T1 from the *Suda*, Marsyas and Philip of Pella in FGrH 135–6; see Marasco (2011) p.45 for discussion of Antipater's identity and the opinion of C. Bearzot on misidentification. Roisman-Worthington (2010) pp.85–86 for Theagenes.
100. A citation in Strabo 11.530 suggested Medius wrote to some extent on the nature of the lands he campaigned in. See Billows (1990) p.401 for discussion. Billows (1990) p.400 for Medius' possible Aleuadae roots at Larissa.
101. Kebric (1997) p.42 for discussion of Idiomenias' work. Pearson (1960) pp.250–251 for discussion of Menaechmus' work. Brown (1949) p.106 for the account of Androsthenes mentioned in Strabo 16.32 (citing Athenaeus 3.93b). His role in the Hydaspes-Indus fleet mentioned at Arrian, *Indica* 18.4.6. Billows (1990) pp.334–337 for Duris' fragments and style.
102. Athenaeus 4.146c for the title of Ephippus' book. Pearson (1960) is rightly dubious about the corruption of the title and suggested it could equally have been titled *Five Books of Diaries on the exploits of Alexander*. Bosworth, A.B. (1988), *From Arrian to Alexander: Studies in Historical Interpretation* (Clarendon Press) p.181 discussed the issue and reminds us many attributions made in the Suda are questionable. Strattis of Olynthus was cited in the Suda as the author of *Five Books of Commentary on the Diary* (*Ephemerides*). The title is probably corrupt. Pearson (1960) p.260 suggested the dating but Hornblower (1981) p.252 rejected it noting many people called themselves Olynthians much later. Nevertheless we may assume Strattis was born before Olynthus' destruction by Philip II in 348 BC, making him a possible contemporary and eyewitness to campaign events, while the destruction of his city would have explained any hostile reporting. Pearson (1995) p.437 suggests the attachment to Olynthus was to reinforce the authenticity of forged diaries.

103. Tarn (1948) proposed the source was a Greek working for Darius, see discussion in Atkinson (1963) p.133.
104. Gudeman, *Greeks* (1894) p.52.
105. Discussion of the steles in Bosworth (2002) pp.20–24, 241–242. For a detailed transcription of the Satrap Stele, see Bevan (1968) pp.28–32; its propaganda discussed in Marasco (2011) pp.70–72.
106. Berossus' *Babylonaica* was written around 290–278 BC for King Antiochus Soter, son of Seleucus. It is not extant, but a number of classical writers referenced it in their works. See discussion of the dating of Berossus in Pearson (1960) p.231; he dated Berossus' writing to between 293 and 281 BC. Drews (1975) p.50 ff for Berossus' contribution to 'history'.
107. Verbrugghe-Wickersham (2000) for discussion of the writings of Berossus and Manetho and their influence.
108. Aristobulus' account of the sophists at Taxila captured by Arrian 6.22.4–8 included reference to Phoenicians 'who had been following the expedition in search of trade' collecting spikenard, myrrh, gum and other roots.
109. Ada was reinstated as satrap of Caria and she adopted Alexander; see Arrian 1.23.8. Alexander addressed Sisygambis, Darius' mother, in terms that suggest he adopted her as his second mother; see Curtius 5.2.22. Curtius 8.4.26 for the comparison to Briseis and Achilles; see Homer, *Iliad* 2.688–694 for the capture of Briseis. Plutarch 21.7–9. Rhoxane was Bactrian or Sogdian; the campaign and siege of the so-called Rock of Sogdia, the Rock of Sisimithres (Chorienes) and the Rock of Ariamazes are confused; see Heckel (2006) pp.241–242 and 187 for identifications, and Heckel (1987) p.114 for discussion. Barsine and Parysatis were from Persian royal lines, see Arrian 7.4.4–7 The prominent non-Macedonian drinking partners mentioned at Alexander's final banquet were Medius from Thessaly, Heracleides the Thracian, Ariston of Pharsalus, Nearchus the Cretan and Stasanor, a Cypriot; Heckel (1988) p.10 for a further list of those present. Holcias may have been Illyrian and Lysimachus was originally Thessalian but became a naturalized Macedonian; Heckel (2006) p.153.
110. Perdiccas and Craterus were from Orestis, Leonnatus from Lyncestis, Polyperchon from Tymphaea, Ptolemy from Eordaea and Seleucus from Europus.
111. Justin 13.1.
112. See Grant, *Last Will and Testament* (2021) and in particular chapter 9 for full discussion.
113. Grant, *Last Will and Testament* (2021), chapter titled 'The Overlooked Evidence', for Seleucus' 'hidden' inheritance of power.
114. See Grant, *Last Will and Testament* (2021), especially chapter 9, for explanation.
115. See discussion in Green (2007) p.46.
116. Euripides, *Ino* fragment 413.2 quoted by Plutarch, *On Exile* 16 and *Moralia* 506c.
117. Quoting Bosworth A to A (1988) p.266 and for full discussion pp.260–270.
118. According to Pseudo-Lucian, *The Long Lived* 10–13, Lysimachus was over 80 when he died, Ptolemy 84 and Seleucus 80.
119. For the opening of hostility between Ptolemy and Seleucus post-Ipsus, see Diodorus 21.5–6.
120. Discussed in Errington (1969) p.233.

121. Memnon's work is preserved in an epitome by Photius FGrH no. 434 F 7.3 and detailed the city's history and the influences upon it, dating from the tyranny of Clearchus (ruled 364–353 BC) to the city's capture by Rome in 70 BC.
122. Discussed in Bosworth-Baynham (2000) p.287. See Billows (1990) p.339 for sources.
123. Following and quoting Pearson (1960) pp.86–78.
124. Following Pernot (2000) p.7 quoting Victor Hugo on 'history eavesdropping on legend'.

Chapter 3: The Funeral Games Historian

1. Pausanias 1.13.9.
2. For the funeral games or contests, see Curtius 10.5.5, Diodorus 17.117.4, Arrian 7.26.3 reporting 'other historians'. Justin (so we assume Trogus) 12.15.6–8 gave a darker, more expansive account of the disputes and slaughter that the dying Alexander expected would follow. With this expression Alexander was recalling the posthumous Homeric contests honouring the fallen heroes of Troy, those Achilles had held for Patroclus in the *Iliad*, for example, when the late Mycenaean world seemed perennially at war, and it was a funerary tradition upheld in Macedon. Some scholars believe the Homeric funeral games (pre 1200 BC) led directly to the founding of the Pan-Hellenic athletics contests, the Olympic, Pythian, Isthmian and Nemian Games; see Roller (1981) pp.107–119.
3. See Grant, *Last Will and Testament* (2021) for full discussion, and in particular chapters 3 and 9.
4. Plutarch 8.2 quoting Onesicritus' claim that Alexander kept a dagger and the *Iliad* under his pillow.
5. Diodorus 16.89.2 for Philip's declaration against Persia, which Alexander 'inherited'.
6. Justin 13.1–4 commented that after Alexander's death the Bodyguards became princes instead of prefects.
7. The epithet possibly stemmed either from his birthplace, from being 'knock-kneed' or even from the name of a protective iron knee plate; discussion on the epithet Gonatas in Iossif-Chankowski-Lorber (2007) p.418.
8. Anson (2004) pp.3–4 for the lost title. Discussion of Dionysius' opinion in Hornblower (1981) pp.246–248.
9. For Hieronymus' approach, see in particular Roisman (2012) p.18 and pp.9–30 for a discussion of his bias.
10. Quoting Hornblower (1981) p.16. None of the eighteen or nineteen fragments are direct quotations of Hieronymus.
11. Brown (1947) p.691 for discussion and referring to Jacoby's *Die Fragmente der griechischen Historiker* which collected the fragments. Diodorus' books 18 and 22 survive in fragments and yet the era they covered suggest they too would have used detail from Hieronymus, who detailed events down at least to the death of Pyrrhus in 272 BC.
12. Hieronymus' history provided material for Pausanias, Polyaenus (second century) and Appian (*ca*. AD 95–165), as well as for the biographies of Eumenes and the Athenian statesman Phocion (*ca*. 402–318 BC) written by Nepos and Plutarch. His narrative

was the foundation of Plutarch's *Lives* of Demetrius and Pyrrhus of Epirus (*ca*. 319–272 BC), and Hieronymus was the template for several books of Trogus' Philippic History, though Duris' overlapping account is surely woven into these biographical portraits too, sourced directly or indirectly. Hieronymus' was substantially the material behind Arrian's *Events after Alexander*, parts of which exist as an epitome in the encyclopaedic *Myriobiblion* (also named *Bibliotheca*) of Photius, who précised a parallel work by Dexippus (*ca*. AD 210–273), the Athenian historian and hero of the Gothic invasion of AD 262. The *Vatican Palimpsest* (or Codex) contains two extracts from Arrian's seventh follow-on book and the *Gothenburg Palimpsest* houses a fragment from the tenth, all ultimately stemming from Hieronymus' account, as does the *Heidelberg Epitome*. For Pausanias, Polyaenus, Appian (*Syrian Wars*) and Dionysius using Hieronymus, see discussion in Hornblower (1981) pp.71–74 and Rozen (1967) p.41. Nepos used Hieronymus for part of his biography of Eumenes and Phocion. Determining how much of the detail Trogus drew directly from Hieronymus, or through Diyllus, is confused by Justin's compression of detail; see discussion in Heckel-Yardley (1997) pp.3–5. For the length of Hieronymus' work, see Hornblower (1981) pp.97–102. Further fragments of Dexippus' book can be found in the *Excerpta de Sententiis*, a work commissioned by Constantine VII of Byzantium around AD 900 and transmitted in palimpsest Vaticanus graecus 73 in the Vatican Library. Anson (2014) p.10 for a useful summary of Photius' work and the two palimpsests. *Gothenburg Palimpsest* discussion in Roisman (2012) p.147.

13. See discussion in Green (2007) p.xxvii and Billows (1990) pp.333–337, and quoting Kebric (1977) p.9.

14. Kebric (1977) p.46 for the proposition that Hieronymus published in response to Duris' account. For his career and dating, see Kebric (1977) pp.1–5. The conclusions are refuted by Billows (1990) pp.333–336, who sees no evidence of the use of Duris. Diodorus is reckoned to have drawn from Duris rather than Hieronymus for detail that appears in book 19 concerning Agathocles, the tyrant of Syracuse; the logic being that Duris had published a so-named book and had possibly been born in Sicily; Kebric (1977) p.4. While Timaeus, who harboured a special grudge against the tyrant, is a strong contender as a source, as are the pro-Tyrant Callias and Antander (brother to Agathocles) – all mentioned by Diodorus himself (21.16–18) – several episodes found in Plutarch are specific to Eumenes' career, and Duris must be a prime candidate for each.

15. Hornblower (1981) p.10 for discussion. Diodorus cited Hieronymus in action at 18.42.1, 18.50.5, 19.44.3 and 19.100.2, in each case confirming him as historian of the wars. See Hornblower (1981) p.234 for details of Hieronymus' exile from his homeland. Also Diodorus 19.44.3–4 for his wounds.

16. Following Hornblower (1981) p.197 for comparisons to Odysseus and Spartan resourcefulness in which theft was encouraged, for example in Xenophon's *The Cavalry Commander* 5.11. Also Polybius 12.27.10–11 and 12.28.1 for apparently well-known admiration of Odysseus and Pausanias 8.30.8; full discussion in McGing (2010) pp.129–130.

17. See Grant, *Last Will and Testament* (2021) for detailed discussion of the war between Eumenes and Antigonus.

18. Billows (1990) pp.319–320 on Hieronymus' bias, which highlighted Antigonus' ambition. Also see discussion in Hadley (1969) p.149.

19. Roisman (2012) pp.9–30 for a discussion of Hieronymus' anti-Macedonian stance.

20. Examples of Hieronymus' hostile treatment of Peucestas at Diodorus 19.38.1, 42.2, 43.5; discussed in Hornblower (1981) p.155. Hornblower (1981) p.17 citing Pausanias for Hieronymus slandering Lysimachus and Pyrrhus. For Hieronymus' treatment of Peucestas, see discussion in Roisman (2012) pp.13–14. See Justin 13.6.9 and Plutarch, *Phocion* 23–25 for Polyperchon's behaviour after Antipater's death. Diodorus' portrait is one of a man who was manipulated by Cassander; see discussion in Wheatley (1998) p.12. See Diodorus 18.74.1 for Polyperchon's failure at Megalopolis and 18.75.1–3 for his 'lack of energy and wisdom'; 20.20.1–3 for his ambition; 20.28.2 for his fickle character; 20.100.6 for his 'plundering' of Greece; 20.103.7 for his 'failure to come to aid'.

21. Grant, *Last Will and Testament* (2021) for Polyperchon's rile on the post-Alexander years and his actions in alliance with Eumenes.

22. Bosworth (1990) p.330 for discussion of the period covered.

23. Diodorus 20.73.1 for the death of Philip, Antigonus' son, and Diodorus 20.73.1–2 for Antigonus' invasion of Egypt.

24. Diodorus 20.75.1 ff for the bribes and desertions. Griffiths (1935) p.114 for the calculation of 5,000 Macedones at the core of Ptolemy's army. Ptolemy fought at Gaza with 18,000 infantry and 4,000 cavalry, but captured 8,000 of Demetrius' men and had them sent to Egypt; Diodorus 19.85.5.

25. Pausanias 1.9.7–8 cited Hieronymus as a source for the accusation that Lysimachus desecrated the graves of the Aeacids during the war with Pyrrhus. Pausanias – cf Carney (2006) p.77 – did however voice his doubt and reported that Hieronymus was angered by the destruction of Cardia. Pausanias 1.9.8, Diodorus 22.12 and Plutarch, *Pyrrhus* 16.6–7 blamed Pyrrhus' own Gallic troops. Pyrrhus was thrown out of Macedon by Lysimachus two years later; discussion in Stewart (1993) pp.285–286.

26. Diodorus 20.83.1–20.85.5 for the siege of Rhodes. See discussion of Hieronymus' eyewitness role in Brown (1947) p.685; the wounds and his participation in battles detailed at Pseudo-Lucian, *The Long Lived* 22 suggest that Hieronymus could have given an eyewitness account of the battle and Antigonus' death.

27. Hieronymus' whereabouts at the time of Demetrius' death are unknown, but if already serving Antigonus Gonatas he would certainly have known of the captivity of Demetrius, under Seleucus' guard, and would have received regular reports on his hopeless fate. Plutarch, *Demetrius* 1.7: a description given when comparing Demetrius to Mark Antony. Phila had married Balacrus in the mid-330s BC, Craterus in 322/321 BC and finally Demetrius in 320 BC. She bore three sons and a daughter.

28. Quoting W.S. Ferguson in his review of Tarn's *Antigonus Gonatas*, in *Classical Philology*, Volume 9 No.3 (July 1913) p.323. Gonatas had Philochorus the Attidographer executed for his anti-Macedonian stance; see discussion in Hornblower (1981) p.185. He also executed Oxythemis, probably the brother or nephew of Medius of Larissa; Billows (1990) p.414 for discussion. Diogenes Laertius 2.127, 5.58, 5.67, 4.41 for Gonatas' association with philosophers.

29. Quoting Green (1990) p.143 for the 'first Stoic king'.
30. Plutarch, *Pyrrhus* 21.12 for proof that Hieronymus used Pyrrhus' memoirs when constructing his own history, and Plutarch, *Moralia* 119c–d (*Consolation to Apollonius*) and Aelian 3.5 for the death of Gonatas' son and his stoic acceptance.
31. Fuller discussion and original text in Grant (2017) p.524ff.
32. Several other notables from the ancient world, including Pythagoras, are said to have lived to 104. This is probably not coincidence: as pointed out by the historian Truesdell Brown, 104 – thus the 105th year – is a mystical numerical combination and the sum of the first fourteen integers. Photius, *Life of Pythagoras* 1 and Pseudo-Lucian, *The Long Lived* 22 for Hieronymus' age. Brown (1947) pp.685–686.
33. Herodotus noticed the symbiotic relationship of the crocodile and birds which picked leeches from its mouth to clean it, and then flew out unharmed; mentioned by Pliny 6.2.25.
34. Following the argument of Shipley (2000) p.13.
35. Pausanias 1.13.9.
36. See Grant, *Last Will and Testament* (2021) for full discussion.

Chapter 4: The Alexandrian Monopoly

1. Heckel (1992) p.222.
2. Heckel (2006) p.46.
3. Cicero, *Brutus* 11.42–43; Quintilian 10.1.74–5.
4. Tarn (1948) p.43.
5. Cleitarchus was 'Alexandrine' according to Philodemus, *De Sublimate* 3.2 (FGrH 137 T 9). Bosworth (1992) p.2, however, considered the evidence tenuous.
6. 'State within a state' quoting Bagnall (1976) p.4.
7. The comparative lack of information in Arrian's account, for example, compared to the Vulgate for the period after 328 BC, discussed in Bosworth (1981).
8. Cicero, *Brutus* 43. Cleitarchus was popular in Rome and was cited as a source by Diodorus, Plutarch, Strabo, Athenaeus and Diogenes Laertius, to name but a few. Quintilian 10.1.74–5. Cicero, *Brutus* 11.42. Cicero had proposed that orators alone should be entrusted with the care of the past. For other criticisms, see Pearson (1960) p.153 footnote 21.
9. Deinon's account was rich in Persian court customs, as inferred by a fragment in Athenaeus 2.67a. Plutarch, *Artaxerxes* mentioned Deinon nine times as an information source; we assume Deinon's *Persica* was being referenced. Nepos, *Conon* 5 for his praise of Deinon.
10. Diodorus 2.125, 2.129–137 for Ctesias' capture and service under Artaxerxes II. Quoting Plutarch, *Artaxerxes* 1.2 and 6.6, translation from the Loeb Classical Library edition (1926); Ctesias had in fact called both Hellanicus and Herodotus liars.
11. Quoting Pearson (1960) p.213. Ctesias appears a preferred source as he was resident at the Persian court.
12. Diogenes Laertius, *Stilpo* suggested Stilpo 'won over' Cleitarchus, detaching him from his previous teacher Aristotle of Cyrene. See discussion in Bosworth (1996)

p.2. As Bosworth (1996) points out, the meeting would have taken place in Greece, not Egypt. For more on the philosophy and influences of Stilpo, see Brown (1950) pp.136–137.

13. Ptolemy's manipulative or even ruthless character is well demonstrated. As examples: his murder of Cleomenes, a local governor or treasurer, see Pausanias 1.6.3; the forced suicide of Polemaeus, a defecting nephew of Antigonus and who had become 'presumptuous', see Diodorus 20.27; and his annexation of Coele-Syria after a failed bribe, Appian, *Syrian Wars* 52 and Diodorus 18.43.2.

14. For the flattery still visible in Curtius' account of the Babylonian settlement onwards, see Grant, *Last Will and Testament* (2021) chapter 3.

15. As proposed by Tarn and others, though we have little actual evidence.

16. For Cleitarchus' use of Theopompus, see Pearson (1960) Introduction p.19. Following Tarn (1948) p.127 for the proposal of Peripatetic polemic and p.297 for 'under Cassander's shield'. Athenaeus 10.435b–c for an example of Theopompus' treatment of the Macedonian court under Philip II. Brown (1950) for discussion of Diogenes' influence over Stilpo, and thus Cleitarchus. Brown (1950) p.153 disputes there is any proof of Cleitarchean hostility towards Alexander. Flower (1994) pp.98–116 for Theopompus' treatment of Philip and pp.166–167 and 169–183 for his moralizing. Quoting Plutarch, *Demetrius* 10.2 of the Athenian regime. Pausanias 1.25.6 termed Demetrius a 'tyrant'.

17. See Kebric (1977) p.36 ff for Duris' influence on other historians and p.79 for the early publication of the *Samian Chronicle*; Theopompus is not proposed, but if the *Samian Chronicle* was published before Samos was occupied by Ptolemaic forces in 281 BC, then it is possible Samos' struggle under Alexander's Diadochi influenced Cleitarchus, assuming he published late.

18. Quoting Bosworth (1971) p.112.

19. Quoting Spengler on 'organ of history' and cited in Brown (1962) p.257.

20. Lucian, *A slip of the Tongue in Salutation* 10; discussed by C. Bearzot in Marasco (2011) p. 46.

21. In Arrian's account he cited, or implied, there had been discrepancies between Aristobulus and Ptolemy at 2.3.7 (implied), 2.4.7 (implied), 3.3.6, 3.4.5, 3.30.5, 4.3.5, 4.5.6 (implied), 4.13.5 (implied), 4.14.3–5, 5.14.3 (implied), 5.20.2.

22. Polybius 12.3.4c 4–5.

23. Pearson (1960) p.194.

24. Arrian, *Indica* 18.9 for Evagoras' role.

25. Quoting Hornblower (1981) p.153.

26. Noted by Hornblower (1981) p.234. Polybius and Hieronymus could have returned to their native lands but had by then become influential to regimes elsewhere.

27. Robinson (1953) believed Callisthenes himself drew from the diaries, as did later historians, yet paradoxically he believed the 'thin sources' in 327–326 BC were due to Eumenes' loss of the documents in a tent fire rather than Callisthenes' death. This is paradoxical, for while Callisthenes is mentioned as a source in later works, the *Royal Diaries* are never mentioned aside from the fragment dealing with Alexander's death.

28. Quoting Robinson (1953) Itinerary, pp.70–71.

29. Grant, *Last Will and Testament* (2021) for full discussion.
30. A summary of the earlier chronology debate is given in Pearson (1960) pp.152–154, 172–173 and 226–233; also Brown (1950).
31. Droysen, *Geschichte Alexanders des Grossen* (1833). Fused with later 1836–42 work on Alexander's successors as *Geschichte des Hellenismus* (Gotha, Perthes, 1877–87).
32. Bosworth more recently proposed that Cleitarchean publication was as early as 310 BC, citing the research of Badian, Prandi and Schachermeyr, who believed it was published within twenty years of Alexander's death (thus before 303 BC). Bosworth (2002) p.43 citing G. Droysen (1877), *Geschichte des Hellenismus* (Gotha); E. Schwartz, *Aristobulus*, Pauly-Wissowa, R.E. II, 911 ff (1957), H Berve (1926), Hamilton (1961), Prandi (1996) p.28. Jacoby Pauly-Wissowa R. E. XI, 622 ff (1921). Heckel (1988) p.2 for Schachermeyr's view.
33. Tarn (1948) p.101 described the relationship between Curtius and Cleitarchus' underlying source as *obscurum per obscurius*, though on pp.124–125 he did concede Trogus' use of Diodorus and a common source.
34. Hammond (1993) p.195, citing the earlier research by Goukowsky. Pearson (1960) pp.212–242 for the profile and dating of Cleitarchus and in particular his use of Aristobulus. Arrian Preface 1.2 for his claim that he wrote when a king. As with the claim that Lysimachus was a king when Onesicritus read aloud to him, we do not need to take this too literally; both became kings.
35. The geographical argument is based on Cleitarchus' comment on the relative sizes of the Black and Caspian Seas; see Tarn (1948) pp.16–29 and his use of Patroclus' geography. The titular argument surrounds Ptolemy's investiture with the title Soter. The chronology argument is based around Cleitarchus' time studying with Stilpo of Megara. Well summarized in Pearson (1960) pp.212–242 and Brown (1950) pp.137–139 and Hamilton (1961).
36. For Alexander's entry into the Mallian city and subsequent wounds, see Arrian 6.8.4–6.13.5, 6.28.4, Curtius 9.4.26–9.5.30, Diodorus 17.98.1–17.100.1, Plutarch 63.5–13. Curtius 9.4.15 for the mutinous behaviour before entering Mallia.
37. Arrian 6.11.8 and Curtius 9.5.21 for their polemics on other historians reporting the events, including Timagenes and Cleitarchus.
38. Tarn (1948) p.27.
39. See Robinson (1953) pp.183–243 for the fragments, especially in Arrian, detailing their conflicting accounts.
40. Arrian 6.11.8 and Curtius 9.5.21 for the lines referred to.
41. See discussion of the similarities in Robinson (1953), *The Ephemerides* pp.69–71.
42. Arrian 6.6.3 for the slaughter of unarmed men and Arrian 6.11.1 for the women and children.
43. Arrian, *Indic*a 19.8; *hyperaspizantes* are hypaspists who protected their king or colleague with a shield. Plutarch 63.5 has Limnaus instead of Leonnatus in the role, but this could be a manuscript corruption. An aspis is a small light shield, though a larger hoplon-style shield is implied.
44. See discussion in Hammond (1993) pp.268–269, citing Arrian 6.10.2, who in turn cited Ptolemy as his source. For Leonnatus' actions, see Arrian 6.4.3 and Curtius 9.4.15; for

Peucestas' actions, Curtius 9.5.14–18, Arrian 6.9.3, 10.1–2, 11.7–8, 6.28.4, Diodorus 17.99.4. The arrowhead was allegedly four fingers in breadth; Plutarch, *Moralia* 341C gave Aristobulus' equally detailed account of the wound. Curtius 9.5.24–28 for Critobulus' role; this is the same name as Philip's physician at the siege of Methone twenty-eight years before; Pliny 7.37; Arrian 6.11.1 called him Critodemus.

45. Athenaeus 13.576e.

46. Briant (1974) p.108 for the chronology of Persepolis' fall, looting and burning. Plutarch 37.6 mentioned a four-month stay. Diodorus 17.72 and Curtius 5.7.3–7 embodying Cleitarchus' version of events; Justin 11.14.10 is too brief for any analysis. The report of Strabo 15.3.6 and Arrian 3.18.12 didn't mention Thais but focused on Alexander's political decision to please the Greeks. Plutarch 38 reported both versions. Arrian 6.30.1 claimed Alexander regretted his action upon returning to Persepolis on his way back to Babylon after the Indian campaign.

47. Diodorus 18.70.3, translation from the Loeb Classical Library edition (1963).

48. Plutarch 38.2–5 captured the heroic theme but commented that her speech urging on Alexander was not in keeping with her place. Diodorus 17.72 followed closely, clearly putting Thais in the lead role. Athenaeus 13.576d–e confirmed Cleitarchus was his source for the reporting of the fire.

49. Plutarch 3.5. Valerius Maximus, *Memorable Deeds and Sayings* 8.14.5 recorded that the arsonist of Ephesus was found. The Ephesians decreed that his name never be recorded, according to Aulus Gellius 2.6.18. It was Strabo 14.1.22 who revealed it. Originally the name had been preserved by Theopompus in his *Philippica*, but that work is now lost. See Plutarch 3.5 for the links to Alexander's birth.

50. Athenaeus 13.576e. A daughter, Eirene, married Eunostus of Soli, King of Cyprus, and a son by Thais fought at Salamis in 307/306 BC against the Antigonids according to Justin 15.12. Bosworth (1996) p.3 disagrees that Cleitarchus would have dared change Ptolemy's version of events at Persepolis.

51. Plutarch 46.4–5, translation from the Loeb Classical Library edition (1919).

52. Following Jacoby's statement in Brown (1949) p.6.

53. Heckel (2006) p.183 and Pearson (1960) pp.84–85 for discussion on Onesicritus' age.

54. Discussion in Pearson (1960) pp.224–225 for Cleitarchus' use of Nearchus.

55. Brown (1949) p.7 for the comparison of the length of Onesicritus' work with that of Xenophon's on the *Education of Cyrus*, its model, which was similarly divided into eight books, as was the *Anabasis* of Arrian. Pearson (1960) pp.83–84 for discussion of Nearchus' criticism of Onesicritus, citing Arrian 7.20.8–10 and *Indica* 32.9–13. A more specific rebuttal of Onesicritus' claims appears at *Indica* 3.5 and Strabo 15.1.12.

56. See discussion on the relative chronology of Nearchus' and Onesicritus' publication dates in Brown (1949) pp.4–5, Pearson (1960) p.84 and Brown (1950) pp.5–7. Plutarch 46.4 for the reference to Lysimachus. Heckel (2008) p.7 brings to our attention the fact that the Journal claimed Nearchus read an account of his voyage to Alexander in his final days in Babylon, thus suggestive that he published soon after. However, the Journal citations are spurious and reading excerpts from a diary does not imply an immediate publication when events that followed were so calamitous.

57. For Onesicritus' fear, see *Metz Epitome* 97. The theme of 'fearful historians' is reiterated in the Vulgate texts at Curtius 10.10.18–19, Diodorus 17.118.2, Justin 12.13.10. Grant, *Last Will and Testament* (2021) for full discussion.

58. Noted by Tarn (1948) p.4, citing Diodorus 17.118.2.

59. Though Ptolemy I Soter, the Egyptian dynast, had married Cassander's sister Eurydice in 321/320 BC, he was to repudiate her in 317 BC in favour of Berenice, Eurydice's lady-in-waiting, who 'had the greatest influence and was foremost in virtue and understanding'; Plutarch, *Pyrrhus* 4.4. Pyrrhus singled her out for his affections knowing she held sway with Ptolemy. Berenice was nevertheless of the Antipatrid house; her paternal grandfather was the brother of the regent Antipater, the father of the accused Cassander. Cassander's own sons were exploited by Pyrrhus, the 'Eagle of the Epirotes' (Plutarch, *Pyrrhus* 10.1), and executed by Demetrius and Lysimachus for their internecine intrigues; by 294 BC, the power once wielded by the house of Antipater, the former regent and his offspring was finally spent; see Plutarch, *Pyrrhus* for Pyrrhus' relations with the sons of Cassander – though he had provided aid to one brother (Alexander) against the other (Antipater), he ultimately made both pay. Moreover, Ptolemy II Philadelphus, who succeeded his father in 282 BC (he had been co-ruler with his father from 285 BC), put to death his half-brother by Cassander's sister, Eurydice, who was based at Miletus in Caria by 287 BC, where she formed a dynastic alliance with Demetrius The Besieger, Cassander's old enemy (Eurydice offered her daughter, Ptolemais, to Demetrius in 298 BC – Plutarch, *Demetrius* 32 and 46). Philadelphus allegedly murdered his half-brother for inciting the Cypriots to revolt (Pausanias 1.7.1); the half-brother might have been in league with Ptolemy the Thunderbolt, another son of Eurydice, to oust Philadelphus. Lysimachus, once married to another of Cassander's sisters, Nicaea, died at Curopedium in 281 BC. Eurydice's oldest son, Ptolemy the Thunderbolt (thus Cassander's nephew), who had been passed over for the kingship in Egypt, died in the Gallic invasions in 279 BC, and her second son, Meleager, followed him soon after. Between them they had held the Macedonian throne for less than three years (281–279 BC) at the court based at Cassandrea. Antipater Etesias, the son of Cassander's brother, soon followed them as his reign lasted just forty-five days – 'as long as the Etesian Winds blew'.

60. Arrian 4.13.5–6, also Curtius 8.6.16 for the Syrian prophetess.

61. There is a lacuna in Curtius' account preceding Alexander's death, but Justin (so we assume Trogus) and Diodorus captured the supernatural detail. Hammond (1998) pp.420–421 assumes Curtius drew directly from Aristobulus for some portentous incidents, but he could equally have taken the detail from Cleitarchus. And Curtius never mentioned Aristobulus as a source elsewhere.

62. Cleitarchus' reference to the embassy from Rome was recorded by Pliny 3.57–58; many scholars doubt Rome could have sent the embassy as early as 323 BC, whereas in Cleitarchus' day, Rome was clearly on the rise, which argues for a late Cleitarchean publication date. Refuted by Tarn (1948) pp.22–23, who believes Pliny was mistaken in identifying Cleitarchus as its source.

63. Arrian 7.15.4–6 for the embassies to Babylon and sources behind them. He was doubtful on the report; Aristus is further mentioned as a historian of Alexander in Athenaeus 10.10 and Strabo book 15.

64. Well summed up by Tarn (1949) pp.374–378; see Justin 12.13.1 for Trogus' list of embassies.
65. Polybius 3.22. Polybius' view was possibly duped by Fabius Pictor's propaganda. Momigliano (1977) p.104 for discussion; the *Pyrgi Tablets* relating to *ca.* 500 BC suggest an Etruscan–Carthaginian relationship which may be the basis of Polybius' claim.
66. See Justin 12.2.12–13 and Livy 8.17.10 for the peace treaty with Rome in the Varronian years, so 332 BC. The date of the death of Alexander of Epirus is uncertain, though Livy 8.24.1 credited it to the year of the founding of Alexandria, thus 332/331 BC, yet Livy dated these events to 326 BC, so uncertainty remains. Alexander Molossus had married Alexander's sister, Cleopatra, his own niece.
67. Justin 12.3.1 for the funeral games. Justin 12.2.2–4 and 12.1.14–15 for the oracle of Dodona that warned Alexander to beware of the city of Pandosia and the River Acheron.
68. Strabo 5.3.5, Memnon FGrH 434 F.
69. In Arrian 7.15.4–6, the Tyrrhenians, alongside Lucanians and Bruttians, were reported to be sending ambassadors to Babylon, and this could have referred to Etruscans or other Latins bordering the Tyrrhenian Sea. Arrian 7.1.3 for the alleged plans to campaign in Sicily and Italy.
70. Diodorus 17.113.2, Justin 12.13.1.
71. Chugg (2009) p.11 for a discussion of Rome's emergence after Pyrrhus' campaigns, and for the Rhodian trade discussion, see Berthold (1984) p.80.
72. For Tarquinus' heritage, see Pliny 35.152, Livy 1.34, Dionysius of Halicarnassus 3.46; discussed in Boardman (1964) p.202.
73. Plutarch, *Camillus* 22.2–3. The date of the sacking of Rome is often stated as 390 BC, based on the faulty Varronian chronology. This stems from Heracleitus' claim that Hyperboreans descended on a Greek city named Rome; Aristotle apparently credited Camillus as its saviour.
74. Pliny stated that Theophrastus was the first foreigner to write about Rome in detail, though Theopompus had mentioned the capture of Rome by Gauls; discussion in Pearson (1960) p.233. The coverage of Rome in Timaeus and Callias came from their associations with Agathocles, tyrant of Syracuse; Diodorus 21.17.1–4 for their relative positions; Momigliano (1977) pp.52–55 for discussion.
75. Hieronymus' portrayal of Pyrrhus necessarily brought Pyrrhus' clashes with Rome into his narrative, and thus he was one of the earliest Hellenistic authors to bring Rome into mainstream Hellenic history. See discussion in Hornblower (1981) pp.71–72. Dionysius of Halicarnassus, *Roman Antiquities* 1.5.8 claimed Hieronymus was the first historian to give an account of Rome and Timaeus the second. Yet an 'account' might suggest the definition of something fuller than the mention of an embassy; perhaps something of a background history to their origins, which fits Hieronymus' style. Discussion in Tarn (1948) pp.22–23.
76. Discussed in Boardman-Griffin-Murray (1986) p.234.
77. Aristotle, *Politics* 1.1253a2–3 proposed that men are by nature political animals.

Chapter 5: Secondary Sources: the Roman Alexander

1. Cicero, *On the Orator* Book 2.13, translated by E.W. Sutton (Cambridge Harvard University Press, 1942), quoting Marcus Antonius.
2. Momigliano (1977) p.115.
3. Polybius 8.10.11 for 'numerous historians', who probably included Duris, Diyllus and Demochares; see Bosworth-Baynham (2000) p.302. The oft-cited works of the pro-Athenian Diyllus (early third century BC, his history spanned 356–297 BC, in twenty-six books), along with Timaeus' thirty-eight-book history of Sicily and then Pyrrhus of Epirus (which reached to the Punic War of 264 BC), fell into that hole. As did the accounts of Phylarchus (third century BC), the memoirs of Aratus of Sicyon (lived *ca.* 271–213 BC) and Philochorus the Atthidographer (*ca.* 340–261 BC), all of which are lost bar fragments. Extracts of Euphantus of Olynthus (whose *On Kingship* was likely dedicated to Antigonus Gonatas), Nymphis of Heraclea and Demochares the nephew of Demosthenes, whose history might have stretched back to Philip's reign *ca.* 350 BC, suggest they also narrated the events of the early Hellenistic world. Discussion in Tarn (1948) p.63, and for Diodorus see Pearson (1960) p.239. Hammond (1994) p.16 for Diyllus and Diodorus 21.5 for Diyllus' twenty-six books.
4. Polybius 8.8.8–9, translation from the Loeb Classical Library edition, vol. III (1922–1927). See discussion in Walbank (1962) p.4.
5. Diodorus 1.3, translation from the Loeb Classical Library edition (1933).
6. The lack of interest is an observation made in Shipley (2000) p.7; quoting McGing (2010) p.6.
7. A theme discussed in Hornblower (1981) p.236. Also see Bosworth-Baynham (2000) p.296.
8. Plutarch, *Aemilianus* 22.7 for Scipio's deeds at Pydna. Plutarch, *Aemilius* 23–24 for Perseus fleeing. Pausanias 7.10.7–12 for the 1,000 hostages. Polybius was on the wrong side of the equally hostile Callicrates and his policy of obeisance to Rome. Polybius' father had advocated strict neutrality in the Roman war with Macedon and he was a victim of that political divide, thus deemed of suspect loyalty. Polybius 28.6.9 for his Achaean command. Polybius 24.8–10 for his presence in Rome pleading his case. In contrast, Polybius' father, Lycortas, believed the Achaean League should state its case and relied on Roman common sense to be reasonable with demands. Rome wanted the Achaeans onside against Macedon, as evidenced by their embassy at Polybius 28.3–7, and 30.13 for the political motivation.
9. Polybius 45.6–47.4. Polybius admitted Cleoxenus and Democleitus had conceived the torch system, though he perfected it. The alphabet was broken into five lines and referenced by numerals 1–5 of each axis. McGing (2010) p.142 for discussion of the dating of Polybius' *Tactics*. Polybius 31.23 for Scipio's petitioning. Quoting from an inscription seen by Pausanias; Momigliano (1977) p.68. Polybius was uniquely in Rome (31.23.5) whereas other hostages were in provincial towns. McGing (2010) p.140 for his probable presence in Africa in 151/150 BC. Polybius 38.10.8–10 for the reasons for the war of 146 BC; he returned to Rome in 145/144 BC to plead the league's case, Polybius 39.8.1.

10. Polybius 29.21.1–9, translation from the Loeb Classical Library edition, volume VI (1922–27).
11. This extract is repeated almost word for word at Diodorus 31.10.1–2 and shortened in Livy 55.9.2.
12. Polybius 1.2.8 for *pragmatike historia*. Polybius 9.1–2, translation by I. Scott-Kilvert (Penguin Classics edition, 1979).
13. Quoting Billows (1990) p.2 and 'dissected parts' from Polybius 1.4.7–8. Flower (1994) p.148 ff for discussion of Theopompus exampling this. McGing (2010) p.51 ff for the works influencing Polybius.
14. Polybius 8.11.4. See discussion in Walbank (1962) p.2 ff for Theopompus' treatment. The criticism might be unfair, as Philip V of Macedon reduced the work to sixteen books when excerpting detail on only Philip II from it, so much of Theopompus' fifty-eight-book work must have dealt with other matters.
15. Polybius 1.3 stated that the main narrative commenced at 220 BC, the 140th Olympiad, and at 1.5 he explained the Roman starting point as Rome's first overseas venture in the 129th Olympiad, so dovetailing with Timaeus' history. Discussed in McGing (2010) pp.21–22, 97, and in Hornblower (1981) pp.183–184.
16. Callisthenes is mentioned at Polybius 6.45.1 and 12.17–22, where he is termed 'ignorant' and unable to distinguish the impossible from the possible. See Robinson (1953) p.55 for the full entries.
17. Bosworth-Baynham (2000) pp.286–306 for a useful summary by R. Billows of Polybius' view of Alexander; p.289 for the passages concerning Alexander. Polybius 12.23.5 for his summation on Alexander's soul.
18. Polybius 1.4 for 'entire network of events'.
19. Polybius' critique didn't deter him from extracting detail from their works; Philinus had lived through the First Punic War (264–241 BC), adopting a pro-Carthaginian perspective, while Pictor fought for Rome in the Second Punic War against Hannibal (218–201 BC); Polybius 1.14–15 for Philinus' role with Hannibal. Polybius also attacked Xenophon, Plato and Demosthenes, but Timaeus in particular, dedicating much of his twelfth book to a polemic on his methods.
20. Polybius 1.1.5; Polybius 12.11 described Timaeus' comprehensive cross-referencing of Olympiads with a list of ephors, kings, Athenian archons and priestesses of Hera at Argos in the form of tables; Momigliano (1977) pp.49–50. Pseudo-Lucian, *The Long Lived* 22 for Timaeus' age.
21. Polybius 3.59.2; discussion and translation in Walbank (1962) p.1.
22. See discussion of Polybius' polemics against Timaeus in Walbank (1962) pp.8–11 and Momigliano (1977) pp.50–51. Pseudo-Lucian, *The Long Lived* 22 claimed Timaeus lived to age 96.
23. Strabo 14.1.22 for Timaeus' epithet. Also discussion in Walbank (1962) p.3. For Polemon's *Against Timaeus*, see discussion in McGing (2010) p.65. Timaeus' invective spawned a twelve-book (or more) retaliatory work by the antiquarian Polemon, a contemporary of Polybius, suitably titled *Against Timaeus*. Momigliano (1977) pp.54–55 for the founding date of both cities, upheld by Timaeus.
24. Quoting Polybius 12.25a1–12.25b4 (Loeb) and 12.27.10–11 for his emphasis on the importance of military experience when writing about war.

25. Discussion in Pitcher (2009) pp.106–107 on Polybius' critiques and method. Also Green (1990) was particularly scathing about Polybius' partisan approach. For discussion of Polybius' speeches, see Champion (2000) p.436 quoting F.W. Walbank for 'subjective operations'. Quoting Walbank and discussed in Momigliano (1977) p.71 on Polybius' final chapters. Following McGing (2010) p.15 for 'writing himself into Roman history'.

26. Quoting Hatzopoulos (1996) p.265.

27. Polybius provided his own explanation of anacyclosis at 6.3.5–6.4.13; following Bosworth-Baynham (2000) p.308 for Herodotus' empire progression. Building on the discourses of Plato and Aristotle, as well as the sequence of empires described by Herodotus, his system of cyclical inevitability saw the rise and fall of city-states and their empires from 'primitive' monarchy through to (developed) monarchy, tyranny, aristocracy, oligarchy, democracy, ochlocracy (mob rule) and finally back to the beginning of the cycle with some form of monarchy. Ironically, Polybius considered Athens at its prime as verging on ochlocracy (Plato might have agreed, for its *demokratia* had overseen the death of his friend and mentor, Socrates). He further believed that Rome's republican system of government, a 'mixed constitution' (a hybrid that contained elements of a monarchy, aristocracy and democracy), had broken the chain, and though he was not suggesting that this would prevent its natural decline, signs of which he pointed to even in his day, Rome was, in fact, to become a fine example of the *politeion anakyklosis*. Polybius 6.43.1, 6.44.9 and 6.10–18 for the 'mixed constitution' discussion. Polybius 6.9.12–14 for the prediction of Rome's decline and 6.9.10 for *politeion anakyklosis*.

28. Polybius 1.3.3–6, translation by I. Scott-Kilvert (Penguin Classics edition, 1979).

29. Polybius 3.59.3 ff for credit to Alexander, quoting 1.1.3, and for 'Fortune's showpiece' 1.1.4. He was referring to the years 200 BC – the beginning of Rome's war against Hannibal – down to 168/176 BC and the defeat of King Perseus of Macedon at the Battle of Pydna.

30. Polybius 12.4b.2–4; for his attitude to Rome and use of *barbaroi* discussed in Champion (2000) pp.425–444.

31. Quoting T. Mommsen and cited by Walbank (1981) p.19.

32. The *Annales Maximi* were city records kept by the Pontifex Maximus; Cicero in his *On the Republic* 1.25 claimed they were legitimate until 400 BC, when an eclipse was mentioned. They were assembled into eighty books and finally published by Publius Mucius Scaevola in 130 BC; for full discussion, see Frier (1979) chapter 8 p.162 ff, and for their dating see Crake (1940) p.379.

33. Gudeman, *Romans* (1894) p.145 for the unlikely speech, as an example, of Scipio Africanus recorded by Livy, though Cicero informs us that Scipio left no written commentary on his activity.

34. Quoting Hegel (1837) II, *Reflective History, 1, Universal History*.

35. Quoting Momigliano (1977) p.79 on Livy's use of Polybius.

36. Livy 1.1 and Livy Preface 1, translation by Rev. Canon Robert, E.P. Dutton and Co. (1912) and Livy 6.1 for his comments on the fire and loss of genuine public records.

37. These early republican historians, nevertheless, had advantages the later annalists did not: before imperial edicts closed them to public eyes, public records provided a first-hand account of events, for the *Annales Maximi* of the Pontifex Maximus, the

Commentarii of the censors and the *Libri Augurales* too had all been available to consult. Discussed in detail in Seeley (1881) pp.12–14. One of the outcomes was the avowed later use of the so-called *Libri Lintei*, 'Linen Rolls' supposedly kept in the Temple of Juno Moneta, a doubtful documentary source supposedly consulted by the historian Licinius Macer (died 66 BC), for example, when nothing else was at hand.

38. Macaulay, *The Lays of Ancient Rome*, Introduction.
39. Quoting Malthus (1798) 2.20.
40. The expression first seen in Aulus Gellius 19.8.15.
41. Hesiod, *Theogony* 83–87, based on the translation by M.L. West (Oxford World Classics, 2008 edition) p.5.
42. Hesiod, *Theogony* 22–34. Hesiod, *Theogony* 27 claimed the Muses instructed him as he tended his lambs in his mountain pastures. Translation from Jaeger (1939) p.75.
43. Cicero, *On the Orator* 2.36, translation from Dominik (1997).
44. Strabo 9.2.40.
45. Cicero, *On the Orator* 2.62–63, translation by A.J. Woodman and appearing in Pitcher (2009) p.15. This was set after the death of Marcus Licinius Crassus (91 BC) and shortly before the Social War and the war between Marius and Sulla commenced. Cicero's house had already been sacked and he himself had recently returned from exile.
46. Cicero, *Brutus* 11.42.
47. Suetonius, *Julius Caesar* 56.2, drawing from Cicero, *Brutus* 262, for Cicero's likening rhetoric to curling irons; the analogy repeated in Quintilian 2.5.12, 5.12.18–120. Cicero, *On the Orator* 2.57–2.94 for the comment on Isocrates. For the dating of Cicero's treatises, see Dominik (1997) pp.13–15 and *On the Orator* 1.5 for Cicero's own description of his adolescence. The view that these historians – Flower (1994) p.46 for a list – attended Isocrates' school is rejected by Schwartz and Flower (1994) pp.44–62 and put down to Hellenistic-era invention or Cicero using the term 'school' in a metaphysical sense.
48. Pseudo–Plutarch, *Isocrates*, Pseudo–Lucian, *The Long Loved* 23, with a similar tradition in Dionysius of Halicarnassus, *Attic Orators*, *Life of Isocrates* 3.2, Pausanias 1.18.1, Flavius Philostratus, *Lives of the Sophists* 17. Other corroborating claims in anonymous 'lives' remain.
49. Cicero, *On the Orator* 2.57–2.94; Flower (1994) p.43 for the accreditation of the quote. Pseudo–Plutarch, *Isocrates*: Isocrates was asked how, not being very eloquent himself, he could make others so? He answered: 'Just as a whetstone cannot cut, yet it will sharpen knives for that purpose.'
50. Quoting and following Grant (1995) pp.27–28. Polybius 2.56.10–12; discussed by T.P. Wiseman in Gill–Wiseman (1993) p.134.
51. Quintilian 3.1.19 recorded that neither Cicero nor the rhetor Marcus Antonius (died 87 BC) completed their works on rhetoric.
52. Diodorus 1.76.1. Bagnall–Derow (2004) pp.206–211 for Ptolemaic papyri detailing legal procedures.
53. Momigliano (1977) p.47 for Timaeus' view on rhetoric.
54. In the *Iliad* 9.442, Achilles' tutor, Phoenix, was appointed to teach him about the art of public speaking as well as fighting. At 3.212–223 there is a description of Odysseus'

skill at public speaking. Homer. *Iliad* 9.343–344; *Psychagogia* was used by Plato in his *Phaedra* 261a and defined a positive aspect of rhetoric in persuading souls to see truth.

55. Diogenes Laertius, *Empedocles* 3, also Diogenes Laertius, *Zeno the Eleactic* 4. The origins of rhetoric in Pernot (2000) pp.21–23.
56. Cicero, *Brutus* 46.
57. Guthrie (1971) p.270; for Gorgias' label, see Wardy (1996) p.6. Antiphon's *On Truth* is preserved in *Oxyrhynchus Papyri*, xi, no. 1364, quoted in Kagan (1965) p.2965. In translation the Rock of Ares, also called Areopagus, situated north-west of the Acropolis, functioned as a Court of Appeal for criminal and civil cases in ancient times.
58. Pliny 7.30 claimed Isocrates could charge 20 talents for a single oration.
59. Plato, *Theatetus* 151e (and *Sextus Against the Mathematicians* VII.60) attributed the phrase to Protagoras' *Truth*. For the fees charged by the Sophists, see full discussion in Worthington (2007) pp.306–307. Aristotle, *Rhetoric* 1402a23–5 recorded Protagoras' claim to 'make the weaker argument the stronger'.
60. For Anaxagoras, *On Nature*, see discussion in Boyer (1991) pp.56–58. For Anaxagoras' imprisonment, see Plutarch, *Moralia* 607f or *On Exile* 17 and *On the Opinions of Philosophers*, *Anaxagoras*. Anaxagoras claimed the sun was a red-hot stone the size of the Peloponnese and not a deity.
61. Cato, *Maxims Addressed to his Son*, quoted by Pliny 29.13–14.
62. See discussion of Cato's familiarity with Greek rhetoric and educating his sons to its principles in Dominik (1997) p.6, quoting Quintilian 3.1.19, who stated Cato was the first he knew of to 'handle' the topic.
63. See Polybius 31.25.5, quoting Cato.
64. Suetonius, *Lives of Eminent Rhetoricians* 25 for the expulsion of rhetoricians from Rome. For the banning of coins, see Atkinson (2009) p.39.
65. Plutarch, *Cato* 22–23.
66. Athenaeus 213d. Athens had sided with Mithridates of Pontus in his revolt against Rome and the city felt the Senate's backlash. The so-called brain drain quote from Potter (2006) p.528.
67. Quoting Macaulay (1828).
68. Horace, *Epistle* 2.1.156–157: '*Graeci capta ferum victorem cepit et artis intulit agresti Latio.*' Virgil's line from the *Aeneid* book 2 was in fact 'fear the Danaans, even those bearing gifts!' In full, '*Equo ne credite, Teucri! Quidquid id est, timeo Danaos et dona ferentis.*' It referred to the wooden horse at Troy.
69. Based on the quote by Whitmarsh (2002) p.175 on paradigms.
70. Quoting Pernot (2000) p.128.
71. Discussed in Pitcher (2009) p.53.
72. Livy 38.17.12.
73. As noted and proposed by Bosworth-Baynham (2000) Introduction pp.7–8.
74. Livy 38.17.12. The dating of Livy's work is uncertain; he commenced the *Early History of Rome* mid-life and completed it much later. He is thought to have been born *ca.* 60 BC and to have died *ca.* AD 17/18, possibly the same year as Ovid, as claimed by St Jerome (Eusebius Sophronius Hieronymus *ca.* AD 347–420). Diodorus published sometime between 36 and 30 BC.
75. Livy 9.17–18.

76. Quoting Lucan, *On the Civil War* 10.20–52 and 10.1. Seneca, *Epistles* 113.27–30, 83.18–25 and *Suasoria* 1.5–6 are good examples of vitriol hurled at Alexander; cited by Spencer (2002) p.89 and discussed at pp.140–143; Lucan 10.22–45, cited by Stewart (1993) p.14; for other polemics against Alexander, see Livy 9.18.1–7, Cicero, *Letters to Atticus* 12.40–13.28, also cited by Spencer (2002) pp.53–60.

77. Suetonius, *Nero* 19.

78. The caging episode was retold in Justin 15.3.3–9, Plutarch, *Demetrius* 27.3–4, Pausanias 1.9.5, Curtius 8.1.14–19, Valerius Maximus 9.3 etx.1, Seneca, *Concerning Anger* 3.17.2, 3.23.1, Pliny 54.

79. Heckel (2006) p.154 for the alternative identification of Lysimachus.

80. Seneca, *Concerning Anger* 3.17.1–4 and *Concerning Clemency* 1.25.1. See citation in Curtius 8.1.17. The Lysimachus episode discussed in Heckel (1992) p.249.

81. Athenaeus 598b–c mentioned his being caged but does not mention the mutilation of the ears and nose that Seneca recounted. Plutarch, *Symposiacs* 2.634f had the story almost identically transmitted about Timagenes making the fatal quip, but no punishment was mentioned.

82. Valerius Maximus' use of Alexander as an exemplum discussed in Wardle (2005).

83. See discussion in Spencer (2002) pp.15–21 for Rome's dictators and their emulation of Alexander; also p.37 for the Trajan-era admiration. Following discussion of I. Worthington in Carney-Ogden (2010) p.167 for the return of philhellenism.

84. Teuffel-Schwabe (1892) pp.4–5.

85. Cruttwell (1877) p.6.

86. From Gore Vidal's 1959 review of Robert Graves' *The Twelve Caesars*.

87. Arrian Preface 1.1–2 translation by A. de Selincourt (Penguin Books edition, 1958).

88. Diodorus confirmed the wealth of literary materials when he arrived in Rome. Plutarch used at least twenty-four sources for his Alexander biography alone.

89. Arrian Preface 1.2 and 6.11.2, translation from Hammond-Atkinson (2013).

90. Pearson (1960) p.218.

91. Quoting Stewart (1993) p.10 and Green (1974) p.479.

92. Ephorus earned Polybius' praise as the 'first universal historian': Polybius 15.24a.

93. Diodorus 1.3.

94. Diodorus 1.74.7 and 12.95.1 for his own comments on democracy. Quoiting Sacks (1990) p.26 on 'moral utility'.

95. Polybius 8.24.1.

96. Diodorus 1.4.1.

97. Sacks (1990) p.171 ff for discussion of Diodorus' intended terminus.

98. See Goralski (1989) p.81 for reference to the 280 surviving works of Photius. Bosworth-Baynham (2000) p.311 for Diodorus' chronological scope.

99. St Jerome, *Chronicle*; the entry was cited under the Year of Abraham 1968 (49 BC).

100. Diodorus' complex attitude to Rome discussed in Sacks (1990) p.212 ff; p.129 for Sicilian loss of enfranchisement. Caesar has proposed *sine suffragio* for the whole island, though Mark Antony claimed he had requested *Latinitas* for Sicily, before Sextus Pompey; discussed in Sacks (1990) p.207 ff.

101. Diodorus 1.4.4 for Agyrium and 4.24 for its Heraclean cult. Diodorus 4.24 for Heracles' visit. Quoting Polybius 12.26 on Timaeus; discussed in Momigliano (1977)

p.48. Diodorus 16.82.5 and 16.83.3 for hints of Agyrium's former importance; Sacks (1990) p.165 for discussion.

102. See discussion in Barber (1993) pp.84–90.

103. In his *Chronicle*, St Jerome stated Diodorus was in his prime in the year of Abraham 1968, which would suggest 49 BC. His presence in Egypt in 59 BC is suggested at 1.83.8, and further references to Egypt at 144.1–4 indicate he started composing as early as 56 BC, whereas at 16.7.1 his references to Tauromenium (modern Taormina) and Caesar's removal of the citizens relates to activity of 36 BC. Diodorus 1.4.3 for the statement on Rome's expansion; Bosworth-Baynham (2000) pp.312–314 for a summary of Diodorus' attitude to Rome.

104. See Diodorus' comment at 40.8 on filching and earlier publishing by third parties; his comment on 'before they were ready' rather than before the 'whole Library was completed' does, nevertheless, suggest he may have published packets himself.

105. Diodorus 1.4.4 for his claim to a 'considerable familiarity' with Latin. Herodotus 2.16 for Europe and Asia. Diodorus' geography of Mesopotamia put Nineveh on the Euphrates, for example. He never mentioned the Acropolis at Athens. At 1.4.2, Diodorus mentioned Rome as the only other place he visited apart from Egypt. Diodorus 1.83.8–9 for his eyewitness account of an incident in Egypt and 3.381 for mention of the 'royal records' in Alexandria. Sacks (1990) p.189 for Diodorus' seeming lack of affiliations in Rome.

106. Discussion in Barber (1993) pp.14, 17. See Green (2007) p.IX for the term 'kaleidoscopic disjunctiveness', though applied to the earlier Hellenistic period.

107. See discussion in Pitcher (2009) p.115 for his method and p.127 quoting Dionysius of Halicarnassus, *On Thucydides* 9.

108. Diodorus 20.43.7. Translation R.M. Greer (Loeb Classical Library edition, 1954).

109. Polybius 5.31.3–5 for his recognition of the problem.

110. Diodorus 17.117.5 commented that Alexander had accomplished greater deeds than any of the kings before or after his own time.

111. Diodorus 17.117.5.

112. Diodorus 32.27.3 for his eulogizing Caesar; discussion in Sacks (1990) p.74 ff.

113. Discussed in Heckel (1984).

114. Quoting Hadley (2001) p.3 for the 'uneasy agreement'. Errington (1970) on the other hand sees the exclusive use of Hieronymus in books 18–20.

115. Sacks (1990) p.18 for the contradiction between Diodorus' prologues (*proemia*) and narratives.

116. Discussed in Hornblower (1981) p.263. Diodorus 19.29.2 for the unique reference to *asthippoi*.

117. See full discussion in Grant, *Last Will and Testament* (2021), chapter 5 in particular.

118. Proposed and discussed by Hornblower (1981) p.26.

119. Tarn (1948) p.92 for his description of Diodorus as an 'honest plodding Greek'.

120. Diodorus 1.3.6 for 'immense labour'.

121. In 1865, Heinrich Nissen reasoned Diodorus habitually followed single sources; discussed in Pitcher (2009) p.72. For his plagiarizing of Polybius, 1670 John Henry Boecler and later Petrus Wesseling in 1746. Discussed in Hornblower (1981) p.19.

122. Examples are discussed at length by Simpson (1959) pp.370–379 and Hornblower (1981) pp.62–75. The degree to which Diodorus adhered to a single source and plagiarized its content is still debated, yet it seems clear he followed single authors where he could. Much of his history of Alexander closely correlates with Curtius' work, suggesting Cleitarchus as a common link. For discussions, see Anson (2004) pp.1–33, Hornblower (1981) pp.1–75 and also discussion in Baynham (1998) p.85. Following the views of Brown (1947) p.692 for the fortunate lack of creativity. Detailed discussion of Diodorus' methodology in Sacks (1990) p.21 ff, citing Agatharchides as a possible intermediary source.

123. 'Not entirely mechanical' following Hornblower (1981) p.63. Also referring to Hegel (1837) and its contention that only a recorder of contemporary events merits the title 'historian'. Recorders of events of the past are deemed 'compilers'. His *Lectures on The Philosophy of History* were originally delivered as lectures at the University of Berlin in 1821, 1824, 1827 and 1831.

124. Quoting Pitcher (2009) p.116.

125. Justin Preface 1 described Trogus as *vir priscae eloquentiae*; discussed in Baynham (1998) p.30.

126. Quoting P.A. Brunt (1980) p.494.

127. 'Philippic' may have come to mean 'encyclopaedic in proportion' after early *Philippics*, by Theopompus for example.

128. See discussion in Heckel-Yardley (1997) Introduction pp.2–3.

129. Justin 12.13.1 for the embassy from the Gauls; the succession of empires discussed in Alonso-Núñez (1987) pp.62–70. Heckel-Yardley (1997) introduction p.2. quoting Justin 43.5.11–12.

130. Justin 11.6.3, 12.13.1 and 12.16.9 for Alexander's quest to become king of the universe or the entire world.

131. See discussion in Heckel-Yardley (1997) Introduction pp.6–7.

132. Duris is also reckoned to have been anti-Macedonian in his treatment of Alexander and his successors. See Shipley (2000) p.161 for discussion. Also Hornblower (1981) pp.68–70. This is largely disputed by Billows (1990) p.336.

133. See full discussion on Trogus' style and content in Alonso-Núñez (1987) pp.56–72.

134. The study by Yardley (2003) suggests Justin's creativity.

135. Discussed in Heckel-Yardley (1997) Introduction p.9. Also Baynham (1995) p.61.

136. Quoting C. Thomas in Carney-Ogden (2010) p.178.

137. Tarn (1948) p.125. Also see Tarn's summation of Justin in Watson-Miller (1992) pp.106–110.

138. Discussion in Baynham (1995) p.15.

139. Curtius 10.5 ff. Discussed in full in Grant (2017) chapter 9 and in more-summarized form in Grant, *Last Will and Testament* (2021) chapter 5.

140. Thorough treatment has been given to Roman themes in Curtius' final chapter in Atkinson (2009). Also a discussion of Curtius' independence of thought in Errington (1970) pp.72–75.

141. McKechnie (1999) pp.59–60. A *contio* was a Latin term for a public gathering, though Livy for example used the term for a meeting, its audience and its speeches.

Historians have reconstructed speeches given at public ceremonies when, inevitably, little real-time recording took place. Thus *contio* speeches are often nothing more than approximations, at best, of the spirit behind the original. See discussion in Frolov (2013). Hammond (1978) p.341 for the *contio* in the manner of Scipio.

142. As an example see Curtius 4.14.9–26 for the speech provided before the battle at Gaugamela. Also Justin 11.9.9–10 for Darius' pre-battle rhetoric. Quoting Tarn (1948) p.92.

143. Curtius 9.1.34.

144. Renault (1975) p.412.

145. Tarn (1948) pp.91–92.

146. Curtius' relative merit discussed by Schachermeyr and Sibert and cited in McKechnie (1999) p.47, as well as in detail in Baynham (1998). For Errington's comments on Curtius, see discussion in McKechnie (1999) p.47 and Errington (1970) pp.49–77.

147. Summarizing Baynham (1998) p.14. Romane (1987) observed Curtius' technical account of the siege of Tyre was superior to Arrian's.

148. Quoting Olbrycht (2008) p.233.

149. For Cleitarchus' popularity, see Pearson (1960) p.213; he was cited by Diodorus, Plutarch, Strabo, Cicero, Athenaeus, Pliny, Quintilian and Diogenes Laertius, to name but a few, alongside references from many rhetoricians. The extant fragments can be read in Robinson (1953) pp.171–183.

150. Quoting Atkinson (2009) p.19.

151. Chapter 9 argues that Curtius most likely published in the term of Nero; this preceded, or marked the very beginnings of, the Second Sophistic when Greek writing and culture once again became popular.

152. Quoting Longinus, *On Sublimity* 22.1 – full extract in Gray (1987) pp.470–471 – and Diodorus 1.2.

153. In an analogy of his method, Plutarch 1.3 explained he relied mostly on the face, the expression and the eyes and paid less attention to the other parts of the body. Quoting Tarn (1948) p.296 for 'best to worst'.

154. In Plutarch, *Alexander* he referred to personal letters of Alexander at 7.6, 8.1, 17.8, 19.5–8, 20.9, 22.2, 22.5, 27.8, 39.4, 39.7, 39.13, 42.1, 46.3, 47.3, 55.6, 55.7, 60.1 and 60.11. No other historian seems to have had access to them, and how genuine they were remains open to speculation. Plutarch, *Demosthenes* 2.1.1–4 for his limited library. The various themes of letters to and from Alexander discussed in Pearson (1955) p.449. In 1873, Hersher published his *Epistolographi Graeci* (*Greek Letters*) containing some 1,600 examples. Discussed in Ehrman (2014) p.43.

155. See discussion on the unravelling of Plutarch sources in Hammond (1993) pp.1–2, citing Powell (1939) pp.229–240 and Tarn (1948) p.296.

156. Such as his *Moralia*, containing the possibly spuriously assigned *On the Fortune or Virtue of Alexander*.

157. Following Whitmarsh (2002) for 'virtual history' and noting the diptych comparisons.

158. Plutarch, *Moralia* 404d or *The Pythian Responses* 21, translated by Sir Thomas Browne, and Plutarch, *Coriolanus* 75, cited in Clement, *The Stomata* (Miscellanies) 5.88.4.

159. Plutarch 73–76. On reincarnation, see *Moralia, Consolation to his wife*, Loeb Classical Library edition, vol. VII (1959) pp.575–605 and J. Rualdus, *Life of Plutarch* 1624. In a letter to his wife concerning the death of their daughter, Plutarch firmly suggested his belief in reincarnation or at least the survival of the soul.

160. See Grant, *Last Will and Testament* (2021) chapter 4 for portents; Arrian 7.18 and 7.23. Aristobulus is cited several times as author of the mysterious portents.

161. Plutarch 1.2.

162. Compare his treatment of the meeting with the Amazon Queen and his account of Alexander's pre-death portents.

163. Polybius books 10 and 11 for the detail on Hannibal and Scipio. 'Cradle-to-grave' quoting S.R. Asirvatham in Carney-Ogden (2010) p.201.

164. Quoting Tarn (1948) p.297.

165. Quoting Mossman (1988) p.85.

166. Macaulay (1928).

167. Arrian 1.12.2–3 for a digression on the relative fame of Alexander and (in his opinion) lesser men whom Rome favoured.

168. Discussion of Arrian's relegation of Philip by S.R. Asirvatham in Carney-Ogden (2010) pp.202–204.

169. Quoting Atkinson from Hammond-Atkinson (2013) Introduction p.xxxvi for 'public intellectual'. See Hamilton (1971) Introduction: Plutarch had been granted Roman citizenship with possibly an honorary Roman consulship, and was also a Greek magistrate and archon in his municipality; also A.H. Clough, *Plutarch's Lives* (Liberty Library of Constitutional Classics, 1864) Introduction. For Polybius, see the Introduction to *The Rise of the Roman Empire* (Penguin Classics edition, 1979) pp.13–15 for his career in Achaean federal office and in Rome.

170. Quoting Arrian 7.30.3. As an example, Arrian 4.28.2–3 and 5.1 and 5.3 for his doubt surrounding the legends of Heracles and Dionysus and India, and his doubt on the claimed geography of the Caucasus. Following S.R. Asirvatham in Carney-Ogden (2010) p.203 for the comparison of Arrian to Homer; Arrian 1.12.2 for his understanding of Alexander's self-comparison.

171. Arrian opened with a polemic against previous works, asking the reader to compare them against his own. See the introduction by Hamilton to the Penguin Books edition (1971) p.9 for references to the style used in the *Indica* and Pearson (1960) p.112.

172. Photius' epitome 93 was a summary of Arrian's *Bithynica*.

173. See Bosworth (1976) p.118 for discussion of Dio Chrysostom's earlier book.

174. Following Hammond-Atkinson (2013) Introduction p.xv.

175. Photius epitome 58.4 for the 'young Xenophon'.

176. Quoting Bosworth (1976) p.137 on Arrian's errors.

177. Arrian Preface 2 for his accepting that 'as a king he would have been honour-bound to avoid untruth'.

178. Bosworth-Baynham (2000) Introduction p.4 for the quote. Tacitus had worked his way through to military tribute, questor, praetor and proconsul of Asia, serving with legions under Domitian, Nerva and Trajan; Pernot (2000) pp.128–129 for Tacitus' oratorical career.

179. Arrian 1.12.5.
180. Pliny's Preface to his *Natural History* included a Livian quote nowhere found in Livy's extant texts, and which must have come from a later work, which read 'I have now obtained a sufficient reputation, so that I might put an end to my work, did not my restless mind require to be supported by employment.'
181. Thucydides 1.22.4.
182. For Arrian's deliberate omissions of the darker episodes, see Baynham (1995) p.70. Quoting McInerney (2007) p.429.
183. Arrian 3.27.4–5 and here referring to the Ariaspians.
184. See discussion of Arrian's politics in the introduction by Hamilton (1971) Introduction.
185. Arrian 7.14.5–6
186. Arrian 3.18.11–12. Arrian 7.29.4 for his acceptance of the reason, following Aristobulus, of Alexander's drinking.
187. Arrian 5.21.6, 5.23.5, 5.24.3 (500 dead when retreating), 5.24.4 (17,000 deaths, 70,000 prisoners), 5.24.7–8, 6.6.3, 6.6.6, 6.7.1–4, 6.7.6, 6.8.3, 6.8.8, 6.11.1, 6.16.1–2, 6.16.5, 6.17.1–2, 6.18.1 and 6.21.4–5. Specific numbers of dead were not recorded for most operations, but the numbers we do have make it clear than tens of thousands died.
188. Diodorus 17.104.6–7 for the Gedrosian campaign.
189. Quoting and following Tarn (1948) p.286.
190. Arrian 1.12.1–3 for references to Homer and Xenophon. Arrian's use of the title 'Xenophon' in his own name discussed in the 1958 Penguin edition of *The Campaigns of Alexander*, Introduction p.1; refuted by Stadter (1967) p–155 ff, who argued it was a genuine part of Arrian's name.
191. Quoting Pearson (1960) p.123 for the form and content of the *Indica*.
192. As proposed by Highet (1949) p.105.
193. Preface to the *Discourses of Epictetus* by Arrian headed 'Arrian to Lucius Gellius, with wishes for his happiness', translation by George Long from the 1890 edition published by George Bell and Sons. Arrian expressed (somewhat confusingly) his efforts with: 'I neither wrote these *Discourses of Epictetus* in the way in which a man might write such things; nor did I make them public myself, inasmuch as I declare that I did not even write them. But whatever I heard him say, the same I attempted to write down in his own words as nearly as possible, for the purpose of preserving them as memorials to myself afterwards of the thoughts and the freedom of speech of Epictetus.' Only four of the eight books are extant.
194. Arrian's stoic interpretations of kinship following Pearson (1960) Introduction p.7. The original title of the *Discourses* is unknown; it has been variously named the *Diatribai* and *Dialexis* amongst others.
195. Quoting Shipley (2000) p.236.
196. Polybius 1.4.
197. Quoting Grant (1995) p.53.
198. Discussion of the papyri in Bevan (1913) pp.22–25.
199. Pitcher (2009) p.171 for a discussion of Athenaeus' diversity.
200. Flower (1994) p.48, quoting Photius' *Life of Theopompus* F25, and p.157. Billows (1990) p.333. Following Flower (1994) Introduction p.2 for Athenaeus' preservation

of Theopompus; we have eighty-three verbatim quotations (598 lines of text) with 412 lines in Athenaeus. Flower (1994) p.156 for Photius paraphrasing Theopompus, who claimed the 'first place in rhetorical education'.

201. Nietzsche, from an unpublished manuscript on Diogenes Laertius and his sources, a contribution of the history of ancient literary studies; quoted by Glenn W. Most, Speech at the Israel Society for the Promotion of Classical Studies 42nd Annual Conference.

202. Quoting the comment of J.R. Lowell (1867), see Loeb Classical Library edition (1937) Prefatory Note p.vii.

203. Momigliano (1966) pp.3–4 for the reference to antiquarians.

204. This was first made possible by Reitzenstein's 1888 translation of the two single leaves (a bifolium) of the Vatican palimpsest (ms. Vaticanus 495) and more recently Oxyrhynchus fragment PSI 11 1284; see Simpson (1959) p.377. This was published as *Arriani τῶν μετὰ Ἀλέξανδρον libri septimi fragmenta e codice Vaticano rescripto nuper iteratis curis lecto*, Breslauer philologische Abhandlungen Bd. 3, H. 3 (Breslau, 1888) S. 1–36. See Bosworth (1978) for full discussion. The fragment found at Oxyrhynchus in 1932 gave a detailed description of Eumenes in battle against either Craterus or, in Bosworth's opinion, Neoptolemus, which appeared to come from Arrian, *Events After Alexander*. For details of the extract from the Vatican palimpsest, see discussion in Goralski (1989) p.81, and for additional detail on surviving fragments of Arrian, *Events After Alexander*, see Goralski (1989) pp.81–83.

205. Errington (1970) p.73 and Bosworth (2002) p.22 for discussion on Arrian, *Events After Alexander* filling ten books, covering three years to Antipater's return to Macedon sometime after Triparadeisus.

206. Goralski (1989) p.82 and Kebric (1977) p.52.

207. See discussion in Hornblower (1981) p.101 and Warner (1966) p.30 for dividing up the campaign year.

208. The Roman Consular Year was set at 1 January to 29 December from 153 BC onwards. It had previously commenced in March, and before that May. See explanation in Polo (2011) p.15. We have no idea how extensively Hieronymus covered events in Greece, for example when based in Asia; the coverage of the double-burial of Philip III and Eurydice at Diodorus 19.52.5, as an example, seems Diyllus-sourced as it closely matches Athenaeus 4.155 citing Diyllus.

209. See Anson (2004) p.18 for discussion of Diodorus' chronology. For the archon dating, see Hornblower (1981) pp.108–109. Also expanded in Anson (1986) pp.208–217. Full discussion of the chronological problems and the omission of archon years in Anson (2004) p.77 footnote 2 and Smith (1981) p.283 ff; also Goralski (1989) p.102.

210. See discussion in Anson (1977) p.251 for the dating of the battle at Orcynia.

211. 'Passed over in silence' quoting Billows (1990) p.347. Diodorus occasionally confused himself with his method. One result is the conflicting claim that Eumenes' victory over Craterus in 321 BC provided Perdiccas with the confidence for his invasion of Egypt (18.33.1), whereas just several pages later he stated that news of that battle arrived only after Perdiccas' death in May/June 320 BC (18.37.1), although Eumenes' victory could refer to that over Neoptolemus some ten days before. Plutarch, *Eumenes*

8.2 supported Diodorus' latter claim. Earlier, a more generalized approach to time-framing by Diodorus placed Alexander's Exiles Decree 'a short time before his death' (18.8.2), and yet he went on to state it was proclaimed at the Olympic Games of 324 BC (17.109.1), thus almost a full year earlier.

212. Anson (2014) pp.58–59 and 116–121 for the relative chronologies. Also Hauben (1977) pp.85–120. He cites Manni and others who date Triparadeisus to 321 BC (the 'high' chronology, supported by Diodorus' event order). The date of Perdiccas' death, May/June 320 BC, is backed up by the *Babylonian Chronicle* extract BM 34, 660 Vs 4, which suggests 320 BC for the conference (the 'low' chronology, also backed by the *Parian Chronicle*). Also discussed in Errington (1970) pp.75–80. Anson (1986) pp.208–217 made a convincing case that Triparadeisus took place in 320 BC. For references to the astronomical records of Babylon, see Geller (1990) pp.1–7.

213. See Bosworth (2002) pp.20–21 for discussion, and in particular pp.55–81 and p.74 for the inaccuracy of the *Parian Chronicle*; also Wheatley (1995) p.434. Goralski (1989) p.103 for a full translation of the *Parian Chronicle*.

214. Plutarch 15.8–9, Diodorus 17.17.3, Arrian 1.12.1–2, Aelian 112.7 for Alexander's behaviour at the ruins of Troy. Plutarch 16, Diodorus 17.19–2, Justin 11.6.8–13, Arrian 1.13–16 for the Granicus battle itself.

215. Callisthenes, Ephorus, Damastes, Phylarchus and Duris agreed that Ilium fell on the 24th of Thargelion (May–June); confirmed in Plutarch, *Camillus* 19.7; others claimed 12th or 22nd; see Pearson (1960) pp.60–61 and full discussion in Lincoln (2002) pp.1–18. Fragments from ancient historians suggest the following dates BC: Duris 1334, *Life of Homer* 1270, Herodotus *ca*. 1240, Cleitarchus 1234, Dicearchus 1212, *Parian Chronicle* 1209, Thrasyllus 1193, Timaeus 1193. Apollodorus and the so-called *Canon of Ptolemy* also dated the fall of Troy; Eratosthenes and his disciples (Apollodorus, Castor, Diodorus, Apollonius and Eusebius) 1184/1183; Sosibius 1171, Phanias *ca*. 1129, Ephorus *ca*. 1135; detail taken from Mylonas (1964) p.353.

216. Diodorus 17.17.3–5 for troop numbers crossing to Asia. Following the Loeb Classical Library edition (1963) 17.17.4 footnote 4: Diodorus is our only source for the detailed troop list of Alexander. Justin 11.6.2 gave 32,000 foot and 4,500 horse; Plutarch 15.1 cited 30,000–43,000 foot and 4,000–5,000 horse; Arrian 1.11.3 stated 'not much more than' 30,000 foot and 5,000 horse. Plutarch, *Moralia* 327d–e reported that Aristobulus stated 30,000 foot and 4,000 horse, Ptolemy 30,000 foot and 5,000 horse, and Anaximenes 43,000 foot and 5,500 horse.

217. Curtius 4.13.3 for 'the best tactician'.

218. Arrian 1.15 ff; Diodorus 17.20 ff; Plutarch 16.1 ff for the initial onslaught. Arrian 1.115.3 for 'cut to pieces'.

219. Diodorus 17.19.4–5.

220. Arrian 1.14.4.

221. Justin 11.6.11. This may be a manuscript corruption of 60,000.

222. Diodorus 17.21.6.

223. Plutarch 16.7; Arrian 1.16.2.

224. Justin 1.6.2; Arrian 11.116.4; Plutarch 16.7.

225. Plutarch 16.2–16.

226. Modern interpretations suggest more like 5,000 mercenaries were present; discussion in Parke (1933) p.180, Green (1974) p.179 and in detail pp.499–500.
227. Arrian 1.116.2 for laying among the dead and 1.16.2 for the hard labour camps.
228. Diodorus 17.31.2 and 33.4, Justin 11.9.1 for the total numbers. Plutarch 20.8 for the vastly inferior numbers.
229. Arrian 2.8.6–2.8.8. Arrian stated Aristobulus was his source for numbers at the next battle at Gaugamela: Arrian 3.8.3–6 and 3. 11.3. Also Curtius 3.9.2 for mercenary numbers
230. Diodorus 33.6–7.
231. Diodorus 17.33.3–4 for the missiles
232. Plutarch 20.8 for the wound correspondence and Chares' claim. Also Diodorus 34.5, Curtius 3.11.10 and Arrian 2.12.1 for the wound.
233. Curtius 3.11.5.
234. For the Battle of Issus, see Arian 2.8–11; Curtius 3.9–11; Diodorus 17.33–34; Plutarch 20.5–10; Justin 11.1–10
235. Arrian 2.10.7.
236. Arrian 2.11.8 for 100,000; Diodorus 17.36.6; Plutarch 20.10; Curtius 3.11.27 added 10,000 cavalry to make 110,000. Justin 11.9 for 61,000 infantry and 10,000 horsemen.
237. Curtius 3.11.16–17.
238. Curtius 3.11.27 stated 504 wounded, thirty-two infantrymen killed and 150 cavalrymen. Justin 11.9 130 infantry and 150 horsemen; quoting Curtius 3.11.27.
239. Arrian 2.13.1 for mercenary escapees.
240. It is reckoned Darius had 20,000 Greek mercenary infantry at the Granicus and Alexander 10,000, according to Arrian 1.12.8 and 1.14.4. Also at Issus, Darius had 30,000 Greek mercenaries facing 10,000, according to Arrian 2.8.6, and a fragment of Callisthenes from Polybius 12.17–18 has 30,000 mercenaries facing the Macedones. Diodorus 17.9.5 for the Theban proclamation.
241. Anson (2004) p.235 for discussion of the exiled mercenaries. Curtius 5.11.5, Pausanias 8.52.5 for 50,000, and discussed in Parke (1933) pp.179–185, Green (1974) p.157 footnote; a similar figure was given by Pausanias 8.52.5, but for returning mercenaries under Leosthenes before the Lamian War. Arrian 1.16.6–7 for their fate if captured.
242. Quoting Diodorus 17.6.3 on Darius' genius. According to Curtius 5.11.5, Darius III had some knowledge of Greek. Three distinct offers from Darius were recorded in the extant accounts, and confusion between dates exists. Justin 11.12.1–2, Arrian 2.14–15 and Curtius 4.1.7–14 stated Darius demanded Alexander withdraw from Asia after Issus. Arrian mentions no financial offer for the return of the royal family. Arrian 2.25.1 cited the Euphrates, not Halys. The offer of marriage to Barsine and the division of empire is positioned in Curtius after the capture of Tyre. See Curtius 4.5.1–8 and Justin 11.12.3–3. The third offer comes after Alexander departed Egypt and sometime before Gaugamela. See Diodorus 17.39.1–3, 17.54.1–6, Curtius 4.11–12, Arrian 2.25–26, Justin 11.12.7–16, Plutarch 29.4. Some scholars such as Briant (1974) p.52 doubt Darius ever made such an offer.

243. For Darius' peace offering(s) and Alexander's rejection, see Curtius 4.11.1–14, Arrian 2.25.1, Plutarch 29.7–9 and Diodorus 17.54. *Romance* 2.14–15 and 2.22 for examples of the embellished correspondence between Alexander and Darius.

244. Diodorus 17.39.1–3 alone recorded the forgery.

245. Thersippus is mentioned as the envoy in Curtius 4.1.14, and he confirmed the camp was at Marathus at 4.1.6.

246. Lucian, *A Slip of the Tongue in Salutation* 3 has 'Philippides'. Plutarch, *Moralia: On the Fame of Athens* 3 stated it was either Thersippus of Erchea, or Eucles, who ran to Athens with news of the victory at Marathon. Lucian's name appears to have been taken up by Robert Browning into Pheidippides.

247. See Heckel (2006) p.264 for discussion. Thersippus seems to have survived the incident, no doubt because Alexander had Darius' family as hostages and was later honoured by the Nesiotic League for services to Philip and Alexander.

248. Arrian 3.11–15; Curtius 4.13–16; Diodorus 17.57–61; Plutarch 31.6–33.11; Justin 11.13.1–11.14.7; Polyaenus 4.3.6, 4.3.17 for the battle details.

249. Arrian 3.8.6 for numbers; Plutarch 31.1 simply stated 'a million men'.

250. Justin 11.13 for Darius' speech to his men on numbers.

251. Justin 11.14 for the Persian resolve.

252. Diodorus 17.59.1–4.

253. Arrian 3.15.6 for Persian troop losses of 300,000, again far higher than Curtius 4.16.26 at 40,000 and Diodorus 17.61.3 at 90,000. For the 100 men lost on the Macedonian side, Arrian 3.15.6, 300 according to Curtius 4.16.26.

254. Plutarch 32 for Alexander sacrificing and his deep sleep.

255. Curtius 4.10.1–8 for the eclipse and interpretations. Discussion in Hammond (1993) pp.269–270 and Pearson (1960) p.162 with footnote 70. The time between the eclipse and the battle (eleven days), Plutarch 31.8, Pliny 2.180, though 'some days' before battle in Arrian 3.7.6. Polcaro-Valsecchi-Verderame (2008) pp.55–64 for discussion of the dating of the eclipse. The Babylonian cuneiform tablet recording the eclipse is referred to as BM 36761 along with 36390. Modern calculations place the eclipse after sunset on 20 September 331 BC, whereas the battle commenced on 1 October 331 BC.

256. The Goddess Selene represented the Moon in Greek mythology and was termed 'the far shining' in the *Homeric Hymns*.

257. Plutarch 33.2 for Aristander riding before the lines at Gaugamela.

258. Herodotus 7.37. A translation of the relevant cuneiform table in the British Museum, using extracts from Sachs-Hunger (1988). It somewhat backs up Diodorus' account at 17.60.2–4 that Darius himself did not order a retreat, but that the ranks around him collapsed, perhaps due to the earlier drop in morale following the celestial portents. The panic in the camp is strangely dated to the 11th of the month (in the sixth month of Darius) when the battle took place on the 24th, with the eclipse reportedly preceding it on the 13th. Yet the same entry recorded or suggested the armies were encamped opposite one another. This suggests Curtius' source might have been correct and the battle actually took place eleven days earlier.

Chapter 6: The Greek Alexander Romance: Truth and Legend as One

1. Green (1974) p.479.
2. Josephus, *Against Apion* 1.3, 1.11 and *Jewish Antiquities* 20.8.3.
3. Sir William Jones, *On the Gods of Hellas, Italy and India* 3.320–322 (1784). Discussion of Jones' work in Lincoln (2002) pp.1–18.
4. Wallis Budge (1896) p.VI. Also see Stoneman (1991) pp.14–16 on early Alexandrian literature.
5. Stoneman (1991) pp.8–10 for Egyptian origins of the *Romance*. The *Septuagint* derived its name from the seventy-plus translators who, ancient tradition tells us, worked on the manuscripts; see Casson (2001) p.35. For discussions of the various origins of the *Septuagint*, see Jobes-Silva (2001), for the *Corpus Hermeticum* see Copenhaver (1992), Sundberg (1958) pp.205–226 for the *Alexandrian Canon*.
6. A sentiment more recently restated by Momigliano (1966) p.116. Budge's work was published as *The Life and Exploits of Alexander the Great. Ethiopic Histories of Alexander by Pseudo-Callisthenes and other Writers*.
7. Aristander's prophecy is detailed at Arrian 3.1.2, Aelian 12.64 (though here after Alexander's death); he deflected embarrassment at Alexandria's mapping-out when birds flocked to eat the barley-meal being used as the boundary marker. Other 'seer' prophecies regarding the city appear at Curtius 4.8.6, Plutarch 26.5–6 and Strabo 17.1.6. The city bears the inscription 'founder' against Alexander's name in the *Romance*.
8. Diodorus 18.14.1. Ptolemy apparently found 8,000 talents in the treasury amassed by Cleomenes' tax collections. His role is stated as 'money administrator' or 'revenue collector' (*arabarchos*). Cleomenes was eventually executed by Ptolemy, possibly for his Perdiccan sympathies. Heckel (2006) pp.88–89 for 'over-zealous tax collection'.
9. Formerly Heraclion (also known as Thonis) was the dominant seaport positioned on the Nile Delta. Heracles, Paris and Helen are all associated with the city. The city was lost until recent excavations confirmed its legendary status. In ancient texts, Heraclion was mentioned by Diodorus 1.9.4, Strabo 17.1.16 and Herodotus 2.113 amongst others.
10. Quoting Pearson (1960) p.9.
11. Quoting C. Gill in Gill-Wiseman (1993) p.41.
12. Quoting Wood from Gill-Wiseman (1993) Prologue xiii, and de Polignac (1999) p.3 quoting Goukowsky.
13. Following Stoneman (1991) p.10 on 'a process of accretion'.
14. Quoting Stoneman (1991) p.28. Fraser (1996) pp.205–207 for discussion of the origins of the recension A manuscript, p.206 for 'ill-written, lacunose, and interpolated', and p.210 for 'flimsy continuum'.
15. Tarn 1 (1948) p.144 for the numbers of versions and languages.
16. Fuller discussion in Grant (2017) p.231 ff.
17. Discussed in Townsend (1996) p.15, quoting Henry of Ghent's statement on the popularity of the poem with similarities to Curtius account, *Alexandreis*.

18. Strabo 11.11.1 reported the expansion of the Hellenistic kingdoms and expeditions that might have travelled as far as the Seres and the Phryni. The Seres were inhabitants of Serica, the land of silk, so China. Strabo 11.11.1 first referred to them, though their whereabouts and cultivation method remained unknown, as evidenced by Pliny 20, *The Seres*, when he referred to the woollen substance as forest derived.

19. Diodorus 1.37 and 3.36 for Ptolemy II Philadelphus journeying to the Upper Nile and into Ethiopia. Bagnall-Derow (2004) p.250 for a papyrus detailing the elephant hunters.

20. Diodorus 3.36.1 for 100-cubit-long snakes, 3.36 for the length of the live python at Alexandria, 3.39.9 for the ability of the pythons to devour bulls, oxen and bring down elephants. For Ptolemy's hunting expeditions, 3.36–39. The Attic cubit at 18.25in was longer than the Macedonian cubit of 14in. Arrian 3.2.7 for the deportation of pro-Persian tyrants from the Aegean islands to Elephantine.

21. Alexander's lineage detailed in chapter titled 'Gods, Heroes, Sons, Wives, Bastards and Courtesans'.

22. Quoting Macaulay (1828).

23. See Robinson (1953) p.69 for the fragment. It is recorded as a miracle in the *Romance* 1.28. Plutarch 17, quoting the poet Menander, translation from the Loeb Classical Library edition (1919). Arrian 1.26.1 also recorded the incident and mentioned the relation of the winds; Plutarch implied Alexander gave a more sober description of the event.

24. Strabo 17.1.43 (following Callisthenes) for the sacred spring at Branchidae, dry for some 160 years, flowing again once Alexander arrived.

25. Xenophon, *Anabasis* 1.4.17–18 and Herodotus 1.189–190 for the feat of Cyrus the Great, and 7.33–36 and 7.54–57 for Xerxes' bridging of the Hellespont. As for prevailing doctrine, see Herodotus 8.109–110 for Themistocles' warning that no king should rule Asia and Hellas too. Arrian 1.26.1–2; Plutarch 17.6–8. *Romance* 2.14–16 for the River Stranga episode.

26. Quoting Pearson (1960) p.5.

27. Strabo 11.6.4.

28. For the corpus of letters, see below.

29. Diogenes Laertius, *Diogenes* 6.50.

30. Plutarch, *Moralia*: *How to tell a Flatterer from a Friend*, translation by A.R. Shilleto (digireads publishing, 2011).

31. Herodotus 1.134 gave a detailed description of *proskynesis*. See discussion in Stewart (1993) p.13, quoting Curtius 8.5.7–8. Plutarch 45.1 and Curtius 6.6.3 did suggest Alexander initially restricted mandatory *proskynesis* to Asians. Also Arrian 4.9.9, 10.5.12, 6, Curtius 8.5.5–24, Plutarch 54.2–6 for the introduction of *proskynesis* and the repercussions.

32. Curtius 8.5.8.

33. Homer, *Iliad* 2.212, translated into English blank verse by William Cowper (Project Gutenberg edition, 1860).

34. Curtius 8.5.8 for Choerilus' presence with Alexander and *Romance* 1.42. For Alexander's payment to the poet, see Pomponius Porphyrio's commentary on Horace'

Epistles ii. 1.232–4. Also Horace, *Ars Poetica* 357 for the derision of Choerilus as *poeta pessimus*.

35. *Romance* 3.34.106 for the oracles determining the fate of the body.

36. The so-called 'golden age of automata' refers to the period broadly spanning 1860–1910, which itself followed the earlier nineteenth-century automata exported in great quantities to China.

37. See Stoneman (1991) pp.14–17 for discussion. Recensions 'e' and 'g' of the *Romance* include this detail. For Alexander's visit to Jerusalem, see Josephus 11.329–335, and 12.3–10 for Ptolemy's captives. The Jewish Quarter of Alexandria discussed in Vrettos (2001) pp.6–7.

38. Discussion of the numbers in *Philo of Alexandria, Philo's Flaccus, The first Pogrom*, P.W. van der Horst (Brill, 2003) p.136.

39. Quoting Spencer (2002).

40. Argead lineage detailed in chapter titled 'Gods, Heroes, Sons, Wives, Bastards and Courtesans'.

41. Pausanias 9.16.1 for the description of the sanctuary and its roots. Pausanias 3.18.2, 8.32.1, 10.13.3 for the worship of the god in other parts of Greece. Pindar, *Pythian* 4.29 for the reference to Zeus Ammon. Herodotus 1.46, 2.32, 52.6 for references to Ammon being equated to Zeus; discussion in Anson (2013) p.97. Early links to Zeus refuted by Tarn (1948) pp.348–351, who nevertheless confirms the presence of a cult to Ammon in Athens before 371/370; Tarn 1 (1948) p.42. Alexander had spared Pindar's house when he flattened Thebes; Arrian 1.9.10.

42. Diodorus 17.51.2–3, Curtius 4.7.28 for the oracle's answer on Philip's assassins. For the journey to Siwa, see Diodorus 17.49.2–52.7, Arrian 3.4–5, Curtius 4.7.8–4.89, Plutarch 26.3–27.11, Justin 11.11.1–13, Strabo 17.1.43, *Itinerarium Alexandri* 48–50.

43. See Bevan (1927) p.13 for discussion. Recognition of the pharaoh or kings as the son of Ammon-Ra had been common practice since the second millennium. According to Strabo 17.1.43, Callisthenes stated that Alexander received, uniquely, spoken words from the priests confirming that he was the son of Zeus, whereas nods and signs were used elsewhere. See full discussion of the various versions from Plutarch, Arrian, Diodorus and Justin in Hammond (1993) pp.58–60. Anson (2013) p.97 for the origins of Zeus Ammon.

44. Herodotus 3.25.3, 26.1–3, Plutarch, *Cimon* 12.5 and Plutarch 26.12 mentioned Cambyses' earlier journey; Arrian 3.3.1 and Strabo 17.1.43 mentioned that Alexander knew Perseus, and Callisthenes stated Heracles had visited the oracle before him. See also Robinson (1953) pp.62–63.4. For discussion on Heracles and Perseus, see Bosworth (1988) p.281. The remains of the 50,000-strong army that vanished in 525 BC were reportedly discovered in 2012 by Angel and Alfredo Castiglioni after thirteen years of research and desert expeditions; report at http://news.discovery.com/history/archaeology/cambyses-army-remains-sahara.htm

45. Arrian 3.3.6 reported that Aristobulus claimed they were guided by two ravens; see discussion in Robinson (1953) Preface p.xiii. Strabo 17.1.43 for crows.

46. Only the *Romance* 1.34.2 claimed Alexander was given the title of pharaoh. Discussed in Anson (2013) p.104, and Tarn (1948) p.347 accepts this as proof Alexander became pharaoh.

47. De Polignac (1999) p.6.

48. Arrian 4.10.2 and Plutarch 3.2–3, Justin 11.11.3–4 for Callisthenes' claim that Olympia was spreading 'lies' about Alexander's alleged immortal father.

49. Curtius 9.6.26 for Alexander requesting Olympias' consecration to immortality.

50. See Grant (2019) pp.81–84 for fuller discussion of Philip's last, young wife and offspring.

51. *Romance* 1.4–14

52. See Grant, *Last Will and Testament* (2021) chapter 6 for full details of Serapis.

53. Plutarch 2.1–9.

54. Quoting Plutarch 42.1, translation by I. Scott-Kilvert (Penguin Classics edition, 1973). Plutarch cited many letters unique to accounts of Alexander. In Plutarch, *Alexander* the historian referred to personal letters of Alexander he had read or knew the contents of at 7.6, 8.1, 17.8, 19.5–8, 20.9, 22.2, 22.5, 27.8, 39.4, 39.7, 39.13, 42.1, 46.3, 47.3, 55.6, 55.7, 60.1, 60.11 and 68.4. No other historian seems to have had access to them, and how genuine they were remains open to speculation. Arrian 7.12.5, Justin 12.14.3 mentioned slanders from Olympias in letter form.

55. The Hamburg and Florence papyri discussed in Pearson (1960) p.258 and Pearson (1955) p.448 for the Oxyrhynchus papyri. Quoting Powell (1939) p.230 for the earliest sign of the epistolary corpus. Cicero, *On Duties* 2.14.48 for the epistolary corpus; Marasco (2011) pp.45–47 for other references.

56. Cicero, *On Duties*, Book 2, *Expediency*. Arrian 6.1.4 and 7.12.4–7 for examples of a letter from Alexander to Olympias and Antipater that Arrian believed to be genuine.

57. The epistolary collections are discussed in Gudeman, *Greeks* (1894) pp.64–65.

58. Following the comments of Arthur-Montagne (2014) p.1 on the breadth of epistolary forms in the Romance, and p.3 for the reference to 'Pseudo-documentarism', a term emanating with William Hansen. For full discussion of the epistolary corpus in the *Romance*, see Arthur-Montagne (2014) pp.1–31.

59. Plutarch 1.3.

60. Plutarch 6–7; Arrian 5.19.4–6 for other explanations of the name.

61. See Grant (2019) pp.256–261 for fuller account. *Iliad* 23 for Achilles' horses.

62. See Grant (2017) p.17 ff and Grant (2019) chapter 7 for further detail of the rift between Philip and Alexander.

63. Plutarch 6–7. Chares, as recorded by Aulus Gellius 5.2.1, did record the sum paid for the horse (13 talents, broadly $180,000 US dollars today) and the derivation of the name (ox-head), due to the shape of its head, but nothing of its taming. Arrian 5.19.5 attributed the name to a brand mark or white mark on its head; the *Romance* 1.15 suggested its haunch. See full fragment in Robinson (1953) p.85. The *Romance* 3.33 made the comparisons of Alexander and Bucephalus to Bellerophon and Pegasus. See discussion of the taming of Bucephalus in Baynham, *Romance* (1995). Green (1974) p.43.

64. Quoting Powell (1939) p.230; Samuel (1986) pp.433–435 for discussion of the letters in Plutarch's biography of Alexander.

65. Alexander spoke to Bucephalus at the point of his death and recognized that the horse had shared his fate, except in death, *Romance* 3.33. Whitmarsh (2002) p.180 draws the comparison to Plato's *Phaedra*.

66. See Grant (2017) p.742 for more detail on the meaning of Olympias' former names.
67. *Romance* 1.18–22, Plutarch, *Moralia* 331B. In Plutarch, *Moralia* 179D a variant has Philip suggest his son's Olympic Games participation; see Adams (2003) p.214 footnote 1.
68. Plutarch 4.9–4.11.
69. *Romance* 1.20–23. In Recension A it is Antalus, in other texts Lysias.
70. Romance 1.21m, based on the translation by Stoneman (1991).
71. Curtius 8.8.7 obscurely refers back to the episode, but his first two books are missing, in which it would have appeared; Justin 9.7.3, Plutarch 9.7–9, Athenaeus 13.557 d–e.
72. For example Carney (1992) p.179.
73. *Iliad* 2.121–2.129.
74. Strabo's opinions at 15.1.28 and 15.2.9; see Robinson (1953) p.151 for translation.
75. Preserved in detail at Strabo 15.1.63–65.
76. For Calanus, see above fragments plus Strabo 15.1.68 and his death Arrian 7.3.1, Diodorus 17.107.1–6, Valerius Maximus 1.8 ext. 10.
77. *Romance* 3.5 based on the translation from Stoneman (1991).
78. Preserved by Plutarch 14.1–6 and *Moralia* 331f or *Fortune* 10 and Diogenes Laertius, *Diogenes* 6.38, Cicero, *Tusculan Disputations* 5.32.
79. See Brown (1949) pp.27–28 for the background to the dialogue between Alexander and Diogenes.
80. Diogenes Laertius, *Diogenes* 40 and 60 for examples of publicly being called a 'dog'.
81. It remains unclear exactly what he was charged with. Diogenes Laertius, *Diogenes* 74 for his life in slavery. Diogenes 6.20 suggested his father was a banker or moneychanger and he became involved in a scandal concerning defacing currency; possibly a political statement. A number of defaced currencies from Sinope and dating to the middle of the fourth century BC had been discovered; discussion in Seltman (1938). Finlay (1973) pp.166–167 for the treatment of those charged with debasing currency.
82. Diogenes Laertius, *Diogenes* 6.54; Aelian 14.33 for the comparison to a 'mad' Socrates.
83. Plutarch 14.1–6 and *Moralia* 331f or *Fortune* 10 and Diogenes Laertius, *Diogenes* 6.38, Cicero, *Tusculan Disputations* 5.32. Diogenes Laertius, *Onesicritus* 6.75–76 for his acquaintance with the Cynic. Grant, *Last Will and Testament* (2021) chapter 7 for more details on the Diogenes encounter and more hostile traditions.
84. Plutarch 60.1; translation in Robinson (1953) p.158.
85. Plutarch 64–65, based on the Loeb Classical Library edition (1919).
86. Diodorus 17.102.7, Curtius 9.8.15 for the 80,000 and Brahmin involvement.

Chapter 7: Birth and Death: Nature's Cracked Mirror

1. Lucian, *How to Write History* 40–41, translation from Brown (1949) p.5. See discussion of the authenticity of this extract in Brown (1949) p.2.
2. Attributed to Caesar.
3. Martial, *Epitaph to Canace, Epigrams* 11.91.
4. Grant, *Last Will and Testament* (2021) with Alexander's death in detail.
5. Diogenes Laertius, *Empedocles*. See discussion in Gottschalk (1980) pp.14–20. Heracleides reported Empedocles' death in his treatise *On Diseases*.

6. Much of the *Scriptores Historiae Augustae* tends towards romance: examples of pre-death portents can be seen at *The Two Maximini* 31, *Severus Alexander* 60, *Caracalla* 11 and *Commodus* 16.

7. See Pitcher (2009) p.29 for discussion on the spurious sources used by the *Historia Augusta*; also Syme (1971) and Baynes (1926). Momigliano (1966) p.147 for the 130 documents cited and their breakdown and groupings. Quoting Momigliano (1966) p.145 and pp.143–166 for the authenticity of the *Historia Augusta*. His full dissection of the *Historia Augusta* can be read in Momigliano (1954) pp 22–46. The *Historia Augusta* is also discussed in Pitcher (2009) p.153. The quote is from Momigliano (1954) p.23.

8. Empedocles is considered the first philosopher to bring all four basic elements in a creation theory; see discussion in Collins (2008) p.32.

9. Aelian 2.26, citing Aristotle's lost work, *On the Pythagoreans* (Fr. 191 R). Russell (1946) p.60 ff for Empedocles' career. Felix Martí-Ibanez, *A Prelude to Medical History* (MD Publications Inc, New York, 1961) Library of Congress ID: 61-11617, for Hippocrates' legend.

10. For Democritus' age at death, see Pseudo-Lucian, *The Long Lived* 18 citing 104 and Diogenes Laertius 9.43 for age 109. The 'pseudo' attached to Lucian here denotes that the prosopography is possibly another spuriously assigned work. For reference to Aristotle's claim, see Jones (1886). For several deaths, see Margotta (1968) p.66. Soranus penned a doxography and the Suda has further conflicting detail.

11. Photius, *Life of Pythagoras* 1 and Pseudo-Lucian, *The Long Lived* 22 for Hieronymus' age.

12. Brown (1947) pp.685–686.

13. Diogenes Laertius, *Pythagoras*.

14. Quoting Huffman (1993) pp.1–16.

15. Diogenes Laertius, *Chrysippus* 3.

16. Diogenes Laertius, *Chrysippus* 7.

17. Diogenes Laertius, *Zeno* 7.28.

18. Lucian, *The Long Lived* 19.

19. See chapter 5 for Alexander's encounter with Diogenes.

20. The various deaths outlined through Diogenes Laertius, *Diogenes*.

21. Epicurus, *Letter to Menoeceus* for nature's mirror. Lucretius preserved much of Epicurus' doctrine in his epic poem *On the Nature of Things*. The 'symmetry' argument was supposed to take away the fear of death.

22. Plato, *Phaedo* 117e–118a.

23. See discussion in Griffin (1986) p.199 for reference to Socrates' alleged last words in Plato's *Phaedo*.

24. Plutarch, *Moralia* 607f or *On Exile* 17, translation from the Loeb Classical Library edition, Vol. VII (1959).

25. Plutarch, *Demosthenes* 29.3 translation from the Loeb Classical Library edition, Vol. VII (1919).

26. Plutarch, *Demosthenes* 30.5–6.

27. Diogenes Laertius, *Aristotle* 8, translation from the Loeb Classical Library edition (1925), and *Aristotle* 7 for his death by aconite. Chroust (1970) p.650 footnote 90 for the

alternative traditions. Eurymedon (or Demophilus) had tried to associate Aristotle's encomium (or hymn) to Hermias with impiety for casting Virtue as a goddess and for the inscription on his statue at Delphi; Diogenes Laertius, *Aristotle* 5–6.

28. Plutarch, *Phocion* 36.3–4. The executioner refused to 'bruise' more hemlock unless he paid 12 drachmas. Blackwell (1999) p.63 for discussion of Phocion's career. Aelian 11.9 for Phocion's gift from Alexander.

29. Aristophanes, *Frogs* 116–126.

30. The nature of Socrates' poison has been disputed since the publication of Johannes Weepers' treatise *Cicutae aquaticae historia et noxae* (Basel, 1679). See full discussion in Brickhouse-Smith (2001). Full paper of the authors titled *Hemlock Poisoning and the Death of Socrates: Did Plato Tell the Truth?* can be read in the *Journal of the International Plato Society*, State University of New York at Buffalo.

31. Theophrastus, *Enquiry into Plants* 9.16.8.

32. Suetonius, *Caesar* 82.2 and Plutarch, *Caesar* 66.9. *Kai su* is more convincingly a threatening accusation than a philosophical lament. Ovid, *Metamorphoses* book 15 lines 794–797 for 'upheavals'.

33. Discussion in Wright (1995) and also Roller (1997) pp.109–130. A fulsome account of the death is Plutarch, *Cicero* 46.3–5. For the proscriptions, see Cassius Dio 47.8.4.

34. Cicero, *Second Philippic* 12.

35. Cicero, *Letter to Friends* 10.28.

36. For Callisthenes' death, see Lane Fox (1980) chapter 3, footnote 15.

37. Livy claimed both hands were cut off. Appian, Cassius Dio and Valerius Maximus claimed just one.

38. Cassius Dio 47.8.4.

39. Seneca the Elder recorded that Cicero's death was a popular oratory topic.

40. Suetonius, *Nero* 33, confirmed by Cassius Dio 60.35, who stated Nero's quip meant that once Claudius had eaten the mushrooms he joined the gods.

41. Suetonius, *Claudius* 44 claimed he was in Rome, whereas Tacitus 12.66 stated he was in Sinuessa. His death is additionally recorded by Josephus 20.148 and 151, Cassius Dio 60.34, Pliny 2.92, 11.189 and 22.92 citing Halotus, his taster, Xenophon, his doctor, and Locusta as the assassins.

42. Suetonius, *Nero* 35–39, and for his planned poisoning of the Senate, Suetonius, *Nero* 43.

43. Suetonius, *Nero* 49.1.

44. The goblets were smashed in a rage when Nero heard of the defection of his northern Italian legions. The goblets were termed 'Homeric' as they were engraved with scenes from Homer's poems. For recent reinterpretations of Nero's exclamations, see Pitcher (2009) pp.50–51.

45. Ovid, *Metamorphoses* book 15 lines 87–90.

46. Pythagoras allegedly forbade the consumption of kidney beans. The Egyptians did the same, relating its shape to the male testicle. There may have been sound medical grounds for the advice, or it may have been religious and to do with transmigration: 'eating broad beans and gnawing on the head of one's parents are one and the same'; Grmek (1989) p.218.

47. Lucian, *The Double Indictment* 5.
48. Pliny 10.3.6–8; Aelian, *On the Characteristics of Animals* 7.16, Valerius Maximus, *Nine Books on Memorable Deeds and Sayings* 9.12.2 also has a version in which, blinded by the sun's reflection from Aeschylus' bald head, the eagle was dazzled into dropping the tortoise. For his part at Marathon, see Lattimore (1953) pp.1–3. Aeschylus' reference to Homer is at Athenaeus 8.347e.
49. Plutarch, *Pyrrhus* 8.1. Translation from the Loeb Classical Library edition (1920). Plutarch, *Pyrrhus* 1.4 and Justin 17.3.4 for Pyrrhus' descent.
50. See discussion in Green (2007) pp.46–48. Pyrrhus allegedly exclaimed 'another such victory over the Romans and we are ruined!' after the battle at Asculum; Plutarch, *Pyrrhus* 17.4 and 21.4 ff. The ancient Greeks would have termed a self-defeating victory 'Cadmean' after Cadmus' loss of all his companions when trying to slay the water-dragon. For Pyrrhus' death, see Hornblower (1981) citations p.248, Plutarch, *Pyrrhus* 34, Pausanias 1.13.8 gave two accounts; Hieronymus provided another derivative.
51. Plutarch, *Pyrrhus* 5.3–7. Pyrrhus always wore a helmet with goat horns protruding.
52. Plutarch, *Pyrrhus* 34 for Pyrrhus' death in Argos and Pausanias 2.22.8–25.8 for the Homeric story attached to the tomb of Licymnius. He was the illegitimate son of Electryon, the son of Perseus and Andromeda, and was finally killed by Heracles' son, Tlepolemus, who was then banned from the state for the homicide.
53. Plutarch, *Demosthenes* 28.4, Arrian, *Events After Alexander* 1.13 for the cutting out of Hyperides' tongue, and Plutarch, *Moralia* 849f or *Life of the Ten Attic Orators* 9, *Hyperides*, for linking that to his proposing honours for Iollas.
54. Plutarch, *Demosthenes* 29–30.
55. A claim possibly inspired by or backed up by Plutarch 28.4, in which Alexander claimed Anaxarchus wanted to see a row of satrap heads on the dinner table, rather than humble fare. Diogenes Laertius 9.59 and Valerius Maximus 3.3 ext 4 for the 'tale' of his biting off his own tongue.
56. Diogenes Laertius, *Anaxarchus* 9.2–3. Also Zeno 9.5. According to Hermippus he was crushed with mortar and pestle, but the common tradition was that Zeno bit off his own tongue and spat it at 'the tyrant'.
57. Borza (1995) pp.175–176 for discussion of the Eudaimonic school of philosophy.
58. Plutarch, *Marcellus* 19.4–6. The text describes how Archimedes defied arrest, telling the soldier he was in the middle of a mathematical problem. These were Archimedes' last words. The reply has since evolved.
59. Pausanias 1.23.9 claimed Thucydides was murdered on his return to Athens, which, due to his exile, must have been after the city's surrender in 404 BC. However, evidence exists that he lived past 397 BC. Plutarch claimed he was interred in Cimon's family vault; Plutarch, *Cimon* 4.1.
60. Plutarch, *Camillus* 19 for the date of Marathon; Plutarch dedicated the paragraph to how unlucky the month of Thargelion was for 'barbarians'. Plutarch 3.5 for Alexander's birthday. Callisthenes, Ephorus, Damastes, Phylarchus and Duris agreed Ilium fell on the 24th of Thargelion (May–June); confirmed in Plutarch, *Camillus* 19.7; others claimed 12th or 22nd; see Pearson (1960) pp.60–61 and full discussion in Lincoln (2002) pp.1–18. Fragments from ancient historians suggest the following dates BC:

Duris 1334, *Life of Homer* 1270, Herodotus *ca.* 1240, Cleitarchus 1234, Dicearchus 1212, *Parian Chronicle* 1209, Thrasyllus 1193, Timaeus 1193. Apollodorus and the so-called *Canon of Ptolemy* also dated the fall of Troy; Eratosthenes and his disciples (Apollodorus, Castor, Diodorus, Apollonius, Eusebius) 1184/3; Sosibius 1171, Phanias *ca.* 1129, Ephorus *ca.* 1135; detail taken from Mylonas (1964) p.353.

61.   Plutarch 1–4.

62.   Diodorus 16.1.5.

63.   Plutarch 1 gives us Alexander's Aeacid descent on his mother's side from Neoptolemus, and Justin 17.3. Neoptolemus was also known as Pyrrhus; Plutarch, *Pyrrhus* 1.1–4 for his origins and Pausanias 1.11.1, 2.23.6 for Neoptolemus, rule of the Molossians; Anson (2004) p.211 for detail, also Carney (2006) p.5. The mythical association is confirmed by Pindar in his Nemean Odes 4.51–53 and 7.38-39. See Arrian 1.11–12 for Alexander's sacrifice to Priam to avert anger against the family of Neoptolemus. Molossus inherited Epirus after the death of Helenus, the son of Priam.

64.   For Perseus, see Arrian 3.3.2. Also discussed in Thomas (2007) p.200. At Herodotus 7.150, Xerxes claimed the Persians were descended from Perseus, whose father was Danae's son, Perseus. The full text is 'Men of Argos, this is the message to you from King Xerxes. Perseus our forefather had, as we believe, Perseus son of Danae for his father, and Andromeda daughter of Cepheus for his mother; if that is so, then we are descended from your nation.' Thus Xerxes claimed to be of the same blood as the Greeks. Heracles was a Perseid four generations after Perseus, so claimed Isocrates in the *Busiris* 8.36.

65.   Lineage discussions in Hammond (1996) and Roisman-Worthington (2010) pp.1–39, Green (1970) pp.20–21, Hammond (1993) pp.5–6, Hammond (1991) pp.12–13, Plutarch 1 and Greenwalt (1985). Plutarch 2.1 for Caranus founding the Argead line, with similar claims in Satyrus FGrH 631 F1, Theopompus FGrH 115 F 383 and Marysas FGrH 135-6 F14; Roisman-Worthington (2010) p.128. Herodotus 5.22.1, 7.73 and 8.137.8–9 for the link from Temenus to King Perdiccas of Macedon; Justin 7.1.6 for Caranus' invasion and the refounding of Aegae. Diodorus 7.17 for Caranus' Argive origins. There is uncertainty of the lineage of the early kings of Macedon; discussed in Greenwalt (1985) pp.43–49. Thucydides 2.99.3 and Herodotus 8.137–9 reported on the Temenid origins from Argos.

66.   Arrian 2.5.9 confirmed Alexander's descent from the Argive Heracleidae. Isocrates, *To Philip* 32: 'Argos is the land of your fathers.' Also Isocrates, *To Philip* 115 for his descent from Heracles. Hammond (1994) p.1 for discussion of the Spartan and Aleuadae connections.

67.   Herodotus 5.22 for the story that Alexander I of Macedon was allowed to compete after proving his Argive roots; Justin 7.2.13–14. Macedones were at that time not permitted to enter the games and only allowed Greeks to compete.

68.   Justin 7.1.6 for Midas' expulsion. Herodotus 1.14 for the son of Gordias, and at 8.138.3 he mentioned the Gardens of Midas in Macedon. It is certain Alexander would have read Herodotus, for Aristotle had and it would have surely been an educational study topic; see Aristotle, *Rhetoric* 1409a 27, where Aristotle opened with 'Herodotus of Thurii hereby publishes the results of his enquiries.' Callisthenes FGrH 124 F 24 for Midas' wealth coming from iron ore, cited in Hammond (1994) p.5. Hammond

(1996) for discussion of early Macedon and Midas' dynasty, and (1991) p.31 for early genealogies.
69. Homer, *Iliad* 2.204 for the wording of Odysseus to quell an uprising in the Greek camp.
70. Quoting Borza-Palagia (2007) p.108. Grant, *Last Will and Testament* (2021) for full discussion of the Vulgate version of Alexander's death.
71. Plutarch 75.5.

Chapter 8: Illegitimate Sons, Rogue Wives, Forgotten Bastards and Courtesans

1. Diodorus 17.77.7, Justin 12.3.10; for the concubines and numbers, Curtius 3.3.24.
2. Plutarch 21.7–11
3. Curtius 10.6.13–15.
4. Some consider that Alexander had Illyrian blood himself: Carney (2006) p.90 for Philip's Illyrian blood through his mother, Eurydice, though contested. Plutarch, *Moralia* 14b–c and Libanius through the *Suda* stated Eurydice was Illyrian of the Taulanti tribe, but Eurydice's father, Sirrhas, was probably of Lyncestian (so Upper Macedon) origin, which makes sense when considering his recent defeat at Illyrian hands.
5. Justin 7.4–6 and Diodorus 16.1–2.
6. Justin 7.4.
7. Justin 7.5.
8. Diodorus 16.2.4. Diodorus 14.92.3–4, 14.19.2, 16.6.2 for Illyrian incursions, and following Anson (2013) p.44. Diodorus 16.2.4–5 for the death of Perdiccas III and his losses. Hammond (1991) pp.25–30 for a summary of Perdiccas' challenges. After the death of King Amyntas III in 370/369 BC, Ptolemy of Alorus, a possible envoy to the king (an alliance with Athens in 375–373 BC mentioned the name) and possibly the son of Amyntas II (Diodorus 15.71.1; thus descended from the line of Menelaus, son of Alexander I), started a liaison with Amyntas' widow, Eurydice, and he may have married her and ascended to the throne. In 368/367 BC, Ptolemy allegedly assassinated Alexander II (Diodorus 16.2.4 and 15.71.1–2, but Demosthenes, *On the False Embassy* 19.194–195 stated an Apollophanes was executed for the murder) after less than two years on the throne (Diodorus 15.60.3 stated one year), and became guardian (*epitropos*) for the immature Perdiccas III (Aeschines, *On the Embassy* 2.29, Plutarch, *Pelopidas* 27.3), a role that saw him become regent of the kingdom until Perdiccas killed him in 365 BC and then reigned for five years (Diodorus 15.77.5). Diodorus 15.71.1, 15.77.5, Eusebius, *Kronographia* 228 stated Ptolemy was in fact *basileus*, king, for three years, but the use of the demotic, Alorus, and the absence of coinage in his name speak otherwise. Moreover, his marriage to Eurydice (Justin 7.4.7, Aeschines 2.29) and previously to her daughter, Eurynoe (Justin 7.4.7–7, 7.5.4–8 stated Ptolemy and Eurydice were lovers even then), suggest he needed legitimacy his heritage did not provide. According to Justin, the intrigue was revealed by Eurynoe. Why Eurydice intrigued with Ptolemy remains unclear (Justin 7.5 claimed she had previously plotted against Amyntas, who spared her for the sake of their children); it may have been to undermine Alexander

II, or the line of Amyntas on behalf of a foreign regime, or simply lovers intriguing to put Ptolemy in power, even above her sons. However, neither Diodorus nor Plutarch included her in any plotting with Ptolemy, so her involvement may be fiction; Carney (2006) p.90 argues that there is evidence she was a loyal and devoted mother. Pelopidas, who had already driven the Macedonian garrisons installed by Alexander II from Thessaly, was called in to arbitrate (Plutarch, *Pelopidas* 26.3, Diodorus 16.67.4). Pelopidas was offered, or took, hostages for good behaviour, including Philip II.

9.   Justin 7.5.9 for the guardianship of his nephew and for people demanding Philip take on the kingship; Athenaeus 13.557b (his acting first as regent implied by a reign of twenty-two years); Diodorus 16.1.3 for twenty-four years and 16.2–3 for the hardships facing Philip. Satyrus stated twenty-two years, Athenaeus 557C, which conflicts with Justin 7.5.9–10 (who stated Philip acted as guardian) and Diodorus 16.1–3, via Diyllus, stated twenty-four years. The scholiast to Aeschines 3.51 suggests 359 BC (archonship of Callidemus in the first year of the 105th Olympiad, thus 359 BC). Heckel (2006) p.211 for the calendar explanation.

10. Diodorus 16.2 6. Green (1974) p.22 for discussion of the five usurpers; see Justin 7.4–5 and 8.3.10 for the half-brothers.

11. Diodorus 16.3.8 for Theopompus' books.

12. See Grant (2019) pp.59–60 for fuller discussion.

13. Plutarch, *Pelopidas* 26.3 for his intervention; while not mentioned, Eurydice may have summoned him if she was not scheming with Ptolemy against her own son; also Diodorus 15.67.4. Aeschines, *On the Embassy* 2.28 claimed Eurydice placed Perdiccas in Iphicrates' arms and Philip on his knee when pleading for his support as her stepson.

14. Athenaeus 13.557 for Satyrus' quote.

15. Grant (2019) pp.226–227 for full explanation of the source on Philip's wives.

16. Grant (2019) p.227 for discussion.

17. Diodorus 19.52.1–2, Justin 14.6.13, *Heidelberg Epitome* FGrH 155 F2.4, Diodorus 19.61.2 for Antigonus' accusation that the marriage was forced upon Thessalonice. Events well covered in Plutarch, *Demetrius* 36.1–2. Grant (2017) p.148 for a summary.

18. Athenaeus 13.557c (from Satyrus), Plutarch 10.1.

19. Athenaeus 13.557c (from Satyrus), Justin 9.8.2, 13.2.11 for Philinna, Plutarch 10.1 for Olympias giving him drugs. For Philinna's questionable background, see Justin 13.2.11. For his mental Illness, Appian, *Syrian Wars* 52, Plutarch 10.2, Plutarch, *Moralia* 337d, Justin 13.2.11, 14.5.2, Diodorus 18.2.2, Porphyry of Tyre FGrH 260 F2. The *Heidelberg Epitome* 1 called him epileptic. Socrates' *daimonion* was described in Plato's *Apology* 31c–d, 40a which has been postulated as epilepsy. Caesar's fits have likewise been posthumously attributed to epilepsy; see Plutarch, *Caesar* 17, 45, 60, and Suetonius, *Julius* 45. The symptoms exhibited by Caligula and described in Suetonius, *Gaius* are likewise suggestive of epilepsy.

20. Carney (1992) p.179 footnote 27 cites the doubting scholars.

21. Plutarch 10.1–10.5, based on Loeb Classical Library edition (1919).

22. Following the proposals of S. Ruzicka in Carney-Ogden (2010) pp.4–11 for the importance, timing and implications of the Pixodarus affair. Justin 9.7.7 for Alexander's plans to overthrow his father and Plutarch 10.4 for Thessalus' presence on Corinth;

Philip demanded he be returned in chains. Demaratus' role at Plutarch 9.12–14, *Moralia* 197c.

23. Justin 9.7.
24. Arrian 3.6.5.
25. Diodorus 16.75.1, 16.77.2, Plautarch, *Moralia* 850A, Pausanias 1.29.7 for Pixodarus' actions against Philip. More in Sears (2014) pp.214–215 and Carney (1992).
26. Carney (1992) p.179.
27. For Alexander's meeting with Ada, see Strabo 14.1.17, Arrian 1.23.7–8, Diodorus 17.24.2–3, Plutarch 22.4
28. See Grant, *Last Will and Testament* (2021) chapter 9 for more on the faked court correspondence.
29. Plutarch 74.2–6, Plutarch, *Moralia* 180 f for the hostility between Cassander and Alexander.
30. Curtius 10.7.2 for Arrhidaeus' religious role. Grant, *Last Will and Testament* (2021) chapter 3 for detail of the settlement at Babylon
31. See Grant, *Last Will and Testament* (2021) chapter 3 for discussion.
32. Curtius 10.8.16–19.
33. Diodorus 19.11.5 stated six years and four months as Arrhidaeus' reign, and Justin simply six years. However, the date of the formal commencement of his reign is not specified. Arrhidaeus is later attested to have 'received Phocion', but this was in essence an embassy to Polyperchon, Arrhidaeus' regent and his guardian. In an outburst of anger, he almost ran Hegemon through with a spear; again, this suggests he was neither self-controlled nor predictable; Nepos, *Phocion* 3.3, Plutarch, *Phocion* 33.8–12 for thee episode with Arrhidaeus and the Athenian ambassador.
34. There is uncertainty; he may have acted as regent for his nephew, Amyntas Perdicca, initially; see Grant (2019) p.226.
35. Athenaeus 10.435a, quoting Theophrastus; see Heckel (2006) p.77 for discussion of the sources.
36. Aelian 12.34.
37. Pliny 35.86.
38. Pearson (1960) pp.27–28 for discussion on Theophrastus' epitaph to Callisthenes. Heckel (2006) pp.77–78 and 189 for sources and the confusion of women.
39. Diodorus 17.16.2 for Antipater and Parmenio pleading with Alexander to produce an heir before departing Macedon.
40. Justin 12.12.11 for 'compliance to the king's wishes' in intimate context. Athenaeus 13.603b for his love of male youths.
41. For Alexander's intimacy with Bagoas the eunuch, Curtius 6.5.23, 10.1.26, 10.1.22–38, also Plutarch 67.7–8, Athenaeus 13.603a–b.
42. Plutarch 22.1–6; Plutarch *Moralia* 180F and 760c; Plutarch, *Sayings of Alexander* 19–20; Athenaeus 13.603b–c.
43. Plutarch 22.7.
44. Arrian 7.28.
45. *The Campaigns of Alexander* (Penguin edition, 1971), J.R. Hamilton, Introduction p.23.
46. Plutarch 21.7–9.

47. Plutarch 21.5.
48. Diodorus 17.77.7 and Justin 12.3.11–12 for Alexander's incorporation of concubines into his retinue, and Justin 12.3.7–8 and Diodorus 17.77.3 for his thirteen-day tryst with Thalestris.
49. Plutarch 70.3, 77.6, Curtius 4.5.1, Diodorus 17.107.6, Justin 12.10.9, Plutarch, *Moralia* 338 d for Stateira; Aristobulus names her Barsine; Arrian 7.4.4 for Barsine and Parysatis.
50. For the eighty marriages at Susa, Arrian 7.4.6, and 7.4.8 for the 10,000 total Macedones who had married Asian wives, a suspiciously high number. Arrian 7.12.2 for Alexander's refusal to let the Asiatic children be repatriated to Macedon. This is reinforced by Diodorus 17.110.3 detailing the fund Alexander left for their upbringing and schooling.
51. The *epigonoi* referenced here are distinct from the 30,000 Asiatic soldiers who had been trained and armed in Macedonian style. Here, sons of Macedonian soldiers are being referred to under the same general heading as 'offspring'. Diodorus 17.110.3 for their education funding, Justin 12.4.1–11 for Alexander's payment to men with Asiatic offspring, Arrian 7.4.8 and Plutarch 70.3 for the newlyweds receiving gifts. For Alexander considering them replacements for their fathers, see Arrian 7.12.3, Plutarch 71.9 and Curtius 8.5.1. Full discussion in Roisman (2012) p.58.
52. See Grant (2019) chapter 13 for the typical roles of Athenian women.
53. Quoting Heckel (2006) p.90, Cleophis. Curtius 8.10.32–36 for the whole Cleophis affair and siege of Massaga; *Metz Epitome* 45 for Cleophis' beauty, and Justin 12.7.9–11 for the further scandal. See Heckel (2006) pp,90–91 and Curtius (Penguin Classics edition, 1984) p.294 footnote 68 for discussion of its authenticity. *Romance* 3.18–24 for the Candace episode.
54. For the massacre of the mercenaries at Massaga, see Diodorus 17.84.1–6 for the most damning version, though it was captured by Plutarch 59.6–7; Arrian 4.28.7–4.30.4 claimed Alexander killed them as they planned to desert. Quoting Plutarch 59.6.
55. *Romance* 3.18–3.24.
56. For the origins of the name, see full discussion in Arthur-Montagne (2014) p.9.
57. Dalley (2013) pp.121–124 for discussion of the widespread use of Semiramis. The title 'Semiramis' potentially included the second wife of Sennacherib, Naqia. Herodotus 1.184–191 for additional references to Semiramis. Strabo 16.1.2 for the attachment of the name Semiramis to monuments across the western Persian Empire.
58. *Romance* 3.25–3.27.
59. Quintus of Smyrna, *Posthomerika* 18 ff for Penthesilea's arrival at Troy and Diodorus 2.46 for her legend; Pseudo-Apollodorus, *Epitome of the Bibliotheca* 5.1 for her death at Achilles' hand. Pausanias 10.31.1 and 5.11.2 for the art that suggested Achilles repented the death of a woman he had fallen for.
60. Bosworth A in the East (1996) p.81 for the female warriors amongst Sacan nomads. Arrian 4.15.2–5 suggested this was close to Colchis on the Black Sea, where Curtius 6.5.24–26 for example suggested Hyrcania in the plains of the River Thermodon. Fully detailed in Mayor (2014) pp.34–52. It is also worth noting that over 112 weaponry-filled graves of Scythian women aged 16–30, previously identified as men, have been

discovered at tombs between the Danube and River Don; see Antikas–Wynn Antikas (2014) p.7. Tarbell (1920) for the Amazonomachy in Greece. Hanson (1991) p.25 for Amazon light battle-axes.

61. Plutarch 46.1–3 for Thalestris' meeting with Alexander; also, Curtius 6.5.24–32, Justin 12.4.5–7, Diodorus 17.77.1–3. Justin provided an alternative name, Minithyha.

62. Thalestris is otherwise named Minithya; Plutarch 46; Diodorus 17.77.1–3; Curtius 6.5.24–32; Justin 12.3.5–7. Fuller discussion of the episode in Hammond (1993) pp.293–294.

63. Plutarch 46.4–5 for the episode involving Onesicritus and Lysimachus.

64. Arrian 7.13.2–6 for the other Amazon affair. Arrian 4.15.2–5 for the earlier encounter with the Scythians and offers of marriage with the daughter of the Scythian king or the regional chiefs.

65. For Heracles' link to Barsine, see Diodorus 20.20.1, 20.28.1, Justin 11.10.3, Plutarch, *Eumenes* 1.3, Curtius 10.6.11, 10.6.13, Justin 13.2.7, 15.2.3, Pausanias 9.7.2. Heracles' authenticity discussed in Billows (1990) pp.140–141, citing the initial work by Tarn and Brunt. Also see Tarn (1948) p.330 relating to his earlier article: Tarn (1921). Whereas Errington (1970) p.74 and Brunt (1975) pp.22–34 accept the child could have been legitimate, Pearson (1960) p.117, Jacoby, Berve, Beloch and Hamilton concluded he was an imposter. Tarn dismisses the boy on a number of principles: his age, and conversation between Polyperchon and Cassander that Tarn concluded alluded to the boy as a 'pretender', along with the boy's previous long-term obscurity. However, these contentions are open to reinterpretation. As has been pointed out, Tarn took a moralistic stance in his interpretations of Alexander's career, here defending him from accusations of a liaison (and its outcome) with an unofficial concubine, Barsine. Heracles' existence and/or his relationship to Alexander was recorded by Diodorus 20.20.1, 20.28, Justin 11.10.3, Dio, *Crysostom Discourse* 64.23, Pausanias 9.7.2, Appian, *Syrian Wars* 52, Curtius 10.6.11, 10.6.13 and Plutarch, *Eumenes* 1.3.

66. Diodorus 18.2.1, translation from the Loeb Classical Library edition (1947).

67. Diodorus 19.64.3–5 for Cassander's turning of Polyperchon's son and Diodorus 19.66.7 for his son's assassination. See Heckel (2006) p.230 for 'retirement'. Billows (1990) p.140 for his powerlessness. Following Tarn (1921) p.22 for Polyperchon's isolation.

68. Diodorus 19.67.1. For Cratesipolis' actions at Sicyon, see Diodorus 19.67 and 20.37, Polyaenus 8, Plutarch, *Demetrius* 9.

69. Antigonus' likely role in the affair as stated in Tarn (1921) pp.18–21, Tarn (1948) pp.330–337 and restated in Billows (1990) p.141.

70. Antigonus' likely role in the affair as stated in Tarn (1921) pp.18–21, Tarn (1948) pp.330–337 and restated in Billows (1990) p.141.

71. Diodorus 20.20.1–2 for Polyperchon's reintroduction of the boy and Diodorus 20.28.1 for the reception in Macedon. Justin 15.2 suggested both mother and son must have travelled to Macedon as both were later secretly killed.

72. Tarn (1948) p.332.

73. Arrian, *Events After Alexander* 1.43 for Cassander urging his father not to 'get too far from the kings'. Arrian, *Events After Alexander* 1.38 suggested Antigonus took custody

of the kings, but this should more logically read Antipater as there is no evidence of this; he was after all heading for war with Eumenes, and it was Antipater who took the kings back to Macedon. However, Antigonus' custody might be a reference to Heracles, based in Pergamum. Cassander urged his father not to 'get too far from the kings'. The one occasion Antipater may have given them up, temporarily, is when confronting Eumenes in a short campaign uniquely mentioned in the *Gothenburg Palimpsest*.

74. Tarn's theory proposes that Nearchus' own book promoted the boy as genuine, and so too his part in the boy's promotion at the Assembly, when he was writing at the Antigonid court some years later. It has been argued that Antigonus' influence over Nearchus, who operated under him from 317/316 BC onwards, paved the way for a publication that perpetuated the claim of Heracles; inevitably it was for Antigonus' own dynastic ends, care of a compliant Polyperchon who was by then desperate for alliances in Greece.

75. Brunt (1975) pp.22–34 concurs.

76. For Cassander's actions, see Diodorus 20.28.1–4. Curtius 10.6.10–13 preserved Nearchus' speech proposing Heracles be recognized as an heir. Errington (1970) p.74.

77. Plutarch, *Moralia* 530b–d and Diodorus 20.28.2 for Polyperchon's murder of Heracles: Polyperchon handed him over to Cassander for 100 talents and a share of power, which amounted to little.

78. Curtius 3.11.24–25 for their respective ages, Diodorus 17.36.2, Justin 11.9.12, Plutarch 21.1 and Arrian 2.11.9 for the confirmation that Darius' wife was his sister.

79. Athenaeus 13.608 for the harem numbers of 329, Curtius 3.3.22 for 360.

80. Curtius 3.13.12–17 for the captive list. Diodorus 17.23.5 for Mentor sending his wife and children to Darius' care. Diodorus 16.52.3–5 and Arrian 2.1.3 mentioned Memnon appointed Pharnabazus, son of Artabazus, as his own replacement. See Heckel (2006) p.70. Mentor was last heard of in 342 BC; for Memnon's death, see Diodorus 17.29.3–4, Arrian 2.1.3, Curtius 3.1.21 and 3.2.1. Diodorus 16.52.4 for the eleven sons and ten daughters; Curtius 6.5.4 mentioned nine sons (Arrian 3.23.7 named three of them) were with him when he surrendered to Alexander in Hyrcania at age 95; perhaps two had died earlier or were operating elsewhere. Ilioneus is named 'Hystanes' by Hedicke in some Curtius editions; amended by Heckel (2006) p.143.

81. Curtius 5.9.1 and 6.5.2 for Artabazus taking refuge in Macedon. The date of the arrival at Pella is uncertain; see Heckel (1987) p.116 footnote 4. Alexander would have still been young (perhaps 8) when Artabazus and family departed *ca.* 348 BC as suggested at Diodorus 16.52.1–4 (16.5.2.3 for Memnon's presence in Macedon); the archonship of Callimachus is referred to 349/348 BC, though communications, pleas and exonerations would have taken time, so we may add a year or so to the departure of Artabazus from Macedon. Heckel (2006) p.275 (F12) for discussion of the wife captured at Damascus.

82. See Heckel (2006) pp.55, 70 for discussion, as well as Diodorus 16.52.3–4.

83. For Barsine's intimacy with Alexander, see Curtius 3.13.14, Plutarch 21.7–9, Justin 11.10.2–3, Plutarch, *Eumenes* 1.3. For Artabazus' surrender, see Curtius 6.5.2–6, Arrian 3.23.7, and for Bactria, see Curtius 8.1.10 and Arrian 3.29.1. Artabazus was the son of the daughter of the Great King Artaxerxes II; see Plutarch 21.9.

84. See Heckel (1987) for a list of these and other *anonymae* and their backgrounds, and Heckel (2006) pp.274–275.

85. For the Rhodian connection for Artabazus' wife and family links, see Demosthenes 23.154, 23.157 (these suggest an 'in-law' relationship). Diodorus 16.52.4 was more specific that Artabazus sired his children with their sister; Heckel (2006) p.275 for details. Heckel (1987) pp.114–116 provides a study of these interwoven lines. Also Mentor had married a daughter of Artabazus, who was himself the son of an Achaemenid princess.

86. Quoting Justin 11.10.2–4; for Rhoxane's misidentifications, see Justin 14.6.2 and 14.6.13, Porphyry fr.3.1; see Tarn (1921) p.27 for discussion. *Romance* 2.20, 2.22 for the daughter of Darius; Stoneman (1991) pp.110, 113, 114 – she became the daughter of Darius.

87. Curtius 3.12.21–23 for Barsine's descriptions and Arrian 4.19 for similar descriptions of both Rhoxane and Darius' wife. Discussed at Tarn (1948) p.333, Plutarch 21.6.

88. Plutarch 21.6–7.

89. Arrian 7.4.4 for naming Darius' daughter Barsine. Tarn (1948) p.334 disagrees with her having royal blood, and this is one of his principal arguments for Heracles being a 'pretender'. Brunt (1975) p.24 reversed the claim. She (a daughter of Darius) cannot have been the mother of Heracles for various reasons: Stateira was reportedly murdered by Rhoxane in Babylon, as Plutarch 77.6 claimed, and if Heracles' mother was murdered with him in Macedon fourteen years on, as Justin 15.2.3 stated, then obviously Heracles cannot have been Darius' grandson. It would also fail to explain Nearchus' promotion of the boy at Babylon and why Perdiccas did not have the boy killed when Antigonus vacated Asia Minor. We would further imagine that Heracles' descent from the Great King would have been a widely discussed *topo*s. And it was not.

90. Tarn (1948) pp.335–336.

91. Brunt (1975) pp.28–29 refutes Parmenio's advice and sees it as fiction. Tarn (1948) p.335 sees it differently and argues Parmenio was referring to the Persian princess, citing a mistaken identification by Plutarch. The offer of marriage to Barsine and the division of empire is positioned in Curtius after the capture of Tyre. See Curtius 4.5.1–8 and Justin 11.12.3–3.

92. Plutarch 29.4, Curtius 4.5.1, Justin 11.12 for Alexander's reply; quoting Plutarch 21.5.

93. Diodorus 17.67.1.

94. Curtius 6.5.4 stated Artabazus was 95 when he surrendered to Alexander *ca.* 330 BC in Hyrcania; Heckel (2006) p.55 for age discussions. Curtius 8.1.19, Arrian 4.17.3 for his retirement due to old age.

95. Plutarch 21.8–9, translation from the Loeb Classical Library edition (1919). Tarn (1948) p.333 for the Duris link and p.334 for a similar (possible) misidentification at Strabo 13.610. See below for Arrian 7.4.6 linking Barsine to Mentor.

96. Diodorus 17.77.7 and Justin 12.3.11–12 for Alexander's incorporation of concubines into his retinue and Justin 12.3.7–8 and Diodorus 17.77.3 for his thirteen-day tryst with Thalestris.

97. Curtius 3.13.14, Diodorus 17.23.5.

98. Tarn's statement in the *Journal of Historical Studies* xli 18 ff, quoted in Todd (1985) p.283, considered this 'a purely unfounded conjecture of modern writers'. Heckel supposes two separate Mentors are being referred to. Brosius (1996) p.95 has Barsine as the daughter of Arses.

99. Tarn (1948) p.333 for the generation statement. Arrian 1.15.2 for Memnon's sons at the Granicus. Tarn (1921) p.24 for discussion of Mentor's son; an Athenian inscription honouring a 'Memnon' may also suggest Mentor's son was old enough to have seen action, though he could be from an earlier marriage. This fragmentary stele on pentelic marble dating to 327 BC seems to support 'a family relationship', though not conclusively this one. Full details of the inscription in Todd (1985) pp.281–284; it honours a Mentor for saving Greek lives in Egypt during the Persian invasion in 343 BC; see Heckel (2006) p.162 for discussion and p.318 footnote 42, and Brunt (1975) pp.26–27.

100. Diodorus 20.20.1 for Heracles being aged 17 and Justin 15.2.3 has Heracles in his fifteenth year; Tarn (1948) pp.333–334 concurs, yet sees this as proof that the boy was an imposter, terming the links a wholesale 'tissue of absurdities'.

101. That Barsine had a daughter sufficiently old enough for marriage by 325 BC only need, in extremis, put her in her mid-20s in 333 at Issus, assuming, for example, she gave birth to that daughter when she was 16 and that daughter in turn was 16 when being married to Nearchus in 325 BC. But the reference to several children and the ages of Mentor's children, if by her, would clearly make her far older, unless sources only assumed she birthed the other children with the brothers.

102. Arrian 7.4.6, translation from the Oxford World Classics edition (2013).

103. Plutarch, *Eumenes* 1.3, translation from the Loeb Classical Library edition (1919).

104. The name 'Apame' was attested in Artabazus' family; his own mother had been so called: Plutarch, *Artaxerxes* 27.4, Xenophon, *Hellenica* 5.1.28, Plutarch, *Agesilaus* 3.3. Plutarch, Arrian and Strabo were unclear over the identity of the bride of Seleucus. Arrian 7.4.6 stated he married the daughter of Spitamenes of Sogdia-Bactria, but he failed to mention her name. In his *Life of Demetrius* 31.5, Plutarch named Seleucus' wife 'Apame' 'the Persian', the correct name for a number of Seleucid cities that were later named after her, but Plutarch failed to say whose daughter she was. Strabo thought Apame was a daughter of Artabazus, and the above text explains why. The *Metz Epitome* termed her *quaedam Bacrtrina*; see Heckel (1987) p.117 for discussion. While Alexander was able to forgive and elevate those who opposed him (Rhoxane's father, for example) accounts of Spitamenes' death, and the unique detail of Spitamenes' flawed character at Curtius 8.3.1–12 (he took concubines and banished his own wife), make his daughter a strange choice of bride; unless this Apame was really Achaemenid and her true identity was hidden by Ptolemy?

105. Arrian 7.4.4–6 named Aristobulus as his source for the name matches at the Susa weddings. Sources of the Susa wedding lists discussed at Tarn (1948) p.333 footnote 1. Aristobulus is not mentioned by name as a groom in Arrian 7.4.6, but eight pairings are, as well as a reference to Companions. Chares' description of the wedding banquet suggested ninety-two marriages were to take place for ninety-two bedchambers were prepared, see Athenaeus 12.54P, 538B–539A, full text in Robinson (1953) p.79. Aelian 8.7 claimed ninety brides.

106. Justin 11.9.13.
107. Arrian 1.15.7 mentioned Mithridates was Darius' son-in-law. Thus we assume he had a daughter apart from the 'virgins' Stateira and Drypetis, both from his second wife Stateira. Heckel (2006) p.274 (F5) for Darius' previous wife and F8, F9 for other unnamed daughters. Heckel (2006) p.206 for Pharnaces' possible identification.
108. The contention at Curtius 6.5.3 that Artabazus was 95 by the time he surrendered to Alexander is termed 'absurd' by Tarn, see Brunt (1975) p.25. Tarn suggested he was 'well over sixty'. As he married before 362 BC and had twenty-one children by 342/341 BC, as nine of his sons were old enough for military campaigning against Alexander and as we have no gender order for their birth, it is quite possible Mentor's daughters by Barsine, who was possibly an earlier older child of Artabazus, could have been past puberty.
109. Curtius 4.11.5–6 stated Darius demanded the return of his two daughters, *duas virgines filias*.
110. Based upon Arrian 7.4.6 and incorporating the claims of Plutarch, *Eumenes* 1.3.
111. Strabo 15.8.15 for Apame being a daughter of Artabazus.
112. Plutarch, *Eumenes* 7.1 for Pharnabazus' support for Eumenes.
113. Also Heckel (2006) p.54. Artabazus' father, Pharnabazus, had been the satrap of Hellespontine Phrygia. Justin 13.2 for Heracles at Pergamum.
114. Demosthenes, *Against Aristocrates* 23.154; Strabo 13.1.11.
115. Curtius 8.1.19, Arrian 4.17.3 for Artabazus' retirement. Heckel (2006) p.187 (Oxyartes) and pp.241–242 (Rhoxane) for a summary of the confusion with dates and sieges surrounding the capture of Rhoxane and her father. Curtius 9.8.9–10 referred to Oxyartes as *praetor Bactrianorum*. This makes more sense than appointing him to a foreign province: Paropanisadae, according to Arrian 6.15.3; was Arrian's source, Ptolemy, undermining Rhoxane's family power? See Heckel (2006) pp.187–188 for discussion of Oxyartes' appointment.
116. Arrian 7.4.4 and Curtius 10.3.11–13 for Alexander's additional marriages to Parysatis and the daughter of Darius III.
117. See Heckel (2006) p.379 for the stemma of Artabazus.
118. Curtius 10.3.11–12, a highly rhetorical speech, in which Alexander is chastising his men at Opis and explaining his integration of Persian troops (and wives) into his ranks, only mentioned Rhoxane and 'a daughter of Darius', failing to mention Parysatis too; this could have come from his sources (or Cleitarchus alone) or from his own understanding of events.
119. Arrian 7.4.4. For the marriage of Stateira, see Arrian 7.4.4. Justin 12.10.9, Diodorus 17.107.6, Plutarch, *Moralia* 338d, Curtius 10.3.11–12. Heckel (2006) p.341 footnote 695 suggested Aristobulus was Arrian's source, and that when writing 'late in life' (well after Ipsus in 301 BC, we propose) he was no longer clear on detail; thus, he had confused the great king's daughter with Alexander's mistress.
120. Brosius (1996) p.185.
121. Brosius (1996) p.95.
122. Adea's own grandmother, Philip's Illyrian wife, had probably been renamed 'Eurydice' before her; Arrian, *Events after Alexander* 1.22; discussed by O. Palagia in Carney-Ogden (2010) p.35. Arrian 3.6.5 named Cleopatra, niece of Attalus, as 'Eurydice', where elsewhere she was named Cleopatra; discussed in Heckel (1978).

123. The change of name discussed in Heckel (2006) p.181 and Heckel (1978) pp.155–158; also Carney-Ogden (2010) p.35 for Olympias' changes of name as well as Tarn (1948) p.334 footnote 4; Plutarch, *Moralia* 401a–b, Justin 9.7 and Carney (2006) pp.93–94 for the adoption of the name 'Myrtale', and p.95 for Olympias.
124. Discussed at length in Grant, *Last Will and Testament* (2021).

Chapter 9: Forgery, Philology and Meddlesome Morphology: Battle on Papyrus

1. Momigliano (1954) p.22.
2. *Collected Works of Erasmus, Letters* 1–141 (1484–1500) Vol. 1, p.134, translation by R.A.B. Mynors and D.F.S. Thompson (University of Toronto Press, Toronto-Buffalo, 1974).
3. Quoting Grafton-Blair (1998) p.32.
4. Discussed in detail in Casson (2001) p.138; it was Edward Gibbon who proposed the material fuelled the 4,000 baths for six months.
5. Galen *Corpus Mediocorum Graecum* 9.1; full text in Heller-Roazen (2002) p.146; 'self-proclaimed' as Galen wrote a work titled *The Best Physician is also a Philosopher*.
6. Discussed in Grafton (1990) pp.12, 73–77; Callimachus' catalogue's full title was *The Tables of Persons Conspicuous in every Branch of Learning and a List of Their Compositions*.
7. Casson (1971) p.45. *Ex ploion* meant literally 'from the ships'.
8. Galen reported competition between Pergamum and Alexandria. For references to Ammonius Saccas, see Gudeman, *Greeks* (1894) p.61. Full discussion in Metzger (1972).
9. That is if Diogenes did not simply plagiarize Diocles of Magnesia (second or first century BC), as Friedrich Nietzsche supposed. Galen, *On His Own Books* 2.91–92. Galen is said to have written over 600 treatises; see Kotrc-Walters (1979). A reading of the *Life of Diogenes* will, for example, illustrate the number of times a story was additionally credited to other individuals.
10. Diogenes Laertius, *Life of Aristotle* 13.
11. Eusebius, *Praeparatio Evangelica* 10. As further examples, Eusebius accused Theopompus of stealing entire passages from Xenophon; Apollonius suggested he plagiarized Isocrates word for word. Lucian, *How to Write History* 59, Eusebius, *Praeparatio Evangelica* 10.3.1, Porphyry, *The Study of Philology Book* 1: *On the Greeks as Plagiarists*, cited in Shrimpton (1991) p.5. Grafton (1990) p.78 for Apollonius' criticism of Theopompus.
12. Eustathius published extant commentaries of the Homeric works, the *Eustathii archiepiscopi Thessalonicensis commentarii ad Homeri Iliadem* 1194 (Hildesheim, G. Olms, 1960).
13. Quoting Macaulay (1828).
14. Plato, *Republic* 377d 4–6.
15. Aristotle, *Poetics* 1451a36–8; translation from Gill-Wiseman (1993) p 182.
16. Diogenes Laertius *Heraclitus*. Herodotus 2.2.23; Herodotus' father discussed in Pitcher (2009) p.156. Thucydides' criticism of Homer discussed by J.L. Moles in Gill-Wiseman (1993) pp.100–101, citing Thucydides 1.9.3, 10.1, 10.3–5, 11.1–2.

17. In the fourth century, Q. Septimius published *Dictys Cretensis Ephemeridos belli Troiani*, in six books, a work that professed to be a Latin translation of the Greek version. Dares' work was published as *Daretis Phrygii De excidio Troiae historia* and is dated to the fifth century. Aelian 11.2 reports that Dares' original *Iliad* predated Homer. Quoting Heckel (1987) p.114 on 'charlatans' referring to deceptive *anonymae* in general.

18. Discussion of Nero's part on the translation of Dictys' diary in Gudeman (1894) p.152.

19. Translation of Nepos' letter by R.M. Fraser from Martinez (2011) p.17. There is however a warrior named Dares in Homer, *Iliad* 5.9; discussed in Highet (1949) pp.52–53.

20. Benoit de Sainte-Maure's *Le Roman de Troie* was one of the inspirations for Chaucer's *Troilus and Criseyde*. For full discussion, see Nolan (1992). Highet (1949) p.55 for discussion of the later adaptations and p.104 for the Latin *Odyssey*.

21. Highet (1949) p.114 for Samxon's edition of the *Iliad*.

22. Plutarch, *On the Malice of Herodotus* 43, or *Moralia* 873f.

23. Plutarch, *Agesilaus* 15.4 for a 'battle of mice'.

24. Strabo 9.1.10 and also implied at Plutarch, *Solon* 10.1. The inserted verse referred to the *Iliad* 2.557–558.

25. Herodotus 7.6.

26. Casson (2001) pp.29–30 for discussion. The reference to Lycurgus comes from Pseudo-Plutarch, *Lives of the Ten Orators* 841f. Metzger (1972) p.9 for *dramatis personae*. Also discussed in more detail in Gudeman, *Greeks* (1894) p.55. Plutarch, *Solon* 29.4–5 for Thespis' lies.

27. Aulus Gellius 3.3 quoted in Grafton (1990) p.13; termed Varronian as Varro used a sound method to detect the genuine plays.

28. Kenyon (1899) p.14 for the dating of the oldest extant papyri.

29. Pliny 13.74–82; as an example see Theophrastus, *Enquiry into Plants* for the many uses of papyrus.

30. First argued by Theodor Birt in his *Das Antike Buchwesen* (1882) and discussed in Madan (1893).

31. Pliny 13.74–82.

32. Discussed in Madan (1893) pp.8–12. Pliny 13.17 claimed parchment was invented at Pergamum but the differentiation to vellum is unclear. Pliny 13.21 for *charta Pergamena*. Herodotus 5.58 for its earlier development by the Ionians.

33. Martial first described the codex format and its handy compactness for travel in a series of poems written between AD 84 and 86. Full discussion in Needham (1979) p.4 and following Casson (2001) p.126.

34. Kenyon (1899) pp.17–18 for the lengths of unrolled papyri.

35. Theopompus' epitome detailed in Flower (1994) p.35.

36. Discussed in Heckel-Yardley (1997) Introduction p.1.

37. Quoting Hornblower (1981) pp.19–20, 28–29.

38. Aulus Gellius 7.17 for the fate of the Pergamum library. Mark Antony gifted Cleopatra much of the Pergamum library; Plutarch, *Antony* 58. Archaeological excavation suggests the library at Pergamum may have been large enough to hold 160,000 scrolls.

39. Discussed in Momigliano (1966) p.124.

40. Casson (2001) pp.125–127. Over 70 per cent of Oxyrhynchus finds have been on papyrus, and less than 1.5 per cent in total were in the codex format.
41. Neleus' activity detailed in Athenaeus 1.4.3a–b, Strabo 13.1.54, Plutarch, *Sulla* 26.1–2, Diogenes Laertius 5.52–56. Discussed in Fortenbaugh-Schütrumpf (2000) p.344 and Casson (2001) p.35.
42. Athenaeus 5.53.214d–e.
43. Quoting Harris (1999) pp.40–41.
44. Strabo 13, Plutarch, *Sulla* 26. Also discussed in Casson (2001) pp.70–71.
45. Porphyry, *Life of Plotinus* 24 mentioned the classifications and arrangement that Aristotle's and Theophrastus' works were subjected to by Andronicus.
46. Diodorus 1.4.2.
47. Plutarch, *Lucullus* 74.3 described his rule of Africa as carried out with 'the highest degree of justice'.
48. Plutarch, *Caesar* 49.8. Aulus Gellius 7.17. Ammianus Marcellinus and Orosius concur that Caesar started the fire, though the burning of the library was accidental.
49. Also Shipley (2000) p.235 for discussion and Casson (2001) p.138. The earthquake and subsequent tsunami were recorded by Ammianus Marcellinus 26.10.15–19.
50. Caesar, *Civil Wars* Book 3.111. For Cassius Dio's claim, see discussion in Casson (2001) p.46.
51. Caesar, *The Alexandrian War* 1 and Lucan, *On the Civil War* 10.440 ff; 486–505. Full discussion in Heller-Roazen (2002) p.148.
52. Discussed in Casson (2001) p.79. Detailed discussion of the damage caused by Caesar and the final destruction of the library at Alexandria in Heller-Roazen (2002) pp.147–149. There is some doubt as to whether the fire actually affected the library at all; see Heller-Roazen (2002) pp.150–151.
53. Augustus later favoured Varro and his writing was again encouraged.
54. Suetonius, *Life of Julius Caesar* 56.1 and 56.3 for confirmation of Hurtius' praise.
55. The lost *Codex Fuldensis* discussed in Rolfe (1913) p.207.
56. Suetonius, *Caesar* 55; the *pro Metello* speech, for example.
57. Other sources for the fire and book numbers destroyed are Orosius 6.15.31–2, Aulus Gellius 7.17, Seneca, *On the Tranquillity of the Mind* 9.5, Ammianus Marcellinus, *Roman History* 22.16.13–15; other citations: Pseudo-Aristeas (200,000 increasing to 500,000, echoing Demetrius of Phalerum's promise to Ptolemy), Orosius 6 (400,000), Epiphanius ,*Weights and Measures* 9 (54,800), Isidore of Seville, *Etymologies* 6.3.3 (80,000), John Tzetezes, *Prolegomena to Aristophanes* (490,000). Full discussion of the size of the library and its traditions in Bagnall (2002).
58. Discussion of the composite scrolls in Heller-Roazen (2002) p.140. Following Bagnall (2002) p.356 for the doubt that Callimachus could have listed all the works. Boardman-Griffin-Murray (1986) p.392 for the Serapis library. Vrettos (2001) p.34 for the Serapeiana. Vrettos (2001) p.40 for the mixed rolls.
59. Athenaeus 5.203e.
60. Polybius 38.5.21. Also recorded in Appian, *Hannibalic Wars* 132. Scipio's quote is from Homer, *Odyssey* 6.448
61. The fate of the Metz Epitome discussed in Baynham (1995) p.62. Texts now rely upon the editions of D. Volkmann (Nuremberg, 1886) and O. Wagner (Strasburg, 1900); more on the surviving editions in Thomas Review (1963).

62. An acrostic is a writing format in which the first letter, syllable or word of each line, spells out a word or message.

63. Following and quoting from Nisetich (1980) pp.15–16. Highet (1949) pp.222–224 for Pindar's stanzas.

64. Discussed in detail in Casson (2001) p.43.

65. Discussed in Gudeman, *Greeks* (1894) p.69. Fitzgerald (1998) p.xii for the multiple-author theory behind the *Odyssey*.

66. Following Robbins (2001) p.79.

67. Discussion of the Bronze Age references in West (2008) p.76.

68. Robbins (2001) p.66. Herm (1975) p.180 for *phoinikia grammata* and its early Greek usage.

69. Discussed in Robins (1987).

70. The *Suda* identified a work titled *Selection of Attic Words and Phrases* that likely belongs to the grammarian.

71. Strabo 15.2.8 suggested the people of Ariana (Iran and Central Asia), including Persians, Bactrians, Medes and Sogdians, as 'speaking approximately the same language. With slight variations.' Discussed in Olbrycht (2008) p.243.

72. Onesicritus' conversations with the Indian sages are preserved at Strabo 15.1.63–65; full discussion in Brown (1949) pp.38–39, 44 for the translation discussion.

73. Polybius 3.22, translation by Ian Scott-Kilvert (Penguin Classics edition, 1979).

74. Livius Andronicus' translation discussed in Highet (1949).

75. Discussed in Baker-Saldanha (2009) p.35.

76. Quoting Grant (1995) p.97 and Suetonius, *Life of Horace*.

77. Many of the Greek city-states used different names for the calendar months. Caesar abolished the lunar year and intercalary month, reverting to a solar year. Diodorus tried to synchronize the archon changes in Athens with the campaign years during the Successor Wars, causing as much as six months' slippage along the way. Discussion and citations for Caesar in Hannah (2005) p.98.

78. Discussed in Shipley (1903) pp.1–25.

79. Following Shipley (1903) pp.7–8.

80. Following Madan (1893) p.2.

81. Quoting West (2008) Introduction p.viii. The 'erratic' nature of the early manuscripts Erasmus had to work with is discussed by Metzger (1992) p.102.

82. Discussed in Shipley (1903) pp.1–25.

83. Full detail of Symmachus in Hedrick (2000) pp.181–182; for detail of the later recensions, see Foster (1874) p.32. For details of the Nichamachean recensions, see Hall (1913) pp.246–247 and Kraus (1994). The new copy bore the subscription *Victorianus emendabam dominis Symmachis* ('I Victorianus emended (this) by the authority of Symmachus'), thus anticipating the useful colophons, the publication and production notes, of the Middle Ages.

84. Discussed in Gregory (1886) pp.27–32.

85. Horace, *Ars Poetica*.

86. Quoting Niebuhr (1844) p.38, who proposed scribes refused to copy the later books of a by then 'old and loquacious' Livy.

87. A dittography is a scribal error in which a letter, syllable or word is accidentally repeated in the text; a haplography is an error where a word, syllable or letter is written just once

instead of twice, a parablepsy is an error resulting from a distraction to the eye which causes an omission in the text.

88. Plutarch, *Demosthenes* 14.4.
89. Discussion in Cook (2000) pp.537–547.
90. Discussion of Demosthenes' spuriously assigned speeches in Worthington (2000) p.1.
91. Erasmus, *Adagia* (III, IV, 96) 'collection of proverbs' published first in Paris in 1500.
92. Following Grafton-Most-Settis (2010) p.30 for Petrarch's treatment of Alexander.
93. Following the observation of Momigliano (1977) p.109.
94. The Latin translation was by Boccaccio, a friend of Petrarch, aided by Leontius Pilatos, the first professor of Greek in Western Europe; quoting Highet (1949) Introduction p.15 for 'wooden'.
95. Following comments in Gibbon (1776), *The History of the Decline and Fall of the Roman Empire*, cited in Highet (1949) Introduction p.17.
96. Highet (1949) Introduction p.16 for the first professor of Greek.
97. Highet (1949) pp.106–111 for the impact of purer Greek and Latin on the vernacular languages and following his observation on the reasons for the 'poorer' vocabulary, and p.85 for 'positive paganism'.
98. Quoting Momigliano (1977) p.76.
99. Quoting Highet (1949) Introduction p.15, following Bracciolini. Highet (1949) pp.91–92 for Boccaccio's visit to Monte Cassino.
100. Highet (1949) pp.17–18 for the origins of the Vatican Library.
101. Many books printed after 1500 followed this format, but Bernhard von Mallinckrodt in his *prima typographicae incunabula* chose an arbitrary date of 1500 as the end of the 'infancy of printing', thus *incunabula*, Latin for 'cradles'.
102. From the German publication titled *Gutenberg-fest zu Mainz imjahre* (1900), quoting a letter Mark Twain had sent them to celebrate the opening of the Gutenberg Museum.
103. Quoting from the Preface (line 1) to *Tacitus and Bracciolini, The Annal Forged in the XVth Century* by J.W. Ross, originally published anonymously in 1878.
104. Quoting *Tacitus and Bracciolini, The Annal Forged in the XVth Century* chapter 2.3 by J.W. Ross. Also Hochart (1889).
105. Quoting Homer, *Odyssey* 11.362–6.
106. Annius was made Master of the Palace by Alexander VI. Ligota (1987) p.50 for discussion of Annius' claim to read Etruscan. Etruscan is not an Indo–European language and has not been fully deciphered. The *Pyrgi Tablets*, written in both Etruscan and Phoenician (Punic), have helped translate some rudimentary phrases and vocabulary. According to Suetonius, *Claudius* 42.2, Claudius wrote a history of the Etruscans in twenty books; this has led some people to assume he spoke Etruscan, but there is no corroborating text.
107. Full discussion of Annius' methods is given by Ligota (1987). Annius' *Antiquitatum Variarum* was first published under the title *Commentaria super opera diversorum auctorum de antiquitatibus loquentium* (Eucharius Silber, Rome, 1498); discussed in Temple (2002). Also a series of essays on various aspects of Annius' career and his influence on Renaissance myth, and the first interest in the Etruscans, was collected in *Annio da Viterbo, Documenti e ricerche, Multigrafica Editrice* (Rome, 1981).

108. Discussed in Ligota (1987) p.44.
109. Herodotus 2.53 claimed Homer lived some 400 years before his own time, thus *ca*. 850 BC. Estimates of the dating of Homer vary across sources, with some preceding this by 250 years.
110. Discussion in Borchardt (1986) pp.27–35. Quoting Grafton (1990) p.61.
111. Quoting Weiss (1962) pp.101–120.
112. For full discussion see Borchardt (1986) pp.27–35.
113. Quoting Grafton (1990) p.23.
114. Discussed in detail in Grafton (1990) pp.78–81.
115. Momigliano (1966) p.145. Most educated Romans were expected to have mastered Greek.
116. Seneca, *Natural Questions* 7.16, translation by J. Clarke (1910).
117. Scaliger's work was published as *De emendatione temporum*, discussed in Grafton (1975) pp.164–166.
118. Grafton (1990) p.116 for the legacy of Goropius. Valla exposed the fraud in 1440 in his *De falso credita et ementita Constantini Donatione*. For discussion of the *Donation of Constantine*, see R. Fubini (1996) p.80.
119. Discussion in Mallory (1989) pp.9–10.
120. Quoting Syme (1971) p.265 and taking Annius' contention from Ligota (1987) p.46.
121. Excerpt from the *Catalogue of the Exhibition Alexander the Great in European Art*, edited by Nicos Hadjinicolaou (Thessalonica, 22 September 1997 to 11 January 1998).
122. Ligota (1987) pp.52–53.
123. Ligota (1987) for 'organon of the truth'. See discussion in Grafton (1990) pp.95–97. Casaubon, Porphyry and Reitzenstein each exhibited bias in their critiques.
124. Rational analysis fought stubborn faith, quoting Glenn W. Most, speech at the Israel Society for the Promotion of Classical Studies 42nd Annual Conference. Following Russell (1946) p.462 for the unpopularity of the Renaissance.
125. Scaliger (1583) *De emendatione temporum*, with a second edition in 1598. Between them, Scaliger had published his *Epistola de vetustate et splendore gentis Scaligerae et JC Scaligeri vita* (1594). The *New Testament* preacher called into question was Dionysius the Areopagite. The Jesuit reply came in the form of Gasparus Scioppius' *Scaliger Hypobolimaeus* or *The Supposititious Scaliger*, a polemic against his character. A complete list of his works appeared in a biography by Jakob Bernays (Berlin, 1855). Discussed at length in Grafton (1983). Scaliger's response included the *Confutatio fabulae Burdonum*.
126. Digory Whear, *De Ratione et Methoda Legendi Historias* (October 1623). Further discussion in Levine (1991) p.279.
127. Quoting Ehrman (2014) Introduction and Momigliano (1954) p.23.
128. This appears in the bibliography as Speyer (1971).
129. Following the observation made by Ehrman (2014) p.31 and Metzger (1972) p.13.
130. Full discussion at *The Freethought Exchange*, no. 37–38 (1998), article titled 'Thirty Centuries of Forgeries' pp.1735–1837 now available online at christianism.com. The so-called Angel Scroll is an example of newly emerging deceptions. Summarizing N.C. Gross, *The Mystery of the Angel Scroll: Find of the Century or Elaborate Hoax?*

(Jerusalem Report, 11 October 1999). For a full discussion of their authenticity, see Berry (1999) and Pagels (1979). The definitive study of the Decretals of Pseudo-Isidore is H. Fuhrmann, *Einfluß und Verbreitung der pseudoisidorischen Fälschungen*, 3 vols, Schriften der Monumenta Germaniae Historica 24, i–iii (1972–1973).

131. Eusebius, *Ecclesiastical History* 8.2.
132. E. Gibbon, *Vindication*. It was an attack on Eusebius' treatise on pseudos in his *Praeparatio Evangelica* 12.31.
133. Eusebius, *Praeparatio Evangelica* 9.5.1. For Theotecnus, see Metzger (1972) pp.3–24.
134. Discussed in Attridge Oden (1981). References to Sanchuniathon are found in Eusebius, *Praeparatio Evangelica* 1.9–10.
135. Quoting Blackburn (2006) p.1.
136. Discussed in Grafton (1990) pp.14–16.
137. *The Letter of Aristeas* 10–11, translation from Bartlett (1985) pp.20–21.
138. Full discussion in Heller-Roazen (2002) p.141.
139. Digory Whear, *On the Plan and Method of Reading Histories* (1623).
140. Translation from J.F. Healy, *Pliny the Elder on Science and Technology* (Oxford University Press, 1999) Preface p.VIII.
141. Following Bishop (1983) pp.360, 366.
142. Discussed in J.F. Healy, *Pliny the Elder on Science and Technology* (Oxford University Press, 1999).
143. P.G. Naiditch and R. Resinski, *Philodemus and Greek Papyri* (UCLA University Research Department, Exhibition Catalogue, 1994), quoting Sir William Gell.
144. Quoting Deane (1918) p.41 for 'antiquarian sentiment'.
145. Momigliano (1977) p.79 ff for discussion of Pausanias' reintroduction into Europe.
146. J. Dryden, *Preface Concerning Ovid's Epistles* 16.
147. Ovid, *Metamorphoses, Epilogue*, lines 871–874.
148. Bentley's comment appeared in Samuel Johnson's *The works of the poets of Great Britain and Ireland* (1804) p.568.
149. *The Miscellaneous Prose Works of Sir Walter Scott* (1848) Volume 1, 'Life of John Dryden' p.318.
150. J. Dryden *Preface concerning Ovid's Epistles* 16.
151. Following the observation of D.S. Carne-Ross in Fitzgerald (1998) pp.lxi–lxiii on poetic structure.
152. Quoting Shelmerdine (1995) Preface p.iii. Highet (1949) p.200 for the loss of lyric poetry.
153. J. Dryden, *Preface Concerning Ovid's Epistles* (1683 text) sections 12 and 19.
154. The comment on Bardon's edition came from W.S. Watt and is discussed in J.E. Atkinson's commentary p.23 on Curtius in *A Commentary on Q. Curtius Rufus' Historiae Alexandri Magni, Books 5 to 7*, 2, Acta Classica, Supplementum 1.
155. Grant (1956) p.25.
156. Quoting Wolfgang Schwadewaldt in the *Bryn Mawr Classical Review*, June 2010, review of *Mindt N (2008) Manfred Fuhrmann als Vermittler der Antike: ein Beitrag zu Theorie und Praxis des Übersetzens* (Transformationen der Antike, Bd5, Berlin, New York).

157. The earlier model being in the form of J.F. Bielfeld, *The elements of Universal erudition, Containing an Analytical Abridgement of the Science, Polite Arts and Belles Lettres*, Vol. III (J. Robson, London, 1770).
158. Quoting Cruttwell (1877) p.7.
159. Quoting Teuffel-Schwabe (1892) pp.4–5.
160. Discussed by Momigliano (1954) p.27.
161. Hammond (1993) p.154.
162. Hammond (1993) p.190 and Pearson (1960) p.213.
163. Syme (1987) pp.111–114 and discussed by Baynham (1999) p.201. The *Metz Epitome* dating discussed in Bosworth-Baynham (2000) p.65; Baynham (1995) pp.63–65. *Testudo* also appeared in the *Metz Epitome*, although the text is corrupt. However, Wagner suggested the reference to the king's tunic employs a phrase rarely used in Latin and argues for a Hellenic original; for discussion, see p.65. For the unique citations of the *Metz Epitome*, see Heckel-Yardley (2004).
164. Curtius used *testudo* at 5.3.9 and implied its formation again at 5.3.21 and 7.9.3. Xenophon, *Hellenica* 3.1.7.
165. Wheeler (1902); Mahaffy (1888) and quoting Goralski (1989) p.83 on Rooke.
166. Taken from P.G. Naiditch and R. Resinski, *Philodemus and Greek Papyri: an exhibition 1 April–31 August 1994* (UCLA, University Research Library, Dept. of Special Collections, April 1994). This was read in a review of 1847, some eleven years after Gell had died. The Caliph Omar of Damascus is one of the suspects for the burning of the Library at Alexandria. Its actual fate is unconfirmed.
167. Aristotle's work is thought to be preserved through his lecture notes. The current organization into treatises and sequences was certainly not his. Diogenes Laertius, *Aristotle* 12 for the calculation of lines. For Demetrius of Phalerum, see Reeve (2001) Introduction p.15; Diogenes Laertius, *Demetrius* for detail of his output.
168. Diogenes Laertius, *Plato* 55–61 mentioned Thrasyllus' collection and identifications. Well discussed in Gibson (1998).
169. Pliny preface 24.
170. Cicero, *Ad Quintum*, fr 2.11.4 The full citation is '*paene pusillus Thucydides*' or 'almost a miniature Thucydides'.
171. Flower (1994) Introduction p.1. Diodorus 16.3.8 for the loss of five of Theopompus' books.
172. Diogenes Laertius, *Diogenes* 24.
173. Plutarch, *Nicias* 29.
174. Full discussion in Balme (2001).
175. Discussed in Gudeman, *Greeks* (1894) p.72.
176. Discussed in Gudeman, *Romans* (1894) p.161. Aulus Gellius on the other hand suggested there had been another comedian named Plautius and hence the confusion.
177. Details in Gudeman, *Romans* (1894) p.159.
178. Casson (2001) p.57. For Aristotle's prejudice evidenced in the *Constitution of the Athenians*, see Grant (1995) p.125
179. A point made by Flower (1994) p.42. The 'Attic Bee' quote is from Digory Whear's historical treatise in 1623, a term previously used for Sophocles: see Athenaeus

13.598c. Barnes (2000) p.12; see discussion of the Oxyrhynchus historian in Warner (1966) pp.16–17 and Shrimpton (1991), Introduction, p.XVIII. Warner (1966) p.30 for the suggestion that Cratippus may be the author. The historians appear to criticize Thucydides' use of speeches as part of the narrative; Sacks (1990) p.94 for Cratippus' opinion, from Dionysius of Halicarnassus, *On Thucydides* 16.349. As the work appears to be a continuation of Thucydides' account (410 BC onwards), a link is further established.

180. See further discussion of the finds at Oxyrhynchus in Green (2007) pp.xxxiv–xxxv.
181. They are listed by Dosson in his *Etude sur Quinte Curce* (1887) pp.315–356.
182. McKitrerick (2004) p.28. Also a comprehensive summary of the Curtian manuscripts given in Curtius' *History of Alexander* (Loeb Classical Library edition, 1971 reprint) Introduction pp.IX–XIV, translation by J.C. Rolfe.
183. J. Mutzell had already published an influential well-informed edition in 1842 in Berlin in two volumes; discussed in Timpanaro-Most (2005) p.53. The two traditions was a distinction first made by Nikolaas Heinsius, the Dutch philologist and son of Daniel Heinsius, Joseph Scaliger's pupil.
184. Following Baynham (1998) p.37.
185. Discussed in Atkinson (1997) pp.3448–3449; also Curtius, *History of Alexander* (Loeb Classical Library edition, 1971 reprint) Introduction pp.IX–XIV, translation by J.C. Rolfe.
186. Following discussions in Baynham (1998) pp.4–5, Berzunza (1941) p.133 and Curtius, *History of Alexander* (Loeb Classical Library edition, 1971) Introduction pp.XXXII–XXXIII.
187. Quoting Higbie (2003) p.222.
188. Following Berzunza (1941) p.133.
189. 'Anonymous fluidity' taken from Townsend (1996) Introduction p.23.
190. Full discussion of the supplements in Curtius and the associated MSS can be found in Smits (1987) pp.89–124.
191. Details in Smits (1987) p.90. The 1946 Loeb Classical Library edition of Curtius still houses Freinsheim's added text. The comment on Freinsheim's efforts preserved in the preface by W.H. Crosby in the 1854 Cellarius edition.
192. Quoting M. Wood from Gill-Wiseman (1993) Prologue p.xiii.

Chapter 10: Mystery Historian, Mystery Agenda

1. Tarn (1948) p.91.
2. Quoting Bosworth (1996).
3. Quoting Fears (1976) p.214.
4. Curtius referenced Cleitarchus as a source at 9.5.21 and 9.8.15. The stylistic accord of Diodorus, Curtius and Justin's epitome of Trogus suggested a common source for much of their works.
5. The 123 manuscripts are listed by Dosson in his *Etude sur Quinte Curce* (1887) pp.315–356. The titles are discussed in *Quintus Curtius Rufus, The History of Alexander* (Penguin, London, 1984), Introduction by W. Heckel p.1. An author-owned 1623 edition from Mattaus Rader in Germany carries this final title.

6. Printed English editions of the *Ab urbe condita* range from *The Early History of Rome* to the *Dawn of the Roman Empire*. Arrian's *Anabasis* is most commonly named *The Campaigns of Alexander*, though 'campaigns' is far from a literal translation.

7. Cassius Dio 60.35; thus the title suggested Claudius had an apotheosis into a pumpkin, though modern interpretation suggests it implied 'pumpkin head'. Full discussion in Sullivan (1966).

8. A comprehensive list of studies dedicated to the theme can be found in Atkinson (2009) Introduction pp.3–19, Baynham (1998) pp.200–219 and *Quintus Curtius Rufus, The History of Alexander* (Penguin Classics edition, 1984) Introduction pp.1–4.

9. Quoting Steel (1905) pp.402–423 and following Hamilton (1988) p.445 for the dating.

10. Dating arguments well summed up by Atkinson (2009) pp.3–9 and Baynham (1998) p.206, especially for Claudian supporters. Also see Tarn (1948) pp.111–116 for late dating arguments.

11. Pliny the Younger, *Epistles* 7.27.2–3, Tacitus 11.20.4–11.21.4. See full discussion in the introduction of Heckel (1984). For similar arguments, see Fears (1976) p.447.

12. Tacitus 11.21.2.

13. Suetonius, *On Grammarians and Rhetoricians*, Index 1.28. Q. Curtius Rufus appeared between M. Porcius Latro and L. Valerius Primanus in Suetonius' *De Rhetoribus*.

14. Milns (1966) p.504 for the dating based on the list of rhetors. Suetonius' father was a tribune of equestrian rank and he himself became an intimate of Trajan and Hadrian. A further Q. Curtius (not Rufus) is thought to have been mentioned by Cicero, who complimented his prosecution skills, though his letter dates to *ca.* 55 BC. But as Milns points out, this on 'stylistic grounds, though inconclusive in many ways, must also exclude him, since it is obviously post-Ciceronian and has strong affinities with the Latin of the rhetorical schools of the first century AD'. Moreover, as another scholar comments, the name was actually penned as Q. Acutius, not Curtius! Nevertheless, in Milns' view, due to 'the comparative rarity of the name in Imperial times there is a strong possibility' that the historian is one of these three. Milns (1966) pp.504–505. The rejection of the name comes from J.W. Bussman, Quintus Curtius Rufus' *Historiae Alexandri: The Question of Authorial Identity and Intent*.

15. Augustus had fixed the sestertius value at 1/100th of an aureus, thus 1 million sestertii equated to 10,000 aureii, each of which was approximately 8 grams in weight of gold. At a gold price of US$40 per gram (the aureus was almost pure twenty-four carat gold), that gives a present-day gold standard value of over US$3.5 million. Later emperors melted down the 'old' sestertius to reissue the coins, by then debased with bronze and lead, inevitably with an inflationary impact.

16. The loans of the Roman nobility discussed in Finlay (1973) pp.53–57.

17. Tacitus, *Histories* 1.1; Pliny Preface.

18. Ovid, *Metamorphoses* book 15.745–870.

19. Parthian references can be found at Curtius 5.7.9, 5.8.1, 6.2.12, 7.12.11 describing their dominance over former Macedonian territory and 'everything beyond the Euphrates'. Following Milns (1966) for the broad dating argument, though he mentioned AD 227 as the fall of Arsacid Parthia. R.T. Bruère, C.Ph. 47 (1952) cited in J.W. Bussman, *Quintus Curtius Rufus' Historiae Alexandri: The Question of Authorial Identity and Intent*. Silius Italicus' knowledge of Curtius also discussed in Fears (1976) p.215 ff.

20. Curtius 4.4.21.
21. The statement that archery was still a widely practised skill at Curtius 7.5.42. Curtius 3.11.15, 4.9.3 for *cataphracti*; impact on dating arguments discussed in Fears (1976) pp.222–223.
22. Quoting Wilkes (1972) p.178.
23. Tacitus, *Histories* 1.1, translation from the Loeb Classical Library edition (1925).
24. Tacitus 2.1.
25. Cassius Dio 53.19.2 ff; cited in full in Wilkes (1972) p.186.
26. Discussion of the less-than-frank rendition of speeches by Tacitus and Livy, for example, in Gudeman, *Romans* (1894) p.145.
27. See discussion in Morford (1973) p.210. Tacitus 4.43.1 for the comparison to Cordus.
28. Discussed in Scramuzza (1940) p.39.
29. Curtius 10.9.1–6. For a full discussion on the chronology issues, see Baynham (1998) Appendix pp.201–220, Heckel (1984) Introduction pp.1–4 and Atkinson (2009) pp.203–214.
30. For a useful summary of historical references to 'star' and 'last night', see Atkinson (2009) Introduction pp.207–208. Horace, *Satires* 1.7.23–36; following Fears, *Solar* (1976) p.495.
31. Hamilton (1988) pp.459–451 for the use of *sidus* and citing Pliny, *Panegyric* 19.1 for its attachment to Trajan.
32. Lucan, *On the Civil War* 10.35–36. Curtius 9.6.8; for similarities to Virgil, see Steele (1915) pp.409–410.
33. Tacitus, *Histories* 1.38.
34. The theories and sighting are summarized in Barrett (1978). See Atkinson (2009) p.7; Pliny made seventy-five references to comets in his second book and mentioned the allusion to a hairy star frequently; at 2.25 for example.
35. Eusebius, *The Life of Constantine* 28. Recent geological surveys might have pinpointed the crater of a meteorite that could be related to the sighting. Theories suggest a mushroom cloud could have constituted the 'cross' in the sky. See Dr David Whitehouse, 'Space impact saved Christianity', BBC News (23 June 2003).
36. This was first proposed in Steel (1915).
37. Virgil, *Georgics* 1.487–488.
38. Suetonius, *Claudius* 46. The comet following Caesar's death also alluded to in Ovid's *Metamorphoses*, chapter 15, *The Apotheosis of Caesar* line 786. Suetonius, *Claudius* 46, Cassius Dio 61.35 for the comet heralding Nero.
39. Seneca ,*Natural Questions, On Comets* 7.21.3. Quoting Tacitus 14.22. Calpurnius Siculus, *Eclogues* 1.77.79 if they can be dated to AD 60 and not AD 54; discussion in Barrett (1978) pp.99–100. The *Octavia* 231–232, wrongly ascribed to Seneca, also recorded the sighting; discussion in Barrett (1978) p.99.
40. Tacitus 15.47, translated by A.J. Church and W.J. Brodribb (Macmillan and Co., 1864). Seneca also confirmed the sighting 'when Paterculus and Vopiscus were consuls' in his *On Comets* 7.28.3; see Barrett (1978) p.99 for the full entry.
41. Suetonius, *Nero* 36 for the AD 66 sighting. Josephus, *Jewish War* 6.289 for the Jerusalem sighting.

42. As an example of the significance attached to comets, see Suetonius, *Nero* 36. Tacitus mentions two comets, one in AD 60 and the other in AD 64; see *Annales* 14.22 and 15.47.

43. For the works of art, see Pliny 34.84. Suetonius, *Vespasian* described Vespasian's dubious financial dealings.

44. Suetonius, *Vespasian* 5–6 for a list of portents and 7.2 for prediction of his alleged healing powers. Sextus Aurelius Victor, *De Caesaribus* (broadly: *Summary of the Life and the Manners of the Emperors*) 9 recorded it, but appears to be following Suetonius as well as Cassius Dio 66.17.2.

45. Cassius Dio 60.26.

46. Following the proposal of Atkinson (2009) p.209; rejected by Milns (1966) p.502, though neither linked this to Nero's term.

47. Pliny 2.92–93, translation from J. Bostok and H.T. Riley (Taylor and Francis, 1855). This may not relate the comet seen at Nero's accession but to a later sighting.

48. Suetonius, *Claudius* 46; quoting Cassius Dio 61.35.

49. Tacitus 14.22 and 15.47. The sighting of AD 66 might have been a super nova as it had no tail, according to Chinese astronomers.

50. See Atkinson (2009) pp.207–208 for a summary of Nero's relationship to Roman Apollo; discussion in Champlin (2003) pp.112–113 for Nero's associations with the heavens. The view and 'solar monarchy' is challenged by Fears, *Solar* (1976).

51. Seneca, *Apolocolocyntosis* 4, translation from Sullivan (1966) pp.383–384.

52. 'Actor-emperor' was a term used by Pliny the Younger in his so-called *Panegyricus Trajaini* 46.4.

53. Quoting Desiderius Erasmus, *On the Correct Method of Instruction*.

54. For the reporting of the death of Agrippina, see Tacitus 14.1–8, Suetonius, *Nero* 34, Cassius Dio 63.11–14.

55. Seneca, *On Comets* 7.28.3.

56. Trajan's praise of Nero's first five years is mentioned in Aurelius Victor, *Summary of the Life and the Manners of the Emperors*, and in the anonymous *Epitome of the Caesars* 5. For his civic activity, see Suetonius, *Nero* 17 for the limit on legal fees; Tacitus 13.26 for his support for freedmen; and for the impeachment of government officials, Tacitus 13.30, 14.18, 14.40, 14.46. For Otho's emulation of Nero, see Plutarch, *Otho* 3.2.

57. Following the observation of Champlin (2003) pp.116–117.

58. See Atkinson (2009) pp.209–210 for discussion of the similarity of Seneca, *Of Clemency*.

59. As noted by Bosworth (2004) p.553.

60. *Citharoedo principe* was a term used by Juvenal in the *Satires* 8.198.

61. Suetonius, *Nero* 38; Cassius Dio 62.16. Tacitus 15.39. He nevertheless reported there were rumours of Nero playing his lyre.

62. Tacitus 15.40 claimed five days; Suetonius, *Nero* 38 claimed six days and seven nights, and a pillar erected by Domitius claimed nine days.

63. For the use of elephants, see Spartianus, *Life of Hadrian* 19.

64. For Germanicus' attributes and his suspicious death, see Suetonius, *Caligula* 1–5. Tacitus 12.66 and 13.15 recorded that Martina was suspected of poisoning Germanicus and suspicion fell upon Tiberius.

65. For Otho's homosexual relations with Nero, see Suetonius, *Galba* 22.
66. Vitruvius, *On Architecture* 8.6.10–11, Pliny 34, 54.175–178. The principal claim that lead contributed to the fall of Rome was published by J.O. Nriagu in March 1983, titled 'Saturnine gout among Roman aristocrats. Did lead poisoning contribute to the fall of the Empire?' A more recent paper by H. Delile titled 'Lead in ancient Rome's city water' confirmed the high levels (University of Utah, Salt Lake City, March 2014). The claim that lead contributed to the fall of the Roman Empire is generally considered extravagant, though the effects of lead poisoning on long-term users of lead cookware in Rome is not denied; this can result in insanity as well as infertility.
67. Suetonius, *Nero* 35.3. Tacitus 16.6 recorded the same but attributed it to a casual outburst. Cassius Dio 63.27 suggested it could have been an accident. Also see Tacitus 16.6.
68. Following Milns (1966) p.491 for arguments on the use of *trepidare* and an event yet to happen.
69. The main source for the Pisonian plot is Tacitus 15.47–65.
70. Quoting Tacitus 15.62; the 'brother' was a reference to Nero's stepbrother (and former brother-in-law), Britannicus, the heir designate who died mysteriously just a month before he would assume manhood and thus the emperorship, and one day before his fourteenth birthday. Tacitus 13.14–16 and Suetonius, *Nero* 33–34 claimed it was the work of Nero's poisoner, Locusta.
71. Josephus 20.154–156. Compare with Tacitus 2.1.
72. Ker (2009) p.53. Pliny the Younger's citation is from *Epistles* 8.12.4–5 and references Fannius at 5.5.3.
73. Seneca, *Of Clemency* 1.1; there are ten sentences connected to 'swords' (sheathing or drawing) in book 1.
74. Suetonius, *Nero* 24.2. *Romance* 1.18–19 as an example of Alexander's charioteering.
75. Champlin (2003) p.55 for fuller discussion on Nero's entries into the games of Greece.
76. Suetonius, *Nero* 25, Cassius Dio 63.20–21.
77. Tacitus 13.40 for the role of the archers against Tiridates in the campaign.
78. Lucan, *On the Civil War* 10.2.
79. Bosworth (1983) p.152, citing Lucan, *On the Civil War* 9.439–444 and Curtius 4.7.19.
80. See full accounts of Tiridates' entry into Rome in Champlin (2003) pp.228–234, and also Cassius Dio 62, Tacitus 15, Pliny 30.6.16 all recorded elements of the events. For Nero's attachment to Apollo, see discussion in Champlin (2003) pp.276–286. The Greek Helios was Latinized to Helius and Apollo remained Apollo; both were associated with the Sun.
81. Cassius Dio 63.1–6.
82. Virgil, *Aeneid* 5.190, 6.502, 6.513; Bosworth (2004) p.553 for discussion.
83. The episode of Lysimachus' caging with a lion appeared in Justin 15.3, Seneca, *On Anger* 3.17.2, *On Clemency* 1.25, Pliny 8.16.21; he was most likely Alexander's schoolteacher, not the Bodyguard. Heckel (2006) p.154 for the alternative identification of Lysimachus. For other similarities between Seneca and Curtius, see Hamilton (1988), though Hamilton proposes Seneca followed Curtius.

84. If Seneca was following Curtius (as Wiedemann argued a century-and-a-half ago), then it was Curtius who wrote in the untroubled days of Nero's early term, though this argues against much we find in his encomium. What seems clear from other similarities is that one of them borrowed phraseology from the other. Hamilton (1988) p.447 for discussion of Wiedemann's views. Seneca, *Epistle* 94.62 '*Toto orbe arma circumfert*' and Lucan, *On the Civil War* 10.31 ff, '*gladiumque per omnes Exegit gentes*'. Hamilton (1988) pp.447–456 for the similarities, especially Seneca's *Epistles* 56 and 59. For Chrystrom's orations, see S.R. Asirvatham in Carney-Ogden (2010) pp.196–200.

85. Curtius 10.5.26, translation from the Loeb Classical Library edition (1946).

86. For discussion on the use of these terms, see Balot (2001) pp.XI, 291. Also see McKechnie (1999) p.103 for Curtius' necrology and its vocabulary at 10.5.26–34.

87. Curtius 10.5.37.

88. See Whitmarsh (2002) p.175 for the comment on Trajan and the transition in Roman opinion. Aelian 3.32 for Alexander playing the cithara.

89. Suetonius, *Nero* 19 for the phalanx. Suda α 1128= FGrH 618 T2 for Alexander of Aegae.

90. Pausanias 10.7.1 and 10.19.2 for the looting of statues, and Cassius Dio 63.14 for the blocking up of the fissure. Full discussion of other sources in Champlin (2003) pp.133–134.

91. Ammianus Marcellinus 4.8.10; discussed in Fears (1976) p.221.

92. Josephus, *Jewish Wars* 2.95, and Josephus 17.319, 18.28 for the renaming to Neronia.

93. See discussion in McKechnie (1999) p.49.

94. See Errington (1970) pp.50–51 for comparisons between Arrhidaeus and Claudius. For Tiberius' reticence to assume power, see Suetonius, *Tiberius* 24 and for the quip, *Tiberius* 21.2. Discussed in more detail in Grant, *Last Will and Testament* (2021) chapter 5.

95. Tacitus 11.2.1–11.5 for the trial of Asiaticus and the indictments that followed and following the discussion in Baynham (1998) p.174.

96. Curtius 10.9.1 and quoting Atkinson (2009) p.205 on its relevance to Nero's suspicions of conspirators, if indeed Curtius' words were related to the encomium.

97. For arguments against Seneca and Lucan drawing from Curtius, see Fears (1976) pp.216–217. In contrast, their use of Curtius has been recently upheld by Hamilton (1988) p.445. Also see Bosworth (2004) p.553, citing Seneca's *Epistle Morales ad Lucillium* 59.12 for more arguments.

98. See discussion of the sources and dates in Champlin (2003) pp.38–44.

99. Revisiting the comment by Wilkes (1972) p.178.

100. Syme (1987) pp.111–114 and discussed by Baynham (1998) p.201.

101. Quoting Baynham (1998) p.20 on 'no one doubting' Curtius used Livy. A full discussion of Livian influence can be found at pp.20–25, 35, 75–76. Also see Oakley (2005) pp.661–662; and especially the introduction to Atkinson-Yardley (2009) and also well summarized by W. Heckel in the introduction to the 2004 Penguin Books edition of Curtius and quoting Heckel on 'modes of expression'. Fuller discussion of the similarities to Livy in Steele (1915) pp.402–409.

102. Arrian 2.7.5 for the effeminacy of the Asian troops, the 'most warlike' of those Europeans would face.
103. Livy 9.19.10 for the comparisons of the foes of each Alexander and Curtius 8.1.37 for its reiteration at Cleitus' death.
104. As an example of Curtius taking phrases from Virgil, see Curtius 4.6.25–29 and Alexander's treatment of Baetis following the siege of Gaza, which emulated Virgil's treatment of Hector's mutilated body.
105. Curtius 10.10.5–6. As for Curtius' own dismissal, and reiterating Chugg (2009) p.5 who refuted the use of the first personal singular in favour of the first-person plural, in other translations 'we' is used; as an example, the translation by J.C. Rolfe in 1946 published by the University of Michigan. Nevertheless, it was not unusual for an author to use the plural 'we' when referring to his own efforts, and this does not convincingly argue that Curtius paraphrased Cleitarchus, for example. Diodorus (for example 1.83.9) and Polybius, in particular, switched between singular and plural where emphasis demanded it, and in particular to stress the veracity of either eyewitness reporting or personal vouching for facts; discussion in Marmodoro-Hill (2013) pp.199–204. Of course 'we' is still commonly used today, and by the author in this book.
106. See Suetonius, *Claudius* 43–46, translation from the Loeb Classical Library edition (1914). Britannicus had become the heir designate of Claudius under the name 'Tiberius Claudius Germanicus'.
107. Milns (1966) p.502.
108. Following the observation in Bosworth (2004) p.551.
109. The 600 examples identified by F. Walter, *Studien zu Tacitus Und Curtius* (H. Kutzner, Munich, 1887). For discussion of the similarities, see Bosworth (2004).
110. Bosworth (1994) p.559, and for the mourning p.562.
111. Macaulay (1828).
112. Tarn (1948) pp.91–92, see McKechnie (1999) pp.44–46 on Tarn's treatment of Curtius.
113. Tacitus 11.21, translation from the Loeb Classical Library edition (1937).
114. Tacitus 11.20 for Curtius' mining activities and 11.21 for the summation; translation from the Loeb Classical Library edition (1937).
115. Following the title and theme of Bosworth (2004).
116. 'Insider' and 'outsider' quoting Champlin (2003) p.44.
117. Suetonius, *Vespasian* 6.3 for the July accession.
118. Suetonius, *Vespasian* 1.
119. Milns (1966) p.491 for *trepidare*, and quoting Bosworth (1983) p.151.
120. Suetonius, *Vespasian* 8–9.
121. Cassius Dio, *Vespasian* 59.12.3.
122. Suetonius, *Vespasian* 18.
123. 'Oh dear' is a Robert Graves translation from the Penguin edition of the *Life of the Twelve Caesars – Vespasian* (1957) of what is more traditionally worded 'woe is me'.
124. Josephus' comments in *Against Apion* 9 are a good example of Vespasian's tolerance to historical works that painted him in a favourable light. For the siege at Jotapata, see Josephus, *Jewish Wars* 3.6 ff.
125. Josephus' treatment in Rome discussed in Wiseman (1991) Introduction p.ix.

126. See discussion on Vespasian's censorship in Townend (1964) pp.340–341.
127. Suetonius, *Vespasian* 15.
128. Milns (1966) p.493 for Tyre's stance in the war.
129. Fears (1976) p.220.
130. Josephus, *Jewish War* 3.3 ff.
131. See discussion in Heckel's introduction to the Penguin edition of *Quintus Curtius Rufus, The History of Alexander the Great* (London, 1984) pp.1–4.
132. References to Cluvius Rufus are found at Josephus 19.1.13, Suetonius, *Nero* 21, Pliny the Younger, *Epistles* 9.19, Plutarch, *Otho* 3, Tacitus 12.20 and 14.2, Tacitus, *Histories* 1.8, 2.58, 2.65, 3.65, 4.39 and 4.43, Cassius Dio 68.14.
133. Josephus' account and his sources are discussed in detail in Wiseman (1991) Introduction p.XIV.
134. Proposed by Syme and discussed in Townend (1964) pp.337–377. Rejected by L.H. Feldman (ed.) *Josephus the Bible and History* (EJ Brill, Leiden, 1988) p.404.
135. Suetonius is rumoured to have had an affair with Vibia Sabina, who was married to Hadrian, according to the *Historia Augusta* 11.3. Suetonius was dismissed from office for it. This may be rumour and he may have simply been disrespectful, for we would have expected harsher treatment if true.
136. Tacitus, *Histories* 1.76.1 for his support of Vitellius and 2.65.1 for the charges brought against him, 3.65 for Cluvius' presence with Vitellius.
137. References to a 'Marcus' Cluvius Rufus appear unfounded, and the sources mentioned a 'Cluvius Rufus' only. See Cornell (2013) p.550 footnote 3, citing a mistranslation of Tacitus, *Histories* 2.65.1 from which the 'Marcus' stemmed. It is possibly because the translator had Marcus Caelius Rufus, protégé of Cicero, on his mind. His identity is discussed later in the chapter.
138. Suetonius, *Nero* 21.1 and Tacitus, *Histories* 1.8.1. See Wiseman (1991) p.111 for the *nobilis* discussion.
139. Suetonius, *Nero* 21.1, Cassius Dio 62.14.3 for Cluvius' ex-consulship. See below for 'Cluitus'; Tacitus, *Histories* 1.8 for his role in Hispania.
140. Full chronology discussion for dating Cluvius in Wiseman (1991) p.111. Pliny 33.
141. Josephus 19.1.13. Taken from *Iliad* 14.90–91.
142. Plutarch, *Roman Questions* 107; Livy 7.2 recorded the same incident.
143. The disapproval – and its origins – is the opinion of Shorter (1967) pp.370–381.
144. Pliny the Younger, *Epistles* 9.19.5, translation from Marchesi (2008) p.146.
145. As an example of the interpretations, see the opinions of Levick (1985) pp.318–346.
146. Pliny the Younger, *Epistles* 2.1.2, translation from Marchesi (2008) p.146 and quoting Marchesi on 'double vocation of history'.
147. Discussed in Marchesi (2008) pp.145–146.
148. The origins of the Cluvii discussed in Wiseman (1991) p.111, and Cornell (2013) p.550 for the early Capua origins.
149. Tacitus, *Histories* 1.52–54.
150. Tacitus, *Histories* 2.65.1 for Cluvius' oratorical skills.
151. Tacitus 1.1.

152. See Townend (1960) pp.98–100; the theme was picked up again in Townend (1964) p.342 for discussion on sources on AD 69.
153. Townend (1964) p.346.
154. See Wiseman (1991) p.115 for discussion of Townend's conclusions.
155. For Cluvius' lenient treatment of Nero, see Wilkes (1972) p.202. Cornell (2013) p.558 for 'golden mean'.
156. Pliny 7.45 ff.
157. For a full discussion of Pliny's use of Greek, see Deane (1918) pp.41–44.
158. Discussed extensively in Teuffel-Schwabe (1892) and Sandy (1921) pp.824–826.
159. Suetonius, *Nero* 21.
160. For Cluvius' age, see discussion in Wiseman (1991) p.111.
161. Suetonius, *Vespasian* 4.4.
162. Tacitus 14.2; also discussed in Wiseman (1991) p.112.
163. For 'food of the gods', see Suetonius, *Nero* 33. Pliny 7 reported that Agrippina used poisoned mushrooms on Claudius; also Tacitus 12.66; Suetonius, *Claudius* 44, Cassius Dio 61.34 for the account of his death. Josephus 20.8.1 was more ambivalent. Additionally Cassius Dio 61.35 and Suetonius, *Nero* 33 claimed Nero knew of the murder, while Tacitus 12.65 and Josephus 20.8.1 mentioned Agrippina only and not Nero's involvement.
164. Tacitus, *Histories* 4.43.1, Pliny the Younger, *Epistle*s 2.11.17.
165. Tacitus, *Histories* 4.39.4, following Cornell (2013) p.552.
166. Townend (1964) pp.111–113 and Wiseman (1991) p.111 for a list of fragments and anecdotes. The four fragments appear in Tacitus 13.20, 14.2, Plutarch, *Otho* 3, Plutarch, *Roman Questions* 107 and the anecdote in Pliny the Younger, *Epistles* 9, 19.5.
167. Quoting Champlin (2003) p.50.
168. Discussed and developed through Townend (1964) and Wiseman (1991) pp.114–115.
169. Confirmation that he wrote a history comes from Pliny the Younger, *Epistles* 9.19.5.
170. Mommsen (1870) pp.320–322, republished in *Gesammelte Schriften* 7 (Berlin, 1909) p.248. The extract is from Josephus 19.91–92.
171. Complete discussion of the arguments in Feldman (1996) pp.165–168. Feldman refutes the claim. Also disputed by Wardle (1992) pp.466–482.
172. The identity of a Canius Rufus is also discussed in Nauta-van Dam-Smolenars (2006) pp. 315–328.
173. Excerpt from Martial, *Epigrams* Book 3.20, *On Canius*, sections 1–4 (Bohn's Classical Library, 1897). The translation, modified by the author, comes from Champlin (2003) p.36.
174. See discussion in Williams (2004) p.60. For Caelius Rufus, see Cicero, *On the Laws* 1.7. Cicero also mentioned a Q. Curtius (though not Rufus) in his *Letters to Brother Quintus*, confirming his, and his brothers' liking of the man they were attempting to advance with a military tribuneship from Julius Caesar.
175. Sentiment captured in Cicero, *Letters to Friends* 5.12.4–6; discussed in Dominik (1997) p.218.
176. See discussion in Adrados (2000) p.540.
177. Quintilian 10.1.102–105.

178. Syme (1964) pp.408–424.
179. The codex is also referred to as *Laurentianus 68, II. Langobard*, thus from the Lombards, is also known as Beneventan Script used from around the mid-eighth century until the thirteenth century, although there are later examples. There were two major centres of Beneventan usage: the monastery on Monte Cassino and Bari.
180. Apollinaris Sidonius, *Epistle* 4.14.1 and 22.2.
181. Discussed in detail in Wilkes (1972) pp.179–180 and quoting Momigliano (1966) p.131.

Chapter 11: Through the Cyclical Looking Glass

1. Pearson (1960) pp.240–241.
2. Macaulay (1828).
3. Aristotle, *On Magic* fragment 6 cited in Diogenes Laertius, *Lives of Eminent Philosophers* book 1 Prologue, section 8–9 *On Philosophy*. Aristotle's lost work, *On the Pythagoreans*, is also said to have discussed the Magi and/or magic. See discussion in Chroust (1964) p.572 and Momigliano (1977) pp.18–19.
4. With calendar changes and recalibrations, it is not possible to support the exact dating of this event to the modern calendar with any certainty, despite the accuracy of astronomical observations.
5. Scholars disagree on whether the text on the Cyrus Cylinder really portrays a tolerant regime; see discussion in Kuhrt (1983) pp.83–97 and below.
6. The tablets are labelled BM 36761 and 36390. For full discussion, see Polcaro-Valsecchi-Verderame (2008) pp.55–64. Sprague de Camp (1972) p.141 for a description of the Processional Way.
7. Arrian 3.16.4, 7.17.2, Diodorus 2.9.9, Strabo 16.1.5 for the destruction; Xerxes melted down the gold statue of Marduk for his depleted treasury.
8. Following P. Briant, *Rois, tributs et paysans: études sur les formations tributaires du Moyen-Orient ancient* (Pu Franc-Comtoises, 1989) p.330; discussed in Briant (1974) pp.183–184; the contention was also re-asked as a question by R. Lane Fox in 2007.
9. Quoting Bosworth (2004) p.553.
10. Quoting Heuss. A good summary of the relative views of these modern historians is given in Baynham (1998) pp.63–66.
11. Following the details in Hadjnicolaou (1997) for the printed editions in France.
12. Nicolas de Soulfour, *L' Alexandre francois* (1629).
13. Quotation from N. Beauzée, *Histoire d' Alexandre Ie Grand par Quinte Curce* (1781).
14. Dante, *The Divine Comedy: Inferno*, Circle 7, Canto 12.
15. Rodrigo Borgia took the title Alexander VI in admiration. He, and later Alessandro Farnese, pope from 1534–1549 under the name Paul III, decorated the Vatican apartments with scenes from Alexander's life. See discussion in Hadjinicolaou (1997).
16. Avcioğlu (2011) p.126 for emulation of Alexander by Louis XIV and Mehmet II.
17. In his 1748 *De l'Esprit de Lois* (*On the Spirit of the Laws*).
18. Droysen (1877); detailed discussion of biographer opinions in Green (1974) p.481 ff.
19. Tarn (1948).
20. Schachermeyr (1949).

21. Badian (1958), Green (1974).
22. Atkinson (1996) pp.xvi, 218, and Atkinson (1963) p.125.
23. Polybius 12.23.5; Green (1974) p.487. Lane Fox's view appears to have influenced Oliver Stone's 2004 movie, to which he consulted; discussed by G. Nisbet in Carney-Ogden (2010) pp.217–231; 'historiophotic' was a term coined by Hayden White in 1988 in his 'Historiography and Historiophoty', *American Historic Review* 93, to describe the 'representation of history' and our thoughts about it in visual images and filmic discourse.
24. Green (1974) p.487.
25. Heckel (1993), final page of the review.
26. The word literally means 'policy of fusion' and was first used by Droysen in his *Geschichte Alexanders des Grossen* (1833) to describe Alexander's supposed plan.
27. For Alexander's refusal at Opis to let veterans return to Macedon with their Asiatic children, Arrian 7.12.2, for the eighty marriages at Susa, Arrian 7.4.6, and 7.4.8 for the 10,000 total Macedones who had married Asian wives, a suspiciously high number.
28. Athenaeus 12.537e cited Ephippus as claiming Alexander dressed as Ammon, Artemis and Hermes. Tarn (1948) p.97.
29. Blackburn (2006) p.18.
30. Quoting De Polignac (1999) p.3, translation by Ruth Moriss.
31. Aristotle, *Sophistical Refutations* 1, discussed in Reeve (2001) p.208.

Index

The Index relates to names appearing in the main chapter text only, not the footnotes, book titles, image captions, or the bibliography.